COOLING THE TROPICS

T0314507

ELEMENTS *A series edited by*
Stacy Alaimo and Nicole Starosielski

COOLING THE TROPICS

ICE, INDIGENEITY, AND HAWAIIAN REFRESHMENT

HIʻILEI JULIA KAWEHIPUAAKAHAOPULANI HOBART

DUKE UNIVERSITY PRESS   DURHAM AND LONDON   2023

Library of Congress Cataloging-in-Publication Data
Names: Hobart, Hiʻilei Julia, author.
Title: Cooling the tropics : ice, indigeneity, and Hawaiian refreshment /
Hiʻilei Julia Kawehipuaakahaopulani Hobart.
Other titles: Elements (Duke University Press)
Description: Durham : Duke University Press, 2022.
| Series: Elements | Includes bibliographical references and index.
Identifiers: LCCN 2022028078 (print)
LCCN 2022028079 (ebook)
ISBN 9781478016557 (hardcover)
ISBN 9781478019190 (paperback)
ISBN 9781478023821 (ebook)
Subjects: LCSH: Cold storage industry—Social aspects—Hawaii—19th
century. | Cold storage industry—Hawaii—History—19th century. |
Ice industry—Hawaii—History—19th century. | Ice industry—Social
aspects—Hawaii—19th century. | Food habits—Hawaii—History—
19th century. | Americans—Hawaii—History—19th century. | BISAC:
SOCIAL SCIENCE / Ethnic Studies / American / Native American
Studies | SOCIAL SCIENCE / Anthropology / Cultural & Social
Classification: LCC HD9999.C683 H3 2022 (print) | LCC HD9999.C683
(ebook) | DDC 621.5/809969—dc23/eng/20220902
LC record available at https://lccn.loc.gov/2022028078
LC ebook record available at https://lccn.loc.gov/2022028079

Cover art: Rawley's Ice Cream advertisement, *Paradise of the Pacific*,
December 1921.

Publication of this book is supported by Duke University Press's
Scholars of Color First Book Fund.

CONTENTS

Wherever possible, I have sought to represent Hawaiian viewpoints as they are expressed in ʻōlelo Hawaiʻi, the Indigenous language of Hawaiʻi. The translations within this book are my own (unless otherwise indicated), and I include them alongside the originals so that others may interpret them otherwise. I am a beginner learner of ʻōlelo Hawaiʻi and acknowledge that there are certainly other ways to understand what these sources convey, contexts that I have missed, or references beyond my purview.

Throughout this book, words in ʻōlelo Hawaiʻi are not italicized in recognition that, in this context, it is not a foreign language. All quotations from Hawaiian newspapers are transcribed as they appear in print, often without diacritical marks. Likewise, citations of various works reflect the spelling of Hawaiian words as they are presented in that particular text (for example, *Hawaiʻi* often appears instead as *Hawaii*). Otherwise, and unless noted, my spelling of Hawaiian follows the conventions in Mary Kawena Pukui and Samuel H. Elbert's *Hawaiian Dictionary*.[1]

Kanaka (countable pl. *Kānaka*; infinite pl. *Kanaka*) refers to the Indigenous people of Hawaiʻi. I tend to favor the term *Kanaka Maoli* here, though I also variously use *Kanaka ʻŌiwi*, *Native Hawaiian*, and *Hawaiians* to refer to those who are descended from seafaring people who arrived in these islands nearly two thousand years ago.[2]

I never intended to write about Hawai'i. The idea of it—even now—feels audacious to me: it is my piko (umbilicus), my very center, even though I have lived most of my adult life on the US continent. The pages of this book are filled with love and longing for the place of my ancestors, which will forever drive the work that I do.

A full decade in the making, this book would simply not be in the world without beloved mentors under whose guidance the earliest iterations of this project took form. Audra Simpson showed me the importance of writing to, and from, my community. Lisa Gitelman modeled good mentoring by always giving me clear, concise, and generative feedback exactly when I needed it. Krishnendu Ray's brilliant theoretical mind helped me to imagine taste beyond flavor—an idea that is central to this book's argument. Dean Itsuji Saranillio was one of my first teachers of Hawai'i's history, and I could not have been more fortunate for his arrival in New York City at a time when I had so much to learn.

The Department of Nutrition, Food Studies, and Public Health (as it was called when I began my doctorate) at New York University gave me tools for thinking about the world through food, and I am grateful to the people there who continue to nourish my first intellectual love. I owe thanks to Krishnendu Ray, Amy Bentley, Carolyn Dimitri, Marion Nestle, and Jennifer Berg for their loving guidance and training. I was especially lucky to have a doctoral cohort that felt like a family. I cherish the invaluable insights and feedback I received from Christy Spackman, Scott Barton, Shayne Figueroa, Jackie Rohel, and Sara Franklin, on early drafts, in cubicles, and over meals.

The research for this book brought me home in more ways than one. In Hawai'i's archives I ran my fingers over the handwriting of my kūpuna, our monarchs, and our lāhui (people) who defended the sovereignty of our homeland with tender and fierce love. I wept with them in these repositories. I am especially grateful for the work of the librarians and archivists who safekeep these records. At the University of Hawaiʻi's Hamilton Library, Dore Minatodani guided me through the library's massive collection, always pulling materials that I would not have even known to ask for. At the Hawaiʻi State Archives, Melissa Shimonishi's greetings by name across years of visits made me feel seen in the best kind of way; Luella Kurjistan always welcomed me back home and kindly showed me many beautiful dining artifacts belonging to ʻIolani Palace. Heather Diamond and Zita Cup Choy opened up the ʻIolani Palace curatorial files to me and gave me a bounty of references to follow. Estee Tanaka, the archivist for the Hawaiian Electric Company, went above and beyond by putting together packets from the company's collections for me when I wasn't able to come to her in person. At the Bishop Museum Archives, I owe thanks to DeSoto Brown for sharing with me his encyclopedic knowledge of Hawaiian history and technology, and to librarians Tia Reber and B. J. Short for helping me make the most of my research appointments.

I began the work of expanding and editing this book at Northwestern University. There I had the privilege of working and thinking alongside an incredible cohort of early career folks, including Douglas Ishii, Elizabeth Schwall, Michelle Huang, Sarah Dimick, Kaneesha Parsard, Umayyah Cable, Doug Kiel, Beatriz Reyes, Nell Haynes, Danny Snelson, and Emrah Yildiz, who all gave me encouragement, community, and sharp feedback. I was furthermore supported—both intellectually and personally—by the wonderful people who work at the Alice Kaplan Institute for the Humanities, especially Jill Manor, Tom Burke, and Megan Skord, as well as two of its directors, Wendy Wall and Jessica Winegar, who coached me through early academic parenthood. While these thanks may seem incidental to the making of a book, they are assuredly not. I want to thank beloved and generous colleagues Josh Honn, Kelly Wisecup, Mary Weismantel, Helen Tilley, and Daniel Immerwahr for their friendship and guidance. Northwestern also connected me with Nitasha Sharma, an extraordinary mentor and dear friend, who has held my hand through every step of the publishing process and taught me that academia can be a place for someone like me.

I had the rare privilege of coming full circle with this project at Columbia University, where its first seeds were planted, when I was invited to return as a postdoc under the mentorship of Audra Simpson and Paige West. These women opened doors for me in ways that I will never lose sight of, including organizing a manuscript workshop that provided me a crucial road map for revisions. At that workshop, I had the transcendent honor of also receiving feedback from J. Kēhaulani Kauanui, Karl Jacoby, and Andrew Needham, which was as humbling as it was useful.

While I'm using a temporal frame to guide my thanks, the accrual of intellectual debts is not linear. A long list of colleagues helped me deepen and broaden my scholarly practice across many phases of my career. David Chang's unwavering championing of my work has forever marked me. Maria John has been my sounding board, inspiration, and faithful "conference wife" since the earliest years of graduate school. Nicole Starosielski saw this project's potential in ways that even I could not imagine. About icy things I am particularly grateful to have learned from Joanna Radin, Rafico Ruiz, Jen Rose Smith, Thomas Wickman, and Rebecca Woods; about eating things I have learned from the brilliance of Stephanie Maroney, Kyla Wazana Tompkins, Sarah Tracey, Nadia Berenstein, and Jessica Hardin. Invitations to present or workshop portions of this manuscript were invaluable, and I am deeply grateful to Tracey Deutsch, Erin Suzuki, Melody Jue, Sean Brotherton, Aanchal Saraf, Joyce Chaplin, Ty Kāwika Tengan, and Cynthia Wu for providing forums for me to share my work with the many scholars across continents and oceans who have, in turn, shaped this work with their questions and insights. The Nutrire CoLab's invitation to workshop what would eventually become this book's conclusion helped me to see beyond the edges of the project toward something larger.

The final pushes to complete this book have been deeply informed, energized, and supported by beloved colleagues at the University of Texas at Austin. Ashanté Reese read final drafts with a keen eye and wit; Jason Cons, Pauline Strong, Alex Beasley, Circe Sturm, Pavithra Vasudevan, and my cohort of Humanities Institute fellows offered key insights into the broader interventions of the work. A special thank you to my department chair, Anthony DiFiore, for taking such care to protect my time and energy as I muscled my way to the finish line.

Publishing a book with Duke University Press has been one of my greatest professional dreams. To Ken Wissoker, who first saw a potential home for this project, even in its earliest stages, thank you. To Courtney Berger, whose first meeting with me took place when I was fully nine months pregnant at the 2017 American Studies Association conference in Chicago, and whose second meeting with me, about six months later, was held as we sat on a baby blanket on the floor of a Los Angeles Hotel at the 2018 Native American and Indigenous Studies Association conference with a fussy infant, I am so grateful for your steady support and graciousness. You allowed me to come to our conversations exactly as I am. Courtney sought out and secured two anonymous reviewers who read an imperfect draft with the rare kind of thoughtfulness, generosity, and expertise that gives a writer fresh energy to revise. Thank you for your selfless gifts of close and critical reading. Sandra Korn moved the review process forward with diligence and cheer; Liz Smith kindly saw this book through to production; Susan Ecklund edited the text carefully. The wonderful people at Ideas on Fire helped me as I revised the book in full, and I owe thanks to Cathy Hannabach and especially Micha Rahder, whose sharp eye for narrative arcs helped my ideas shine. Josh Rutner not only provided indexing but also stepped in at the last minute to help edit my introduction: thank you for squeezing me in! Samantha Aolani Kailihou double-checked the ʻōlelo Hawaiʻi throughout this entire book with stunning attention to detail. Finally, I owe my love and thanks to Christy Spackman and Aimee Bahng for volunteering to be the very last set of eyes on this book's introduction as I got ready to hand it in for typesetting.

The genealogy of a book can feel more defined than the genealogy of an idea, which comes from places we are sometimes not even aware of when they first take hold. Mine is anchored in a childhood in Hawaiʻi, with a Kanaka Maoli mother who epitomized Hawaiian grace and a second-generation Irish father who expressed his devotion to her by researching and writing our family histories. My mom, Tessa Kamakia Magoon Dye, lived just long enough to see me to adulthood, but not to see what I would do with it. In many ways, this work attempts to teach myself what I was not able to learn directly from her. I wonder every day what conversations we might have had together about being Hawaiian, sovereignty, and love. My dad, Robert Paul Dye, whose dream for me was to one day get a doctorate, lived long enough to know that I had applied to PhD programs, but not to know that I would be accepted everywhere I had applied. My deepest hope is that my parents would be proud of how I channeled my love for Hawaiʻi. My siblings, Tom, Steve, Ahia, and Kekapala, have welcomed me home for visits, research trips, and conferences. They watched me learn how to become an academic with exceptionally good humor and, at times, great patience.

As many know, the nuclear family is a fiction in Hawaiʻi. The researching and writing of this book have been sustained by many lifelong friends who are better described as ʻohana. Jill Abbott opened her home to me when I came to Hawaiʻi for my first extended research trip and has kept her door open for every visit back since. Being with her has come to feel like home in the deepest sense. Samantha Aolani Kailihou tutored me in ʻōlelo Hawaiʻi as I researched this project, for which she gets thanked several times in this book. She and her husband, Peni, have hosted me for many conferences and research trips to Hawaiʻi Island and—especially—when I came in 2019 to Puʻuhonua o Puʻuhuluhulu with my childhood friend, and now beloved colleague, Amanda Shaw.

Finally, I owe my deepest thanks to my partner, Jake, whom I have now known and loved for more than half of my life on this earth, and with whom I have the privilege of parenting our luminous daughter, Hauanuawaiau May. I am so lucky to have a person who not only dreams with me but builds that dream, too.

In the middle of a Honolulu summer in 1876, the weekly Hawaiian-language newspaper *Ka Lahui Hawaii* ran an advertisement for the Bonanza Saloon's new menu items:

> Ke kali nei ka hoa J. W. Crowell (Keoni Kolowela) o ke keena Bonanza, ma alanui Moi, o ke kipa ae o kona mau makamaka hanohano o ka Ahaolelo e hooluolu ia lakou iho me na kiaha hau i hoopaa ia a i awili ia hoi me na momona. Ilaila makou a hoomano ae la i ka "ono maeele ka puu i ka wai o ka lehua," ua hele kela a "anu e, anu i ka wai o ka Ice."[1]

> Our friend J. W. Crowell of Bonanza Saloon, on King Street, is currently waiting for his prestigious associates of the Legislature to visit [and] they will be refreshed with glasses of ice that has been frozen and mixed with sweet flavorings. It is here that we all will be reminded of "the throat's delicious numbing feeling due to the water of the lehua blossom," which became "strangely cold, cold due to the water of the Ice."

At a time when few establishments in the growing city offered ice, the Bonanza used it to draw in patrons. Its rarity meant that the pleasures of the cold needed to be explained, and Crowell painted a vivid picture: beads of dew nestled within a lehua, the endemic flower of the 'ōhi'a tree that thrives at misty mountain elevations.[2] Kanaka Maoli (Native Hawaiian) readers would have immediately connected the flower's imagery to the fiery passion of the akua (deity) Pele. Crowell accordingly calls the sensation of drinking iced water "mā'e'ele"—a numbness associated with shivers of pleasure.[3] To have simply described the ice as cold—"anu"—would not have fully captured the concept of refreshment. Instead, employing language that overlapped sensory, intellectual, and emotional aspects of feeling—and all within the space of a brief newspaper advertisement—Crowell leveraged Indigenous cultural and environmental references in order to sell Hawaiians on a foreign commodity.

These descriptive choices mark a vibrant and distinctly Hawaiian brand of empiricism, which was increasingly obscured by the pressures of Westernization that encroached on the growing port city in the second half of the nineteenth century. Where once the novelty of consuming cold in Honolulu was introduced with images of dewy lehua, this mode of refreshment would soon become matter-of-fact. Since Hawai'i became enfolded into the American nation-state at the cusp of the twentieth century, images of golden beaches have replaced misty mountains, and American honeymooners sipping iced Mai Tais in hotel lobbies have edged out Crowell's Hawaiian legislators in their urban saloons. In the span of about 150 years, the desire for frozen refreshment would become fully naturalized into Hawai'i's foodscape as a necessary and pleasurable form of recreation—particularly as the islands emerged as the paradigmatic example of a tropical "paradise."

This, however, is not a story about how ice first arrived in Hawai'i.

Kānaka Maoli have long described the cold through mo'olelo (storied histories)—especially those referring to the summits of the island chain's tallest mountains, where snowfall is common in the winter months. Its *commoditization*, however, is imported. Today, ice and refrigeration—that is, the technological production and regulation of cold temperatures—underpin sensory, aesthetic, and logistical experiences of everyday life for most people in Hawai'i, just as they do for many people around the world. Middle-class Americans are quite literally "conditioned," moving daily between climate-controlled homes, transportation, and offices; shopping for food (kept fresh from field to factory to market); and relaxing—perhaps with a cold drink in hand.

This book examines how such normative thermal relationships between bodies and environments have developed as a function of American imperial power, arguing that they continue to operate today as embodied expressions of ongoing settler colonialism. I explore this dynamic as it unfolds in the Hawaiian Islands, paying attention to how discourses about the cold encapsulate ideas about race, modernity, and the senses and in turn help rationalize Indigenous dispossession. Beginning in the mid-1800s, Americans hauled frozen pond water, then glacial ice, then ice machines to Hawaiian shores—all in an effort to reshape the islands in the service of white pleasure and profit. Marketed as "essential" for white occupants of the nineteenth-century Pacific, ice quickly permeated the foodscape as technological advancements facilitated its mechanical production. Into the twentieth and twenty-first centuries, infrastructures of the cold became so deeply embedded that they faded into the background of Hawaiʻi daily life.[4] I follow this trajectory to show how the related concepts of freshness and refreshment mark colonial relationships to the tropics.

Again, this is not a story about how ice first arrived in Hawaiʻi; it is an analysis of how people make sense of temperature under conditions of colonization. By looking at how Hawaiians—and others living in or traveling to Hawaiʻi—used ice to talk about difference and assimilation across the nineteenth and twentieth centuries, this book asks: What does the infrastructural unremarkability of ice today tell us about the normalization and tenacity of settler colonialism? What are the implicit understandings of environment, climate, and embodiment that underpin human needs and desires for the cold within the tropics? Finally, how can a thermal analysis of Indigenous dispossession help us to envision decolonial futures for Hawaiʻi beyond the artificial cold?

PERFECTION AND DESIRE

For many people, Hawaiʻi is synonymous with paradise.[5] Almanacs describe its temperate climate as hospitable for a remarkably broad spectrum of plant and animal life—and this includes humans. The Hawaiian archipelago, which constitutes a portion of the Hawaiian-Emperor seamount chain, is situated roughly at the center of the Pacific Ocean, between 18 and 22 degrees north latitude and 154 and 160 degrees west longitude.[6] Its geolocation means that Hawaiʻi experiences little variation in daylength or median temperatures throughout the year, producing a relatively stable climate with a nearly continuous growing season.[7] The edited volume *Prevailing Trade Winds: Climate and Weather in Hawaiʻi* (1993) states in the opening paragraph of its introduction that, "for most people, the essence of Hawaiʻi is its year-round pleasant climate, never too hot and never too cold, with moderate humidities and air-conditioning trade winds."[8] Hawaiʻi, it suggests, is so ideal that it comes with its own cooling mechanism.

But perfect environments, historians explain, are not natural.[9] They are produced. Paradisial imaginaries about Hawaiʻi have been shaped over nearly 250 years since Western contact, when white people first began theorizing the tropics as a source of pleasure, exploitable labor, and profit.[10] These ideas can be found in the earliest written records of Hawai'i, when, for example, George Gilbert, a midshipman on Captain James Cook's third voyage (1776–80), reported, "The joy that we experienced on our arrival here [in Maui] is only to be conceived by ourselves or people under like circumstances; for after . . . the space of near ten months we have come into a delightful climate were [sic] we had almost everything we could wish for, in great profusion."[11] Hawai'i would go on to measure up to (or fail to meet) expectations of the islands as nothing less than a modern-day Eden. James Jackson Jarves, an early editor for the *Polynesian*, a popular Honolulu-based newspaper, wrote in 1843 that, "to foreigners, and particularly to children, the climate has proved of the most salubrious nature. It may be doubted if any more conducive to general health can be found."[12] By contrast, colonialists reasoned that Hawai'i's climate was so ideal that Native Hawaiians had evolved into a people without industry, and thus without desire for self-governance or civilization. As Manley Hopkins, Hawai'i's consul general in London, explained in 1862: "Indolence is another grand fault attributed to the Hawaiian race. It is very true that the delicious, equitable climate engenders in those constantly within its influence a lotus-eating habit, a love of the *dolce far niente*. Their absolute wants were few; and as the chiefs would have pounced down on any little surplus the people could have acquired by labour, they lost the powerful stimulus of a desire to accumulate."[13] Consistent with theories of geographic determinism at the time, the mental gymnastics used by colonialists to justify their presence in the tropics—and, simultaneously, to racially disassociate themselves from Indigenous and enslaved people—butted up against colonial desires for land and, eventually, settlement.

During the nineteenth century, the tropics operated as a racial imaginary as much as a physical place, with the theory of acclimatization used to rationalize white supremacy.[14] Claiming that climate produces race over time, the theory aligned with the racialization of plantation labor, for which nonwhite people were imagined to be better adapted than white people.[15] Colonialists contorted their understandings of tropical habitability—for plantation overseers, researchers, and entrepreneurs—in order to accommodate ideas about the unsuitability of white people for warm places, as well as their entitlement to the resources and capital extracted from them.[16] As David Livingstone explains, a combination of "medical science, imperial politics, evolutionary theory and moral principle . . . helped produce in the minds of the Victorian public an imagined region—the tropics—which was, at once, a place of parasite and pathology, a space inviting colonial occupation and management, a laboratory for natural selection and racial struggle and a site of moral jeopardy and trial."[17] For Hawai'i, the racial hierarchies of the plantation included poorly paid immigrant workers (largely from Asia) who were seen as better suited to hard agricultural labor than white settlers. As Jessica Wang notes, this racialized labor system would eventually bump up against Jeffersonian ideals of private property ownership in the early twentieth century, when white homesteaders sought to establish small farms in the islands as way of extending continental manifest destiny.[18] Climatic perfection, as it is praised in Hawai'i, has thus never served all bodies equally, but instead belies deep anxieties about race, belonging, and mobility across the tropics.

Envisioned as simultaneously exotic and familiar, Hawai'i offers valuable insight into the ways that settler colonialism moves through the Pacific. Scholars like Patrick Wolfe, Lorenzo Veracini, and numerous others working across Native and Indigenous studies have theorized settler colonialism as a political formation of Indigenous dispossession that relies on land as its primary currency. In order for settlers to claim space as their own, territories are "emptied" of original occupants using various strategies, including projects of assimilation, forced removal, and enclosure, as well as rhetorical and aesthetic forms of elimination.[19] In turn, settlers understand themselves as the sovereign "inheritors" of Indigenous lands and resources.

Within Oceania, settler colonialism manifested in the development of what Teresia Teaiwa describes as a "militouristic" economy, in which the military and tourism industries mutually reinforce Indigenous dispossession—with military networks supporting and facilitating tourism, and tourism, in turn, masking military force. While the impact of militourism on land use in Hawai'i is profound—Hawai'i's economy today is completely overdetermined by these industries—Teaiwa uses this phenomenon as a heuristic for showing how "Polynesian" bodies become fixed in space and hierarchies of power. "Although military forces and tourism provide employment and social mobility for many Islanders," she writes, "they also drain or pollute natural resources, endanger sacred sites, and introduce unhealthy 'convenience' goods."[20] These dynamics not only organize Indigenous people according to settler colonial economic and spatial logics but also produce a complex aesthetics of Polynesian sexualization, exoticism, assimilability, and subservience.[21]

For Hawaiʻi, climate is embedded deeply within its racial logics: the Edenic imaginaries of the late eighteenth century helped settler colonialists of the nineteenth and twentieth centuries envision white belonging despite ongoing Indigenous presence. Kanaka Maoli scholar Maile Arvin describes how American claims to territory maneuvered around the shifting racializations of Polynesian people across the nineteenth and twentieth centuries: at times too brown, at times almost white, but never close enough for self-governance.[22] Imaginaries about Hawaiʻi's inherent whiteness amalgamated racial and environmental theories that were then brought to bear on territorial claims. Narratives produced in the 1880s by Abraham Fornander, and again in the 1950s by Thor Heyerdahl, imagined that the Pacific had originally been settled by a "white race," simultaneously suggesting that Hawaiians were once white themselves (even if they would never again be so) and that Hawaiʻi was a place primed for reclamation by white settlers as a kind of long-awaited homecoming, in part because of its ideal climate.[23]

Questions that would eventually emerge about Hawaiʻi's political future in relation to the United States—as sovereign nation, plantation colony, or American state—frequently drew on the ideological interplay between climate and race that shaped much of Victorian-era colonialism in the tropics across Caribbean and Pacific spaces. As theories of land, labor, and territorial entitlement continued to shift over the nineteenth and twentieth centuries, material objects offered concrete and performative avenues for resolving the racial, moral, and epidemiological ambiguities of the settler colonial tropics. Namely, the circulation of ice and iced refreshment in Hawaiʻi helped code hierarchies of power, even as they remained unfixed across time.

THERMAL COLONIZATION AND SETTLER REFRESHMENT

As part of a larger set of strategies employed by settlers to calibrate thermal environments to the aims of territorial expansion, resource extraction, and settler habitation, the mediation of temperature helped to exert domination and control over Indigenous environments. Such forms of thermal colonialism, a phenomenon examined by scholars like Nicole Starosielski, Rafico Ruiz, and Jen Rose Smith, reflect the ways that environments are made friendly to settlement alongside ideas of temperate normativity, or the notion that geographies of extreme heat or cold are uncomfortable or uninhabitable for the civilized (and, in turn, that temperate climates are exceptionally hospitable to Western settlement).[24] This has been the case since European settlers first worried about how their bodies would adapt to life in the "new world"; as Alfred Crosby presciently noted in his classic text on the ecological impact of North America's colonization, "The crux of the problem was temperature."[25] Anxieties over what could take root in tropical or ice geographies became, in turn, intimately related to capitalist expansion through sensorial concerns about bodily comforts and pleasures for white settlers and economic concerns about bodily labors for everyone else, particularly the enslaved.[26]

Histories of ice and refrigeration constitute an important facet of thermal colonialism. The American ice trade—in which great blocks harvested from lakes in the Northeast circulated the globe—peaked between 1840 and 1870.[27] Packed in sawdust, an otherwise valueless byproduct of the lumber industry, ice would serve both as a ballast and a revenue generator for ships sailing abroad to collect goods produced by slave labor, such as sugar, fruit, and cotton.[28] Forms of thermal settler colonialism generated by the American ice trade stretched out across the globe, making a profound impact on plantation spaces. As Marc W. Herold argues in his article on early ice exportation from the United States to Brazil, the ice that went to the tropics—places like Calcutta, Havana, New Orleans, Jamaica, and British Guiana—was a luxury product, used in cocktails, to chill wines, and for service at fine hotels (as opposed to being used as a food preservative, which was more common in the American Northeast).[29] Set against the contexts of plantation labor and colonial dispossession, iced refreshment within the tropics articulated sensory pleasure as a particularly embodied form of thermal colonization.

In tandem with the global success of the nineteenth-century ice trade, Americans developed an obsession with coldness. Settler colonial logics of inevitability, irreversibility, and belonging come to be naturalized through thermally mediated experiences of place. Historians of Western ice manufacture, air-conditioning, and refrigeration describe how such technologies responded to frontier desires for mastery over nature—forms of territorial domination expressed through the distributive reach of fresh meat and produce, regardless of season or distance.[30] "Ample perishable foods," writes Jonathan Rees, "became a symbol of American plentitude [and] the wide availability of this bounty at first seemed like divine intervention."[31] In particular, American political investments in the cold engaged ideas of manifest destiny, casting political expansion across Indigenous lands as a God-given right, suturing race, refrigeration, and refreshment as thermal expressions of territorial entitlement. Histories of air-conditioning, such as Marsha E. Ackermann's *Cool Comfort* (2002), furthermore argue that the use of temperature control to mitigate climatic discomfort resonated especially with American national identity, which treated air-conditioning as a cornerstone of civilization. In this way, technologies of artificial cold addressed not only the spatial but also—and perhaps more crucially—the biopolitical concerns of colonial settlement.[32]

Americans came to see this as their legacy. Such technological approaches to "mastery over nature" manifested an everyday sense of comfort and freshness across a vast body politic despite—or perhaps in suppression of—spectacularly variable geographies and embodiments. It is no wonder, then, that Mark Rifkin begins and ends his influential essay "Settler Common Sense" discussing Henry David Thoreau's *Walden* (1854), a book that theorizes sovereignty through one's ability to feel at home in nature—a sense of entitlement conditioned by white privilege.[33] Readers might recall that the backdrop of Thoreau's peaceful commune was the Tudor Ice Company's employees chiseling out ten thousand tons of pond water to send to "the sweltering inhabitants of Charleston and New Orleans, of Madras and Bombay and Calcutta."[34] To that end, the feelings of comfort that so affirm Thoreau's de facto relationship to "nature" are triply premised on settler colonialism (the theft of Native lands in the Northeast), racial capitalism (plantation slavery in the American South), and empire (global trade with colonial India).[35] Rights to freshness, abundance, and energy resources became baked into what it means to be American. Put simply, these investments in the cold produced a normative condition of American life fundamentally premised on settler colonial desire.

Tracking the impact of ice and refrigeration on Hawai'i as a distinctly American endeavor offers insight into the mutability of colonial formations across time and the changing nature of Hawai'i's relationship to the United States. Dean Saranillio explains in *Unsustainable Empire* (2018) that by the early twentieth century, "Hawai'i's occupation by the United States, and the specific forms of settler colonialism there, was thus composed of a complex constellation of federal, territorial, military, Hawaiian, and settler interests."[36] Because colonialism's forms are not static but instead adapt to the site-specific exigencies of territorial occu-

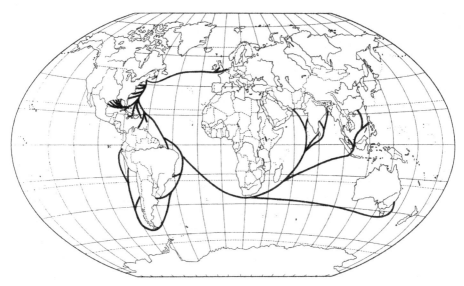

Figure I.1. Global ice trade routes in 1856, in which the Pacific is unaccounted for. From David G. Dickason, "The Nineteenth-Century Indo-American Ice Trade: A Hyperborean Epic," *Modern Asian Studies* 25, no. 1 (1991): 58.

pation, understanding Hawai'i and its relationship to the United States requires accounting for the ways that the islands have been constituted through multiple power structures: American empire in the Pacific (and thus in relation to Guam, Samoa, and the Northern Marianas); settler statehood (and thus in relation to Indigenous territory on the North American continent); and plantation labor (and thus in relation to the movement of people and capital across these lands and oceans in ways that subordinated, racialized, and dispossessed).[37]

Tracing ice and the cold offers a sensorial through line that connects power to pleasure as it traverses the racial and economic terrains of these multiple configurations. Thermal technologies, like air-conditioning and refrigeration, affirm normative subjectivities as they are deployed across public and private spaces and, in turn, mark difference.[38] This phenomenon is akin to "settler common sense," as Rifkin calls it: the lived conditions of settler possibility that appear self-evident.[39] The supposed neutrality of temperature obscures not only personal percep-tions of hot and cold but also the political power of thermal manipu-lation to differentiate raced, classed, and gendered bodies.[40] By paying attention to how the sociotechnical work of calibrating temperatures produces idealized environments as well as ideal subjects for those environments, one can see how thermal comfort operates as a function of settler colonialism.

TEMPERATURE AS PREFERENCE AND POWER

This book's concern with cold temperature and embodied desire is premised on an understanding that while temperature is measurable, "cold" is subjective.[41] Within the sciences, coldness might be recognized as anything within a range of degrees above and below the freezing point of water (0°C or 32°F).[42] It also signifies a negative value: the movement of energy in the form of heat away from an object (when you touch an object that feels cold, what you are actually feeling is the transfer of energy from your body to that object).[43] But beyond these measures, coldness as we know it is just that: as *we* know it. In the English language, coldness is experienced relative to the human body; according to the *Oxford English Dictionary*, "cold" is an intuitive state.[44] But while the measure of cold feeling belongs to the individual, the values attributed to it—pleasure, discomfort—coalesce through social practices that are acutely influenced by things like race, class, and gender.[45]

Language translates these cultural ideologies as forms of feeling. For example, even though the word *anu* most commonly describes low temperatures in ʻōlelo Hawaiʻi, a multiplicity of words elaborate on specific valences and interpretations of the cold—like ʻāmuʻemuʻe, which refers to both bitter cold and bitter taste.[46] In both English and ʻōlelo Hawaiʻi, cold also metaphorically reflects emotional states: love, displeasure, affection, callousness, isolation, hipness.[47] For Hawaiians, the relationship between temperature and emotion is sometimes inverted, with coolness illustrating happiness or sexual passion, as opposed to Western ideas of coolness as disaffectedness and detachment.[48] Importantly, the tourism economy relies heavily on the language of warmth as one of the dominant descriptors of Hawaiʻi and its people, equating its climate with romanticized notions of Hawaiian hospitality—what is commonly referred to as the "spirit of aloha."[49] This thermal language articulates affective states of being that underpin the environmental logics of colonial settlement.

So, what transpires across states of affective and sensory coldness that helps us to understand power? You might wonder: Aren't cocktails and ice creams and shave ice inherently delicious?[50] Here it may be useful to linger a moment on the biology of refreshment.[51] Unlike immersive activities like swimming, consuming cold things doesn't substantially affect internal body temperature. Instead, studies show, the pleasure most associate with iced refreshments is the feeling of thirst satiety.[52] But even that response is psychological: water, hot or cold, hydrates just the same. Take, for example, a set of scientific studies conducted in the 1980s and 1990s designed to test the relationship between drink temperature and palatability. Researchers found that while multiple factors determined the volume of fluid intake (including environment, container type, and ease of access), temperature preference stood out.[53] Many studies tellingly showed that thermal preferences diverged sharply across national lines. For example, a test conducted in 1984 found that American subjects, when offered water at a range of temperatures, overwhelmingly selected the coldest available (5°C/41°F).[54] Yet another study, conducted in 1983, found that French subjects preferred water just cooler than room temperature (16°C/60.8°F)—even after warming their bodies up with vigorous exercise designed to make them thirsty.[55] Still more studies highlighted the important role of things like expectation in shaping temperature preference: in 1988, American test subjects consumed various "unfamiliar juices" at both cold (read: appropriate) and warm (inappropriate) temperatures. Subjects then rated the palatability of each juice, consistently ranking cold juices higher than those served warm. Their rankings shifted, however, when they were informed that some juices were *meant* to be consumed warm.[56] Taken together, these studies not only indicate that thermal expectations are culturally determined; they reflect a contemporary American notion that cold consumption is both universally necessary and desired.[57]

Histories of sugar and sweetness offer a useful correlation for understanding settler colonial desires for ice and coldness. Flavor scientists, for example, who have documented the hedonics of sweetness argue that humans are evolutionarily "hardwired" to like sugars.[58] Even so, this supposed human propensity for sweetness cannot sufficiently account for the differential impacts that sugar has had on communities of color, especially Black descendants of the enslaved.[59] Sidney Mintz's groundbreaking *Sweetness and Power* (1985) reveals how Western desires for sweetness are in fact products of colonial plantation economies and industrial labor formations.[60] Following Mintz, this book similarly troubles the ahistorical way that contemporary Americans presume that hedonics of cold are solely driven by universal biological desire, rather than being conditioned by colonialism. Understanding what this means for a study of settler colonialism, indigeneity, and race-making in Hawai'i requires, then, looking beyond the biology and physics of taste, and toward how the sensorium develops as a function of global power.[61]

SENTIMENTALITY IN THE SETTLER COLONIAL CITY

In order to detail the broad cultural and political meanings of the cold as a form of thermal settler colonialism within the imperial Pacific, the heart of this book focuses on urban Honolulu as a rapidly evolving technological and cosmopolitan center of Hawai'i in which ice had an early and long-standing impact.[62] Honolulu's transformation into a bustling metropolis began in the early 1800s with the arrival of missionaries and whalers who took advantage of its generous harbor, which could accommodate the deep draft vessels used for whaling. It quickly grew from a small village of about a dozen households in 1803 to ten thousand or so people (including several hundred foreigners) by 1850, when it became designated as Hawai'i's capital city.[63] Since the kingdom era, it was usually the first point of contact for the people, goods, and ideas that flowed into Hawai'i, and so the city's residents had no choice but to accommodate that diversity, for better or worse. The intimacies that the city forced between Native Hawaiians and newcomers also became contested spaces of civility, morality, and national identity.[64] Honolulu's development as one of the Pacific's largest cities was thereby shaped by the quotidian as much as it was forged in geopolitical fires.[65]

Often mistaking Hawaiian cosmopolitanism as evidence of its colonization, Westerners homed in on Honolulu as an attractive location for settlement. By the time the United States annexed Hawai'i in 1898, Honolulu had around thirty thousand residents. They lived modern, cosmopolitan lives: they traveled by rail car, called each other on the telephone, patronized stores advertising in five different languages, and kept their food fresh in iceboxes.[66] It was, in fact, these same cultural and technological amenities that compelled American settlers to draw equivalencies between Hawai'i and the continental United States.[67] In travel guides like *Appleton's Illustrated Hand-Book of American Winter Resorts* from 1895, for example, readers were informed that "the aspect of [Honolulu] is surprisingly like that of a thriving New England town, and Americans in particular soon feel quite at home."[68] And so, in the nineteenth century, biologically deterministic ideas about race, climate, and human geography gave way to settler embodiments governed in part by what Kyla Schuller calls a "plasticity of feeling" that traversed the sensory and the sentimental.[69] This logic allowed settlers to imagine themselves as racially distinct from Native Hawaiians, and yet paradoxically at home in Hawai'i, thus producing populations of "civilized" settlers, "uncivilized" Natives, and opportunities—however limited—to traverse those categories.[70]

The technological and cosmopolitan development of Honolulu occurred within the context of Hawai'i's political economy more broadly. Between 1850 and the present, Hawai'i's primary economic drivers have shifted from whaling to sugar to the military and tourism, and its population has expanded and diversified accordingly.[71] Immigrant laborers —Japanese, Chinese, Filipinos, Koreans, Portuguese, Puerto Ricans, and Okinawans—who arrived in the 1800s to work the sugar and pineapple plantations had, by the second quarter of the twentieth century, begun to find economic footholds that allowed them to start small businesses and expand family networks, often intermarrying and making kin with Hawaiian families. By the 1930s and 1940s, "local" identity came to reflect Hawai'i's multiethnic working class and constituted a strong counterpoint to the haole (white foreigner) domination of the plantation era. Once Hawai'i transitioned from a US territory to a state in 1959, multiculturalism emerged as one of the most celebrated features of the islands, proffering American Dream ideologies and structuring Indigenous erasure. In this way, American setter colonial sentimentalities of the nineteenth century matured into state-generated "liberal settler multiculturalism" that insisted on Hawai'i's particular suitability for all seeking acceptance and belonging.[72]

By the time of statehood, Hawai'i would be envisioned variously as a crossroads, a melting pot, and a haven for nonwhite Americans (though this sentiment has a longer genealogy).[73] As members of a multiethnic society celebrated for its tolerant approach to newcomers, Native Hawaiians have been simultaneously centered and sidelined in thermal narratives about Hawai'i's welcoming warmth. A 1993 article published in a political and social science journal, for example, argued that Hawai'i's racial tolerance stemmed from "the value of *aloha kanaka*, the love of one's fellow human beings [which] often translated into public policy."[74] Such attitudes are pervasive across academic work (particularly throughout the 1980s and 1990s), tourism literature, and fiction, which erroneously naturalize practices of welcoming as extensions of Kanaka Maoli core values.[75] In turn, the downplaying of local resistance—by both Hawaiians and non-Hawaiian allies—in favor of multiethnic belonging *as a form* of American nationalism importantly reveals how tightly the racial paradigms of the late twentieth century were bound up in claims over land and power.[76]

Today Honolulu is home to nearly 40 percent of Oʻahu's total population, though suburban sprawl blurs the boundaries between the city and the rest of the island (Oʻahu is designated as the City and County of Honolulu).[77] Honolulu—the city—stretches between the ahupuaʻa of Moanalua to Waikīkī (roughly from Daniel K. Inouye International Airport to Makapuʻu Point at the easternmost tip of the island).[78] It contains many of the state's major financial, educational, and governmental institutions, as well as Waikīkī, the crown jewel of Hawaiʻi's tourism industry.[79] Much of the state's ongoing appeal for visitors, on which its economy fiercely relies, is Hawaiʻi's unique culture and natural beauty—even though Native Hawaiians themselves face significant economic, political, and social challenges, the effects of which are reflected in disproportionately high rates of impoverishment, incarceration, and out-migration to more affordable cities in the continental United States.[80] The example of Hawaiʻi thus follows the contours of a broader phenomenon articulated by Elizabeth Povinelli, Audra Simpson, and others in which settler domination operates through a politics of recognition that aims to hold dispossessive structures in place.[81] To that end, corporeal, spiritual, and emotional expressions of indigeneity are celebrated as "traditional culture" only when they appear in politically neutral ways that affirm settler colonial dominance—often coded as multicultural coexistence.

Notions that anyone would find themselves naturally at home in Hawaiʻi underpin many post-contact histories of the islands, from Captain Cook's arrival to Hawaiian statehood. Only in recent decades have the tireless organizing and resistance of Kānaka Maoli been written back into mainstream accounts of contemporary Hawaiian history—from the signing of the Kūʻē petitions in protest of US annexation, to anti-statehood solidarity movements across the midcentury, to the Black Lives Matter movement's impact on addressing antiblackness within state multiculturalist and Hawaiian sovereignty discourse.[82] Dynamics of ongoing resistance despite settler refrains about colonial inevitability bring to mind Patrick Wolfe's important reminder that, in order "to get in the way of settler colonization, all the native has to do is stay at home."[83] This is, however, made all the more challenging when settlers believe they have arrived "home" in that very place.

HOME IS WHERE THE FRIDGE IS

Food systems are networks of intimacy. Across two centuries of Western presence in Hawai'i, freezing and refrigeration technology facilitated its integration into a complex global food system that functions, in large part, through the manipulation of temperature in order to keep foods fresh over vast distances.[84] Jonathan Rees refers to the United States as a "refrigeration nation," citing its outsize contributions to the development of freezing and refrigeration technology.[85] Early forays into American ice exportation eventually became a cold chain that made perishables commonly available in nearly every corner of the first world. Susanne Freidberg argues that refrigeration not only lengthened the global supply chain but also "fundamentally challenged the everyday power relations and knowledge that governed commerce in perishable food."[86] The development of the cold chain revolutionized how the world eats, from large-scale food systems to the intimacies of domestic life.[87]

Infrastructures of the cold determine the very conditions of life in the Hawaiian islands—as they do elsewhere—linking the global cold chain to the mundane hum of kitchen refrigerators.[88] Despite its history of agricultural abundance, nearly everything that Hawai'i residents eat is imported; real estate development has encroached on arable farmland to such an extent that a mere 11.6 percent of food is locally grown.[89] Natural disasters serve as painful reminders of the connection between thermal technologies and Hawai'i's food security: were the refrigerated container ships to stop arriving, Hawai'i would run out of fresh produce in ten days.[90]

Hawai'i's dependence on imported food, along with the additional built-in cost for perishables, makes its groceries the most expensive in the United States.[91] Analysts explain that it is not shipping per se that sets the high prices of Hawai'i's produce, meats, and dairy (as shipping cargo is relatively cheap); rather, its cost is determined by the energy required to keep food fresh in Hawai'i's warm climate, and the price of electricity is significantly higher than anywhere else in the nation.[92] A sense of precarity thereby pervades how Hawai'i residents understand their food system both in terms of supply (worrying that they will run out of food if the ships don't arrive) and in terms of cost (worrying about affordability).

While arguments about settler colonial intimacies may seem at first incidental to a history of ice and cold in Hawaiʻi, refrigerators importantly mark the conceptual and bureaucratic boundaries of domesticity within the settler state.[93] The social and fiscal pressures of Hawaiʻi's cold chain terminate in the refrigerators and freezers of homes, linking settler colonial regimes of private property and imposed expressions of normative family life.[94] This system has, over time, effectively altered the material shape of domestic space. In the late 1970s, the cost of living in Hawaiʻi soared as poststatehood in-migration from the continental US grew, resulting in a dire housing shortage.[95] By 1981, the State of Hawaiʻi began permitting the construction of ʻOhana Units—residential home additions designed to support the expansion of multigenerational households. While the ability to more comfortably house several generations under the same roof was said to appeal to Asian and Hawaiian cultural sensibilities, this change in residential zoning laws operated more as an economic pressure valve for local families. The permitting constraints for the unit determined the familial limits of their habitation: the home addition had to share a roof and a kitchen—including a full-size refrigerator—with the main house, and the tenancy would be restricted to people legally recognized as family through marriage or blood.[96]

Forty years later, the multigenerational single-family home no longer suffices. The cost of living in Hawaiʻi is currently the highest in the nation, and homeowners must wring out additional incomes by renting their extra space to nonfamilial tenants.[97] In 2015, Honolulu mayor Kirk Caldwell signed an accessory dwelling unit ordinance that permitted the construction of detached units with their own kitchens, including full-size refrigerators.[98] Through these legal frameworks, appliances not only come to define what counts as a kitchen but also delimit the family structure according to settler conventions of relatedness. This, in turn, shapes the forms of care made possible (or not) through practices of cooking and feeding.

Where refrigerators once evoked Americanness as the cold chain developed in the twentieth century, those nationalistic sensibilities have since dropped away in accordance with their ubiquity. Refrigerators have, in fact, become exceptional in their universal normativity; they are what those trained in econometrics call a "normal good," an item that marks economic wealth thresholds within a household (i.e., as income rises, so too does the likelihood that a household will own or purchase that item). A prizewinning research paper from 2013 argued that refrigerators are, in fact, *the* normal good by which global health inequality can be measured across time and space precisely because of their universality.[99] In describing this phenomenon, Emily Yates-Doerr points out that equating progress and wealth is itself a form of harm, writing that "refrigerators, taken by the global health community as evidence that people have been successfully inserted into the cold chains of global connection, are evidence in other communities of the very failure of these chains."[100] Where refrigerators appear, then, they do not necessarily measure a community's capacity for health but, instead, express capitalism's reach. By contrast, the absence of refrigerators signals spaces of habitation that exceed or sit beyond the capitalist economy's cold chain infrastructures.

Hawai'i is home to one of the largest houseless populations in the United States—a population in which Kanaka Maoli are demographically overrepresented.[101] Hawai'i's houseless, who live, according to news reports, "in public spaces not meant for human habitation," also affront Western private property regimes by reasserting claims to stolen land.[102] Bianca Isaki, describing tensions between the houseless and local fishing communities in Ka'ena Point on O'ahu, argues that settler colonial homemaking eschews Indigenous forms of kinship and relationality in favor of Indigenous dispossession.[103] Here, "legal" forms of residency and belonging become demarcated and legitimized through things like refrigerators, as well as access to running water, ice for fishing coolers, and electrical grids for powering appliances. As such, domestic reproduction and the "domestication" of foreign territories become public/private forms of the same political project of which ice and refrigeration sit at the heart.

COOLING HAWAI'I

Organized into five chapters, *Cooling the Tropics* attends to the cold's broad social meaning in Hawai'i. I draw from diverse source materials in both English and 'ōlelo Hawai'i that describe ideas about, and experiences of, the cold as it was recorded in business records, treaties, cookbooks, menus, mo'olelo, advertisements, travelogues, newspaper editorials, periodicals, and photographs. While this history is mapped out in roughly chronological order, the first and last chapters provide a contemporary frame for the historical chapters that make up the heart of the project. I use these chapters to highlight the cold's ongoing significance both as a form of dispossession and as a site of decolonial practice.

Chapter 1, "A Prehistory of the Artificial Cold in Hawai'i," highlights long-standing Kanaka Maoli relationships with the cold by looking to those places in the islands where water freezes naturally. Focusing on Maunakea's summit, it contextualizes recent struggles against the construction of the Thirty Meter Telescope (TMT) through epistemological frameworks that have sought to exclude Native Hawaiians. Slated to become the most powerful telescope in the world, the stadium-sized facility threatens to desecrate one of the most sacred sites for Kanaka Maoli. Significant within discourses in favor of summit development is the persistent belief that Maunakea is, and has always been, devoid of Native people and therefore is a kind of terra nullius, unmonitored and available for development. In particular, I locate the genealogy of logics used in favor of the TMT within nineteenth-century literatures that imagined the alpine climate of the summit as unsuitable for Kanaka 'Ōiwi. This chapter analyzes these logics across the nineteenth and twentieth centuries as they variously seek to produce Maunakea as not-for-Hawaiians, as not-Hawai'i, and as not-Earth—all in the service of scientific "progress." By drawing connections from historical ideas of race and temperature in the Pacific to the settler frontier logics of space exploration, this chapter identifies the violence of settler colonialism that alienates Kanaka 'Ōiwi from their homelands and sets up the underlying assumptions about Hawaiian relationships with the cold that shape the consumption practices that emerged with the arrival of comestible ice in the middle of the nineteenth century.

Chapter 2, "Vice, Virtue, and Frozen Necessities in the Sovereign City," looks at the brief presence of foreign ice in Hawai'i as a failed but significant chapter in the history of the American global ice trade. It begins in 1850, when a shipment of ice arrived in Honolulu from Boston, Massachusetts, after journeying for several months down the east coast of the Americas and across the Pacific Ocean. It would, like the handful of other ice shipments that arrived over the coming decade, be sold to Hawai'i consumers who craved ice-cold refreshments in the warm, tropical port city. Imported ice, used for chilling fine wines and sweet desserts, was sold in the hotels and saloons where American sugar planters, European tourists, and Hawaiian elites mingled—and from which maka'āinana (the general populace) were excluded. The legal, cultural, and economic structures that shaped Hawai'i governance during this time underpin desires for cold refreshment, provoking public discourse about temperature and climate in the context of American settlement and laying the groundwork for the infrastructural projects that followed the eventual failure of the ice trade to Hawai'i in 1860.

Chapter 3, "Making Ice Local: Technology, Infrastructure, and Cold Power in the Kalākaua Era," examines intersections between technology and taste through the establishment of ice-making machines and factories around Honolulu's urban periphery during the 1870s and 1880s. Placed against the backdrop of an increasingly formalized political relationship with the United States, it focuses on affective relationships with infrastructural development: electricity, steam engines, sewer systems, and roadways all contributed to Hawai'i's agricultural economy while at the same time supporting Honolulu's growing global modernity. The business of making artificial ice emerged as part of this broader technological landscape, offering greater availability and access to the fast-melting delicacy. The Hawaiian monarchy embraced the serving of ices and ice creams at government events—gustatory displays of state power that engaged with the complicated press of Western desires. As ice grew in popularity throughout the city, discourses turned toward the maka'āinana body to consider how Hawaiians responded to consuming the very cold. Such discourses produced hierarchies of taste premised on deeply racialized concepts of civility as a measure of climatological comfort.

Chapter 4, "Cold and Sweet: The Taste of Territorial Occupation," examines ice in the context of the territorial foodscape between 1898 and 1915. One of the consequences of US annexation was the transfer of American laws onto Hawaiian society, including the 1906 Pure Food and Drug Act against the adulteration of edible products. A few years later, in the wake of a 1911 cholera outbreak in Honolulu, when poi came under legal scrutiny as a food dangerous to public health, the newly appointed food commissioner decided instead to focus on a campaign to increase the overall butterfat content of the city's ice cream. The food commissioner's efforts to regulate ice cream, which also fell under the umbrella of pure food, served to privilege Western tastes over Indigenous public health. These legal and gustatory legacies continue to reverberate in more current projects around the revitalization of Native Hawaiian staple foods—particularly within the legalize pa'i 'ai movement of 2011.

Finally, chapter 5, "Local Color, Rainbow Aesthetics, and the Racial Politics of Hawaiian Shave Ice," places the previous chapters into conversation with more contemporary discourses of multiculturalism, postracialism, and American state power by examining visual representations of Hawaii residents who perform cool refreshment as an expression of local identity. The emergence of mixed-race identity becomes, in this case, aestheticized through the image of the shave ice cone precisely because of the food's ability to be an edible rainbow. Contrasting media representations of shave ice in a poststatehood context, first in the decades immediately following statehood in 1959 and then in the present day, I explore not only how shave ice has come to act as a metonymy for Hawaiian multiculturalism but also how it becomes used to accessorize American nationalism and Indigenous dispossession in Hawai'i as an affective and an ideological project.

Across these five chapters, which examine the evolving social meaning of the cold in Hawai'i, I seek to understand the ways that thermal relationships between race and environment have been shaped by—and continue to be shaped by—Hawai'i's food system. Within it, the cold operates variously as infrastructure, taste, and a sensorial logic of power, producing normative forms of comfort and refreshment that help to organize laboring and leisured bodies in space. Feeling cold in Hawai'i, then, articulates a thermal politics of belonging rooted in empire and settler colonialism, suturing together race-making and taste-making as complementary projects that can—and must—be attended to in struggles for food sovereignty and political self-determination in Hawai'i and beyond.

1

A PREHISTORY
OF THE ARTIFICIAL COLD
IN HAWAI'I

It was the middle of summer in Hawai'i, and snow was falling on the summit of Maunakea.[1] Screen grabs taken from webcams bolted to the exteriors of the powerful telescopes that stand sentinel showed the unseasonal blanket of white that drifted down from the sky on July 17, 2015.[2] One view, taken from the vantage of the Canada-France-Hawai'i telescope, appeared on the Instagram feed managed by @protectmaunakea with a hashtag that read #PoliahuProtectingMaunakea.[3] The commenters on the post agreed that the timing seemed purposeful, with one writing, "The Mauna is protecting itself—at least for a while." These reactions to the snowfall celebrated the fact that freezing conditions had temporarily halted activity and access to the construction site for the Thirty Meter Telescope (TMT), which protesters had already been occupying for nearly four months.[4] Attributing the snow to Poli'ahu, an important akua (deity [or deities]) of the cold who is known to reside atop Maunakea, many Kānaka Maoli recognized the event to be an exercise of her desire to protect the sacred mountain from desecration.

Many summers and snowfalls have since passed, and the threat of the TMT's construction still lingers in Hawai'i. The blockade in 2015 set into motion years of organizing on the ground and in the courts to challenge the process by which the TMT Observatory Corporation received permits to build in a conservation district on the pristine northern plateau of Maunakea.[5] At the time of this writing, these efforts to halt construction have been largely successful, the resistance movement swelling to international visibility with the establishment of Pu'uhonua o Pu'uhuluhulu in the summer of 2019 at the base of the Mauna Kea Access Road (I return to the site of the encampment in the book's conclusion). Kanaka Maoli scholars Iokepa Casumbal-Salazar, David Uahikeaikalei'ohu Maile, Noelani Goodyear-Ka'ōpua, Emalani Case, and others have written rich and fierce analyses of Kanaka Maoli protectorship of Maunakea.[6]

Notable within these works that unpack the political relationships between Kanaka and the state, laid bare through the ongoing development of Maunakea, is the attention paid to the presence of the Mauna's akua, who communicate through weather patterns. Maile, for example, in writing about the day on which thirty-eight kūpuna were detained for obstructing the Mauna Kea Access Road on July 17, 2019, described the arrival of law enforcement that morning: "There must have been 500 kia'i already present. Police from the Division of Conservation and Resource Enforcement, Hawai'i County, Sheriffs, and Attorney General's Office emerged behind the kūpuna tent, lurking around as their shadows stretched on the ground in clear morning sun. But, when police began moving in, grey clouds thickened, and quickly blanketed the blockade, perhaps in protection for the long day ahead. The mauna and its elements were responding, animate as always."[7] Descriptions like these, of the affective signals of Maunakea's snows, mists, and rains, importantly signal Kanaka Maoli perspectives on the agential forces of the elements, not just as atmosphere, precipitation, or temperature but as intention, ancestor, and spirit. These are forms of environmental knowledge that Kanaka Maoli share with many other Indigenous peoples who maintain interdependent and—to echo the words of Leanne Betasamosake Simpson—diplomatic relationships with the nonhuman world, including plants, animals, and elements.[8] This chapter analyzes how elemental agency takes on particular importance on the summit because it is there that animacy most challenges how modern-day formations of terra nullius have been employed toward capitalist ends in the name of science.

In the context of the TMT controversy, and Native Hawaiian resurgence more generally, animacy has emerged as a potent point of resistance that contends with Western colonialism's aestheticization of the cold as objective, rational, empty, and capitalistic.[9]

Western spatial and thermal imaginaries underpin development projects imposed on Indigenous lands. Desolation—narrated as uninhabitability or, at the very least, not inhabited by humans of consequence—conceptually anchors infrastructural and extractive logics, which pump resources and materials from one place to another determined to be in greater need. From uranium mines and nuclear test sites in Nevada, to the construction of oil pipelines across unceded Native territories in countries now called the United States and Canada, extractive and infrastructural regimes operate under disingenuous presumptions of environmental desolation.[10] These imaginaries are, as Nick Estes argues, an extension of the American founding myths of manifest destiny that have rationalized the settler occupation and development of Indigenous lands.[11]

In turn, Maunakea's landscape has suffered a process of de-animation across the nineteenth and twentieth centuries, where discourses of absence have systematically produced the Mauna as a place without humans, spirituality, nation, or even atmosphere. Such a conceptual vacating of Indigenous space, in turn, allows the summit to be envisioned as a bridge to a new, otherworldly frontier of colonialist and capitalist expansion. I locate this process in three phases: first, the earliest, in which Western visitors summited the mountain in the nineteenth century and communicated written accounts of its desolation to Western audiences; second, in the mid-twentieth century, when US military infrastructures increased access to the mountain and consequently facilitated a boom in both leisure and scientific activity, particularly in the form of winter sports framed as tourist novelty and National Aeronautics and Space Administration (NASA) spacewalk simulations; and finally, in the present moment, when the astronomy community and other political and economic beneficiaries have cast Maunakea as a crucial point of access to the galaxy, using the summit as a place for both celestial observation and an ongoing earthly simulation for Mars and the moon. Each of these moments is a plot point on a timeline of cumulative efforts to frame Maunakea as empty and thus available for occupation by enacting Indigenous erasure through the recasting of place itself.

This chapter anticipates those that follow in that it considers the role that environmental cold has played in Hawai'i, from mo'olelo to sport to science. It offers an important counterpoint to other portrayals of the islands that foreground warm, beachy tropicality and shows ways that Hawai'i's cold terrains have been exceptionalized as non-Hawaiian spaces precisely because of their climatic features. And so, while examinations of landscape may, at first blush, seem out of place in a book largely concerned with ice consumption, I draw attention here to how ideas about the environment both historically and in the present have organized thermal relationships within, and to, Hawai'i. The summit space becomes a prime site for the masculinist aesthetics of imperialist and settler colonial power precisely because of its environment.[12] The cold, in turn, becomes metaphorically indexical to the overlapping military, tourist, and scientific activities on Maunakea through thermal articulations of Western "rational thought," objectivity, and emotional detachment.[13]

Beginning a history of ice in the Hawaiian Islands with the arrival of New England pond water to Honolulu in the 1850s would suggest that Kanaka were only just beginning to encounter the cold in the middle of the nineteenth century. To the contrary, mo'olelo about ice were well known across the islands by way of oral transmission and later through published works that articulate theories about Hawaiian environments that stretched the length of the archipelago.[14] As Candace Fujikane describes in *Mapping Abundance for a Planetary Future*, Maunakea, also known as Mauna a Wākea, is "the sacred firstborn of the union of Papahānaumoku, she who is the foundation birthing islands, and Wākea, he who is the wide expanse of the heavens."[15] This creation story places the mountain into relation with kalo, elder sibling to Kanaka Maoli and staple food, illustrating the important links between environment and sustenance, including the value of watersheds for robust and resilient food systems.[16] In this way, ice would arrive in Hawai'i as a foreign commodity, even if its existence in the islands predated early shipments. Within Hawaiian epistemology, coldness is often feminized because of its intense and generative power. The waters of Maunakea, represented as four sisters, Poli'ahu, Lilinoe, Waiau, and Kahoupokāne, are, as Fujikane writes, examples of Kanaka frameworks of abundance that extend beyond capitalist notions of scarcity, which are often used to bracket discussions of Maunakea's past and potential future development.[17]

Thermal imaginaries about ice in Hawai'i—as an environmental and elemental medium for Western science and leisure—profoundly overlook its central role in Kanaka Maoli place and thought. Exploring discourses of the cold beyond capitalism and commoditization pushes back against narratives about ice that are solely dictated by Western paradigms; seeing consumption as distinct from environmental elements is a product of Westernization. While this book is primarily concerned with comestible ice and how Kanaka Maoli, migrants, and colonialists sensed and made sense of frozen refreshments, I use this first chapter to honor deeper genealogies of the cold in Hawai'i, and to acknowledge that multiple registers of meaning have accumulated over time, in both the refusal and the service of settler occupation.

SUMMIT ANIMACIES

It is most appropriate, then, to start with Kanaka Maoli epistemology. In ancient times only a portion of the island chain's inhabitants—those in view of the mountains on Hawai'i Island—would have seen the white caps throughout winter months; even fewer would come into contact with frozen water on the summit. Traditionally, spiritual and royal elites used these mountaintops as highly restricted sacred spaces for healing, worship, and burials. This usage is reflected in archaeological records that have identified at least 263 historic and culturally significant properties on Maunakea.[18] Understandings of summit conditions nevertheless permeated Hawaiian consciousness as a central point for Kanaka Maoli origin stories, as the piko (navel) of the universe and a dwelling place of important ancestors and akua.[19]

Mo'olelo of akua and the spaces they inhabited circulated widely throughout the islands, acting as a framework for cultural memory and placemaking.[20] Prominently located within this framework is Poli'ahu, the god known to reside at Maunakea's snowy summit. She figures most centrally in the well-known *Ka Moolelo o Laieikawai*, which S. N. Haleole initially recorded in his journal in 1844 and later published as a Hawaiian-language serial in *Nupepa Kuokoa* between 1862 and 1863.[21] In one particular version of the mo'olelo (I use Beckwith's here, though there are several), Aiwohikupua, a young chief from Kaua'i is traveling between the islands when he falls in love with a chiefess from Maui, Hinaika-malama, whom he encounters surfing waves at Pūhele in Hāna. Later she falls in love with him, too, when he bests her at a game of kōnane (Hawaiian checkers). Quickly they are betrothed, and he promises to return to her after a journey on to Hawai'i Island. However, upon arriving there he meets and falls in love with Poli'ahu, who has come down from her abode on the mountain and appears to him as a chief. Aiwohikupua regrets his recent commitment, "claps his hand before his god" to relieve himself of it, and soon he and Poli'ahu happily wed and return to Kaua'i in celebration. The jilted Hinaikamalama, not to be forgotten, hears of what has happened, arrives from Maui to assert her prior claim, and compels Aiwohikupua to renounce his union to Poli'ahu.

That night, as the reunited Aiwohikupua and Hinaikamalama lie in each other's arms, a biting cold settles over them. Poli'ahu has draped her snow mantle over them to make her displeasure felt. Hinaikamalama responds with a chant that asks the reason for this "very strange cold." "Perhaps," she wonders, "sin dwells within the house" ("Ua hewa ka paha loko o ka noho hale").[22] The lovers embrace tighter and are once again assaulted by freezing temperatures. Hinaikamalama then knows where the cold is coming from, chanting: "It is cold, cold as the snow on the mountain top . . . it presses upon my heart." Alternating burning heat with freezing cold, Poli'ahu punishes them until the couple relents and separates.[23] Poli'ahu's command of the heat and the cold thus emplaces her at the summit of Maunakea, where the characteristics of the mountain blend with her appearance; the white mantle of snow she famously wears either travels with her or returns to the mountain when she casts it off. In another version of *Ka Moolelo o Laieikawai*, the wedding party is overcome with coldness after Poli'ahu wraps her betrothed in her mantle to signify their union. After the procession is, essentially, frozen—"aole e hiki aku lakou no ke anu"—she sets aside her cape and the snow is returned once again to its usual place on Maunakea.[24]

Newspaper readers of the mid-nineteenth century would have appreciated the multiple layers of meaning encoded within this story, including lessons about the natural world, social and ancestral relations, and history.[25] In this way, Kanaka Maoli came to know the conditions of Maunakea intimately, even if they were not able to clear the summit. Just as Poli'ahu is not confined to her snowy realm, Kanaka Maoli need not go to her realm to comprehend the ecological and spiritual importance of Maunakea. The altitude and the ice are thus embedded within a complex genealogy that connects akua, humans, and nature under a single worldview.

References to Poli'ahu today, through the retelling of mo'olelo and the affirmations of her animacy through snowfalls that halt construction crews, reveal that Maunakea embodies a living history through its elemental forms and vibrant and peopled mo'olelo.[26] This presence is further explained by the Hawaiian concept of kinolau—"a literature of body forms that moves stealthily and metamorphically within the Western preoccupation with the human and animal (and plant as well as land, sea, and sky forms)."[27] The concept, elaborated by Jonathan Goldberg-Hiller and Noenoe Silva, is central to understanding how interconnectedness among human, nonhuman, and spiritual beings creates an epistemological fabric by which Hawaiians construct ideas of belonging within their ancestral homeland. Fujikane, in her readings of moʻolelo, mele, and oli (chants) about the waters of Mauna a Wākea, emphasizes the many layers of ecological, historical, and political meaning embedded within them: "[They] are all love songs that provide lessons in the ecological continuities necessary for the vibrancy of life on the mountain."[28] Moʻolelo about the mountain thereby refute claims of its desolation, instead revealing the elements on the summit to be animate, agential elements that exceed the space of the mountain itself and extend across the pae ʻāina (archipelago).

These historical narratives not only trace genealogies of being and belonging but also link the summit space to other areas of the island chain, underscoring Maunakea as a space that is deeply connected to, rather than set apart from, Hawaiʻi's lower elevations. Fujikane illustrates this point by describing that ways that Kānaka petitioners advocated for the protection of Maunakea during a series of contested case hearings against the TMT in the Hawaiʻi Supreme Court in 2011. Quoting E. Kalani Flores's testimony on behalf of Moʻoinanea, the moʻo guardian of Waiau, Fujikane underscores how akua, as elemental beings, guide pono (righteous and balanced) approaches to environmental protection. Flores describes this guidance as consciousness, stating, "Our ancestors understood this very clearly, that when we talk of akua, our akua, in the context, they are the natural elements around us. That's why our kūpuna gave them names. So it's not just the rain or the snow of the ocean and the waters; these elemental forms were the akua of our people. And it's not just elements, these elements have a consciousness. And when I say a consciousness, they have an ability to interact with us as humans."[29] Protectorship is thus characterized as a practice of deep listening based in relationality. Today, Kānaka Maoli recognition and celebration of the cultural significance of kinolau and spiritual presence on Maunakea present challenges to the settler state's ongoing development and desecration of the summit through continued insistence of cosmological relations to spiritual beings, plants, and elemental land forms. In turn,

Western characterizations of Maunakea as a lifeless void produce violent erasure by circulating narratives of emptiness at the summit rather than recognizing the beings that have occupied Maunakea since time immemorial, enacting wants, needs, desires, and displeasure.

ATMOSPHERES OF ABSENCE

Western descriptions of Maunakea take on a different tenor. At 32,000 feet from ocean floor to summit, Maunakea is the tallest mountain on the planet, with an altitude of 13,796 feet from sea level, rising above 40 percent of the earth's atmosphere. With low light pollution, low humidity, and high atmospheric stability, the mountain provides ideal conditions for celestial observation.[30] Since the 1967 establishment of the Mauna Kea Conservation District (now known as the Mauna Kea Science Reserve), it has also become one of the world's premier sites for astronomy.[31] Measurements of altitude, saturation, and degrees become, in turn, measured expressions of the mountain's scientific utility. The idealized characteristics of the mountain, presented as simple rationale, produce the mountain as a site through the stripping of its cultural significance; moʻolelo of the cold disregarded in favor of cold reason.

Although snowfall is relatively unusual on Maunakea's summit in the summer months, the impressive altitude of the dormant volcano produces its characteristically cold and dry conditions year-round. Today there are thirteen telescopes operating on Maunakea, which are collaboratively funded by government agencies from eleven different nations.[32] The land on which they sit is leased by the University of Hawaiʻi (UH) from Hawaiʻi's Board of Land and Natural Resources. In 2011, UH approved a new sublease for the construction of the TMT, slated to become the most powerful telescope on the planet. Named for the diameter of its mirror lens, the TMT is a giant among its peers, to be housed by a cycloptic dome standing eighteen stories tall at a cost of $1.4 billion.[33]

While Hawaiʻi residents have been protesting scientific development on the mountain since at least the 1960s, resistance to the building of the TMT garnered international attention in October 2014, when the telescope's groundbreaking ceremony was halted, surrounded by protectors bearing protest signs, chanting, and waving Hawaiian flags.[34] Since then, the construction project has languished while courts examine and reexamine master leases, subleases, environmental impact statements, and testimonies in a series of contested case hearings.[35] At the heart of the argument are several core issues: that the construction of the TMT would have significant negative environmental impacts that go against stewardship agreements held by UH, the lessor; that development of the summit has already desecrated, and will continue to desecrate, one of Hawai'i's most sacred sites; that the ongoing mismanagement of the Mauna Kea Science Reserve is but another act of the ongoing violence against Kanaka Maoli and the pae 'āina at the hands of the settler state.[36] To date, several excellent analyses have been published on the spiritual importance of Maunakea and the cultural significance of the TMT controversy for larger efforts toward Indigenous sovereignty and self-determination.[37] Here I build on and extend those critiques by focusing on specific elemental discourses that have made possible continued development of the summit space in the name of science.

Characterizations of atmosphere and environment have privileged the occupation of the mountain by certain bodies and for certain purposes, effectively dismissing deep histories of Indigenous knowledge and presence at the summit. Rhetorics of absence thereby operate as a function of settler colonialism rather than its product: in the state's refusal to recognize ancient and ongoing Indigenous presence on Maunakea, Kanaka Maoli are forced to make themselves "visible" and thus vulnerable to the dispossessive violence of US state power. Within the current context of Maunakea's ongoing development with the TMT, it is possible to locate the politics of recognition that Glen Coulthard articulates within liberal settler states that seek ways to accommodate Native resistance without dismantling colonial structures themselves.[38] In this case, erasure extends beyond human bodies and is pushed into the cosmological networks that connect Native Hawaiians to the very elements of place itself.

For many visitors to Hawai'i, who have come to know the islands for their sunshine and beaches, Maunakea offers a stark and often overlooked geographic contrast. Since the 1900s, when American capitalism tightened its grip on the archipelago, Hawai'i has been subject to environmental idealizations that have sustained the agricultural and tourist sectors of its economy: its temperate climate permits a year-round growing season for commodity crops like pineapple and sugar and makes it a honeymooner's fantasyland. Indeed, these two economies form a symbiotic relationship through advertising and packaging that sell the idea of a "tropical paradise."[39] First, Hawai'i is presented as a place of natural abundance: lush, sweet, and life-giving. Second, Hawai'i is a place of leisure: romantic, languid, and pleasure-giving.[40] In addition to the colonial utility of such notions of paradise or even an earthly Eden, which worked to both racialize Native Hawaiians and empower haole, these characterizations produced a vision of Hawai'i relegated to shorelines and lush valleys, where "natural" elements assert themselves in the service of aesthetic beauty and sensory pleasure.[41] And just as Hawai'i has been relegated to its sunny shores, so have Native Hawaiians: as "beach boys," resort performers, or agricultural laborers.

Together, interlocking tropes stand in contrast to Western characterizations of Maunakea as an inverse landscape, empty and desolate and unsuitable for beach-bound Kānaka. From early encounters to present-day developers, the summit has been rendered a profoundly empty space: a desolate hinterland not-quite-of Hawai'i. Indeed, the inhabitability of the summit for humans, nonhuman animals, and plants has long been a common refrain in descriptions of the landscape. Take, for example, an astronomy textbook published by Springer in 2013, in which the caption for a photograph of Maunakea's summit states, "Although Hawai'i has a reputation as a tropical paradise, the mountain of Maunakea is a desolate volcanic site. This view of Maunakea can easily be mistaken for a picture of the surface of a lifeless Mars."[42] Indeed, in the early 1970s, when Maunakea's development was still in its infancy, scientists deployed this rhetoric to confirm the site's ideal conditions for stargazing. "Mauna Kea is an extinct volcano . . . above 3000m there is little vegetation and the summit area is a barren alpine desert," went one 1973 evaluation published in the journal of the Astronomical Society of the Pacific. "The low population density [of Hawai'i] together with the high elevation effectively insulate Mauna Kea from most sources of atmospheric, electronic, and light pollution."[43] While such observations are meant to simply act as notations, it is nevertheless arresting to see how observatory construction has been predicated on ideas and measurements of absence: of geological activity, of bodies, of humidity, and of light. Narratives of emptiness here have a double effect, at once reifying a particular notion of terra nullius that has been reformulated to legitimize its use as one of the world's premier sites for modern astronomy and, simultaneously, setting up the conditions through which outer space imaginaries can be thought through the paradigm of Maunakea.

In the past few years, stakeholders in the Maunakea science community have, however, come up against insistent reminders that the summit's emptiness—as a pristine site for both development and preservation—is a historical fiction. Dismissals of Maunakea's significance for Kanaka Maoli, whether as a site of worship for aliʻi (royalty) and kahuna (spiritual leaders) or as a dwelling place for akua, remain deeply implicated in a commitment to imagining the summit as an empty space without Native peoples or Native worlds to contend with. The violence of such counternarratives about Maunakea, and the beings who do or do not occupy the summit, surfaces clearly in discussions of sacredness by Kanaka Maoli cultural practitioners, who endeavor to explain its importance from every conceivable vantage point, from ceremonial rights to natural resources.

Outstanding in a cacophony of voices protecting Maunakea from development is the manaʻo (wisdom) of Pua Kanakaʻole Kanahele, who provided the following explanation in an interview with Iokepa Casumbal-Salazar:

> The tops of the mountain have never belonged to man. In the mind of intelligent Hawaiians, it's never belonged to man . . . that's the different hierarchy in sacredness. So there's that sacredness that's totally natural, that totally belongs to the elements and our elemental deities. We have nothing to do with shaping it. And we have nothing to do with it being a benefit to us. . . . We have nothing to do with the snow that falls up there and the water that it gathers. So, it's out of man's realm. That's the whole idea to me of the sacredness of Mauna Kea.[44]

Indeed, beyond the spiritual significance of the summit, researchers have today come to grasp what Native Hawaiians have long articulated through moʻolelo: that Maunakea is full of life forces, even if they are not immediately observable. As journalist Jamie Winpenny explained to the *Big Island Weekly*: "Despite its severe, arid environment, Mauna Kea's summit is a rich ecological system. It is home to numerous, uniquely adapted native plants and creatures that include moths, caterpillars, spiders, and the tiny, predatory wekiu insect, which can survive temperatures far below freezing. The habitats in which these species thrive are fragile and delicate in the extreme. A single human footfall can cause irreparable harm. The construction of the TMT will irrefutably accelerate the loss of species and habitats that are even now on the brink of extinction."[45] The telescope's development has the potential to fully realize a colonial project that has been in motion since the early 1800s, when Westerners first set foot on the summit: a final blow to the "hidden," nonhuman animacies of Maunakea.

DE-PEOPLING AND THEN REPOPULATING THE MAUNA

By the nineteenth century, barriers to summit access instituted in ancient Hawai'i began to change when curious foreign visitors to the islands employed Native guides to accompany their treks to the summit.[46] Authors of travelogues unsurprisingly depicted Kanaka Maoli as being averse to or uncomfortable in the cold. In an account of one such expedition in 1841, American Charles Wilkes describes his party's descent from Mauna Loa as a hurried affair. "Every one was engaged in taking down and packing up the instruments and equipage," he wrote, "loaded with which the native laborers scampered off. Some of them, indeed, were unable to bear the cold any longer, and hoping to obtain loads afterwards, withdrew without burdens."[47] The idea that "natives" refused mountain ascent was established as early as 1823, when William Ellis, a British missionary, reported, "They [Hawaiians] have numerous fabulous tales relative to its being the abode of the gods, and none ever approach its summit—as, they say, some who have gone there have been turned to stone. We do not know that any have ever been frozen to death; but neither Mr. Goodrich, nor Dr. Blatchely and his companion, could persuade the natives, whom they engaged as guides up the side of the mountain, to go near its summit."[48] Framing spiritual belief as superstition, Ellis creates one of several explanations for why Hawaiians should not, or could not, claim the summit as their own: that they simply refused to occupy it. Echoing similar refrains from the continental United States, which based Indigenous claims on the literal counting of visible bodies (and ignoring the conditions under which Native people are subjected to violent processes of erasure), he instead suggests that only monetary compensation would induce guides to go with them.[49]

In 1825, not two years after Ellis's travelogue, another account produced by James Macrae more deeply entrenched these same ideas about whether or not Indigenous bodies belonged on Maunakea, even after locating evidence of Native Hawaiian human activity near the summit. After declaring the summit "too cold for natives," and then paradoxically narrating severe bouts of altitude sickness experienced by the haole contingent of their party, Macrae made a discovery at the peak (which is worth quoting at length):

> On 26th August 1823 [Goodrich] reached the summit of Mauna Kea. This is the first recorded instance of the ascent of this mountain, although Mr. Goodrich mentions that on reaching the top of one of the terminal cones that encircle the main plateau of Mauna Kea, he discovered a heap of stones, probably erected from some former visitor. Who this former visitor was is unknown, but he was probably one of the white men that in the early years of the nineteenth century got a living by shooting wild bullocks. . . . It is very unlikely that any native had reached the top of the terminal cones on the summit, owing to being unprovided with warm clothing to resist the great cold and also to the fact that the natives had a superstitious dread of the mountain spirits or gods.[50]

The passage, later added as a lengthy footnote to his journal entry, marks an important pivot in Western perspectives about life and liveliness at the summit. First, it memorializes Western conquest of the mountain's temperatures and altitudes; second, it establishes an originary presence of white bodies at the summit. The intentionality of establishing such a presence is underlined by this interpretation of the ahu (shrine) as a simple cairn found at the highest point. Dismissing a logical presumption that the stones signal a longtime Native Hawaiian presence, it instead attributes them to a vague notion of nineteenth-century haole hunters, who wouldn't have reason or need to venture that high. A commitment to white presence on Maunakea thus makes it easy to ignore the struggles of all bodies to adjust to the summit and instead focus on only Native shortcomings (despite the fact that on the day of Macrae's summiting, the infamous Goodrich was "laid up with mountain sickness").[51]

While early nineteenth-century visitors to Maunakea were quick to imagine only the presence of white male bodies on the mountain's summit, later excursions seemed to acknowledge evidence of Kanaka Maoli activities, though these activities were always placed in a distant and forgotten past. A report published in the *Pacific Commercial Advertiser* on October 23, 1862, described how Dr. William Hillebrand, physician to the Hawaiian royal family, located Native Hawaiian artifacts during his summit of Maunakea that same year:

About 1500 feet below the top, on a side of the mountain seldom visited by either foreigners or natives, they discovered an ancient manufactory of stone implements. It consists of a cave, in front of which was a pile of stone chips 25 feet high, which had evidently accumulated from the manufacture of stone adzes, maika balls, &c. &c., which lay scattered about in an unfinished state. In front of the cave was found a wooden idol, in good preservation, which with the pedestal attached to it, measures nearly five feet high. . . . Bones of pigs and dogs, kapa, pieces of cocoa-nut shells, fragments of hewn wooden implements, sea shells, and many other curiosities were also found.[52]

After plundering the site and returning to Waimea with as much "as they could carry," Hillebrand's party reported that the quarry—rich as it was with many signs of everyday living that suggest a greater significance than their title implies—was unknown to any of the Kānaka Maoli they consulted. He stated, "On inquiry among them, no person appears to have heard of the existence of the manufactory,—even the oldest natives were ignorant of it."[53] While it is impossible to know the dynamics at play by which the residents of Waimea claimed to not know about the rock quarry, it is entirely possible that nondisclosure was chosen as a response to a group of outsiders, or simply that Hillebrand spoke to the wrong interlocutors.

What is clear is that the group of hikers sought validation for their decision to rob the quarry site by reporting that no person claimed the items or the space. Audra Simpson's theory of ethnographic refusal offers insight into both the lack of prior knowledge professed to Hillebrand by those he queried *and* Hillebrand's refusal to see any connection between human-made objects and the presence of Indigenous humans. As Simpson explains: "Historical perceptibility is used, and is still used, to *claim*, to define capacities for self-rule, to apportion social and political possibilities, to, in effect, empower and disempower indigenous peoples in the present. Such categorical forms of recognition and mis-recognition are indebted to deep philosophical histories of seeing and knowing."[54] If claiming summit space required apparent emptiness, early encounters on Maunakea sought to validate a view of the mountain as one without spirits, people, or knowledge itself. This required Western visitors either to ignore evidence of Kanaka activity or instead to explain them away by improbable interpretations of non-Native presence. This refusal to acknowledge Hawaiian emplacement on Maunakea, begun in the nineteenth century, would go on to underpin the logics of Maunakea's development as a premier place of, and for, Western science, military, and leisure that emerged potently in the second half of the twentieth century. In this way, terra nullius, even as an imaginary, operates as a form of placemaking that sets the foundation for future colonial projects.

HAWAI'I/NOT HAWAI'I

Astronomy, military activity, and tourism cohered on Maunakea in the midcentury, with the construction of summit access roads meant to facilitate military transit across Hawai'i Island. The Saddle Road, which connects Hilo to Waimea (and then on to Kailua-Kona), was laid in 1943 to service the newly established Pōhakuloa Training Area—a site that continues to be the largest US Department of Defense training ground in the Pacific. In the 1960s, under interest from the University of Arizona's Lunar and Planetary Laboratory, improvements to the Saddle Road began in earnest, and the newly added Mauna Kea Access Road was dedicated in 1964.[55] It offered unprecedented access for those who would capitalize on Maunakea's distinct atmospheric and topographic attributes. In addition to telescope construction, beginning with UH88 for the University of Hawai'i proposed in 1965 and entered into service in 1970, NASA and civilian usage of the slopes flourished. The key activities that emerged were space mission training and skiing—two overlapping articulations of the summit as an exceptional and masculinized space that initially emerged in the 1960s and 1970s and solidified in the 1990s. Each explicitly served to recast Maunakea as a place both not-for-Hawaiians and also, perhaps, not even *of* Hawai'i itself.[56]

Maunakea's use in the second half of the twentieth century as both outer space and play space mirrored Hawai'i's broader and increasing reliance on a militouristic economy, in which tourism obscures and scaffolds the American military occupation of the Pacific.[57] As Vernadette Gonzalez explains in *Securing Paradise*, the military's "masculinized mobilities" included the capacity to travel not only across highways, roads, and oceans but also up and over landscapes in ways that simulate an omniscient "god's-eye" view.[58] These experiences in the air become, in turn, complemented by promises of respite and recuperation at the shore, on beaches, and in tiki bars or dives. Connecting World War II and Vietnam War–era "aerial fields of vision" to the astral projections of the US space

"Oh, is that today?"

Figure 1.1. The Hawaiian shirt operates here as the uniform of the "off-duty" astronaut. Robert Leighton, "Oh, Is That Today?" (cartoon), *New Yorker*, April 16, 2007.

program, it is no accident that portrayals of extreme-altitude activities in film, television, and news media are frequently paired with midcentury Hawaiian aesthetics forged in the Pacific theater.

While the tropics might initially seem to have an oppositional relationship to the lunar, histories of military aerial forays into the Pacific reveal the two spaces, instead, as cherished complements. Hawaiian shirts, for example, frequently adorn the figure of the aeronaut once the space suit has been hung up—a phenomenon most recently exemplified in 2018 by the incumbent crew of the International Space Station, who wore matching blue plumeria-patterned shirts to welcome the arrival of new crew members.[59] Cape Canaveral tiki bars, to use another example, that serve cold beers and frozen cocktails against a backdrop of Polynesian kitsch to NASA crews on their off-hours draw precisely on the racialized, gendered, and thermal discourses of military pasts projected into a scientific future. In a third and most recent instance, billionaire en-

Figure 1.2. "Apollo Valley," Hawai'i Island, December 1970. NASA Photo Archives.

trepreneur Elon Musk's SpaceX program has developed a spaceport and resort village in Brownsville, Texas, that features Starship launchpads within a stone's throw of SpaceX's very own Starbase Tiki Bar.[60] As the warm, feminized, and happy host of cold, masculinized, and objective summit activities, Hawai'i offers an intensified expression of the lunar/beach divide collapsed into the same island locale.[61] Namely, the environmental incongruity—or, more precisely, complementarity—of summit and shore stoked fantasies of Maunakea as a space beyond Hawai'i while simultaneously remaining in Hawai'i.

Analog relationships between Hawai'i and the moon/Mars intensified between the years 1965 and 1972, when NASA deployed Apollo mission astronauts across multiple sites on Hawai'i Island, including areas on Kīlauea, Maunaloa, and Maunakea.[62] Photos taken during these years, which resurfaced from the NASA archives in 2014 as part of an effort to celebrate Hawai'i Island's contribution to the US space program, show Apollo 14 and 15 astronauts in sunglasses and short-sleeved shirts bumping across lava fields in a makeshift "lunar roving vehicle" and wearing large white space packs and chest-mounted cameras while "collecting" soil samples from a "lunar-like" landscape. While simulation was not relegated solely to Maunakea, its summit represented a key site on the

Figure 1.3. Maunakea skiing photo detail from Josh Lerman, "Hawaii Not?," *Skiing*, February 1990, 30.

moon, the Taurus-Littrow Valley, where Apollo 17 astronauts would land. Apollo project manager Donald Beattie later recalled that "this Hawaiʻi simulation was about as good as we could get in obtaining a high-fidelity rehearsal before the real mission was underway."[63] A lava field located at 11,500 feet became an especially popular area for training and remains so to this day. For half a century now, it has been known as Apollo Valley.

At the same time that astronauts "explored" Maunakea's "lunar landscape," military veteran Richard Tillson led efforts to map out the summit's potential ski runs by spending two months camping on the slopes while conducting an independent survey. As he saw it, the newly constructed access road also opened up promising avenues for tourism. In an interview published in *Ski* magazine, for example, Tillson explained that if one added the number of residents in Hawaiʻi who already knew how to ski to "the number of tourists who would love to say they have skied in Hawaiʻi . . . there is a good potential for ski development."[64] Over the next twenty years, downhill skiers populated Maunakea's slopes through regularly organized meets and competitions composed of residents and visitors, who characterized their sport as a natural extension of Hawaiʻi's ocean sports that had been recently appropriated on the American continent.[65] To that end, a featurette in the February 1992 issue of *Skiing* magazine, entitled "Hawaii Not?," reported: "Hawaii has a long tradition of reveling in speed, spray, and smiles. After all, surfing was invented there, as was an early form of the water slide. So it's only natural that, despite the tropical clime, Hawaiians would take to snow skiing in whatever way they could."[66] The text is accompanied by a photograph of two men in snowsuits whizzing past one of the Keck Observatories, which the caption jokingly calls "the world's largest high-altitude macadamia nut storage facility."[67] Although written in jest, the caption highlights how images and discourse are layered to produce an idea of "Mauna Kea" as both the natural and exceptional backdrop to a host of exercises of American masculinity—military, sport, and astronautic— filling up raw space and new possibilities for capitalist expansion and observation. Simulation and pantomime, in this case, reimagine the summit as an always already elsewhere of infinite frontiers for the white male body to traverse.[68]

TERRA INCOGNITA, TERRA NULLIUS

Across the course of its development, the summit of Maunakea has been systematically recast as a space both otherworldly and a-national through its utilization for scientific research. This reflects discursive practices within the science community at large, where research sites like Maunakea often become valued as places that transcend international politics in the name of the greater good of humankind—belonging to no one in particular and to everyone in general.[69] It is here that Western perceptions of climate and landscape have historically been mobilized to presume availability via apparent emptiness.

The practice "moon walks" of the Apollo missions, paired with skiing Maunakea's previously uncharted slopes, pantomimed twentieth-century American manifest destiny. Astrophysicist Martin Elvis likens the moon missions to the settlement of the American West, posing a metaphor for explaining why the United States should maintain a robust space program into the twenty-first century: "Imagine that the United States had ignored the territories acquired in the Louisiana Purchase. At first, this was a hostile territory and much of it was considered a desert. Ignoring the American West might have left the Native Americans better off, but the United States would be radically reduced. Other European nations were then actively exploring the territory, as other nations are today exploring space. In the hostile territory of space there is, fortunately, no indigenous population to abuse, and we already know that the resources are there."[70] Drawing clear parallels to the violence of elimination perpetuated against Native Americans throughout the nineteenth century, Elvis envisions space as an uninhabited resource primed for exploitation—if not by the United States, then by another global power. It is, he explains, "time to unleash capitalism in space."[71] Not only did "moon walks" operate as rehearsals for a future that drew on dispossessions of the past, but the logics of its narration rested on an aesthetics of the cold used to underscore affective perceptions of the frontier as hostile and desolate, as a prime site for capitalistic development without emotional concerns.

To better understand how Maunakea becomes positioned as both a settler resource frontier and a neutral international space, affinities (as well as distinctions) might be drawn here between the case of Antarctica, an international research site born from frontier narratives of colonial settlement as a "terra incognita" appendage to Australia in the early twentieth century.[72] Of course, several key points distinguish Maunakea from Antarctica, including how claims to occupation are legitimized, geospatial scale, and material culture evidence of human presence. Even so, for both sites, a presumed lack of human habitation has emboldened international claims to "ice deserts" that can be amicably shared among those for whom the material and knowledge resources of those spaces benefit, thereby enacting colonialism in fundamental ways. While the Antarctic international society envisions itself as exempt from postcolonial critique, "in large part because of an absence of an Indigenous human population and an absence of race-based violence," this rationale sees Indigenous claims to space only through permanent bodily presence and, more precisely, the presence of bodies marked by political difference made only and through settler occupation.[73] The equivalences drawn between people and possession, sport, and militarization, drawn starkly in the Antarctic context, can then be easily superimposed onto sites like Maunakea when prior claims are ignored in favor of "apparent" human absence.

In the cases of both Maunakea and Antarctica, scientific research is mobilized as a rationale for more permanent occupation. Klaus Dodds and Christy Collis argue, in the case of Antarctica, that techniques of measurement, surveying, taxonomizing, and observation are hallmarks of scientific research that are not without colonial politics, even if those politics are not enacted in direct relation to human subjects. "Viewed through a postcolonial perspective," they write, "this ostensibly neutral scientific engagement becomes more complex, and the articulation of scientific practice and colonial geopolitics becomes clear."[74] (Indeed, it is possible to find echoes of colonial impulses to measure in one of the earliest Western accounts referenced earlier when Ellis laments, "We could not but regret that we had no barometer, or other means of estimating the actual elevation of this mountain").[75] With Maunakea operating as an earthly simulacrum of outer space, such desires for capitalism have been extended to the summit space through the TMT's and UH's promises that development of the mountain will attract revenue, employment, and prestige for Hawai'i's people (though, as many have shown, these alleged benefits are limited in scope when compared with institutional and corporate benefits).[76] The telescopes mediate resource extraction, in terms of both data and material lunar resources, as well as operate as a revenue engine for scientific research, facilitating multiple forms of colonial dispossession within the Hawai'i/not-Hawai'i paradigm. Coupled with the formulation that Maunakea's environmental conditions are ideal for scientific observation and data collection, that idealism can then be interpreted as one that supersedes Native claims; that what Maunakea can provide humankind-in-general absolves developers and the scientific community from obligations to respect sacredness and environmental conservation needs.

This orientation toward the summit of Maunakea serves to put its environment in the employ of humankind's greater good by abstracting its emplacement within Hawai'i and Native Hawaiian culture. Such an attitude dovetails with a more general late twentieth-century internationalization of science, which seeks to work in a vacuum of geopolitical conflicts toward the advancement of global research and has been embedded within the trajectory of the summit's development, particularly in regard to the telescopes that currently litter the Mauna Kea Science Reserve. For example, between 1970 and 2010, the summit became home to thirteen telescopes that are comanaged by groups from eleven different nations.[77] A 2013 paper in promotion of the TMT boasted about the level of international cooperation that the project would engender, stating that "with the partnership of the astronomy communities, and their sponsors, of India, Canada, China, Japan, and the USA, TMT represents a scale of global collaboration well beyond the previous . . . projects in Chile and Hawaii."[78] These articulations of the benefits of international cooperation underscore the inherent muddiness of imagining who the "greater good" serves, and how that shifts between Hawaiian and "global" contexts.

This is further reflected in statements made by Native Hawaiian representatives who must appeal to notions of the greater good to advocate for environmental protection over scientific development. In the wake of the contested hearing for the TMT's sublease from UH, Office of Hawaiian Affairs (OHA) trustee Rowena Akana remarked, "The University has taken license to do many, many things that are way out of their jurisdiction . . . this isn't just the mountain, it's the oceans, and it's everything. Ceded lands belong to all of our people, and we have to be the fiduciaries."[79] In another instance, former OHA trustee Don Aweau explained that "the ʻāina [including Maunakea's summit] should be preserved in perpetuity as a public benefit, not only for Hawaiians like myself, but as a public benefit for all."[80] For those concerned with the impact of the TMT on Maunakea's fragile ecosystems, considerations of the greater good—for knowledge of the universe as well as the protection of endangered flora and fauna—hinge on appeals to ideas of benevolence rather than obligations toward Native communities.

EMPTY RHETORIC, EMPTIED SPACES

In September 2019, a few months into the establishment of Puʻuhonua o Puʻuhuluhulu, the encampment and space of refuge established for kiaʻi at the base of the Mauna Kea Access Road, Hawaiʻi Island mayor Harry Kim unveiled a plan for resolving the dispute "in a good way." Outlined in a pamphlet entitled *The Heart of Aloha: A Way Forward Maunakea*, the proposal aimed to embed the TMT within a narrative of Hawaiian cultural and political progress, promising to use Kanaka Maoli educational programs, land conservancies, and governing bodies as a foundation for ethical development of the Mauna Kea Science Reserve going forward. Drawing on discourses of aloha to continue development plans despite vigorous Kanaka Maoli opposition, the proposal draws on strategies documented by Stephanie Nohelani Teves and Lisa Kahaleole Hall, in which the settler state leverages Hawaiian conceptual frameworks of reciprocity—glossed as aloha—under the guise of "cooperation," "hospitality," and "generosity."[81]

Indeed, the title of the document, "The Heart of Aloha," suggested that Kanaka acquiescence to telescope construction would reflect the very essence of the concept, rather than resistance to site desecration. In addition to pledges toward decommissioning and removing a number of under- and unutilized telescopes from the summit, the document includes specific commitments offered by pro-TMT stakeholders in leadership positions, such as University of Hawai'i president David Lassner, who "commit[ed] to establishing a facility to celebrate and honor Hawaiian history, knowledge, culture, and language, *along with modern science and astronomy.*"[82] Summit development plans like these aim to "honor" sacred space in such a way that permits the industries of science and tourism to continue unencumbered. Such narrow understandings of aloha, however, failed to resonate with kia'i. For them, aloha is a concept that encompasses refusal, particularly when expectations of reciprocity violate principles of aloha 'āina.[83]

The weaponization of Indigenous values toward development is not unique to Hawai'i. Instead, it exemplifies the processes by which Indigenous sacred space gets rendered legible through settler capitalism, even when it is deemed worthy of preservation. As Adam Fish describes, the post–World War II infrastructural development of the American West resulted in the careful partitioning and conservation of sites not yet obliterated by dams, mines, and suburban sprawl.[84] With examples like Mount Shasta in California, Mato Tipila and Medicine Wheel in Wyoming, and Caco Canyon and Rainbow Bridge in Arizona, Fish argues that such spaces spared from development become primed, instead, for tourism, in which "the aesthetic qualities of sacred sites are geospatially located and repositioned as nature reserve, wilderness study area, archaeological district, national gateway, or theme park."[85] Echoing arguments made by Robert Nichols about the recursive creation of private property within the settler colonial project, proposals to "set aside" untouched spaces offer settlers experiences of the sublime through Indigenous erasure, all the while scaffolding those experiences with paved roads, gift shops, restrooms, and tours.[86] When Indigenous histories are marked in such spaces (as they often are), they become folded into narratives of the past that, Fish notes, absolve visitors of obligations to the living communities that claim and caretake those lands in the present.

MAKING ICE FOREIGN

Across the *longue durée* of non-Native presence on the summit of Maunakea, ways of imagining its high-altitude environments seek to organize bodies in space. In particular, they frequently imagine where Native Hawaiians belong, and in what capacity they might take on the role of facilitating white presence (as trek guides, and more recently as visitor center docents or construction workers). Kānaka are busy imagining beyond such proscribed positions in an industry premised on the erasure of Indigenous placemaking. In his essay on gender, sexuality, and the settler colonial project, Scott Lauria Morgensen describes an image from a portrait series by Taskigi/Diné artist Hulleah J. Tsinhnahjinnie, which shows a photograph of a young Native child collaged over an image of an astronaut walking on the moon.[87] The portrait, Morgensen explains, suggests "juxtapositions that interrupt any narrative of the moon as *terra nullius.*"[88] His analysis powerfully resonates with the assessment that this chapter outlines: not only that the ongoing presence of Native bodies and epistemologies refutes an imagined emptiness of the moon, or any of its earthly analogues, but also that ideas of terra nullius continue to be perpetuated in spaces deemed unoccupied and available for settlement and/or development. As Morgensen eloquently shows in his reading of Tsinhnahjinnie's portrait, "The ontology of settler colonialism has been premised on its own boundlessness: always capable of projecting another horizon over which it might establish and incorporate a newest frontier."[89] Indigenous peoples disrupt those historical fictions just as much as they get in the way of settler colonial futures by insisting on the ongoing presence of nonhuman kin in sacred spaces.[90]

Discourses that have been used to organize Hawaiian people in space under settler colonial regimes not only reveal the underlying logics of development on Maunakea's summit as ones that emerge from historical ideologies of manifest destiny and terra nullius, but also more broadly inform settler imaginaries about the value of the cold in Hawai'i. Industries of tourism and science put Maunakea's frozen elevations to work in the service of capitalist accumulation—celebrating ice as a remarkable feature of Hawai'i's landscape that, nevertheless, imagines Kanaka Maoli claims to its scaredness as exaggerated, irrelevant, or incidental to development imperatives. Embedded within these discourses, then, is an epistemological cleaving between Hawaiians and the cold that relies on a paradox that treats ice as both natural to Hawai'i and, yet, foreign to Hawaiians.

This idea is tenacious. Many times as I was researching and writing this book, people have wanted to discuss with me the famous first sentence of Gabriel García Márquez's *One Hundred Years of Solitude*: "Many years later, as he faced the firing squad, Colonel Aureliano Buendía was to remember that distant afternoon when his father took him to discover ice."[91] While presented as an earnest connection to the questions I'm interested in exploring, their eyes always shine with the idea of a whole people marveling at the novelty of ice as late as the nineteenth century. The beauty of García Márquez aside, the Indigenous "discovery" of ice in the tropics stands in as a shorthand for a primitive past unimaginable to the modern person.

The following chapters trace the social history of ice as it became imported, marketed, and sold as an object foreign to Hawai'i, distinct from the tundra of its mountain summits. To build on the environmental focus that I take here, I turn now to the historical processes through which the ice on our Mauna and the ice in our drinks become disaggregated as separate objects. The commoditization of ice and the cold, as it developed across centuries of Western contact, occluded more ancient relationships that Kānaka have with the cold—ones that exceed capitalism, Western "cold reason," and terra nullius logics of emptiness and absence. These are embedded within the thermal politics of Hawaiian embodiment that I trace across the nineteenth and twentieth centuries, in which ice transforms from akua into comestible, from Indigenous to foreign, and from element to product.

2

VICE, VIRTUE,
AND FROZEN NECESSITIES
IN THE SOVEREIGN CITY

In contrast to the waters that naturally freeze on Hawai'i's highest summits, some of the first comestible ice to arrive in the islands came by ship from the American Northeast, ready to be chipped off huge blocks and into the drinking glasses of Honolulu's elite. Trying to imagine what it was like—that first moment when ice came off a boat docked in Honolulu Harbor—requires understanding how the cold, even if strange to the Hawaiian sensorium at the time, exemplified long-established Anglo-European relationships to a racialized tropics. Ice arrived in Hawai'i under the auspices of the imagined necessity of cold elsewhere, like so many blocks of ice that Frederic Tudor shipped to India for Britain's sweltering colonial officers at the height of the nineteenth-century American ice trade.[1] Although Honolulu is considerably more temperate than Bombay, those in the city who were privileged enough to hold some of that ice, or perhaps roll it around on their tongues for a few moments, might have nevertheless longed for its sharp coldness because they desired the kinds of relationships that such a rare luxury indicated: status, power, and a command of the elements such that frozen New England pond water might travel a third of the globe for their pleasure.

The economic and social history of the American ice trade as it traversed oceans marks, broadly, how practices of cold refreshment centered and affirmed settler worlds and embodiments; blocks of ice were extracted from colonized territories and sent off by ship to refresh managers, overseers, tourists, and missionaries in tropical climes. Similarly, as ice became domesticated into Hawaiian worlds, the legal and social frameworks that governed its consumption embedded Western gender and racial ideologies within its early arrival to the islands. Across these global transits—to Hawaiʻi and elsewhere—ice took on consumptive registers produced through processes of capitalism and colonialism.[2] An ever-increasing number of Westerners, emboldened by piousness, a sense of racial superiority, or maybe greed, jockeyed for positions of power in Hawaiian society. In turn, they brought their own tastes and desires to bear on the islands, and Hawaiʻi's commercial centers felt their impact most.[3] Enthusiasm or curiosity around ice consumption (even when rarely available) responded, then, to a growing anxiety around the international recognition of Hawaiian sovereignty in a time of expanding foreign commerce.[4]

Consumption practices enlivened the differences—real and imagined—between Hawaiians and foreigners, men and women, and elite and commoner, in the freshly minted heart of the Hawaiian Kingdom. Over two decades in the 1850s and 1860s, ice would sporadically (and unprofitably) arrive from the American Northeast or Alaska to fill the cocktail glasses and water pitchers of Honolulu's social elite. Minor as it was, the ice trade's relationship with the alcohol market created a fertile battleground within a much larger war over political power, including commodity regulation, Native rule, and a vigorous temperance movement designed to civilize. These efforts extended well beyond Hawaiʻi's shores, spreading across Indian Country and into the homes of the American immigrant and lower classes. Within Honolulu, social efforts to restrict alcohol consumption and economic motivations to import alcoholic goods influenced discourses around race, civility, and cold consumption. Ice would be employed in the service of drinking for purity, in the case of the temperance movement's Cold Water Army, and as a catalyst for pleasurable overconsumption, in the case of critiques leveraged against the entertainments of the Hawaiian royalty.

This chapter sets up the outsize impact of the ice trade on nineteenth-century Hawaiian culture relative to the scant tonnage of ice that actually made it to Honolulu's shores, showing the ways that foreigners interpreted the availability of cold consumption through imperial frameworks of religion, commerce, and racial embodiments. The unprofitability of imported ice left a dearth of business records, shipping reports, and news that allowed the ice trade to fade quickly from public memory. Rather than interpret this lack of information as a reflection of ice's irrelevance to Honolulu daily life in the 1850s and 1860s, it instead can be seen as speaking to the pace at which foreign entrepreneurs worked to capitalize on Pacific markets, seeking out potential consumer desires and then discarding them just as fast when early returns didn't come. This section takes stock of Hawai'i's early ice archive in order, first, to chart out a business history that has fallen from view and, second, to underscore the dogged entrepreneurialism that fueled ice's faltering arrival across at least a decade's time.

Keeping ice frozen in a ship's hold long enough to sell in the Pacific took effort. Before the Panama Canal opened in 1914, a trip to Honolulu from Boston, Massachusetts, included a harrowing pass around Cape Horn and usually a stop in San Francisco before crossing the Pacific's expanse, and so merchants tended to carry comestible ice only when they needed extra ballast for light cargo loads. Early shipments to the Pacific coincided with the overall peak of the ice trade in 1856, a distinctly American industry dominated by Frederic Tudor, a determined man of fluctuating finances who developed insulation and packing methods useful for shipping frozen lake water across long distances. He did brisk business out of Massachusetts and Maine throughout the nineteenth century, sending ice to ports in India, the Caribbean, or the American South, where colonial industries already prevailed.[5]

While the ice trade thrived in other areas of the global South, it struggled in Honolulu, in part because of the Hawaiian monarchy's careful control over international trade at the time. Indeed, Kamehameha III's cabinet rebuffed several attempts by would-be ice importers to secure exclusive contracts in the 1850s.[6] Print archives offer up few details for sketching out a business history that never quite got off the ground, but had a lasting impact on Hawai'i's social and gustatory landscape. The lengthiest piece of writing Hawai'i's archives have on the topic, for example, appears in the 1931 issue of *Thrum's Hawaiian Annual*, the long-running almanac of Hawai'i's business, commerce, and people, which summarized the Honolulu ice trade in a few short paragraphs. "Honolulu's introduction to the use and comfort of ice," it states, can be correlated to three specific moments. First, a few tons arrived from San Francisco in June 1852. Less than two years later, a full cargo of ice shipped from Sitka at the consignment of the local ship chandlery Swan and Clifford, which resulted in "an unfortunate loss of several thousand dollars." Finally, a small ice importation business established by C. H. Lewers provided semiregular shipments from Boston between October 1858 and July 1859, from which he failed to profit.[7] Judging from slim newspaper coverage about these various ventures and businesses, Honolulu residents didn't dwell much on ice cargoes after they melted away, even if the shipments did arrive to occasional fanfare.

Here is what historical newspapers do show: contrary to *Thrum's* assertion that ice first arrived in 1852, sources indicate that Honolulu residents had their earliest tastes in 1850. In fact, the first flurries of ice in Hawai'i must have seemed to be happening all at once. On August 24, 1850, Henry Macfarlane published an advertisement for an ice-making machine alongside an announcement for the grand reopening of his Commercial Hotel.[8] Considering that the earliest experiments with freezing technology existed only as prototypes in 1850, the machine's functionality is questionable, but nevertheless the ad exists as the first record of ice in Honolulu.[9] For his clientele, which consisted largely of local and foreign elites, Macfarlane boasted "a patent ice machine having been purposely imported at a great expense, in order to afford this luxury to the frequenters of this establishment."[10] As the advertisement ran throughout the remainder of the year, and the editorials remained silent on whether the alcohol was, indeed, "placed on the table in a state of delicious coolness" at the Commercial, the *Polynesian* announced that ice from Boston had also arrived by way of San Francisco aboard the American brig *Fortunio* on September 14, less than a month after the ice machine appeared.[11] The quantity may have been small, since the papers do not note tonnage—just that the ship proceeded on to Sydney a few months later—and appears to have been quickly forgotten.

When a cargo of ice arrived in late June 1852, the *Polynesian* noted, "This is the first importation of its kind, in any quantity, to this market, and but the beginning, it is to be hoped, of a regular supply of this luxury to the inhabitants of this city," failing to mention either Macfarlane's machine or the *Fortunio*'s cargo.[12] The shipment amounted to only a few tons packed aboard the *Harriet T. Bartlett*, which arrived on June 18 after a thirteen-day crossing from San Francisco and soon went to auction at a minimum bid of twenty-five cents per pound.[13] At the time, Honolulu didn't have an icehouse prepared for storage; this perhaps is why little time was wasted on the arrival of the ice, which was probably scooped up by the few bidders who could afford to spend their money on quick-melting luxury items. The papers do not provide any additional details (who purchased the ice, how long it lasted, how people used it), though it almost certainly came from a Russian settlement in Sitka, Alaska, which traded ice to California from February 1852 to 1859 through the Russian American Commercial Ice Company.[14]

By October 1854 Swan and Clifford busily prepared to offer the city an ice supply with greater regularity. A few days before the arrival of its first cargo of five hundred tons, workers were still rushing to complete the company's ambitious icehouse, a building designed to hold up to one thousand tons that sat near the "Lime Kiln" at the base of Maunakea Street on land leased from the kingdom.[15] On October 17, and again on November 4, 1854, Swan and Clifford advertised in the *Polynesian* that it possessed ice "in quantities to suit," which had arrived from Prince Frederick's Sound, Alaska, by way of San Francisco.[16] While editorials expressed hope that the ice business would finally find its footing, by March 26, 1855, Swan and Clifford closed shop and quietly left behind $40,000 of forged bills of exchange and $80,000 of "other liabilities."[17] These layers of forgetting—despite novelty, fraud, and insulated infrastructures where there were once none in the port city—suggest that proximate experiences with ice belonged to a scarce few. As one Honolulu resident recalled in 1903, "Ice was a cargo, taken only when it was cheap in Boston and when the ships could get no other cargo for the Pacific. . . . The ships bringing ice, from Boston that is, would take home whale bone and oil, and usually made a good thing of it. But they did not come often. Not more than once a year, as I remember."[18] And so, memories of the ice trade faded quickly in Hawai'i's public record, relegated to vague recollections of this ship's arrival, or that failed business venture; inconsistency and inaccessibility overshadowed the impact of those first ephemeral cargoes. Even if imported ice didn't last long, or make much for those who brought it to Honolulu's harbors, it fit right into the imperial narratives that foreigners had grafted onto Hawai'i as a space of colonial possibility.

When commodity ice first reached Honolulu in 1850, those who consumed it lived in a rapidly changing world. In this period identified by scholars as the "critical" era of its modern development, Honolulu bore the brunt of early capitalism in Hawai'i, with the greatest concentration of foreigners exerting their needs, desires, and business interests on the cityscape.[19] It was also where Western ideas about race, class, and gender norms set their deepest roots. The kingdom government, which had been formed in 1795 under the rule of Kamehameha I, Kalani Pai'ea, formally moved its seat to Honolulu in 1850, during the reign of Kamehameha III, Ka Mō'i Kauikeaouli. Kamehameha III steered Hawai'i through a number of key political changes, including the creation of a formal legislature and privy council, the relocation of the capital city from Lahaina, Maui, and the land distribution into private property commonly known as the Great Māhele.[20] Strategically aimed to circumvent Western encroachment, Kamehameha III's changes nevertheless mirrored European conventions. As J. Kēhaulani Kauanui observes, "An adaptation to nineteenth century European conventions of statehood, in which 'civilized manhood' was crucial to the representation of the nation," inscribed Hawai'i's governance with models of Western subjecthood.[21] Individual comportment under the guise of civility served as both gendered and racialized performances of colonial politics that, Kauanui argues, paradoxically disavowed Western power while also embedding its social values into the very fabric of Hawaiian society.

These transitions at both the personal and the political level reflected not only the city's overall orientation toward international business and trade but also an early racialization of the political and economic center of Hawai'i. Between 1845 and 1855, the Māhele made possible fee simple ownership of land by both foreigners and Kānaka Maoli through the dismantling of the traditional Hawaiian land tenure system.[22] In the middle of this process, Honolulu Harbor increased its capacity for trade by widening and deepening, so that larger and more numerous ships could be accommodated.[23] Accordingly, Honolulu became the most populous settlement of the kingdom, with approximately 10,000 of O'ahu's 73,000 or so residents packing in among foreign settlers, of which there were 1,180 (about half being American).[24] Gavan Daws, in his study of nineteenth-century Honolulu development, asserts that "the raw data [of the Māhele] shows that in the down-town area foreigners were awarded about 50 percent of lots, and that the percentage of awards to foreigners decreased steadily as distance from the harbor increased."[25] By the end of the Māhele, the city's population had correspondingly redistributed itself along blurry but discernibly racial lines, particularly where the shipping industry had made land desirable for foreigners seeking business opportunities.[26]

In the span of a lifetime the city's landscape had completely changed. From a few hundred thatched grass hale (houses) and a stone fort in 1818, Honolulu grew into a booming port by the 1850s.[27] Rudimentary wooden structures, cobbled together with lumber imported from the Pacific Northwest, edged in on the traditional Hawaiian homes that lined the city's narrow, unpaved thoroughfares. A courthouse, a market house, and the McKee and Anthon Building, constructed substantially enough that they would last into the mid-twentieth century, accommodated a commercial boom brought by the whaling ships that crowded the harbor.[28] As the city's infrastructure developed, with roads steadily being widened and straightened, and brick-and-mortar businesses erected along them, foreigners started recognizing something familiar in its contours. Many reported back home that the city increasingly resembled a Western—even "semi-European"—town, noting "improvements" under the tutelage of Hawai'i's missionaries and the investment of prospecting businessmen.[29]

Using the built environment as a measure of the civilizing project's success in Hawai'i, assessments like these reflected emergent ideas of who and what purposes Honolulu served.[30] Between 1825 and 1869, over thirty hospitality establishments opened their doors to accommodate visitors, the majority of whom were white men seeking money or pleasure.[31] The lively downtown catered to both highbrow and lowbrow revelers: those seeking relief from the boredom of seafaring attended back alley grog shops selling cheap bootleg, and those conducting business sipped champagne and brandy at respectable hotels. In these establishments, where Hawai'i's foreign political and economic actors took respite, colonialist visions of the islands conformed to their many appetites.

One such establishment was the Merchant's Exchange, a saloon that prominently advertised ice in October 1856. Proprietor Peck Cutrell announced his acquisition of "a quantity of that greatest of luxuries in a tropical climate—*ice*," by listing an impressive repertoire of cocktails: "Mint Julips [*sic*], Mountaineers, Cobblers, Smashes, Punches, Stone

Fences, Queen Charlottes, and numerous others."[32] As one of the few establishments in the city to hold a license for the selling of alcohol—which came at no small cost—the Merchant's Exchange held a degree of social respectability, even in a city where alcohol consumption had become heavily moralized and legally regulated.[33] The drinks conjured up a cool fantasy that promised to transport thirsty patrons: "Straightaway we are in Dreamland, and visions of 'mint juleps,' 'iced punches,' and other delicious compounds float before our enchanted visitor. When we awake, we find Randall Smith, the incomparable Randall, proffering to our eager grasp a snowy 'mountaineer!'"[34] At least three shipments of ice arrived that winter for exclusive use at Cutrell's tavern, for which he had "spared neither pains nor expence [sic] to render the most popular place of resort in Honolulu."[35] Already the addition of ice underscored the coloniality of cocktails using the language of escapism and leisure to set its drinkers apart from Hawaiian consumers, who may not have been so transported.[36]

In this way, ice transited business and pleasure spaces, tracing networks of power across Honolulu's relatively compact waterfront. A lithograph created in 1854 by the Swiss artist Paul Emmert provides a useful guide to both the growing city and how ice might have moved through it after arriving by boat.[37] His view of the city center is given from the harbor, framed by details of notable buildings that include the new constructions mentioned above. The waterfront buildings shown in situ at the lithograph's center housed nearly the entire ice business and everyone in it. Starting from the left of the image, one can see the Honolulu Iron Works, where Hawai'i's first ice machine would be manufactured in the 1870s, and in front of which its first icehouse was built before the year's end; then, to the left, the Customs House, where bills of lading and taxes for ice imports were assessed and applied. The wide building just right of center belonged to the firm Swan and Clifford, which imported ice from Alaska in 1854; the ground floor of the "Waikiki side" of the Swan and Clifford building contained the office of liquor dealer Cyrus W. Jones, who applied for an ice importation license in 1856; and, in that same year, the Merchant's Exchange, from which Peck Cutrell sold iced champagne, was located in the cluster of buildings set back from the harbor, slightly to the left of Swan and Clifford.[38] Finally, just beyond the right edge of the frame sat Kamehameha III's palace, Hale Ali'i. In 1854 a quantity of ice could go from ship to table in a space of no more than about five city blocks.

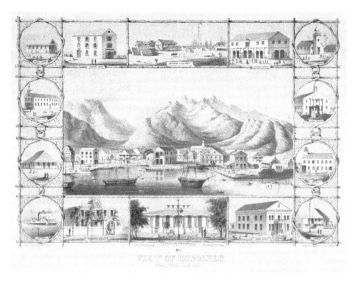

Figure 2.1. Paul Emmert, "No. 1. View of Honolulu. From the Harbor,"
ca. 1854. Popular Graphic Art Print Filing Series, Library of Congress.

Following ice across Honolulu from this vantage reveals two key insights. First, it emphasizes the city's spatial intimacy—a detail important for envisioning life in midcentury Honolulu. Second, it illustrates how imported ice moved through the city along channels of power that explicitly linked foreign capitalism to emergent practices of tropical refreshment. Namely, the urban geography of the burgeoning city allowed for cultural difference, even in a socially stratified capital city such as this one, to be worked out in full view. As ice moved from ship to auction to saloon and home, it accrued meaning for those who handled and consumed it, as well as for those who didn't, sharply defining the racial and class distinctions already charted out by nineteenth-century temperance politics.

THE THERMAL POLITICS OF HAWAIIAN TEMPERANCE

As ice became part of Honolulu's drinking publics, its correlations to whiteness and power resonated with both imbibers and teetotalers: ice helped cocktail drinkers envision respite from plantation oversight; it also offered religious proselytizers an antidote to Indigenous sexualities and the tropical heat. As such, cold refreshment mapped onto racialized ideas of civility in ways that intersected crucially with the robust temperance movement that Hawai'i's powerful missionaries championed. While the dynamics of Hawaiian temperance bore some similarity to calls for alcohol abstinence in the United States, within both settler communities and Native American nations, they were especially shaped by competing imperial maneuvers that sought to control both Pacific trade and Native Hawaiian society.[39] In particular, the religious and economic power struggles between American and European interests in Hawai'i during the 1830s and 1840s produced the legal conditions for the criminalization of Native Hawaiian alcohol consumption into the 1850s, even as the kingdom government permitted alcohol's importation and sale. With ice arriving to a Honolulu divided not only along racial and economic lines but also based on colonial stances toward alcohol, competing social and economic concerns shaped attempts by French, American, and Native Hawaiian entities to restrict or control its consumption.

As early as 1820, missionaries representing the American Board of Commissioners for Foreign Missions (ABCFM) established Native Hawaiian congregations that were decidedly entrenched by the time French Catholic missionaries arrived in 1827.[40] Protestant stances against alcohol consumption differed from Catholic permissiveness about drinking, providing convenient (and, at times, hypocritical) kindling for the ABCFM to stoke anti-French fires, ultimately frustrating their efforts to missionize.[41] Records show that even though ABCFM missionaries maintained stores of alcohol for their personal consumption throughout the early decades of their arrival, they eventually renounced their own drinking habits as a way to contravene Catholic presence and, in turn, maintain influence over Hawai'i's political leaders.

By the 1830s, abstinence anchored the kingdom's stance on alcohol, which missionaries viewed as the result of their own good work. As scholars like Sally Engle Merry and Marilyn Brown have noted, temperance discourse in Hawai'i effected forms of racist paternalism that imagined Kanaka as lacking self-control, and thus in especial need of strong religious and moral guidance.[42] Jennifer Fish Kashay's research on the temperance movement in Hawai'i, however, shows that even as evangelists took responsibility for promoting temperance in the islands, legal moves to restrict alcohol consumption came instead from ali'i seeking to protect the lāhui from Western impingement.[43] This began as early as 1818, when Kamehameha I imposed a strict kapu (prohibition), ordering district chiefs on Hawai'i Island to destroy all liquor stills. About twenty years later, Kamehameha III followed by implementing several laws designed to limit the sale and consumption of alcohol to all kingdom residents, regardless of their race or country of origin.[44] These included an 1835 law against drunkenness and two 1840 liquor laws aimed at limiting the sale of spirits.[45] While makaʻāinana largely followed government prohibitions, haole proved more difficult to manage, with many arguing that such laws should not apply to them; they insisted that prohibition violated their international rights to trade and, furthermore, offended their ability to practice self-restraint.[46] In this way, white residents and newcomers disregarded Native Hawaiian agency and strategic control over alcohol consumption and, simultaneously, took credit for it.

Deploying racial entitlement as exemption from legal authority, Hawaiʻi's missionaries and foreign businessmen used the issue of temperance to leverage political influence on the kingdom and over each other. France, in particular, seemed aware of the economic stakes of Hawaiian faith when, during the late 1830s, French sea captain Cyrille Laplace arrived in Honolulu with a couple of warships, an ultimatum, and treaty demands in response to an ongoing persecution of French Catholics in Hawaiʻi.[47] Signed on July 17, 1839, the treaty included—along with agreements for religious tolerance—the right to import French "wines and brandies," which, Ralph Kuykendall explains, "effectively repealed the liquor law of August 21, 1838.[48] Kingdom laws and regulations pertaining to liquor responded, then, to a multitude of pressures, both within and beyond Hawaiʻi, to appease international relations (to preserve the latitude to import freely) and protect its own citizens (from substance abuse and missionary surveillance).[49] Because of its association with the liquor industry, ice would quickly become folded into importation laws with the 1855 Act to Provide Revenue from Imports, and to Change and Modify Existing Laws Imposing Duties on Imports, which included ice in the tariff schedule for alcohol-related "goods, wares, and merchandise."[50]

Into the midcentury, the Hawaiian government profited substantially from the alcohol trade at the same time that Native criminalization for its consumption climbed. The 1850 *Penal Code of the Hawaiian Islands* stipulated a fine for "whoever shall sell, give, purchase, or procure for, and on behalf of any native of this kingdom, for his use, any spirituous liquor, or other intoxicating drink or substance," essentially creating what Brown describes as "a striking example of a unitary system of legal governance that produced a parallel legal code, one for Whites whose drinking could be regulated through licensing and permits and another for native subjects of the kingdom whose drinking was criminalized."[51] In 1854 (the same year that Swan and Clifford began importing ice, Kamehameha III died under suspicion of alcohol poisoning, and Paul Emmert printed his lithograph of Honolulu's downtown), the Hawai'i Supreme Court's fines for Native drunkenness in Honolulu increased by over 500 percent (from $113 in 1853 to $686).[52] And so, while Daws estimates that liquor licenses and tariffs were some of the kingdom's greatest revenue generators in the midcentury, the cost of alcohol-related arrests, trials, and imprisonments matched those gains "dollar for dollar," essentially canceling out kingdom earnings.[53] The moralization of alcohol consumption created, then, a sociopolitical landscape in which haole could both participate and profit, while maka'āinana increasingly navigated social conditions of exclusion and policing.

Within this complex legal, economic, and religious framework coalesced a logic of Western entitlement to drinking as tropical recreation, and, in turn, Hawaiian abstinence as a necessary corrective to Native indolence. As Brown notes, "The [ongoing] critique of Hawaiian alcohol use was part of a broader colonial discourse that suggested Hawaiians were irresponsible and incapable of governance of the self or, for that matter, political self-governance."[54] This trick, in which alcohol polarized haole leisure and Hawaiian languor, reverberated throughout tourist industry stereotypes that, into the twentieth century, celebrated white comfort at the effort and expense of Native labor. In so doing, Hawaiian temperance politics underscored both race and class distinctions that were used to rationalize the colonial encroachments that followed missionization. Discourses about alcohol consumption and civility thereby laid the groundwork for determining who the pleasures and benefits of the cold would best serve.

VICES AND VIRTUES OF THE COLD

Honolulu's drinking culture flourished across the midcentury despite government and missionary efforts to curb it. Against this, Hawai'i's temperance movement leaders amassed a chapter of the Cold Water Army, a religious organization that performed piety and virtue through the resolute consumption of plain iced water. Founded on the US continent in 1839 by Thomas P. Hunt, a Pennsylvania Presbyterian minister, the Cold Water Army stretched across the United States by the early 1840s, inspiring young people to renounce alcohol through song, children's magazines, and military-style parades and rallies.[55] It quickly played an important role in the recruitment of Native Hawaiian youth into the church. Laura Fish Judd, the wife of noted missionary Gerrit P. Judd, reported in her memoir that "in the years 1838 and 1839 the success of the schools and the prosperity of the churches were at the culminating point. . . . The 'cold water army' embraced legions of valiant champions, who mustered in occasional holiday dress, and marched with flaunting standards of 'Down With Rum,' 'Cold Water Only.'"[56] By 1842, Honolulu's then minister of Kawaiaha'o Church Richard Armstrong counted about seven hundred Native Hawaiian youth in its ranks.[57] The following year, he doubled those numbers and reported to the ABCFM, "Our annual celebration of the Cold Water Army in Honolulu . . . was a happy day among us. Twelve or fifteen hundred well disciplined soldiers cannot but strike terror to the heart of old King Alcohol."[58] The language of soldiers and armies illustrates the forms of religious and moral indoctrination central to the civilizing missions that broadly defined nineteenth-century American settler colonialism, and which also found easy application in Hawai'i.[59]

As a form of discipline, militarization underpinned the work of institutions spanning Oceania and North America that sought to civilize Native youth by reforming their supposed inherent laziness.[60] Echoing strategies used at places like the Carlisle Indian School and others modeled after it, militarized temperance performances also prefigured the kind of colonial gendering that occurred across the Pacific into the twenty-first century, which, as Ty P. Kāwika Tengan describes, "work[ed] to naturalize and maintain systems of gendered, raced, and class-based oppression and domination."[61] Religious and vocational training imposed on Native communities helped to fix Indigenous children into normative and subservient roles. In Hawai'i, Armstrong's work spanned church and school—from Kawaiaha'o he would go on to serve as the minister of public instruction and, then, the kingdom's president of the Board of Education—embedding the value of temperance within Hawai'i's institutions both public and private.[62]

In addition to the racialized and gendered effects of militarized abstinence, the literature of the Cold Water Army drew crucially on thermal discourses that separated figures of pious civility from sinful savagery. The coldness of the water that its members claimed as their preference not only located sensorial virtue (and by extension whiteness) in the global North, but also operated as a corrective to heat's many colonial valences. Climatic heat, theorized by Westerners as a determinant of racial inferiority within the tropics, found dangerous applicability to all kinds of other racist imaginings that associated Black and brown bodies with fecundity, rage, laziness, and hypersexualization.[63] Against the backdrop of Hawai'i's expanding sugar plantation economy, Caribbean histories took on particular salience, especially when it came to the possibilities of salvation through crisp, purifying, bracing glasses of water. With rum production in places like Barbados and the West Indies emerging in tandem with sugar plantations in the seventeenth and eighteenth centuries, alcohol consumption within the tropics became moralized against the nonwhite body, setting up dichotomous relationships between cold and hot, water and rum, white and brown.[64]

Members of the organization's Hawai'i chapter, Pū'ali Inuwai, wore badges and sang chants in 'ōlelo Hawai'i that affirmed their commitment to temperance: "Puali Inuwai / Wai Wale No / Uoki na mea ona" (Cold Water Army / Cold Water Only / Forsake Intoxicating Liquors).[65] On their badges, these words surrounded a woodcut insignia of three roses growing out of a vase, which members would pin to their clothing for large events like one described in 1853 in the village of Kaimū in Hawai'i Island's Puna district. The *Youth's Dayspring*, an American children's temperance magazine produced by the ABCFM, reported on the daylong rally to show how deeply the Cold Water Army's influence had reached into Hawai'i's rural communities. Alongside distinctly Hawaiian feast preparations, with kalo and pigs roasting in an imu (underground oven) and mats laid down for eating, school groups performed their faith: "The schools were seated in ranks; whereupon each read a portion of Scripture; hymns, songs, and chants were sung; and an address was delivered [before] they marched and countermarched . . . in single and double file, in double and single lines, in hollow squares, in triangles, and in solid columns."[66] The article, illustrated with a drawing of the scene that shows children in lines with their banners under a towering grove of coconut trees, indulged American youth with views of Natives brought to literal order under biblical instruction.

Once ice arrived in Honolulu, cold water became more than just a metaphorical antidote to vice in the islands. In 1855, iced water was prominently featured at a Honolulu Temperance League fundraiser for the construction of the Honolulu Sailor's Home Society, which gave alcohol-free lodgings to seamen on leave.[67] After answering a call placed in the

Figure 2.2. Illustration from "A Cold Water Army," *Youth's Dayspring* 4, no. 11 (November 1853): 165.

newspaper by the organization's trustees for donations of "any curiosities which they may possess," Laura Judd's daughters Sybil Augusta and Laura Fish settled on selling home goods and cold refreshments for the public fair.[68] Their iced soda water, Sybil remarked, brought in an especially tidy sum: "The fair has come off, Laura made a pillow and I hemmed six towels and made some fancy lamplighters. Aunt Hattie made a smoking cap and a housewife. Laura and Hattie made some cake which was very nice. Laura sold iced soda water down stairs and father Akay and Ahea sold up stairs. . . . The soda water brought 1 hundred and two dollars."[69] Through the use of coldness, refreshments served at the Sailors' Home fundraiser sent a message of moral purity to its attendees. Not only did it recall the Cold Water Army's activities a decade prior, but using ice to gild soda water also wrestled the consumption of cold away from masculinized saloon contexts and into pious and charitable spaces appropriate for women. These raced, gendered, and classed understandings of iced drinks would go on to inform the body politics of refreshment in the decades to come, which tethered individual healthfulness to questions about Hawaiian capacities to self-govern.

In elite contexts, haole used ice to mark Indigenous difference where wealth threatened to obscure it. When it came to alcohol consumption, aliʻi bore the brunt of missionary surveillance, not only because the ABCFM understood that evangelization of the monarchy offered a pathway to power but also because aliʻi class status seemed to blur the racial lines drawn between Westerners as the bearers of civility and Hawaiians as the perpetually uncivilized. Stories emerged to suggest that consuming cold simply didn't agree with Kanaka constitutions, no matter how elite. To this day, Kamehameha II, Kamehameha III, and Kalākaua's drinking habits are frequently brought to bear on their legacies, implicitly linking personal self-governance to their grasps on Hawaiian political sovereignty.[70]

One particular account of an ice shipment's arrival in Hawaiʻi illustrates how the Anglo-American world stitched together narratives of Indigenous incivility, Western power, and sensorial discontents within the popular media. Entitled "Schemes to Annex the Sandwich Islands," the account was published in the *Californian*, an American journal, in 1881 and looked back to the year 1854 to describe two events the author presents as related: the arrival of ice to Hawaiʻi and the death of Kamehameha III.[71] Kamehameha III's reign is often characterized by his struggle with alcoholism, which haole took pains to catalog because of what it indicated about the limits of their control over the aliʻi.[72] While the elements of the text appear fictionalized (or at least embellished), the details of the account are worth unpacking because of their metaphorical value to American imperialist formations, which leveraged commodity trade for economic and political dominance.

Written by American newspaper journalist James O'Meara, "Schemes" chronicles his journey from San Francisco to Honolulu on the steamer *Sea Bird*, which also happened, on October 2, 1854, to be transporting three unnamed US representatives tasked with negotiating a treaty of annexation. As O'Meara has it, the *Sea Bird* almost didn't make it to Hawaiʻi. It ran out of coal two hundred miles from its destination, leaving the vessel bobbing helplessly offshore until, one day later, a passing whaling ship offered a quantity of blubber scraps that powered the men past Maui Island and into the Molokaʻi (Kaiwi) Channel. With Oʻahu nearly in sight and the blubber spent, the men hoisted sail and began breaking up any spare wood. Desks, trim, and chairs went into the furnace. As they approached land with the ship stripped to its bones, the food stores offered a last resort. At approximately 6:30 p.m. in the dusk of October 14, 1854, O'Meara recalls, *Sea Bird* limped into Honolulu Harbor burning its last keg of butter.[73]

About a month following the *Sea Bird*'s appearance, a cargo of natural ice arrived in Honolulu, imported for exclusive sale at the upscale hotel and saloon Merchant's Exchange.[74] The ice, O'Meara writes, "was a luxury of untold gratification to the American and European residents; a marvel of uncommon curiosity and interest to the natives, from the King to the lowest. . . . Peck Cutrell was shrewd enough to discover and utilize this novelty. He made a large punch-bowl full of champagne cocktail, iced and decocted to appetizing completeness, and sent it to the Palace for the King's own delectation." The king, allegedly enchanted by the iced punch, immediately put in a standing order for regular delivery to the palace and, after a number of days, personally visited Cutrell's establishment.

The coldness of the drink awoke an insatiable desire that, O'Meara writes, caused the monarch's death a few weeks later on December 15, 1854: "On Saturday the King complained of indisposition. . . . Sunday he was recuperating. Monday he was able to sit up. Tuesday morning his faithful personal attendant was giving him a hand-bath of brandy . . . at half-past 11 o'clock the signal announced from the Palace that the King was dead."[75] Kamehameha III apparently sent his servant out during a brandy bath meant to revive him and, unsupervised, consumed it before ultimately perishing.[76] According to O'Meara, the king had been scheduled to sign a treaty of annexation to the United States on Monday, December 14, the day before his death (even though, on the contrary, historian Ralph Kuykendall shows that debates over American treaties had resulted in general opposition to such an agreement).[77] While the story O'Meara tells about iced cocktails and unsigned agreements is unique among accounts of Kamehameha III's death, it draws on some of the core tensions around Kanaka Maoli civility and sovereignty that animated American acquisitiveness, producing narratives that expressed Hawaiian desires for colonization.[78]

Americans reading this magazine story in 1881, nearly forty years after the event in question, would have done so in the context of quickening political intimacy between the two nations. In 1875, a treaty of reciprocity secured an economic relationship between Hawai'i and the United States, establishing commodity trade protections intended to scaffold American sugar interests (I address this treaty in detail in chapter 3). The promise of a permanent stronghold in the Pacific inspired debates about whether Hawai'i might be better annexed, and those would continue until the overthrow of the Hawaiian Kingdom in 1893.[79] Whether or not O'Meara's story contained factual details—the butter keg, the champagne punch, the brandy bath—mattered little compared with the lessons it aimed to teach about Kanaka rulers overtaken by their appetites. Here, Kamehameha III's alcoholism underscored his lack of self-control as a sign of incivility, and his death, catalyzed by his desire for ice, revealed his incompatibility with Western cosmopolitanism. Even as a piece of fiction, this story offers a potent vantage point for understanding how ice, a relatively minor trade commodity in Hawai'i, intersected with the very real and complex ideologies of race and "civility" that shaped nineteenth-century American imperialism in the Pacific.[80]

SENSIBLE FORMS OF COLD PLEASURE

Alongside the formation of ice's social function across spectrums of vice and virtue came ideas about cold refreshment and its embodiments. In 1858, to announce a newly arrived ice shipment, the *Pacific Commercial Advertiser* educated its readership on responsible ice consumption with an article describing its benefits and dangers: "It would be idle to say a word in recommendation of it; it speaks for itself as eminently adapted to gratify the senses, invigorate the system, and lessen the effects of a prolonged or excessive heat, be the same produced by a tropical sun or by an internal fever. But a word of caution against its *abuse* may not be out of place, *particularly for those born on these islands*, who never or seldom have had an opportunity to indulge in iced drinks."[81] Abuse of ice, according to the paper, included drinking cold beverages immediately after physical or mental exertion, or eating ice cream after a full meal when one's body temperature might be warmer than usual.[82] While it deems the pleasure of comestible cold self-evident, those imagined to be of Hawai'i's climate (perhaps Indigenous or acclimatized "by birth") produced an inability to exercise "good sense" when offered cold drinks. This kind of leveraging of environmental discourse to rationalize the sensible suggests that Honolulu-based entrepreneurs took inspiration from colonial elsewheres to plumb untapped consumer markets, imagining wealthy, white bodies in need of a nice cold drink. Likewise, comparisons drawn between the tropics and debility implied that cold refreshment better served more robust (i.e., masculine) foreign constitutions. The passage, which simultaneously presumes universal embodiments and racial difference, importantly anticipates the leisure practices of the tourist body that would go on to define foreign experiences of Hawai'i in the coming decades.

Anglo anxieties about tropical heat carried over from the eighteenth century, intensified, and found fresh salience as women began enjoying iced refreshment in public spaces, like drugstore soda fountains and ice cream parlors, of which Hawai'i had at least a couple by 1854. In the local newspapers, Hoffman's drugstore advertised, "Ice! Ice! Ice!" for its "very delicious" iced sodas; a Mauna Kea Street confectioner sold ice cream near a recently constructed icehouse in downtown Honolulu. Although ice cream was once reserved for the upper class, its emergence as an alternative to alcohol effectively linked these forms of consumption, insofar as both were believed to satisfy similar desires.[83] As Wendy Woloson explains in her book about nineteenth-century confectionary, the ice cream parlor became a space of female freedom, however limited. And, as a result, popular literature frequently characterized parlors as sites of sexual transgression.[84]

Warnings about the pleasures and dangers of iced refreshments circulated through the English-language women's magazines, cookbooks, and domestic manuals that proliferated in the 1850s. On the American continent, railroad expansion and the advent of wood pulp paper made for inexpensive printing and wide distribution; soon a growing middle class eagerly self-educated on idealized Victorian womanhood.[85] A glut of ice cream recipes emerged too, with words of caution about its alleged effect on female or effeminized bodies.[86] Women, children, the elderly, the sick, and the Indigenous all came under shared concern over what desires for ice cream might do to their delicate digestive systems. As Woloson explains: "The (presumably) male writer's identification of women in particular as vulnerable consumers, the female writer's defense of her gender's right to consume ice cream, proved an enduring trope, which recurred with increasing regularity in the ensuing century—women were especially vulnerable to sweets, and sweets had the potential to incite a woman's appetite beyond her control."[87] In 1858, the popular magazine *Godey's Lady's Book* warned readers in its regular "Health Department" column, "In the present mode of living, all who indulge in iced beverages are in great danger . . . [of] *incurable disease* or *sudden death*."[88] Without explaining, exactly, the mechanism by which ice cream incurred disease or death, many publications similarly glossed over medical details and, by doing so, successfully manufactured a general sense of danger and unease.

A temporality of cold emerged that dictated the terms of safe consumption for delicate constitutions, though it lacked consensus. Isabella Mary Beeton, in her ubiquitous domestic treatise *The Book of Household Management* (1861), argued that, while the consumption of ice must be altogether avoided for "the aged, the delicate, and children," "the strong and healthy" could have iced drinks in moderation—though only well after dining, any kind of exercise, or warming of the body.[89] Other books recommended ice cream during or just before a meal to avoid any "injurious" drops in internal body temperature.[90] In Hawai'i, the *Polynesian* printed a story about a Vermonter who eats an entire pint of ice cream in one sitting and soon finds himself doubled up with abdominal pain, "till at last, it seemed as through I'd a steam engine a'sawin' shingles in me."[91] Meant as both humor and warning, narratives about ice cream's effects presumed a reader who required boundaries placed on their desires, whether a white woman ascending into middle-class leisure, a country bumpkin, or a Hawai'i resident. Seemingly contradictory midcentury ideas about ice cream, in which innocence, danger, disease, and purity commingled, found easy importation to Hawai'i's emergent pleasurescape, in which the civilizing project brought white embodiments to bear on Hawaiian bodies.

DOMESTICATING THE COLD

Less than a decade after the initial arrival of comestible ice in Hawai'i, public interest piqued across a whole spectrum of consumers—men and women, traders and churchgoers, adults and children, haole and Hawaiian. But even as desires for ice took hold across the specific economic, racial, and religious contexts of Honolulu, the business of ice failed to find its footing. Entrepreneurs hoping to capitalize on these emergent tastes appealed regularly to the Hawaiian government, knowing that an ice venture required state support if it was to find success in an unpredictable market. Several submitted applications asking for exclusive rights to import and sell, hoping to prevent competition, inspire sufficient confidence to build storage and distribution infrastructure, and stabilize affordable prices. To do so, would-be ice importers appealed to broad accessibility rather than luxury and leisure. In 1858, for example, ship captain John Paty sent a letter to then minister of the interior Prince Lota Kapuāiwa, requesting permission to exclusively import ice-making machines, explaining that "[because] they have become acquainted with a method of fabricating ice by artificial means, at any and every degree of atmospheric temperature in the warmest climates of your Kingdom, . . . the inhabitants thereof can be supplied with an abundance of that healthful and refreshing article, at a rate of cost so cheap as to authorize its general consumption."[92] American businessmen Cyrus W. Jones and Charles G. Davis applied for an exclusive trade license in 1856 and likewise promised that their ice would be kept affordable enough "to furnish to all those willing to buy, the aforesaid article of importation at the most reasonable rate" (or, as they reiterate in the accompanying letter, that ice "may come within the reach of persons of limited income").[93] These appeals suggest awareness that a stable ice market required, ultimately, domestication into Hawai'i's homes, and so license applications strategically proffered inclusive visions of the Hawai'i ice consumer.

The Kingdom Privy Council approved one such application in 1858, exclusively licensing Christopher Hamilton Lewers, a local building contractor, to import ice.[94] While no records explain why Lewers prevailed over other, similar requests, it may have had something to do with a difference in professional background, since other applicants were merchants. Instead, Lewers owned a lumber business, knew council members through his various construction contracts, and had the resources to handily erect his own ice storage facility.[95] Without a vested interest in commodity trade, hospitality, or tourism, he also held no connections to the morally fraught liquor business. That October, Lewers's first shipment of commodity ice arrived at his newly constructed icehouse, which was situated at the foot of Nu'uanu Avenue on leased government land near the boat docks (the Swan and Clifford icehouse had been located two blocks north).[96] One editorial offered, hopefully, "Mr. Lewers deserves credit for his venture, and we are sanguine enough to believe that he will be sustained in it."[97] The *Polynesian*, too, imagined that ice would soon become an everyday item for all of Honolulu's residents: "The great desideratum of civilized life in Honolulu is about to be supplied, and ice is shortly to become a 'household word,' expanding through every ramification of society down to the smallest 'cobbler' and no longer stared at as a curiosity, or monopolized by the gentlemen at the bar."[98] Because ice remained attached to the ideological project of civility (and by extension whiteness and the West), its projected democratization effectively imagined a Honolulu society permeated by cold refreshment and what it represented.

In spite of this (or perhaps consequently), Honolulu residents began to envision a Hawai'i with ice. In the months after Lewers established his ice business, liquor retailers began measuring their spaces for the installation of permanent iceboxes, Hawaiian and English newspapers detailed home delivery options to their readers, and the 'ōlelo Hawai'i newspaper *Ka Hae Hawai'i* approvingly remarked on the quantities coming off the ships, noting that "Ua loaa mamua kekahi hau maanei; aole nae he nui e like me ia, he uuku wale no, a pau koke" (Some ice has been obtained here before, but not as much as this—a little, and was soon gone).[99] Discussions appearing in Hawaiian-language newspapers around this time further underscore expectations that ice would become widely accessible. One of the first editorials in Hawai'i to describe refrigeration, quoted above, appeared in *Ka Hae Hawai'i* alongside an announcement of two hundred tons arriving at Lewers's shop, stating:

> No ka mea, i ke komo ana o ka hau iloko o ka waihona-hau, lilo koke ia i wahi anuanu loa a kupono no na mea a pau e pilau koke i ka wela—Ina e waiho ka io iloko o ka waihona-hau i ma la ekolu paha, aole pilau iki, no ka anuanu.

> By placing the ice in the icebox, it soon becomes a very cold space and becomes suitable to preserve all of the things that spoil quickly in heat. If meat is left in the icebox for even three days, it does not spoil at all because of the cold.[100]

In this description of new ice storage units that kept foods like meat, fish, milk, butter, and pie fresh, the markers of public refreshment—alcohol, cocktails, soda water, and ice cream—are notably absent. Instead, ice emerges as a practical tool for home management, indicating that Kānaka were thinking pragmatically about ice and its utility.

Despite public embrace, the ice trade to Hawai'i ended as inauspiciously as it began. By May 1860, Lewers, more than $7,000 in debt, shuttered an unprofitable ice business.[101] He searched for another firm interested in taking over the business, appealing to the Department of the Interior to forgive his unpaid rent on the land leased beneath the icehouse until new tenants could be found.[102] Honolulu-based merchants Henry Hackfeld and J. Charles Pfluger, who had been running an agency for Russian business interests in Honolulu since the early 1850s, believed that they could use their contacts in Alaska to directly "import into the Kingdom not less than 300 tons of Ice annually, and the price thereof shall not exceed six cents per pound."[103] The government supported their proposal with a ten-year exclusive trade agreement, additional water frontage on the icehouse lot, and free rent, with caveats that the land only be used for ice storage and sale, and that "a constant supply . . . shall be kept on hand"—all indications of their strong desire to keep commodity ice available in Honolulu.[104] Even so, records suggest that Hackfeld and Pfluger never received a single shipment.[105] Honolulu wouldn't see ice again until the 1870s, when its first ice machines began operation.

FAILING FORWARD

The very properties of ice in Hawai'i—its ephemerality, coldness, and newness—and its cultural associations with whiteness, alcohol, and leisure shaped its complicated reception in the islands. In only a decade of sporadic shipments, iced refreshment profoundly influenced the future of Hawai'i's sensorium, from the foreign elite to the maka'āinana. The availability of ice in Hawai'i not only inspired visions of plantation futures for would-be colonialists, who measured white leisure against Black and brown labor, but also placed thermal comfort at the heart of such colonial imaginaries. As a relatively rare and costly accompaniment in the 1850s, ice performed a legitimizing function for the beverages that it cooled. For liquor drinkers, it elevated transgressors to cosmopolitans. For soda water tipplers, it transformed conservativism to indulgence. As such, practices of refreshment emerged as an articulation of whiteness and power, evidenced by the careful policing of social practice that overshadowed Kanaka engagements with ice.

Desires for cold refreshment, which drove the commodity ice trade as it developed across the second half of the nineteenth century, intersected with pressing foreign influences that Hawaiians carefully navigated in their personal and political lives. By linking expressions of vice and virtue to cocktail dreamlands, cold water militarism, and ice cream illnesses, haole newcomers brought colonial sensibilities to bear on Honolulu. Because embodiments of the cold were thought to articulate capacity for civility, civility's promise became implicitly linked to Western economies and social practices that Kānaka were at once implicated in and excluded from. And so even if failure and debt mark Hawai'i's ice trade as a business history, the ideological success of cold refreshment so far from the centers of ice production reveals its social indelibility. In the decades that followed, desires for cold became embedded in the material infrastructures of Honolulu as machines and factories emerged to make ice local.

3

MAKING ICE LOCAL:
TECHNOLOGY, INFRASTRUCTURE, AND COLD POWER IN THE KALĀKAUA ERA

On February 15, 1875, the streets of Honolulu blazed aglow to celebrate the return of Mō'ī Davida La'amea Kalākaua from an important diplomatic journey to the United States. He had been gone for about four months, crossing the continent from San Francisco to Washington, DC, and back. Hawai'i's newspapers, which had been eagerly reporting on the various honors American audiences bestowed on Kalākaua, now printed a commemorative mele:

Anu o Kaleponi
He aina malihini
Kuu pau lia mai
Na hoohiluhilu,
Hoike na moku
Me na Papu
E na kolo na pu
Kowelo na hae

Ole hala na bele [*sic*]
Hone ana na pila
E maki na koa
Kaulele na pahu,
Ulu wehiwehi lua
Na mea a pau

Cold was California, an unfamiliar land
There was much putting on of displays
On the ships and in the forts
The guns roared, the flags waved,
Bells tolled and music played,
The soldiers marched, the drums were beaten
And everything looked so grand.[1]

Like other reports of the king's huaka'i (voyage), this mele invokes the cold in order to characterize diplomatic encounters with America. Here, a chilly San Francisco greets Kalākaua upon arrival; later, a blizzard punctuates his tour of Omaha, Nebraska; from this, Kalākaua comes down with a cold that delays an important meeting with then-US president Ulysses S. Grant. As Tiffany Lani Ing, in her biography of the king, assesses, "The Mō'ī's body was not used to the cold."[2] Subtle thermal discourses about Kanaka bodies—persistent even into the present day, as illustrated by Ing—responded to the sociotechnical and political developments of Hawai'i at the time.[3] The pressures of American colonial interest mounted during the final decades of the nineteenth century, and Hawai'i's diplomacy navigated unforgiving Western ideas about Indigenous civility and modernity, offset against a climate of anti-Indianness and antiblackness.[4] As the cold became increasingly accessible in Hawai'i through the development of ice and refrigeration machines, it expressed imperial relations with the United States as sense and sentiment.

With the support of its monarch, Hawai'i's urban environments transformed across the late nineteenth century as electricity, indoor plumbing, and telephones set the Hawaiian Kingdom's modernity apace with imperial metropoles abroad. Among these technologies, ice machines came into use in the 1870s, filling in gaps left as imported ice ceased to arrive in the 1860s. Even though the trade commodity proved unprofitable, the racialized, classed, and gendered ideas of cold taste that those early ice imports established remained, offering interpretive frameworks for thinking about what locally made ice could mean for Kanaka Maoli. By the 1880s, large ice factories replaced early freezing machines, tapping into expanding urban infrastructures and transforming a once-foreign commodity into a local product.

As ice became embedded in Honolulu everyday life, its use and consumption were linked to forms of social distinction borrowed from Europe and America: home refrigeration, ice cream parlors, and refreshment for tourists. In turn, the existence and use of freezing technologies within the Hawaiian Kingdom became ever more subject to colonialist interpretations—that Honolulu gave the "sense" of being an American city, with entertainments and comforts that privileged Western subjectivities and, by extension, white possession. Importantly, Kānaka resisted these ideas through their own sensory engagements with electric energy, incandescent brilliance, and the artificial cold.

RECIPROCAL RELATIONS

The first of Hawai'i's monarchs to break from the Kamehameha dynasty, Kalākaua ascended the throne on February 12, 1874, after a tense electoral campaign against Queen Dowager Emma, Kamehameha IV's widow.[5] Leaving on his first diplomatic journey less than a year into his reign (1874–91), the new king urgently felt that Hawai'i's commercial relationship to the United States should be formalized with a treaty of reciprocity. This was not a new idea. Drafts of this treaty predated Kalākaua, with earlier versions appearing in 1855 and 1867 under the reign of Kamehameha IV and Kamehameha V, respectively, who also viewed reciprocity as both an economic benefit and a strategic limit to American imperial desires.[6]

Even so, interest in a formal agreement varied in both Hawai'i and the United States. Although it was lobbied against by cane planters in the American South in the 1850s, who saw Hawaiian sugar as unwanted competition, the idea of a treaty was revived in the 1860s, when the American Civil War disrupted supply chains from the South. As wartime economies stimulated investments in plantations overseas and interest in Pacific expansion, the United States' preference for annexation stalled reciprocity.[7] By the 1870s, Hawai'i's American sugar planters began to feel the strain of high trade tariffs and the competition from sugar refineries that emerged on the California coast. They pushed, successfully, for agreements that would buoy their investments.[8] Kalākaua's support for reciprocity thus stemmed from a desire to invigorate Hawaiʻi's industry and economy but also carried with it a firmly grounded awareness of the colonialist agendas of its alternatives.[9]

On a political level, reciprocity yoked Hawaiʻi's future to the United States through its exclusive terms, with Article IV specifying that Kalākaua would not "grant so special privilege or right of use therein, to any power, state, or government, nor make any treaty by which any other nation shall obtain the same privileges."[10] Prominent Kanaka legislator Joseph Nāwahī referred to the highly controversial agreement as a "nation-snatching treaty," predicting that it would lead to annexation because of the way that the document dangerously conferred leverage to the American government.[11] His premonition would come into sharper view during the treaty's renegotiation in 1887, in which the kingdom ceded control of Puʻuloa (Pearl Harbor) for the establishment of a US military base.[12] While Nāwahī may have been referring specifically to legal control when he described the treaty's consequences, it is important to also recognize, as Caroline Elkins and Susan Pederson have noted, that settler colonialism manifests in the marketplace as much as it does through territorial occupation.[13]

Reciprocity shaped everyday life in Hawaiʻi in ways both profound and mundane through its commercial terms. The treaty, as it was written in 1875, articulated schedules of goods that would flow out of Hawaiʻi without taxation—almost entirely sugar and its by-products—and, in turn, American products that would flow back in: construction materials (iron, doors, nails, bolts), apparel (silks, boots, furs), and foods (bread, cheese, butter). Even though ice was no longer shipped to Hawaiʻi by 1875, it appears on the trade schedule, too, having been added during the 1867 draft. While ice never arrived under the terms of this treaty, iceboxes, ice cream makers, and ice pitchers surely did.[14] And so, while reciprocity had been driven by the sugar economy, urban Honolulu felt its effects just as deeply on its changing material culture, from the bones of its buildings to the groceries on its shelves. Soon after the treaty's enactment, American products constituted the vast majority of imports to Hawaiʻi, rising to over 75 percent of the market share by 1890.[15] As an extension of what Anne McClintock has called mercantile imperialism, the increased availability of metropolitan goods—day-to-day commodity exchange—in Hawaiʻi reproduced empire through domestic paradigms. It brought empire home.[16]

At the end of the nineteenth century, Honolulu took on a certain kind of incandescence and cosmopolitanism, championed by Kalākaua and admired by Westerners. The political changes of the 1870s registered in Honolulu through a building and population boom. In the twenty-four years between 1872 and 1896, the number of residents doubled, from 15,000 to 30,000, and as a result, the city became both denser and larger.[17] In short order, an urban trolley system, rural railroad systems, and telephone networks were established; artesian wells and upland valley reservoirs increased the capacity of the city's water system.[18] Unable to fathom how Kānaka Maoli had so quickly taken up these infrastructures of civility, American travel writer Maturin Murray Ballou reported in 1887: "The city, with its twenty thousand inhabitants more or less, has all the belongings of modern civilization, such as churches, charitable institutions, hospitals, schools, gas, electric lights, and the telephone; yet it was forced upon the mind how brief the period that had transpired since this was nearly a wilderness, peopled by a race of cannibals, whose idolatrous superstitions involved frequent human sacrifices."[19] Collapsing together religious, technological, and racial ideologies, Ballou expressed the ways in which mercantile colonialism dovetailed with epistemic and infrastructural colonialism to produce seemingly evident trajectories toward Westernization.[20]

Racist imaginaries about the Pacific in turn limited other conclusions, causing visitors to frequently read the city's development not only as Westernization but more specifically as Americanization. For instance, in 1898, George Leonard Cheney reported that "[Americans] would open their eyes if they could visit Honolulu and see how level with the times its modern conveniences are. It is the largest patron of the telephone in the world. With a population of 24,000, Honolulu has 1,300 telephone instruments to use, or 1 to every 18 people. Streets and houses are lighted by electricity. Cars and carriages are at a traveller's service. The involuntary exclamation of strangers is that this is an American city."[21] Offering these observations in the year of Hawai'i's annexation to the United States (and five years after the American-led coup d'état in 1893), Cheney implicitly connected the dots, despite listing "conveniences" all installed under the direction of the Hawaiian kingdom government.

Nineteenth-century Honolulu's development under the direction of Kalākaua offers an opportunity to grapple with broader questions about

Indigenous political agency in the face of so-called technological progress. The kingdom government, Jonathan Osorio argues, did so under the imperative of survival; according to Osorio, "Intrinsic to this transformation was the haole claim that it was necessary for the kingdom and its Native inhabitants to embrace, or at least deal with, Western conceptions of modernity for it and them to survive."[22] Kamanamaikalani Beamer and Noenoe Silva have also shown how Hawaiian modernity refused capitulation to Western hegemony by also revitalizing traditional Hawaiian cultural forms through a number of state-sponsored projects.[23] Most notably, Kalākaua matched his patronage of new technologies with his establishment of the Papa Kū'auhau Ali'i o Nā Ali'i Hawai'i (Board of Genealogy of Hawaiian Chiefs), the Hale Nauā (a secret society dedicated to ancient knowledge), and the repeal of a missionary-generated ban on hula dancing in public.[24] And so, alongside the very real political and economic pressures under which new technologies came to Hawai'i, kingdom investments in distinctly Indigenous ways of knowing and being scaffolded technological adoption and adaption, reflecting how carefully Hawaiian subjects negotiated ongoing Western influence.

Many of Hawai'i's modern infrastructural systems emerged out of the plantation system, with sugar barons investing in the installation of telephones, telegraphs, artesian wells, hydroelectricity, and trains early and aggressively throughout the 1870s and 1880s. For example, O'ahu's first artesian well pumped water for sugar planter James Campbell's ranch in the 'Ewa district on the Western side of the island, and the kingdom's first telephone transmitted Charles Dickey's sugar business between his Kahului and Wailuku operations on Maui.[25] At the same time, however, Kānaka equally engaged new technology with curiosity and pragmatism. If an artesian well first appeared in 'Ewa in 1879, by 1880 others pumped water through the private homes, stores, and urban ice factories of Honolulu.[26] If Dickey called in orders over his telephone in 1878, by 1880 the Hawaiian Telephone Company of Honolulu had 119 subscribers.[27] Kalākaua's 'Iolani palace famously boasted indoor plumbing, electricity, and telephones before both the US White House and Buckingham Palace—a detail often repeated to this day as a challenge to colonialist narratives that portray Hawaiians as passive recipients of Western imposition.[28] As much as Honolulu's urban development seemed to capitulate to the technological investments that underpinned Hawai'i's growing agricultural economy, these technoscapes also operated as sites of Kanaka innovation and colonial resistance. Of these technologies, the development of freezing and refrigeration worked its way into Honolulu's city infrastructure, connecting Hawaiʻi domestic life to global standards of modernity.[29]

MAKING ICE LOCAL

Honolulu's first machine for freezing water arrived in September 1871 along with its inventor, a retired ship captain named David Smith.[30] Smith, who had been tinkering with freezing systems in San Francisco, California, since 1869 came to Hawaiʻi for its climate, hoping to develop a machine that could reliably produce ice in tropical environments.[31] His interests were at once personal and racial: Smith's wife had died of cholera during an 1864 voyage to Burma, and the physician who tended to her believed that readily available ice would have offered a lifesaving treatment for tropical diseases that tended to afflict white travelers.[32] Within a month's time the machine began producing ice on Honolulu's growing waterfront esplanade.[33] Hawaiʻi's elite soon subscribed to delivery accounts: local homes and businesses were served by a fleet of carriages, with customers on neighboring islands receiving shipments "at same rate" packed in sawdust-insulated boxes.[34] Ice, now available for both refrigeration and consumption, rose prominently within the civilizing discourse as a shorthand for broader paradigms of so-called progress.

Placing Hawaiʻi in this global context, it is important to note how its early ice factories developed largely in response to domestic use, for either refreshment or home refrigeration rather than trade, better aligning Honolulu with the metropoles, rather than the peripheries, of empire.[35] Across the following decades, Hawaiʻi's nascent ice technology kept impressively apace of that of the United States: according to statistics published in the US Census, fewer than ten ice plants existed across the continent in 1867.[36] In 1875, Honolulu city boasted two.

By 1885, the United States exceeded all other countries in the number of operative ice machines, volume of ice production, and ice consumption.[37] At the same time that America invested in cold chain expansion, ice industries also accommodated the routes and appetites of empire.[38] This is how, for example, New Zealand and Australia became major sites for global refrigeration development as their husbandry economies capitalized on Victorian desires for imported meat.[39] These statistics call attention to the role of empire in the development of refrigeration technologies as much as they trouble narratives of imperial dominance within studies of the early cold chain. W. R. Woolrich argues in his history of ice machines, for example, that English and American interest in refrigeration reflected strategies for commercial and colonial expansion by extending the trade of perishable goods.[40]

Within Hawai'i, Honolulu's ice business also expanded rapidly across the 1870s and 1880s, with companies often changing hands several times as single machines turned into manufactories. According to newspapers, local businessman Robert Rycroft took over the city's ice manufacturing when Smith left the islands in 1874. Rycroft had since 1873 already been operating Honolulu's Fountain Saloon, which served cold refreshments out of a small building on Fort Street, and he quickly went all-in on ice.[41] He sold the saloon in early 1875 and opened, instead, Honolulu Ice Works, a large factory in Nu'uanu Valley housing two freezing machines built on commission by Honolulu Iron Works with parts imported from the United States.[42] Rycroft promoted his new products in earnest, sending samples out to Honolulu newspapers so that they might advertise in their editorials, much like the *Pacific Commercial Advertiser* did when it published commentary that stated, "Last Wednesday, rather unexpectedly but very agreeably, the editorial palate was cooled with genuine ice-water, Rycroft having called during our absences and deposited in our pitcher a transparent cube that looked as natural as an old-fashioned winter in latitude of 50 North."[43] Rycroft's machines were fickle but capacious; he managed to send out ice deliveries twice daily, and his cash-and-carry outlet sold ice at half the cost of Smith's.[44]

In 1876, Samuel Gardner Wilder, an entrepreneur with various investments in interisland steamer services, the guano trade, and sugar plantation railways, bought Rycroft's factory and updated the machines.[45] Under Wilder's ownership, supply stabilized and distribution expanded, as was reflected in the proliferation of ice cream parlor advertisements and ice factory updates in both English- and Hawaiian-language newspapers throughout the 1870s.[46] In particular, *Ka Lahui Hawaii* celebrated Honolulu's ice creams and soda waters as local products, noting that "hoohuihui ia e ka hau iniki o Nuuanu"—they were "chilled by the ice of Nu'uanu."[47]

By the early 1880s, W. E. Foster opened the Artesian Ice Works in Mānoa, which took its name from the factory's water supply pumped up by an artesian well.[48] Much like the water that early nineteenth-century ice traders harvested from New England ponds, well water produced ice of much greater clarity than sediment-clouded stream water. Foster likewise borrowed advertising strategies from "Ice King" Frederic Tudor in order to draw in customers who might not yet have established ice accounts. In July 1882, Foster placed in the window of J. W. Robertson and Co.'s downtown storefront a large ice block, which slowly melted under the watch of passersby.[49] Much like a similar promotion of Tudor's Wenham Lake ice melting in a London storefront in 1844, the *Friend* reported approvingly, "With cold at 20 degrees below Zero, we never saw purer or more chrystal-like [*sic*] ice, even in New England, where it is manufactured in a large scale for the India market."[50] The *Daily Bulletin* furthermore remarked on how slowly Foster's ice melted, reporting that it "was exposed from 8am to 4pm, and at the latter hour had diminished very little in size from what it was in the morning."[51] Highlighting values important to natural ice products of decades past, Artesian's business soon took off. In response to the increased competition, Honolulu and Artesian Ice Works merged in 1884 to become the Ice Works Company, which would continue operating into the early twentieth century.[52]

With ice no longer an imported delicacy reserved for the city's elite, its on-demand availability pushed Hawai'i's consumption beyond refreshment, as ice also found use as a refrigerant and medicine. By the mid-1870s, newspapers began running articles describing "ice-bag cures" for various ailments; Boyd's Family Market advertised deliciously tender "meats on ice," with an eight-day shelf life.[53] In March 1875, *Ka Nupepa Kuokoa* described machine-made ice, or "artificial ice," as it was then called, to its readers by stating, "Ua puka hou mai nei keia mea maikai, he hau paa i hana la mamuli o na mea akamai a loaa ai" (This very good thing has just come out, it is ice that has been made due to the technologies that are had).[54] As they became increasingly local, Honolulu's ice businesses drew from the technological landscape of the city, one node in a growing network of materials, power, and distribution: steam engines fired the boilers and condensers; natural waterways flowed in as liquid and emerged solid; and Wilder's interisland steamships ferried enormous blocks of ice to Maui, Kaua'i, and Hawai'i packed in large, black iron chests forged at the Honolulu Iron Works.[55] And as a local product, ice moved through Hawai'i's social landscape, taking on different meanings that cut across race, class, and gender politics. The sections that follow attend to these intersecting hierarchies as they played out, respectively, in haole-, maka'āinana-, and ali'i-dominated spaces. Importantly, ideas and understandings of cold consumption remained unfixed across Kanaka and settler spheres despite Western racial imaginaries of the tropics. Even as ice became available and popularized, its pleasures were by no means agreed upon.

THERMAL DISPLEASURES

By July 1872, Hawai'i's newspapers were already beginning to envision a future filled with ice, with the *Pacific Commercial Advertiser* asking its readers: "How would a 24 hours snow storm suit you in Honolulu? The very thought is refreshing, and so are frozen crab apples, but these are luxuries which our tropical friends can only faintly imagine over a pitcher of iced water. The delightful contrasts of the seasons are all unknown to them, and cocoanuts and raw fish, pineapples and poi don't compensate for the cuckoo's note and the return of spring!"[56] Asserting that contrasts of temperature between food and climate created the very essence of refreshment, the editor identifies the Kanaka through a different thermoceptive register. Acting as a counterpoint to the white settler body, which appreciated comestible ice because it felt *good* to have something cold on hot days, the Native's consuming body performed in this instance a kind of climatological ignorance: the sweet and sour of pineapple and poi did not, and could not, instill a taste for coldness.

These constructions of difference—between race, climate, and taste—may be understood as one example of what Parama Roy describes as the "psychopharmacopoeia of empire"—an alteration of Indigenous sensory worlds driven by the colonial experience. She writes that "colonialism was in important respects a reconfiguration of the fantasmic landscapes and the sensorium of the colonizer and colonized, generating new experiences of desire, taste, disgust, and appetite and new technologies of the embodied self."[57] Settlers in Hawai'i, as I will describe, noted Hawaiian aversions to the cold as a matter of their bodily constitutions. Kānaka Maoli, too, disagreed with the wholesale acceptance of cold pleasure—not as a matter of racial difference but instead through careful epistemic reflections on thermal relationships under the conditions of colonialism.

Even after ice became standard fare within Hawai'i's hospitality industry, with hotels and ice cream parlors regularly advertising frozen refreshments in English- and Hawaiian-language newspapers by the late 1870s, settler reports of Kānaka aversions to ice surface again and again as indictments of their slow path to civility. An article published in the missionary periodical *The Friend* suggested, for instance, that Hawaiians, though curious about ice, simply disliked like it when given the opportunity to try some. Describing an 1870 jubilee celebration for the Hawaiian Mission Children's Society, a benevolent Christian organization, the editorial reported, "Drink for the thirsty was not wanting. Soda water bottles were popping in every direction, and iced water was in profusion. Many Hawaiians drank ice water there for the first time, simply out of curiosity, and made a wry face over it."[58] Likewise, a news story published more than a decade later, in 1886, maintained that the Hawaiian taste for cold had still not developed when it reported on a Sunday school festival in Hoʻokena, Hawaiʻi Island, attended by Kalākaua and then Ke Aliʻi Wahine Liliʻuokalani: "A novel feature at the festival was ice cream, sold by an enterprising Native from Honolulu, but the people did not take to it. Bandmaster Berger and the Rev. Mr. Forbes were the only two white men at the festival."[59] Finally, in one particularly extreme example, Kānaka are portrayed as not only averse to but terrified of ice cream. In a book published as a "reminiscence" of years managing Hawaiian laborers at the Hanalei Sugar Plantation on Kauaʻi, Malcolm Brown describes how Kānaka mistake ice as extremely hot rather than freezing cold: "When ice cream was first seen and partaken of by the natives, terror seized them. It was some time before an explanation would satisfy them. 'Wela loa,' they said, 'ho-o iloko o ka wai'—too hot—place it in water. They could understand how to heat water, but would not understand how anything became so hot that it would solidify."[60] These descriptions of Native encounters with ice, in which they appear to express fear or distaste, illustrate the racial tensions of embodied experience that policed not only the consumption of ice but also life in the islands more generally.

While it may be tempting to dismiss reports like these as straightforward racism couched in the language of taste, some evidence points to a certain amount of agreement between Native and foreign groups on sensorial difference. Hawaiian-language sources indicate that throughout the 1870s Kānaka Maoli grappled with settler orientations toward extreme cold—though hardly through ignorance. From moʻolelo that animated and gave cultural meaning to the snowy environments of Hawaiʻi's tallest mountain peaks to the decades-long involvement in the whaling industry, during which Native men proved themselves as able seamen on the arctic seas, ice featured prominently in environmental discourse about Hawaiʻi as well as around the globe.[61] Even so, ideas of pleasure and leisure continued to trouble discussions about comestible ice, leaving sensorial encounters with the cold unreconciled.

Figure 3.1. Illustration from "Ka Hau," *Ka Lahui Hawaii*, August 16, 1877.

Kānaka Maoli considerations of ice also stretched beyond Hawaiʻi, helping them to envision life on the American continent. More than a decade after the last blocks of imported ice arrived in Honolulu, for example, a lengthy article ran in the Hawaiian language newspaper *Ka Lahui Hawaii* describing an American ice harvest. It educated readers on the process of operating an ice house, cutting, storing, and shipping frozen lake water from which "hoouna ia ai ka hau ma na moku i na wahi a pau o Amerika"—ice was sent on ships to all places in America (though, curiously, without mentioning that some of that water reached Hawaiʻi once).[62] While this description of the ice harvest is a fairly straightforward relay of foreign industry—common newspaper fodder of the time—it also interprets the consumption of ice not only as a foreign practice but also as one that belongs to a foreign place. "In the summer in America, eating things that are iced is necessary for the lifestyle of men," the author notes, underlining, perhaps, the degree to which the ice industry was imagined at a remove from everyday Hawaiian production and practice and, in turn, identifying the commercialization of ice as a specifically American endeavor.[63]

Reports like the ones analyzed here offer glimpses into how Kānaka thought about and understood ice consumption, in the context of both American industry and Western refreshment practices, though the accounts are often filtered through a colonial white gaze committed to racial difference. Hawaiian-language newspapers, however, instead articulated Kānaka Maoli perspectives on ice to Hawaiian readers through epistemological difference, powerfully refuting implications that Kānaka were confused about or afraid of ice. An August 16, 1877, newspaper article entitled "Ka Hau" (Ice), published in *Ka Lahui Hawaii*, exemplifies this important shift.[64] The text describes the cold to readers by imaginatively interpreting an accompanying illustration of a winter scene printed at the top of the page. "He kii maikai loa," the unnamed author begins, asking his readers to regard the quality of the drawing as a good, detailed picture of two young white children, who had stopped their outdoor play in order for some young "chickens" to cross the road before them. Although the snow delights the children, a brother and sister he calls Kale (Charles) and Iulia (Julia), the author expresses grave concern for the plants and animals around them. He describes how the grass is dead, the flowers have withered, and the trees have lost all their leaves. The chicks, apparently without their mother, prompt him to ask, "Mahea ko lakou makua? Make anei lakou i ke anu?" (Where are their parents? Have they frozen to death?) He even wonders about the welfare of Charles and Julia, even though they are bundled up in woolen blankets and gloves. "Auwe! Pehea ko laila kamalii, aole wela lakou?" (How are the children of that place? Are they warm enough?) Although their fingers and toes ache from the frost, and they scream out, "It's cold! It's cold!," the children continue to play happily.

To emphasize how perplexing their joy is, the narrator then places himself in the scene with Charles and Julia. Charles hands him a piece of ice for examination, but he quickly throws it down, away from his hand. "A wela maoli ko'u lima," he explains—the heat of it burned him. The author, perhaps a Hawaiian who had once visited the United States in winter, now explains to his readers in Hawai'i the lesson they might learn from his experience. "Ina paha e lohe i kou kapa ana he wela, akaaka lakou ia oe, a olelo o kea hi ka mea wela." (If perhaps it is heard your naming this as heat, they will laugh at you. They say that fire is what is hot.) (One can see here, too, an echo of the reactions of the Kaua'i sugar plantation workers mentioned earlier.) Not only does the Hawaiian author feel the ice differently than his counterparts, but he indicates that he must also hide his understanding from those whom he believes will mock him for what they wrongly interpret as stupidity. But, he writes, "Owau kai ike" (I'm the one that knows). The haole, represented here as two naive children, only see opportunities for fun and play, but the Hawaiian, an omniscient observer, finds danger in the details. While the scene is initially proclaimed maika'i, or good, by the author, his narration instead reveals a picture of colonial naivete and Indigenous knowing.

In stories like this, Hawaiians offer sharp metaphorical commentaries on the challenges of ongoing American settlement, revealing how Kānaka Maoli were critically aware of imperial encroachments on their felt worlds. Moreover, these examples express the ways that human experience does not begin and end with the Western sensorium. Such approaches to thermal difference detailed in these examples from nineteenth-century Hawai'i are also affirmed in the archives of other people, in other places: the South Africans in Cape Town who, in 1849, reacted to ice cream as if it were "as bad as a fire ball, or a hot potatoe, or a raspberry tart just fresh from the oven"; or perhaps the arctic explorers who described putting alcohol frozen to viscosity into their mouths only to find themselves in a "state as coals of fire," their "tongues, lips, and palate so burned and excoriated."[65] These moments, then, may not be mistakes or instances of thermal confusion but perhaps, instead, may signal ways of feeling that have been trained out to make room for more dominant, more normative understandings of cold pleasure. It's perhaps telling that these moments of what might initially appear as a heat/cold inversion reveal themselves to be deliberate articulations of what cold *felt* like in a culturally grounded context. These articulations disappeared as ice became fully embedded within the Hawaiian foodscape through the final quarter of the nineteenth century.

COLONIAL AESTHETICS OF THE COLD

Once ice became readily available, it began to punctuate public social spaces and functions where haole and elite Hawaiians intermixed. Kaori O'Connor identifies Hawai'i's food culture in these decades as a "hospitable high colonial culture for which the Islands became renowned."[66] In particular, those living in Hawai'i's cities mixed Western food cultures with their own as both an appeal to a growing tourism economy and an expression of global cosmopolitanism that aimed to bridge cultural divides. It was not unusual to find European china and silver adorning the tables of the city's elites, where traditional Hawaiian foods commingled with chilled French champagnes and ice cream desserts. In 1873, William Bliss, a travel writer from the American Northeast, described this blend of Western and Hawaiian culture, reporting that in Honolulu "the doors are always open; the welcome is always hearty. Water from mountain springs flows through the cottages, stopping in baths, escaping in fountains, fertilizing the grass and flowers everywhere. Ice is made to order, and wines are offered from all the vineyards of the world."[67] Linking together Hawai'i's natural environment, infrastructural development, and cosmopolitan luxuries, he envisioned a Hawai'i at the service of white pleasure that appealed to a growing number of travelers to the Pacific. These sensory experiences of Hawai'i were thus spun into imperial fantasies that affirmed haole presence through hospitality services.[68]

A number of newspapers, magazines, and tourist guides in the final three decades of the nineteenth century promoted Hawai'i as pleasurable, healthful, and restorative for Western visitors, circulating editorials and advertisements for businesses like ice cream parlors and soda fountains.[69] The Elite Ice Cream Parlors, for example, took out whole pages in the long-running *Paradise of the Pacific*, which was distributed for free on the American continent.[70] Issues of the *Hawaiian Gazette* featured notices for both the Bonanza Ice Cream Parlor and the Palace Ice Cream Parlor, emphasizing the chaste respectability of such establishments serving women and children. Bonanza, in particular, boasted a newly constructed entrance for female patrons "with or without Gentlemen," who could order "ice creams and iced temperance drinks of many flavors [to] be had 'in quiet' at all hours of the day or evening."[71] For visitors, ice symbolically indexed the growing tensions that animated so much of late nineteenth-century kingdom social politics throughout the elite spaces of Honolulu, in which performances of civility seemed to mark Hawaiian proximity to whiteness or, perhaps more accurately, Hawai'i's proximity to America.

While businesses like these were certainly patronized by elite Kānaka Maoli, Victorian respectability politics overwhelmingly determined the social norms of these refreshment spaces, including gender segregation that policed women's social publics modeled after parlors and saloons on the American continent. Hawaiian engagements with these norms revealed how complicated the racial and cultural terrain of elite public life could be in Honolulu. As Maile Arvin argues of this time period, Kanaka Maoli engagement with Western racial logics "forces us to see that, even as Native Hawaiians were facing colonial violence from haole settlers, Native Hawaiians responded in complicated ways that sometimes internalized and deployed Western notions about Polynesian proximity to whiteness and progress themselves."[72] These dynamics were especially visible in Honolulu's most elite circles, where aliʻi entertained wealthy haole and foreign dignitaries against a backdrop of colonial pressure.[73]

Archived menus for government-sponsored events at ʻIolani Palace show how aliʻi navigated international taste politics and the implicit discourses of civility that came with it. Ice cream featured prominently in palace dinner events, showing up on menus for diplomatic meals as well as in the daily fare at elite hotels throughout the final quarter of the nineteenth century.[74] A dinner at the US legation in August 1875, for example, included a dessert of strawberries and ice cream following courses of mock turtle soup and curry and rice.[75] Menus for the Hawaiian Hotel, printed in French, list *glace à la vanille* and seasonal fruits.[76] In both formal and informal settings, Kalākaua would offer guests selections of chocolate, strawberry, and vanilla ice creams like he did at one 1885 lūʻau held at the Boathouse for plantation owner Claus Spreckels: palace records show expenditures for $6 of flower bouquets, $7 of lei, $30 of pocket money for Kalākaua (presumably for gambling wagers), and $21 of ice cream.[77]

Haole visitors who attended these events as honored guests often described them in writing for audiences abroad in the United States and England, who read with great curiosity about Polynesian sovereigns.[78] The British travel writer and naturalist Isabella Lucy Bird did just this in her book *The Hawaiian Archipelago* (1881), which chronicled six months that she spent touring the islands in 1872. In her rich snapshot of late nineteenth-century Hawaiʻi through a Western woman's gaze, Bird comments at length on Hawaiian civility and the "restorative" charms of the islands.[79] After relaying her daring adventures on the islands of Maui and Hawaiʻi, where she rides horses astride and visits volcanoes, she eventually settles into Honolulu's cosmopolitan society on March 20 of that year. She takes up lodging at the elegant Hawaiian Hotel and is quickly impressed with the city's lively pace: picnics, parties, courtly events, and luncheons in endless succession. While she avoids most of these "socialities," she finds herself unable to resist a picnic hosted by Queen Emma Rooke, the widow of King Kamehameha IV. "I must describe it," Bird writes, "for the benefit of ——, who persists in thinking that coloured royalty must be grotesque." To convince, she spends time admiring the furnishings of the queen's home, the tasteful combination of silks and fresh flowers that adorn the guests, and the graceful music and dancing.

She also notes the refreshments, writing that "tea and ices were handed round on Sévres china by footmen and pages in appropriate liveries. What a wonderful leap from calabashes and *poi*, *malos*, and *paus*, to this correct and tasteful civilization!" Bird then goes on to reveal that the ices offered at Emma's home were not just rarefied dishes but instead everyday fare that could be found produced locally by functional (if not fickle) machines: "There is an ice factory, and icecream [*sic*] is included in the daily bill of fare here, and iced water is supplied without limit, but lately the machinery has only worked in spasms, and the absence of ice is regarded as a local calamity, though the water supplied from the waterworks is both cool and pure."[80] Likely produced by Smith's machine, given the timing of her visit, ice helped Bird organize the racial and gendered politics of refreshment along colonial lines. "It is quite true," she later states, "that the islands are Americanized."[81] For Bird, Honolulu's Americanization was evidenced not only through the material technologies and goods that its society embraced but also through its sensorial effects: smooth silk gowns superseded pāʻū (women's skirts), cool porcelains replaced wooden calabashes, and chilly ices appeared in place of the native poi.

COLD POWER

While visitors read Americanization into the rich textures of social life in Honolulu, the monarchy was forging ahead in its embrace of new technologies on Hawaiian terms, folding them into displays of sovereign power that articulated Hawaiʻi as a peer—not a dependent—of other global powers.[82] Expressions of Hawaiian power through technology culminated on the evening of July 21, 1886, when crowds gathered at ʻIolani Palace for a spectacle that few had ever witnessed. As darkness gradually fell on the city, the building was bathed in "a soft but brilliant light" generated by five electric arc lamps.[83] Kalākaua directed the fanfare on horseback: battalion drills marched to music played by the Hawaiian Band while Hawai'i's high society mingled in the Palace Square. When the volunteer companies broke rank, they stacked their arms and settled under canopy tents for refreshments: tea, coffee, and ice cream.[84] The serving of ice creams (along with teas and coffees that referenced Western imperialism) for 'Iolani's electrification is a small but important detail that reveals how the city's changing sensorium underpinned expressions of political sovereignty.

For several months after their first illumination, the electric arc lamps at Palace Square would go dark so that adjustments could be made to the system. A man named Walter Faulkner arrived in the late fall of 1886 from Lynn, Massachusetts, to install a couple of dynamos shipped to Hawai'i from the Thompson-Houston Company and remove the old gas plant from the palace grounds. Newspapers applauded his efforts when the lights once again returned for the king's fiftieth jubilee celebrations that November. While many contemporary accounts portray this period as one of exuberant progress, a strong undertow of political turmoil rendered this event far tenser than the newspapers allowed: powerful haole elite, including missionary descendants Lorrin A. Thurston and Sanford B. Dole, had grown increasingly resentful of monarchial power within the kingdom government. According to Faulkner's account, recorded as a typewritten transcript in 1925 and tucked into a scrapbook in the Hawai'i State Archives, insurrection felt imminent even as preparations were being made to celebrate the king's authority. He recalled installing the dynamos, "when cannon were placed upon the palace steps behind barricades of sand bags. The only way I could get into the Palace Grounds to continue my work was by a pass word [sic]: 'Kukui Wela Haole' [hot foreign light]."[85] If, to the public, electricity represented political power, then its code word in private suggested that the temperature of technology continued to burn uncomfortably in the nation's heart.

One of several technologies adopted in its infancy by the kingdom, the electrification of 'Iolani is today often held up as a zenith of nineteenth-century Hawaiian modernity. As Liza Keānuenueokalani Williams and Vernadette Vicuña Gonzalez write, the palace holds profound importance for Kanaka Maoli remembrance, trauma, and resurgence.[86] It was the site of the Bayonet Constitution's signing in 1887, which gave suffrage to white settlers, and Lili'uokalani's prison after her deposition as Queen Regent in 1895.[87] Into the late twentieth century, it has remained an important site for the Hawaiian sovereignty movement because it is such a potent reminder of the settler state's violence. For the 1993 centennial of the kingdom overthrow, Haunani-Kay Trask gave her iconic "We are not American" speech on its grounds—now a major rallying cry for Native Hawaiian independence.[88] Given the palace's significance as a discursive and material site of Hawaiian politics, its electrification and the fanfare surrounding it illustrate the complex dynamics of this moment, in which Hawaiian cosmopolitanism indigenized Western cultural forms and, simultaneously, fashioned itself as a proto-Western space through the use of cold refreshment.

Nineteenth-century monarchial displays thus orchestrated sensory experiences of Hawaiian sovereignty: the elegant building aglow against the night sky, notes of the nationalist ballad "Hawaiʻi Ponoʻi" drifting from the bandstand, and the chill of ice cream playing off the evening warmth all interlocking elements of meaningfully crafted pageantry.[89] That the city of Honolulu celebrated electrification using a military display alongside an ice cream social underscores how technological progress sat at the intersections of taste and power. Combining the frozen and the electric invited Hawaiians to embrace modernity on sovereign terms. Marking the affective correlations between sensory embodiment and nationalist sentiment, celebrations of cold power in Hawaiʻi created a prismatic effect, in which nineteenth-century mastery of both Indigenous and imperial cultural forms offered visions of both Kanaka virtuosity and colonization.

SENSORIAL SOVEREIGNTIES

Scholars of the Hawaiian monarchy, and of Kalākaua in particular, have endeavored to understand this embrace of Western culture and technology that characterizes the final decades of the kingdom era.[90] Here, unpacking Kanaka Maoli engagements with modernity and cosmopolitanism shows how infrastructures operated as political tools that pushed against, and negotiated with, American reconfigurations of Hawaiian subjectivities. While these narratives converge through the framework of annexation (especially as it has come to be understood as a looming inevitability in the late nineteenth century), they also pull into focus the ways that Hawaiians consumed nationalism through appetite, spectacle, and incandescent brilliance. Although visitors to Honolulu during this time exclaimed again and again on what they saw as the "Americanness" of the city, this was not the only—nor even the dominant—interpretation of modern technology's role within Hawaiian society. Kanaka Maoli investments in cold technologies were complex, shifting across hierarchies of class, gender, and racialized proximities to whiteness.

This chapter highlights how the sensorium of nineteenth-century Hawai'i came to be defined against the politics of modern technologies, such as ice machines, as they became embedded within everyday Honolulu life. In turn, interpretations of coldness—what it meant, who it served, and what it said about those who consumed it—offer critical insights into Kanaka Maoli urban identity and cosmopolitanism in the late nineteenth century. Contextualizing the cultural import of cold refreshment in late nineteenth-century Hawai'i likewise reflects the deep infrastructural investments—"the natural resources, the production, the commerce, and the monetary circulation"—that made it possible.[91] Though the technologies described in this chapter were adopted and adapted from the United States, Hawaiian engagements with them should not be seen as unilaterally colonizing but rather as contingent on local circuits and circulation where meaning refracted into nationalist and global terms. Ice and its production (which becomes "local" with the advent of ice machines and the commerce that these new energy infrastructures generate) thus constitute a sociotechnical and political process, suturing Hawaii's future to the future of Western expansion in the late nineteenth century.

4

On June 16, 2011, the Hawai'i state legislature voted on and unanimously passed Senate Bill 101, which legalized the commercial sale of traditionally prepared food products made from the corm of the kalo, or taro, plant.[1] Known colloquially as the "poi bill," SB 101 exempted Native Hawaiian staple foods, like poi and pa'i 'ai (a more condensed version of poi), from certain Department of Health (DOH) food safety regulations.[2] The passage of this bill was considered a hard-won triumph by the community activists who had championed it for a long two years, catalyzed by the 2009 arrest of Daniel Anthony, a kalo farmer and O'ahu-based food activist. The "legalize pa'i 'ai movement" included calls to "indigenize the law" through direct, grassroots action, eventually pressuring the Hawai'i legislature to legalize the sale of traditionally prepared poi.

Anthony sells hand-pounded pa'i 'ai at local farmers markets, preparing it in the traditional Hawaiian way, with a pōhaku ku'i 'ai and a papa ku'i 'ai—a poi pounder and board. Because of this, his food sales violated Hawai'i state law on two related counts. First, the tools he uses are made of stone and wood, porous objects that can be difficult to sterilize. Second, he prepares these foods outdoors rather than inside a certified food-processing facility.[3] In the eyes of the state, this method of preparation invites bacterial growth, thus making consumers vulnerable to potential food-borne illnesses.

These are also the methods by which poi gains some of its most valued nutritive qualities. Naturally fermented foods, like yogurt or sourdough, poi and pa'i 'ai develop their characteristically yeasty flavor in conversation with their microbial environment, drawing lactic acid from the hands of the maker. Industrially made poi is available at most grocery stores in Hawai'i, but truly delicious poi is a handcrafted food that fundamentally goes against the Pasteurian sensibilities of the modern American state, which has come to prioritize sterility over the flourishing of microbial life. Poi is, in the words of Heather Paxson, a microbiopolitical object: a food subject to hygienic regulatory governance concerned with health and "safety."[4] Extending Paxson's argument, which she makes through the example of raw milk cheese, the modern-day regulation of poi emerges not only from anxieties surrounding microbial life but also from deep-rooted racism that continues to inform colonial relationships in Hawai'i around food.

This chapter examines the historical and legal precedents of the legalize pa'i 'ai movement by looking to another poi bill from exactly one hundred years prior, in the earliest decades of the territorial period. Responding to a cholera outbreak among Native Hawaiian residents of Honolulu, the Hawai'i Board of Health (BOH) implemented a series of public health measures designed to work in concert with contemporary Progressive Era pure food laws recently imported from the continental United States. Because the BOH believed the virus had spread through a number of downtown poi shops, Honolulu's territorial food commissioner quickly ordered them shut, removing commercial poi and pa'i 'ai from the city almost overnight. However, as Honolulu's kalo markets collapsed, the commissioner became fixated instead on an entirely different issue that would go on to derail the cholera investigation: he believed that Hawai'i's ice creams violated US laws against food adulteration because of their low butterfat content. Eliminating a Hawaiian staple food and enriching another associated with purity and whiteness, such actions reveal how the eliminatory logics of assimilation and dispossession became leveraged through discourses of "safety," pleasure, and taste.

The preferential management of food safety in territorial Hawai'i expressed microbiopolitical forms of settler colonial governance that not only foreclosed Indigenous foodways but also set legal precedents that reverberate into the present day through the bureaucratic management of settler colonialist food politics. The legislation of ice cream and poi in the 1910s makes clear the racial dimensions of such discourses, which deployed ideas of purity in order to embrace encroaching US nationalism, assimilate Kanaka Maoli cultural norms, and disenfranchise local food economies operated predominantly by Chinese and Japanese merchants. As such, the comparative regulation of ice cream and poi in territorial Hawai'i articulates the regimes of taste politics that abet settler food economies as they subtly traverse the language of individual preference, bodily safety, and food epistemologies.

PURITY AND DANGER IN THE TERRITORY OF HAWAII

In 1893, after decades of political maneuvering, the kingdom's haole elite enacted a coup d'état against Mō'ī Wahine Lili'uokalani. The so-called Reform Party, led by a number of missionary descendants, eventually placed her under house arrest in 'Iolani Palace after an attempted rebellion by kingdom supporters in 1895. The Reform Party would then establish the Republic of Hawaii as a provisional government that would maintain control of the kingdom until the US unilaterally annexed the islands in 1898 via the Newlands Resolution.[5] The occupation of Hawai'i was part of a broader set of imperial acquisitions that took place in the final years of the nineteenth century, with American dominion also claimed over Cuba, the Philippines, Puerto Rico, and Guam.

Political desires for Hawai'i emerged out of a number of agricultural, military, and commercial interests related, at least in part, to its location at the "crossroads" of the Pacific, as well as Honolulu's deep and defensible harbor.[6] In 1912, the Australian journalist and travel writer Frank Fox speculated on how imperial power might be distributed throughout the Pacific Ocean in the wake of American imperial expansion. As he saw it, East and West converged in what he speculated had become "an American lake." "Every nation in the Pacific has the same experience," he wrote:

In the Hawaiian Group, the American Power finds the native race helpless material for nation-making. The Hawaiian takes on a veneer of civilisation, but nothing can shake him from his habits of indolence. He adopts American clothes, lives in American houses, learns to eat pie and to enjoy ice-cream soda. He plays at the game of politics with voluble zeal. But he is still a Kanaka, and takes no real part in the progress of the flourishing territory of Hawaii. Americans do the work of administration. Imported Japanese, Chinese, Portuguese and others, are the coolies and the traders. The Hawaiian talks, basks in the sun, adorns himself with wreaths of odorous flowers, and occasionally declaims with the pathetic bleat of an enraged sheep at "American tyranny."[7]

Using cultural practice as a proxy for political sovereignty, Fox articulates the racial hierarchy that many envisioned about the territorial governance of Hawai'i: American oversight, Asian labor, and Hawaiian complacency. His comments on the enduring force and impossibility of assimilation for racialized subjects of empire suggest that the material trappings of Americanization, epitomized by iced refreshment, simply offered a "veneer" of civility smoothed over the surface of indelible brownness.

Hawai'i's annexation to the United States brought new legal, social, and economic regimes to bear on early twentieth-century everyday life, manifesting new forms of control and containment. Scholars like J. Kēhaulani Kauanui, Sally Engle Merry, and David Keanu Sai have documented the profound effects of Western law on Hawaiian culture during the kingdom and territorial periods.[8] From the implementation of eugenics projects at Kamehameha Schools to the establishment of US Department of Agriculture experiment stations that promoted white smallholder agriculture, to the sterilization campaigns proposed by the Board of Prison Directors and the Territorial Conference of Social Work, the governance of Hawai'i embraced what Maile Arvin identifies as the forms of white progressivism that characterized early twentieth-century America more broadly.[9] A set of ideals that marked entitlement to private property ownership through discourses of "civility," white progressivism reflected the raced, classed, and gendered dimensions of the settler colonial project.[10] This phenomenon found particular expression in the governance of Hawai'i's foodscape, which sat at the nexus of the biopolitical and the territorial.

In the year of annexation, the Hawai'i legislature passed its first law against food adulteration through Legislative Act 34, "To Provide against the Adulteration of Food and Drugs."[11] The movement for pure food in Hawai'i drew from a larger set of US-based Progressive Era reform ideals that defined much of early twentieth-century American food politics.[12] Bolstered by the publication of Upton Sinclair's novel *The Jungle* (1906), which exposed deplorable conditions within the meatpacking industry, pure food laws sought to regain control over a poorly regulated industrial food economy.[13] The 1906 Wiley Act became one of the US government's earliest consumer protection acts, working to ameliorate consumer anxieties—both real and imagined—over an expanding national food system.[14] To be sure, instances of food adulteration and spoilage became common as the food chain lengthened and industrialized.[15] More significantly, though, such concerns over food safety also reflected heightened racial tensions surrounding immigration and urbanization. As KC Councilor illustrates, metaphors of digestion, assimilation, consumption, and contamination powerfully framed discourses about non-white migrants who entered American cities and labor forces in great numbers across the late nineteenth and early twentieth centuries.[16] As such, the Pure Food and Drug Act's impact on American foodways was cultural as much as it was political, forging American national identities through consumerism, whiteness, and ideological purity.[17] The legal and bureaucratic application of pure food likewise offered a particular kind of utility in the Territory of Hawaii, a place in which white residents were (and still are) a racial minority.[18]

ASSIMILATING TASTE

Food played an important role in both shaping and narrating the civilizing mission's success in territorial Hawai'i. In 1898, just months after Hawai'i's annexation to the United States, *American Kitchen Magazine* reported to readers that "the things to eat in Honolulu depend on who and what you are."[19] Writing to readers who might be envisioning travel to the newly occupied territory, the article described a tempting array of delicacies available to island visitors and recent residents.[20] "A civilized being," it went on, "can have a conventional menu, from oysters on the half shell—brought in from Baltimore—to Neapolitan ice cream and Nesselrode pudding. For the kanaka there is abundant poi—poster's paste five days old."[21] Ice cream for the haole and poi for the Kanaka represented two important poles of Hawai'i's racial, political, and culinary spectrum at the outset of the twentieth century: American and Hawaiian; modern and traditional; civilized and barbaric; sweet and sour; frozen and fermented.

Politics underpinned the discussions haole had about the taste hierarchies between poi and ice cream: as the expansion of sugar plantations buoyed Hawai'i's economy, concerns over Hawaiian claims to land were mobilized through gustatory logics that would render them either undeserving or uninterested in agriculture and the capitalist economy. John Roy Musick, in his 1898 book about the American Territory of Hawaii, explained, "The comparative ease with which the Hawaiians on their own land can secure their ordinary food-supply has undoubtedly interfered with their social and industrial advancement. Poi, it is said, has proved the greatest obstacle to the progress of Hawaiians. The ease with which the taro, the vegetable from which poi is made, can be grown, relieves the native from any genuine struggle for life, and unfits him for sustained competition with men from other lands acquainted with hardships."[22] Musick offers here a powerful example of the interlocking logics of territory and taste through agricultural labor. In it, Hawai'i's abundance has put Hawaiians at a political disadvantage: they feed themselves too easily.

The languorous problematics of kalo as a crop folded into concerns of taste, too, as a way of talking at, around, and alongside Indigenous difference. Take, for example, a story entitled "The Poi Eater's Progress"—a play on the title *The Pilgrim's Progress*—that circulated in the *Latter-day Saints Millennial Star* in 1893. Referring to poi as "a queer-looking greyish, sticky compound, resembling paper hanger's paste," a histrionic dialogue in the second person describes a missionary encounter with the food:

> As you raise it toward your mouth your nose takes cognizance of a sour smell that harmonises perfectly with the appearance of the poi. . . . By a sublime effort of will you keep your lips closed over the mouthful, while your companion looks on interestedly, evidently expecting to hear your palate scream with delight. . . . The poi is cold and clammy. The poi tastes like stale yeast; it stings your tongue, and an unutterable disgust possesses your soul. . . . You can trace its progress through the œsophagus by the horrified shudder that organ gives as the mouthful passes along it; you can hear the villi in your stomach shriek as the frog-like lump makes its appearance among them, and you think you are going to die then and there.[23]

Others around the same time aren't quite as dramatic—some are even complimentary enough to call poi "not unpleasant."[24] Nevertheless, a consensus formed not only that the texture and taste of poi are overwhelmingly objectionable but that consumption of the food would ignite savagery within.

The taste of poi often compelled descriptions by Westerners that collapsed together anxieties over Hawaiian bodies as both hygienic and copulatory dangers. Mark Twain, who traveled to Hawai'i in 1866, later published a description of eating poi that played on such imaginaries:

> I think there must be as much of a knack in handling poi as there is in eating with chopsticks. The forefinger is thrust into the mess and stirred quickly round several times and drawn as quickly out, thickly coated, just as if it were poulticed; the head is thrown back, the finger inserted in the mouth and the delicacy stripped off and swallowed—the eye closing gently, meanwhile, in a languid sort of ecstasy. Many a different finger goes into the bowl and many a different kind of dirt and shade and quality of flavor is added to the virtues of its contents. . . . All agree that poi will rejuvenate a man who is used up and his vitality almost annihilated by hard drinking.[25]

Here Twain expresses common refrains of the culinary colonial gaze, from texture to body to social practice.[26] What is, for Kanaka, simply eating becomes, in this depiction, gyrations of pleasure: not one finger, but many fingers, swirling around the bowl before entering a swallowing mouth, head thrown back in "ecstasy." At the heart of these discourses sat haole anxieties surrounding the productive and reproductive qualities of bodies and foods. As the very "staff of life," kalo consumption constituted a regenerative act that refused to abide settler civility (for bed and table manners alike).

In turn, civilizing discourse found especially symbolic traction in the consumption and visual marketing of ice cream at the turn of the twentieth century. White, cold, and individually served, ice cream resonated with the goals of American Progressive Era politics. On the continental United States, large waves of immigration, a growing middle class, and a feminist movement for suffrage fomented white desires for racial purity, femininity, and innocence.[27] In much the way that milk emerged, in E. Melanie DuPuis's words, as the "perfect food" of turn-of-the-century social reform, ice cream's milky whiteness and sugary sweetness resonated those same ideals within the public sphere.[28] From the vantage of Europe, the United States became known as a "land of ice cream."[29] Americans themselves claimed ice cream as their "national dish."[30] In Hawai'i, ice cream parlors and manufactories proliferated, catering to everyone, from tourists and haole settlers to urban Kānaka and remote plantation communities.

For some, Honolulu's ice cream shops reflected how rapidly the city had Americanized since annexation. The American travel writer Burton Holmes reported in 1919: "When on King Street [downtown] the traveler can easily imagine himself in the business district of a small American town; he sees familiar articles exposed for sale, reads signs that he has read before, meets people whom he knows at home. . . . We may find in half a dozen drug-stores sizzling soda-water fountains where soft ice-cream and soapy froth are doled out by a Japanese or Chinese clerk."[31] With just a sufficient reminder of Hawai'i's exoticism, the interiors of Honolulu's ice cream parlors and soda fountains affirmed American political dominance in the early decades of occupation. For example, the Palm Café, located on Hotel and Fort Streets in downtown Honolulu in 1913, emphasized bright airiness with a double-height ceiling muraled with palm trees made to look as if the visitor were sitting in an open-air pavilion. Anticipated as "Honolulu's finest restaurant" at its opening in 1912, the café boasted imported fittings, machines, and even a chef from the United States to ensure "the best in the eating line and in the cleanest and most scientific and sanitary manner known to the art." Underneath the dining room, the building's entire basement was devoted to preparing ice creams and ices for the restaurant's five-hundred-person capacity.[32]

Where haole and Kānaka Maoli socialized over meals, ice cream often bridged an ever-narrowing cultural divide. For example, a 1903 lū'au and bazaar to benefit the Kapiolani Maternity Home offered attendees a choice between a "Luau Table" or a "Foreign Table" (consisting of "roast turkey, boiled ham, roast pig, chicken and various salads, rolls and homemade bread"), both of which concluded with ice cream for dessert.[33] Likewise, cookbooks such as *How to Use Hawaiian Fruit and Food Products* (1912) recommended that hosts in Hawai'i serve ice cream as the fourth course in a poi luncheon.[34] Charmian London, the wife of the American novelist Jack London, in her travelogue *Our Hawai'i* (1917)—note the use of the possessive—described a lū'au in Pearl City (Mānana) that they attended "as the only white guests for in these latter days the natives are chary of including foreigners in their more intimate entertainments."[35] While she thrilled at the meal's authenticity, helping herself to poi, raw and salted fish, and laulau, she ate "for dessert, the not unpleasant anti-climax of good old vanilla ice cream to remind us that Hawaii has long been in the grasp of Jack's 'inevitable white man.'"[36] While Hawaiians certainly made their own choices about meal composition—particularly regarding celebrations like lūʻau—such descriptions linked ice cream to imperial power and whiteness, especially when it was folded into Indigenous cuisine.

Hawaiʻi's territorial school system played an especially large role in adapting local tastes to American ideals. The Honolulu Normal and Training School, established in 1895 under the Republic of Hawaii, included ice cream in its school lunch program, offering it as a dessert for an additional 5 cents. One of its pupils, Florence Margaret Lee, reported to the US-based *Journal of Home Economics* that in 1910 the school's lunch menu included "chowders, soups, meats, vegetables, puddings, pastries, ice cream, etc.," and that "a difficult problem in planning this lunch is the consideration of the widely different tastes of the American teachers and the children of various nationalities, for exactly the same lunch is served to all."[37] The serving of ice cream was not limited to the Normal School; a retired nurse, Julia Bryant, recalled in an oral history that during the 1910s, her Kalihi grade school offered a little "already made up cup" of ice cream with meals for an additional few cents.[38] And in 1907, the *Pacific Commercial Advertiser* reported that at a Kamehameha School event, "no one was allowed to miss one course of the lūʻau, typically Hawaiian until the ice cream and cake were served."[39] Records like these reflect the ways that institutional food operated as an educational tool for Hawaiʻi's youngest imperial subjects.

The relationship in Hawaiʻi between ice cream and civility had a visual language, too, as evidenced in the various advertising campaigns of Hawaiʻi's ice cream producers. Rawley's, one of Honolulu's largest and longest-running producers, consistently employed visual fields of whiteness to underscore the purity of its product. A 1917 layout for a movie theater lantern slide, for example, advertised "pure ice cream" at the Kohala Drug Store using an image of a modestly dressed white woman, dainty dish in hand. Rawley's also used Hawaiian-identified images to articulate the same types of messages. One such example comes from the 1921 Christmas edition of *Paradise of the Pacific*, which featured a full-page portrait of a young Hawaiian girl.[40] Presented without title or logo,

Figure 4.1. Rawley's Ice Cream advertisement, *Paradise of the Pacific*, December 1921.

it trades the purity of nature for the purifying embrace of civility. Instead of flowing freely, her hair is styled with glossy bangs and short curls that show off the nape of her neck. Rather than depicted in an outdoor setting, she is posed for a formal studio portrait, sitting with her torso turned toward the camera to create a three-quarter profile, left hand resting in her lap.

The image offers a study in contrasts: the girl's brown skin gleams against a white pinafore. She is smiling, but her lips are obscured by an ice cream cone that sets off her brownness with its milky whiteness. A byline for Rawley's Ice Cream and Dairy Products of Honolulu appears in small type beneath, reading: "Merry Christmas. Santa Claus doesn't forget good little girls just because they live in Hawai'i, where the old fellow's reindeer outfit would have a pretty hard time sledding, and nary chimney exists for his convenience. Nevertheless, as one may easily perceive, he manages to deliver the goods. This child is pure Hawaiian, and furnishes a beautiful example of what Hawaiian eyes can do."[41] While it is unclear exactly what her eyes are able to do in this instance (Entice a pedophilic onlooker? Convince a skeptical Santa of her humanity?), the trappings of whiteness become materially and metaphorically significant to purity's embodiment. The powerful symbolism embedded in ice cream's consumption brought race and gender politics to the forefront of territorial Hawai'i's urban foodscape.

BUREAUCRATIC OVERSIGHT(S)

As Hawai'i's tastes evolved across the early twentieth century, so did the legal frameworks designed to manage them. Edward Blanchard arrived in Hawai'i sometime in 1910 to begin work as the Hawai'i Board of Health's food commissioner and analyst.[42] The third person to hold the position since in 1899, Blanchard had the "power . . . to enter into any creamery, factory, store, salesroom, storageroom [sic], drug store or laboratory, or any place where he has reason to believe food or drink are made, prepared, sold or offered for sale," in the name of consumer safety and protection.[43] Given the racial underpinnings of pure food in the United States, along with Hawai'i's racial demographics, tensions emerged surrounding not only Hawai'i's nonwhite producers and consumers but also the territory's increasing reliance on food imports from the United States.[44] Thus, while newspaper editorials suggested that the Pure Food and Drug Act promised to impart a sense of "commercial morality" in Hawai'i, wherein "the legend 'Made in America' upon food and drink merchandise will stand for honest goods always," those products simultaneously stoked public concerns about the industrialization of Hawai'i's food system as a direct result of annexation.[45]

Less than a year into Blanchard's tenure, the Hawai'i Senate revised its laws on the adulteration of food and drugs in order to specify standards for the three foods believed most susceptible to adulteration in Hawai'i: cream, ice cream, and poi. In 1911, the *Hawaiian Star* reported:

[Blanchard's] idea is to arrive at a standard by tests, and then ask the Legislature to assist him by making that standard law. As it is now, all kinds of poi can be sold, and there is no means of preventing it. Ice cream is another delicacy to have attention. Blanchard does not think that this contains a sufficient amount of cream, and paradoxical as it may seem, some of the ice cream does not contain any cream at all. Ice cream should be pure just as other foods and kindred articles should be, so a crusade against those shopkeepers who sell an inferior article is to be begun, and a standard will be set. The Legislature will then be asked to make . . . a standard for poi and a standard for ice cream."[46]

While the regulation of ice cream was not unique to Hawai'i—studies conducted in New York stemmed from similar concerns over sanitation and ingredient quality—the concurrent regulation of poi shows how gendered, racialized, and classed ideas of taste became embedded in expressions of American governmentality along the edges of its empire.[47] As Blanchard reasoned in 1912, "Ice cream is perhaps as widely eaten as any other food and must consequently be watched carefully."[48]

To that end, Blanchard carried the American ice cream standards over to the territory exactly; Hawai'i simply adopted the same stipulated minimum butterfat content (18 percent for cream; 14 percent for ice cream; 12 percent for "fruit or nut ice cream"). Kalo products, on the other hand, were required to contain a minimum standard of 30 percent "solids."[49] Differential treatment for dairy and kalo prompted the *Hawaiian Gazette* to comment, "Strange to say the bill does not designate just what kind of solids. . . . It is supposed to mean taro while in fact it can mean a brick bat."[50] The *Gazette's* complaint about the legislature's treatment of foods like poi or pa'i 'ai responded to the long-standing and tiresome haole characterizations of the Hawaiian staple as inedible detailed earlier in this chapter, in which newcomers to Hawai'i frequently disparaged poi as "billboard paste" or other inedible adhesives; as "queer" and transgressive; or simply unsanitary in its typical presentation at the center of the meal, to be eaten with one's fingers dipped into a large communal 'umeke, or calabash.[51]

Blanchard's efforts to standardize pure food in Hawai'i picked up on the unfinished work of his predecessor Robert Duncan, who also campaigned to regulate ice creams while struggling to prioritize it over the poi industry. In a government report published in 1907, Duncan apologetically explained that, "owing to the great amount of attention which it was necessary to give the poi shops, the enforcement of the ice cream standard has been somewhat neglected."[52] His tenacity remained through 1909, however, through various campaigns to educate the public on standard butterfat content, including one such story in the *Pacific Commercial Advertiser*. In it, a young couple called "Johnny" and "summer girl" discover that in Honolulu, "they haven't really been eating ice cream all these years, but ice milk." Fortunately, their "Uncle Sam"—described as elderly and no expert on ice cream, but nevertheless sure that it should contain 14 percent butterfat—steps in to replace the "outrageous compounds [that] have been foisted on the public under the guise of ice cream."[53] Embedding legible symbols of US nationalism while simultaneously erasing Kanaka and reducing women to nameless love interests, Duncan's story aimed to underscore the importance of food standards as a matter of political concern in the Territory of Hawaii.

CLOSING UP SHOP

Carrying the previous food commissioner's work forward, Blanchard's efforts to standardize dairy and poi in Hawaiʻi intensified around March 2, 1911, when he supervised the closure of nearly every commercial poi outlet in Honolulu following a deadly cholera outbreak.[54] The Board of Health's president, Ernest Mott-Smith, explained in an internal memo that the poi shops made sense as a locus of the outbreak because Hawaiian foods were known to transmit viruses, writing that "it is a significant fact raw fish, shell-fish, and limu [seaweed], the known [cause] of the outbreak of the epidemic of 1895, and poi, are the distinctive diet of Hawaiians. It is also a significant fact that only Hawaiians thus far have been assailed with the disease."[55] Thus, with at least twenty known cases and eighteen deaths, all Kānaka Maoli, the government quickly shuttered over fifty businesses, destroying in the process more than fourteen thousand pounds of poi and nine thousand pounds of cooked kalo.[56] Only the Kalihi poi factory remained open under a strict government ordinance by which the Board of Health controlled all aspects of manufacture, including full sterilization of equipment, employee quarantines, and stringent medical monitoring for signs of disease.[57] This focus on the poi industry, while responsive to the ways that cholera appeared to move through the Hawaiian community, reflected the territorial government's racialized approaches to public health.[58] Indeed, these measures not only emulated colonial ambivalence toward Native Hawaiian foods but also seized on anti-Chinese sentiments that simmered in urban Honolulu.

The territorial government worked quickly to put some legal measures into place, introducing a poi bill that same March. The bill outlined sanitation requirements in order for businesses to obtain a permit to sell commercial poi, including having cement walls and floors, a fresh water source, sufficient drainage, and regularly sanitized tools. All shops would undergo Board of Health inspections before permit approval, and the permit could be revoked without warning. Although the bill was ostensibly applicable to any and all purveyors in the territory, newspapers reported that it was "for regulation of all *Chinese* shops here," at once reflecting the prominence of Chinese within Honolulu's food industry as well as overt racism against one of Hawai'i's largest immigrant groups.[59]

Since the kingdom era, Chinese had risen in the Hawaiian economy, and by the territorial era, they owned and operated a substantial number of businesses, including rice paddies, fisheries, and many of Honolulu's poi manufactories.[60] Xenophobia's contours, which deepened through the extension of exclusion acts to Hawai'i after annexation, often imagined Asian migrants through paradigms of contagion.[61] Board of Health officials spoke internally about Hawai'i public health as an immigration issue, noting that "from the outside [it] is constantly menaced by the endemic foci of diseases in the Orient."[62] Newspapers like the *Hawaiian Star* furthermore reflected that same analysis as a sentiment of the general public, reporting that "the bureau is keeping the poi shops closed until there is a law under which poi manufacturers can be compelled to be decent and clean, as much as such decency is against the inclination of most of the Chinese shops."[63] Blanchard, who had been tasked by Mott-Smith with sanitation inspections, reported back, "The Chinese shops, almost without exception were found in a more insanitary [*sic*] condition," pointing out that poi manufacture often occurred within domestic living spaces, where families cooked, ate, recreated, bathed, and slept.[64] The racial underpinnings of industrialized America's pure food anxiety unfurled here as a mode of biopolitical control: Hawaiian sustenance limited through paternalistic forms of protection, and Chinese businesses shuttered through xenophobic forms of exclusion.

The Board of Health ordinances to close Honolulu's poi manufactories illustrate the fraught relationship between food and power as it developed in early twentieth-century Hawai'i, particularly as American legal and racial frameworks were brought to bear on the islands. Purity and contamination became the grammar of that relationship. As Blanchard remarked about a month prior to the cholera outbreak, "My investigations have proved to me that there is a great deal of fraud being practiced in the city, and I believe most of it would be made impossible if food standards were adopted."[65] It might have seemed, then, that poi offered a ready medium for testing and applying adulteration standards, given the public health implications of commercial poi that March. And while Blanchard did conduct tests on a few poi samples at the behest of Mott-Smith, they simply indicated whether or not the 30 percent standards for "solids" had been met.[66] As Blanchard clarified in his report, he did not conduct any bacteriological tests that might have detected the presence of cholera.[67]

The issue of food adulteration in the Territory of Hawaii, in Blanchard's view, was more appropriately handled through an investigation of Honolulu's ice cream manufacturers, which, he suspected, had long been selling substandard products. That February, just a month before the poi ordinance went into effect, Blanchard had already begun looking into the issue, estimating that at least 90 percent of Honolulu's ice cream failed to meet American federal standards, and much of it, in fact, did not contain even contain cream.[68] Blanchard sought clarification from Hawai'i's attorney general on whether Hawai'i's manufacturers would be held to US federal regulations. He drew attention to the Department of Agriculture's definitions for ice cream, carefully quoting in his letter that "ice cream is a frozen product made from cream and sugar, with or without natural flavoring, and contains not less than fourteen percent of milk fat."[69] Blanchard wanted to be sure, he explained, because he intended to prosecute.

And he did. Between April 18 and June 15, 1911, he mimeographed and mailed violation warnings to ninety-two ice cream vendors throughout Honolulu. The letters, in fact, constitute almost the entirety of outgoing correspondence archived from Blanchard's tenure.[70] Their contents, which quoted section 1041 of the territory's pure food laws of 1905 and 1911, reported that a sample of the vendor's ice cream had been found deficient in butterfat and that, if this was not resolved, prosecution was imminent. Again, anti-Asian racism determined the direction and force of bureaucratic control. The vast majority of Blanchard's violation warnings went to Chinese and Japanese vendors and, while the food commissioner publicly couched the stakes of the investigation in moral terms, he explained that that Asian vendors required greater retribution than the haole ones.[71] "[Bad] publicity is usually sufficient for the white dealers," he reported, "and, when they see their names printed as violators of the law, they usually bring their ice-cream up to standard, but the orientals are different. They have to be prosecuted and, after they have paid a heavy fine, they realize that they must conform to the law."[72] Echoing xenophobic discourses leveraged against the poi manufacturers, pure food became a racial concern as much as an epidemiological and moral crisis.[73] Given the pressing matter of the cholera outbreak—an issue Blanchard personally oversaw in the same month—the energy spent on regulating butterfat standards for ice cream, which posed no threat to public health whatsoever, makes clear the imperatives of pure food bureaucracy in territorial Hawai'i, in which ideological commitments to purity superseded the very real dangers of foodborne illness.[74]

SETTLER COLONIAL TASTE POLITICS

With poi production halted, debates over food politics expanded to larger power struggles throughout the territory, including over the authority to determine which products were pure, safe, and of good taste. Blanchard's efforts to regulate Hawai'i's ice creams remained energetic well into May 1913, when he reported the examination results of thirty-six samples of milk and twenty-seven samples of ice cream from Honolulu businesses. He found the milk samples to be of consistently high quality, with only three testing below the standard. On the other hand, twenty-four of the ice creams showed evidence of adulteration in the form of gelatin or other commonly used thickeners.[75] A *Hawaiian Gazette* story wryly entitled "Ice Cream Is Now What It Is Called" reported, in turn, "It turned out that not only were the greater part of the manufacturers turning out a very poor imitation of the real thing in the frozen dainty line, but that they even did not know how to make the real thing at all . . . [but] the use of sufficient cream to bring butter fat percentage up to fourteen per cent does away with the necessity of using gelatine to give the required consistency."[76] Suggesting here that Hawai'i's ice cream had long been produced differently than its American counterpart, complaints about the controversy inferred that "adulteration" was less a function of fraud and more about the imposition of US pure food regulations.

Hawai'i manufacturers, it seems, were simply producing their ice cream as they always had. Cookbooks published in Honolulu during the late nineteenth century, for example, regularly included ice cream recipes that didn't call for any cream or butterfat, instead instructing readers to use a combination of Cox's gelatin and milk. A Mrs. Hascall's contribution to *The Hawaiian Cookbook*, published in 1882, stated that omitting dairy altogether was optimal for Hawai'i's climate, explaining that "water ices are more refreshing in hot weather and more delicate than ice cream."[77] Ice cream makers, instead, used broadly accepted ingredients and techniques to sell familiar products to Hawai'i consumers.

Vendors complained that the general public did not even desire ice creams with a high butterfat content, even if the Board of Health demanded American standardization. One unnamed confectioner complained to a news reporter that the quality of its products suffered under the new manufacturing expectations, in terms of both cost and taste:

> The reason that fourteen percent ice cream isn't so palatable is that the butter fats it contains are apparent. Did you ever eat ice cream and have a coating of grease in the roof of your mouth after a mouthful or two? Well, that was high butter fat ice cream. Fourteen percent butterfat in ice cream will give this effect. I know because I have tried it. I think our ice cream is running about eleven percent right now, and although we are making it in exactly the same manner as we always did I have had numbers of persons tell me that our cream was not as good as it was a month or so ago when we aimed to have between eight and ten percent.[78]

When enforcement of a common legal definition began taking precedence over the demands of the local market, producers found themselves caught in ideological crosshairs. Compliance meant a double loss of revenue through increased cost of manufacture and unhappy customers; ignorance tempted fines or incarceration for nonwhite business owners.

The tensions between Honolulu ice cream dealers and the food commissioner peaked dramatically when, in May 1912, Blanchard proposed a public exhibition that might settle the legal standard once and for all. The event he envisioned would gather all of Hawai'i's ice cream in one place sometime before the next legislative session so that the general public could attend, essentially, a massive taste test. "He is not going to open a free ice-cream parlor," the newspapers chided; "the idea of holding the exhibit is to settle a long fought-out controversy as to just how much butterfat should be contained in ice cream—whether the people think that the present stipulated percentage of fourteen is too much or too little."[79] Samples would represent the full range of goods labeled "ice cream"—both above the butterfat standard and below—and consumer preference could then inform pure food lawmakers. The event never came to pass, although it's unclear why not. These seemingly minor details about the local application of pure food laws reveal the complexity of settler colonial taste politics in urban Hawai'i.[80] American federal standards produced bureaucratic forms of racial violence, in which targeted threats of incarceration sought to cast Asian food producers as duplicitous. Localized solutions, in turn, underscored the uneven force of regulation. Blanchard's regard for consumer opinion suggests, at once, his confidence that ice cream preferences would align with pure food standards, as well as acknowledgment in practice that Hawaiian markets operated under a different set of sensory proscriptions.

At the same time that ice cream producers complained that customers didn't like the taste of American ice cream, Kānaka Maoli instead discussed more pressing concerns about the city's poi. With shops still closed and a simmering resentment over the city's new sanitation requirements, a lingering kalo shortage caused city officials to accuse kalo farmers of conspiring with poi shop owners. "They are refusing to sell their taro," the *Hawaiian Gazette* complained, "to any except the owners of the closed poi shops, who refuse to open under the rules of the board of health, and who, consequently, can not buy their taro."[81] While the farmers claimed that they were simply beholden to contracts with certain shops, the dearth of poi in the city resulted in a "famine" for families who relied on the staple food and hesitated to consume what the government offered. The rations from the Kalihi poi factory, many said, tasted suspiciously "off." In May 1911, the *Hawaiian Star* reported, "The poi that the Board of Health is forcing on the community has something in it. Hawaiians say the adulterant is like vinegar. This poi has the unusual faculty of going sour in a day."[82] Leveraging their own charges of adulteration toward the territorial government, Kānaka critiqued the colonialist applications of pure food politics, which seemed to only care about the safety and pleasure of white settlers.

These assessments drew on broad experience with the territorial government's unwillingness to support traditional Hawaiian food systems. As the government prepared to add a poi inspector to the city's payroll in 1901, for example, officials hotly debated whether or not the person to take the position should be Hawaiian, given that "a Hawaiian could not tell the difference between a microbe and a pig."[83] According to a report on the hiring of Honolulu's poi inspector published in the *Pacific Commercial Advertiser*, Jonah Kumalae, a poi manufacturer and member of the legislature, held an entire morning's session in the House of Representatives describing "poi making as an inherited art," arguing that only a Kanaka Maoli could be trusted to determine safety and quality. He explained:

> The poi industry was the means of enriching many Chinese, who, through their unscrupulous methods of adulterating poi were growing rich at the expense of the poor, submissive Hawaiian, who paid the price asked. While a haole might mean all right, he was not to the manner [*sic*] born, when it came to passing judgment on the Hawaiian staple . . . the proof of poi, like that of pudding, was the eating of it. If it made one sick it was bad poi, if one did not suffer, but thrived on it, it was good poi.[84]

Even as Kumalae strategically downplayed Hawaiian political power at the hands of both haole and Chinese, his speech nevertheless advocated for Kanaka rights to self-determination. How could someone without intergenerational knowledge understand the difference between good poi and bad? Kumalae not only privileged epistemology and genealogy but also underscored these qualities as legitimate qualifications for a food safety official serving the Hawaiian public. In addition to upholding common racist tropes of the time—the unethical Chinese, the ignorant Hawaiian, the enlightened haole—his words illustrate the cultural frictions of pure food regulation, which differentially served Hawai'i's people.[85]

TERRITORIAL DESIRES

As Blanchard tracked down ice cream samples around Honolulu, an American disease expert, Dr. Donald Currie, investigated the cholera outbreak by carefully detailing the circumstances of each illness. Presenting his findings to the Board of Health in a special meeting about a month after the outbreak, he traced the source to a stream in Mānoa valley, which irrigated adjacent vegetable farms, including several Chinese-owned lo'i kalo (wetland taro patches) that supplied some Honolulu poi shops.[86] This changed the spatial dimensions of the issue. Several of the infected individuals hadn't even consumed poi but instead had washed clothing in or sourced drinking water directly from the stream. While the *Hawaiian Gazette*, which published the details of Currie's investigation, declared that poi was "proven to be source of Cholera," its framing offered only a partial truth.[87] A second article in the *Gazette*, set alongside the first, reported on a moratorium against "the sale or cultivation of all vegetables raised by irrigation . . . [which] includes everything raised from the head of the valley to the lower fringe of College Hills and applies to everyone."[88] Actions to curb all agricultural production in Mānoa, while maintaining an insistence that the outbreak remained a distinctly Hawaiian problem related to poi, reflected the ongoing racial tensions embedded within broader public concerns about purity and contamination.

News reports on the agriculture moratorium also suggest that the outbreak had the added bonus of cutting off the economic viability of those urban loʻi kalo that supplied Chinese-owned food purveyors. The director of the Hawaiʻi Weather Bureau went so far as to imply that wealthy Honolulu residents had already been looking for opportunities to overtake agricultural lands for residential development; indeed, as the city expanded, the fields began to occupy what could—and did—become prime real estate.[89] In other words, restricting poi distribution in the city necessarily, conveniently, and lucratively collapsed the businesses of nearby agricultural suppliers, eventually making the land available for luxury homes and the flagship campus of the University of Hawaiʻi.

In the following decades, kalo farmers indeed disappeared, first from Honolulu and then from more rural areas, as many abandoned their fields to enter into the commercial workforce, and as Hawaiʻi's people increasingly turned toward a standard American diet. Just as hierarchies of taste became coded by settler dominance in the islands, so too the concept of place would be pulled into capitalist frameworks, effecting what Mishuana Goeman refers to as a "settler-colonial grammar of place," where Indigenous spatial constructions contort in order to accommodate the demands of the settler state.[90] When we consider these landed grammars through the frameworks of food, then the crucial relationships between land, people, and cultural survival become ever more tangible.[91] The dispossessive results of a purported effort to contain the deadly transmission of cholera in Honolulu thereby underscore the profound territoriality of food politics, even when (and perhaps especially when) they are obscured by discourses of safety, purity, and good taste.

Historically, the shared regulation of poi and ice cream—one potentially lethal and the other benign—suggests that Hawaiʻi's pure food laws privileged as much as they classified during a time of enormous political transition. It specifically illuminates how, under the guise of public health, the territorial government prioritized certain kinds of tastes above others, and in turn reproduced distinctly non-Hawaiian ways of living. In particular, colonial officials like Blanchard helped to focus government efforts and funds on the regulation of certain foods that, in a time of cholera, lacked urgency or importance. Through these instances of Hawaiian food regulation, the contours of taste also emerge as a powerful cultural tool to be wielded as a challenge to the state, in much the way that Kumalae insisted that Kānaka know the difference between good and bad poi through intimate knowledges.

One can see that these shifts in taste politics remain unreconciled in Hawaiʻi even today as food activists argue for increased and legally supported access to Indigenous staple foods. Turning back to the legalize paʻi ʻai movement and the events that anticipated the passing of SB 101, however, reveals the ongoing investments the state has made to maintain systems that foreclose expressions of self-determination against regulatory powers that favor global capitalism over Indigenous environmental, cultural, and physical vitality. In the wake of Daniel Anthony's arrest, for example, the sanitation officer for his district tellingly explained the situation by stating, "Mr. Anthony fails to realize that we are not living in ancient times where there were no regulations designed to protect public health. The DOH cannot stand idly by while Mr. Anthony continues to endanger the health of Hawaiʻi's people under the guise of cultural tradition."[92] Setting up a neat dichotomy between a lawless Indigenous past and a safe modern present, the DOH representative drew on stereotypes that imagine Hawaiian worlds as always already receding into the past.[93] In doing so, he made visible the colonialist subtext of an otherwise seemingly benevolent rationale for state force, exposing the ways that Anthony's arrest cut much deeper than health code noncompliance.

Just as the legal precedents of kalo regulation remain present today, the subtle intersections between territory and taste linger in the way that we still talk about the politics of poi, as an agricultural mission to support food sovereignty in Hawaiʻi but also as a form of cultural recuperation. Despite renewed interest in traditional Hawaiian foods and Indigenous food politics, settler taste preferences subtly echo in the language of advocacy, which aims to draw broad public support for kalo-based foods by emphasizing their healthfulness and deliciousness. In one interview, then-UH law student Amy Brinker, who spearheaded the Legalize Paʻi ʻAi project and shepherded the bill through the legislature, emphasized how, because of its taste, paʻi ʻai offered an ideal platform for Indigenous food advocacy because it lacks the flavor characteristics of poi, its more fermented and sourer counterpart. She stated, for example, in an interview for Honolulu's *Civil Beat*, "There are people who may not like poi but find they love paʻiʻai [*sic*], with its mochi-like consistency and milky sweetness. When someone with a newfound taste for paʻiʻai has trouble finding it because there is not enough kalo to meet the demand, the stage is set for more folks to take up farming."[94] In other words, the "milky sweetness" of paʻi ʻai creates a palatable bridge for those who otherwise might not purchase poi or support kalo farming in Hawaiʻi, thus enfolding kalo into the gustatory frameworks established and perpetuated through ongoing settler occupation. While, in one sense, increased consumer interest in kalo may influence agricultural production, perhaps gaining some purchase on farming practices that have been in decline since colonization, the racialized discourses of taste established in the early decades of pure food in Hawaiʻi endure.

5

LOCAL COLOR, RAINBOW AESTHETICS, AND THE RACIAL POLITICS OF HAWAIIAN SHAVE ICE

In 1984, the independent Hawai'i-based energy company Pacific Resources, Inc., took out a simple but bold advertisement in the *Star-Bulletin*. "Local Color," the ad read. Beneath the large type was a photograph of a glistening shave ice. No hand holds it up: just a mound of snow and syrup in a white paper cone and a plastic straw poking out of its side. The copy underneath the image described a well-rehearsed genealogy of what was, by then, an iconic Hawaiian taste.[1] In this ad, and more broadly across the second half of the twentieth century, shave ice and its "rainbow" of flavors offered a metaphor for Hawai'i's success as a multicultural US state. Narratives like the one in this advertisement help to tell a commonplace story about the development of Hawai'i's local identity, wherein a sugar plantation economy produced a racially harmonious society for the only US state with a nonwhite majority population.[2]

The copy below the image underscores how Hawai'i's racial and ethnic histories—both contentious and harmonious—help produce shave ice aesthetics. Here, the "colored" people of Hawai'i are represented by syrup flavors that overlap and mix atop the mountain of ice, engaging "a marketplace of flavors, each competing for its own turf. Coconut invades strawberry. Guava shares a border with lime. But they come together to form that colorful part of our island culture known as Shave Ice."[3] The discursive slippage between flavor, color, and ethnicity is instructive for considering the broad implications of how foods—even those celebrated locally—present as racialized proxies for people in a militarized state.[4] If, in the ad copy, the syrups are described simply as flavors, the political utility of the multiethnic rainbow becomes clearly articulated in the headline when "colors" operate as a linguistic simile for race. The rainbow that results from their mixing becomes, then, the paradigm through which Hawai'i's "local" community becomes imagined and materialized.

Across the twentieth century, the iconography of shave ice increasingly offered an easy shorthand for popular narratives about race and American nationalism in the "Aloha State." In particular, the "ethnic rainbow," in both common understanding and academic analysis, references ideas that Hawai'i offers a model for how American democratic ideals can support racial tolerance, and even acceptance.[5] These metaphorical "rainbows" and "melting pots," Maile Arvin argues, are rooted in colonialism. First generated in the 1920s and 1930s by the University of Hawai'i sociologist Romanzo Adams, and reinvigorated in the 1980s in popular literature, theories of Hawai'i as an island "laboratory" for multiethnic harmony continue to structure the racial imaginary of Hawai'i today. In Arvin's analysis of Adams's research and its lasting legacy, she reveals how twentieth-century narratives about the benefits of racial mixing were formed through anti-Hawaiian racism from their very inception, writing that "the discourse of Hawai'i as a melting pot has always been a salable fiction that masks structural racism against Native Hawaiians and others."[6] Kanaka 'Ōiwi scholars like Haunani-Kay Trask and Lisa Kahaleole Hall have additionally shown how multicultural discourses work to obscure ongoing inequities between racialized Indigenous and non-Indigenous groups in Hawai'i.[7] These tensions, I argue, exist not merely at the political level but also through the aesthetic and sensorial subtleties of everyday life. As the example of shave ice shows, cold refreshment, made local, helps to temper settler colonialism's violence.

Today Hawaiian shave ice can be found in every major American city, distinguished by name and its rainbow iconography from other popular forms of snow cone, piragua, or kakigōri. What makes shave ice particularly "Hawaiian" is not ingredients but textures, tastes, and aesthetics. Unlike similar frozen desserts, its ice is shaved—not crushed—from a large block, which helps to suspend the syrup. A vast array of flavors allows for endless customization, many of which reference tropical fruits: mango, lychee, guava, and liliko'i (passion fruit), alongside cola, vanilla, and blue raspberry.[8] Favorite shave ice spots furthermore operate as shorthand expressions of "localness" that trade on both insider knowledge and claims to authenticity: it's why Hale'iwa's famous Mastumoto's Shave Ice prominently announces the year of its founding (1951); and why folks from Hawai'i Island politely point out that the correct term is *ice shave*; and why *Vogue* magazine publishes trend pieces on Hawai'i's growing artisanal shave ice businesses that "are turning to the 'āina as their muse—creating an exciting farm-to-ice movement."[9]

This chapter explores how shave ice aesthetically expresses racial idealism in Hawai'i in tension with ongoing calls for decolonization and sovereignty by Kānaka Maoli. Distinct from the haole-coded ice creams at the turn of the century and tiki drinks fetishized by the tourist gaze at the early to midcentury, shave ice offers an alternative narrative of Hawai'i's thermal relationship to colonialism and empire, in which refreshment is democratic and naturalized. Reading across historical and contemporary media representations of shave ice throughout the twentieth century reveals how prestatehood anxieties about Hawai'i's racial diversity were not only resolved through multiculturalism's rainbow metaphors but also embraced through nonwhite forms of iced refreshment. Drawing histories of shave ice through to the present moment, I seek to understand how it becomes used to "accessorize" postracial American nationalism in Hawai'i today in ways that obscure or overwrite Kanaka Maoli claims to Indigenous sovereignty.

REFRESHMENT'S RACIAL IMAGINARIES

The multiracial imaginary that local identity and associated foods like shave ice marked represented an important departure from forms of tropical refreshment oriented toward white leisure, like the ice creams that were popularized in Honolulu in the 1910s and 1920s. By the 1930s and 1940s, however, colorful cocktails began to emblematize touristic experiences of the tropics. These changing grammars of refreshment say much about how Hawai'i's tourism emerged out of the plantation economy, with Hawai'i's elites agitating for statehood because of its financial benefits. Prior to World War II, as Dean Itsuji Saranillio explains, statehood meant more lucrative sugar tariffs and, as tourism increased during the postwar boom, US-based insurance and loan servicing—something that territorial status prevented financial institutions from doing—was an attractive benefit for those wishing to capitalize on business expansion and development.[10] While often narrated as an economic shift from one economy to the other, plantation agriculture and tourism worked in tandem throughout these crucial decades, ideologically reinforcing white hegemony through paradigms of racialized labor and service that cut across agriculture and hospitality.[11] For example, advertisements produced in the first half of the twentieth century by pineapple tycoon James Drummond Dole featured Hawaiians variously exoticized while playing on the beach, deferential while serving tourists, and working diligently on the canning floor.[12] These various advertising strategies aimed not just to allay white anxieties about Hawai'i's multiracial communities but to underscore how racial harmony might blossom under factory discipline.[13]

An array of complementary narratives about labor, leisure, and race in Hawai'i became packaged and exported to the "mainland" for consumption, appearing in media representations circulated in magazines and travel books, as well as in the built space of restaurants in the form of tiki bars.[14] Places like Trader Vic's and Don the Beachcomber, some of the original tiki bars, used ambiguously racialized tropes about the Pacific to evoke a sense of tropicality and exoticism in the service of white pleasure: thatched roofs, appropriated religious sculptures transformed into mugs and decor, and menus of "Oriental" food that indiscriminately mixed Pacific and Asian elements together.[15]

The Mai Tai—a rum-based cocktail allegedly invented by Victor "Trader Vic" J. Bergeron—borrows its name from the word for "good" in the Polynesian language family (maita'i in Reo Tahiti; maika'i in 'ōlelo Hawai'i). It quickly became a staple of the stateside tiki bars established on the California coast during World War II. By the 1950s, it had become so popular in America that the rum brand used in the original drink no longer existed. It was the approximated substitute that made its way to Hawai'i in 1953, when Matson Steamship Lines hired Bergeron to produce cocktail menus for the Royal Hawaiian and Moana Surfrider hotels in Waikīkī, where pineapple and orange juice were added to both sweeten the recipe and better reference "local" plantation economies, while rum remained the drink base in reference to Caribbean sugar plantations and the slave labor that sustained them.[16] In doing so, the combined flavors of pineapple and rum largely referenced the economies of empire that relied on racial capitalism to underpin white wealth and leisure, with Hawai'i's predominantly Asian plantation and factory workers rendered at once invisible and central to the settler colonial project, and "Polynesia" reduced to ornament.

As Denis Dutton explains, the tiki bar epitomizes "kitsch" aesthetics —a "self-congratulatory" form of representation that exists to "reassure its consumers of their social standing."[17] The growing American middle class of the mid-twentieth-century embraced a consumer culture that affirmed and celebrated hegemonic Western power through real and imagined vacations to the tropics.[18] While tiki culture's popularity lingers in both Hawai'i and the US "mainland" as a celebration of white power, alternative narratives about race and refreshment, encapsulated by shave ice emerged in the second half of the twentieth century in order to accommodate visions of Hawai'i beyond hegemonic whiteness, even if those visions reinforced the structures of settler colonialism embedded within.

FROM MELTING POTS TO FROZEN CONES

Across the late nineteenth and twentieth centuries, Hawai'i's social power dynamics, once overdetermined by whiteness, shifted to contend with Asian economic and political ascendancy in the poststatehood era. Scholars have theorized that shift as part of a broader settler colonial racial paradigm, using the term *Asian settler colonialism* to refer to the ways that Asian immigrant populations in Hawai'i, once systemically marginalized, today benefit from and reinforce ongoing Native Hawaiian dispossession in favor of their own economic and political advancement.[19] Two particularly salient settler colonial logics are embedded within this formulation. The first is that Asian settler colonialism is contingent on American national identity: as Haunani-Kay Trask writes, "'Locals' want to be 'Americans.'"[20] The second is that local identity, as one that is often mixed-race and may or may not include individuals of Native Hawaiian descent, obscures the political specificity of indigeneity. "Locals," argues Trask, stake their claim to Hawai'i by distinguishing themselves from haole hegemony and, simultaneously, collapse Native Hawaiian indigeneity into a loose panethnic category in order to dissolve prior and politically distinct claims.[21] Local identity formations, forged within the economic and social crucibles of American white supremacy, express how the logics of possession operate through underlying structures of settler colonialism, even in the relative absence of white people.

Although the term *melting pot* did not originate in Hawaiʻi, it continues to hold currency as an expression of Hawaiʻi's racial dynamics. The title of a play by the British playwright Israel Zangwill, *The Melting-Pot* (1908), has come to refer to, as Philip Gleason explains, "a symbol for the process whereby immigrants are absorbed into American society and somehow changed into Americans."[22] Used by sociologist Romanzo Adams to describe processes of nonwhite assimilation in the "racial laboratory" of Hawaiʻi, the idea of the "melting pot" would be brought to bear on discussions regarding Hawaiʻi's suitability for statehood.[23] What had once been regarded with anxiety soon promised, by the late 1930s, to become a unifying asset to the settler colonial project. As Sidney Lewis Gulick, Adams's contemporary, speculated in 1937: "The races are actually growing together—fusing biologically . . . a new race is in the making. . . . The physiological characteristics of the new race will be a mixture of Hawaiian, Caucasian, and Asiatic, while its psychological, social, political, and moral characteristics will be distinctly American."[24] By reframing racial mixing as a tool of colonial acculturation, these early conversations became, as John Chock Rosa argues, the foundation on which later celebrations of Hawaiʻi's multiculturalism were built.[25] Even so, as Arvin describes, assimilationist projections on the future Americanization of Hawaiʻi's people did not always align with sentiments on the ground, in which racial hierarchies remained embedded in how research subjects talked about various ethnic groups and particularly about Hawaiianness.[26]

These frictions were perhaps most famously illustrated by the Massie affair of the 1930s, which made US headlines as readers followed the details of the investigation and trial for the alleged rape of a young, white military wife, Thalia Massie, by a group of mixed-race "local" men in 1931, and the murder of one of those men, Joseph Kahahawai, by Massie's husband and father.[27] While Americans used the case as evidence that Hawaiʻi was a "racial nightmare," within Hawaiʻi, the "local" identity of the falsely accused men was grounded, in part, by a working-class status that most mixed-race brown people in Hawaiʻi shared.[28] By the 1940s and 1950s, the working-class interests of people—many of whom descended from plantation workers or still worked on Hawaiʻi's plantations themselves—importantly manifested a collective political consciousness that galvanized differentially marginalized and oppressed racial groups to unionize against sugar oligopolies like the "Big Five" that controlled Hawai'i's sugar industry.[29]

Statehood in 1959, however, changed the tenor of local solidarities. The transition from colonial subject to American citizenship was an especially fraught experience for Asian peoples in Hawai'i who had, since the 1887 adoption of the Bayonet Constitution in the Hawaiian Kingdom, been ineligible for full citizenship rights.[30] This ineligibility to vote would continue under the US Organic Act of 1900 and until the passing of the Immigration and Nationality Act in 1952, which gave first-generation Asian Americans the right to naturalize and vote in Hawai'i, just as in other US states.[31] As Saranillio explains in his examination of the activities of the Hawaii Statehood Commission, which helped to control narratives about Hawai'i's racial appropriateness for inclusion as an American state, "Hawai'i statehood, narrated as a liberal antiracist civil rights project, facilitated and normalized projects of both settler colonialism and empire" in which Native Hawaiian dissent became all but invisibilized.[32] Placed against the backdrop of US civil rights discourse, Asian American naturalization, and Japanese American heroism in World War II, Native Hawaiian movements for sovereignty and decolonization were often portrayed as racist and antithetical to democratic ideals.[33]

Legal developments like these influenced a growing sense, as Trask put it, that "the vehicle for Asian ascendancy [in Hawai'i] is statehood," with the awarding of long-awaited civil rights and increased political power as both voters and legislators.[34] Upward class mobility—more so for some ethnic groups, like Japanese, than others—meant that mobilization around shared class oppression at times faded into the background in favor of shared cultural characteristics like lifestyle values, informality, and neighborliness as a way of ideologically separating "local insiders" from "haole outsiders."[35] Such forms of local "culture" became implicitly and explicitly underpinned by settler ideology rooted specifically in American nationalism.

Leaving behind the shared sense of ethnic and class oppression that characterized local identity across the territorial period, the common ground among poststatehood locals turned, at times, away from political difference and increasingly toward political sameness.[36] In other instances, however, statehood further bonded Hawaiian and non-Hawaiian locals together in shared struggle as communities organized against their acute displacement in earnest in the 1970s. Along with a cultural renaissance in Native Hawaiian art forms like music and dance, Kānaka Maoli responded to the sharp increases in tourism and development by calling for the protection of, as Davianna Pōmaikaʻi McGregor describes, "Kanaka ʻŌiwi ancestral and national lands and the cultural and natural resources of those lands."[37] The Kalama Valley protests of 1971 stand out as a salient example of such forms of cooperation between Hawaiians and "locals," who occupied the valley in protest of changes to zoning laws that permitted the development of former agricultural land.[38] Antieviction movements such as this galvanized community organizing that articulated class struggles and Native Hawaiian sovereignty struggles, which worked at once in tension and in cooperation during this pivotal historical moment.[39] The emergent state's multiculturalist identity thus formed through a complex and often paradoxical set of phenomena that sought to set Hawaiʻi and its people apart through competing forms of oppression while also reifying American assimilationism and Indigenous erasure.[40]

MAKING SHAVE ICE LOCAL

Just as it took time for Hawaiʻi's immigrant populations to see themselves as local, and eventually American, shave ice would be made, sold, and enjoyed for decades before it became narrativized through multiracial paradigms. This trajectory mirrors broader accounts of Hawaiʻi's food traditions as a story of tolerance, assimilation, and shared values.[41] In Hawaiʻi, so-called local cuisine, of which shave ice is a part, along with distinct regional dishes like Spam musubi, the ubiquitous "plate lunch," and saimin, marks panethnic belonging through its amalgamation and convergence of multicultural food traditions.[42] Rachel Laudan, for example, writes that "local food" functions similarly to pidgin, or Hawaiian creole, which emerged in the early twentieth century to resolve linguistic barriers between plantation workers. She describes the paradigmatic plate lunch as follows: "The plate lunch is truly pidgin (creole) food. The vocabulary of the meal (with the exception of the potato and macaroni salads) is overwhelmingly Asian, but the syntax, the way it's put together, with its large portions of meat, its downplaying of vegetables, and the brown gravy, is haole. The way it is served (heaped on a plate instead of in small bowls) is haole. The way it is eaten (a choice of chopsticks or plastic cutlery) is mixed again."[43] Drawing from structuralist traditions in linguistic anthropology, the metaphor of creole language seems to neutralize cultural admixing in much the same way that the trope of "melt" suggests more of an effortless bleeding than the result of indenture, dispossession, and coercive labor practices.[44]

Food historians like Laudan, Arnold Hiura, and others trace the emergence of Hawai'i's contemporary "local" cuisine through these sugar plantation communities, which depended on overlapping waves of immigrant laborers: first Chinese, then Japanese, Portuguese, Korean, Okinawan, and Puerto Rican people. These ethnic groups brought food traditions with them, cultivating familiar vegetables in modest kitchen gardens and shopping at plantation stores that stocked the rest. Within the cities, a steady influx of business elites and tourists consumed Euro-American fare with some Native Hawaiian elements: often a combination of shelf-stable imported goods supplemented with locally grown fruits and vegetables. Outside of the cities, however, a distinct cuisine coalesced out of the mixed-heritage foods that plantation workers cooked and ate together, out of both necessity and kinship.[45] If ice cream reflected the civility and whiteness of urban Hawai'i, shave ice belonged to rural spaces where non-Hawaiians put down deep community roots. In the decades to come, shave ice would become localized as those who brought it to Hawai'i became "local" themselves.

Even so, and to the degree that shave ice has become an emblematic refreshment of Hawai'i, little scholarly work is devoted to its history. Laudan's award-winning book on the development of Hawai'i cuisine devotes a single paragraph to the topic; Hiura's *Kau Kau* offers a full section with more detail, including some technological context, but it is far from comprehensive or supported by archival references.[46] These writings, along with websites and blogs, offer sketches or brief overviews of the history of shave ice in Hawai'i, which usually trace the origin of the food to Japanese agricultural workers or plantation store owners, who brought the food tradition of kakigōri with them to Hawai'i.[47] Alternately, though in my opinion less likely, some suggest that early door-to-door ice delivery may have inspired Hawaiian shave ice, with the ice man giving children some ephemeral shavings during his delivery rounds.[48]

Most accounts estimate that shave ice arrived in Hawai'i sometime around the turn of the century and was popularized in the 1920s and 1930s.[49] My own extensive searches through historical cookbooks, the Hawai'i Sugar Planter's Association records, the Hawai'i State Archives, and newspaper databases offered up scant resources, providing only brief glimpses into a richly historied working-class refreshment that, in the early twentieth century, was still underexploited by the tourism industry. What archives do detail, however, is how ice became available in Hawaiʻi's rural areas at the beginning of the twentieth century, as electric power spread like capillaries across the islands. Sugar plantations became hubs for technological power, as much as economic power, making local ice production feasible. While, as this book shows, gaps between archival obscurity and contemporary ubiquity are common in the study of ice in Hawaiʻi, this example looks beyond the haole-Hawaiian paradigms that circumscribed cocktail and ice cream consumption in the territorial era, instead illuminating the overlapping and shifting forms of race-making generated outside of urban centers.

The records of the Hawaiʻi Sugar Planter's Association suggest, for example, that once a sugar mill's operations grew large enough, its infrastructures would be put to multiple uses. In 1902, the Pioneer Mill Company on Maui expanded to include the Lahaina Ice Company, which offered both cold storage and electricity to its surrounding community. By 1912, Pioneer also operated an electric light franchise, a moving picture machine, and a soda works, as well as listing livestock as financial assets in its account books.[50] Just a couple of years later, Lahaina Ice received as much revenue from selling electricity as it did from selling ice, having made substantial efforts to install and maintain the necessary infrastructures.[51] Its electric business would only grow as the years went on: the ice company offered house wiring services for those wanting electric lights installed, and it established an agreement with the territorial government to "construct, maintain, and operate suitable poles, lines, wires, cables, lamps, lamp-posts, conductors, conduits, and other such appliances and appurtenances."[52] By the mid-1920s, Lahaina Ice became the main power supplier for one of Hawaiʻi's largest towns, revealing the ways that infrastructures of power and cold worked in tandem to extend American modernity across and through plantation spaces.

The small mom-and-pop stores that served these communities, often owned or operated by immigrant laborers brought over to work on Hawaiʻi's plantations, grappled with new technologies that extended both local and interisland food chains at the same time that the desire for cold refreshment was growing in rural communities. Take, for example, a 1923 dispute between the Honokaa Sugar Company and the Honolulu Dairymens Association that shows how fragile the nascent Hawaiian cold chain was as it expanded between islands. On receiving ten dozen melted Polar Pies from Oʻahu, the Honokaʻa store's manager mailed a complaint:

> We wish to state the only way possible to ship ice cream and have it reach us in good condition, is via Hilo on the S. S. "Haleakala," as this steamer has cold storage facilities.[53]

> We are of the opinion that the blame rests with the Dairymen's Association as, when they took the ice cream down to the "Onomea," the Purser told them he couldn't take it, on account of the steamer having no facilities for carrying ice cream. They asked him to take it any [sic] which he finally consented to do at their risk. . . . It reached here melted and unfit for sale.[54]

This incident illustrates not only the extensive distribution networks required for frozen goods to reach rural townships but also the kinds of expectations that came with increased access to freezing and refrigeration in the second quarter of the twentieth century.

Until electric refrigerators arrived in plantation stores, owners carefully managed their perishable stock. Violet Hew Zane, who grew up in her father's store Hew Fat Kee, remembered when electricity arrived in Lower Pāʻia, Maui, along with their electric refrigerator, in 1924. Before then, daily ice delivery allowed her parents to sell cold drinks and soda water. She recalled, "Maui Ice and Soda Works used to bring ice. They put the ice in the icebox. That's how they could keep things cool." With electricity, she explained, "We could sell ice cream and cold soda water. My mother made some ice cubes and sold ice cubes. There were other things that could be refrigerated." In addition to being able to store whatever foods they didn't sell by the end of the day, her mother could also produce more foods in house.

The refrigerator's arrival significantly shifted the rhythms of labor in the store, exemplified by how the Zane family made refreshments like ice cream and shave ice that they sold to their community. Before 1924, Zane explained, "my mother . . . bought the chunks (of ice) and broke them into pieces. She had the old-fashioned [ice cream] freezer that she ground by hand. She made the mixture of the fresh milk, and sugar, and vanilla extract. . . . She would crank the ice cream until it's hard." After the electric fridge, she recalled, "we bought ice cream to sell. But we didn't have it like we have it today, in separate popsicles or drumsticks like that. You know, separate pieces. They were in a container in a can.

So, we sold it in bulk . . . we bought ice cream every day, because we didn't buy plenty. Just enough that we could sell for the day." Hew Fat Kee made its shave ice "with the big blocks of ice. . . . We had the old-fashioned way of cutting the ice. The shaved ice would be put into cups, then sugar and extracts put in it."[55] Zane's story illustrates how the shifting technological and thermal landscape of rural Hawai'i produced new temporalities for food workers, as well as expanded the availability of refreshments within plantation communities.[56] These instances from the 1920s offer glimpses into how electric power and refrigeration took hold in rural Hawai'i, where cold refreshment was novel but not new. The consumption of ice cream, cocktails, and shave ice reflected the networks of power that funneled into Hawai'i's expanding (and twinned) tourism and agricultural economies.

SHINING COLORS, SIDE BY SIDE

Midcentury efforts toward American statehood shifted Hawai'i's political, economic, and racial relationship with the United States in the 1950s and 1960s. Contextualized by World War II and the Cold War, statehood in 1959 leveraged narratives of harmonious racial diversity as a repudiation of white supremacy. Particular to this moment, historian Tom Coffman argues, a kind of double vision of Hawai'i emerged. From the perspective of the continental United States, Americans saw a tropical dreamland vacation illustrated by the sweet coldness of tiki drinks and tropical cocktails, and Elvis Presley, *Hawaii Five-O*, and airline travel posters portraying lush environments ripe for white pleasure. Within Hawai'i, however, power bent toward new forms of social and political mobility for Asian communities, with major economic shifts away from the indentured labor of the sugar plantation and increasingly toward education, real estate development, and tourism.[57]

In the ensuing decades, a rapid boom and bust in Hawai'i's economy reflected the structural effects of statehood. In the 1960s, Waikīkī hotels sprouted like springtime weeds, and tourists filled them right up. By the early 1970s, Hawai'i's residents were beginning to feel the strains of poststatehood in-migration and development.[58] A surge of "mainlander" tourists and residents primed Hawai'i locals for sentimental expressions of belonging and placemaking that resisted American cultural assimilation while simultaneously embracing statehood.[59] As Coffman explains, "The changing ethnic composition of the population led to a sense of the social fabric unraveling. In the process, the certainties of early state-hood were giving way to questions about what Hawai'i was and where it was going."[60] Ideas of poststatehood belonging likewise recalibrated against the changing economic and social realities that came with American inclusion.

Pro-statehood propaganda aimed to control narratives around race in Hawai'i. State agencies like the Hawaii Statehood Commission (1947–59), which was formed to promote and normalize desires for statehood, sought to gloss over the racial and political tensions between displaced Kānaka Maoli, economically and politically ascendant settlers-turned-locals, and poststatehood haole newcomers. Hawai'i's new "racially diverse but culturally American" citizenry would quickly become iconized as a rainbow, a reference not only to multiethnic harmony but also to Hawai'i's natural beauty. Rainbows soon infused the Honolulu landscape: the iconic Kapahulu neighborhood diner Rainbow Drive-In opened in 1961; the landmark Rainbow Tower at Waikīkī's Hilton Hawaiian Village opened in 1968; the University of Hawai'i's football team became known as the Rainbows in 1974; and vehicle license plates for the State of Hawai'i began featuring a rainbow starting in 1991.[61]

In public forums, the term *rainbow multiculturalism* began to over-shadow the "melting pot" that Adams popularized in the 1920s and 1930s. A several-page spread in the *Honolulu Advertiser* in 1992, for example, mirrored the Pacific Resources advertisement described at the beginning of this chapter with two articles detailing experiences of racial harmony in Hawai'i. "Hawaii's Ethnic Rainbow: Shining Colors, Side by Side," paired with "Growing Up 'Hapa': Interracial Marriage, Chop Suey Society," featured interviews that framed racism as a problem of the US continent.[62] "Wing Tek Lum," the first of these articles reported, "a busi-nessman, community leader, and poet, has written poems and essays about Hawaii's community as a rainbow. Lum likes the rainbow meta-phor: each ethnic group a distinct color. Altogether, everyone doesn't blend into one color, but each exists side by side showing off bands of blue, green, red, yellow or purple."[63] As a symbol of Hawai'i's racial land-scape, the rainbow offered an important vehicle for the affective, and often tense, sentiments of belonging that characterized poststatehood Hawai'i.[64]

Mirroring the urban landscape, shave ice became an edible counter-part to Hawai'i's state multiculturalism, aestheticized by the rainbow. Grounded in the specific racial and economic contexts of sugar plantation labor in the islands, shave ice gestured toward shared histories of oppression at the same time that it appealed to a depoliticized and harmonious present—one that affirmed local identities. Aligning with emergent attitudes about racial harmony, in which Hawaiʻi distinguished itself from the US "mainland" while simultaneously interpellating itself into the nation-state, shave ice championed the economic and political mobility of communities once conscripted to labor, now positioned for middle-class leisure. Returning to the "Local Color" advertisement, one might notice that the copy concludes in a celebration of American power, stating, "In this 25th year of Statehood, let's look to that simple Shave Ice cone to remind us to flavor our lives with ingenuity, imagination, and a belief in ourselves. Take pride Hawaii. The best is yet to come."

SHAVE ICE AS SETTLER COLONIAL NOSTALGIA

As a symbol of Hawaiʻi's multicultural futures, the rainbowed shave ice cone gained symbolic traction in the early decades of statehood. Hawaiʻi's newspapers offer particularly useful insight into multiculturalism's aesthetic and gustatory convergence in shave ice. Although shave ice had already been popular for decades, sold out of beach carts and mom-and-pop stores, its existence barely registered in the news media until the 1970s. After that, and quite suddenly, across the 1970s, 1980s, and 1990s, newspapers began championing shave ice as both an emblem of prestatehood nostalgia and a promise for harmonious poststatehood futures. The keyword frequency of *shave ice* in the digital archives of the *Honolulu Star Advertiser* (the umbrella name under which Hawaiʻi's two highest circulating newspapers—the *Advertiser* and the *Star Bulletin*—have been combined since their merger in 2010) shows that lifestyle reporting on shave ice emerged about a decade after statehood and increased throughout the 1990s.[65] Prior to this era, shave ice tended to appear only in the city's classified sections, where machines and equipment were bought and sold.[66] After that, shave ice began appearing with more frequency, often featuring in editorials about Hawaiʻi's distinct 'local' society.

In 1988, the *Honolulu Star Bulletin* reported on the development of Hawaiʻi's shave ice businesses and their expanding commercial success beyond working-class neighborhoods. In what was by then a pattern of requisite lament for days gone by, the article begins "You want a shave ice so bad you can taste it. Your kid, who was in a stroller when she had her first shave ice wants one, too. And she isn't going to settle for hearing you explain that shave ice is no longer available in (sob) Kaimuki, (choke) Kapahulu, or (scream) at the Honolulu Zoo. So you decide the shave ice business is dying."[67] Bookending its report with the figure of a sobbing child lamenting a simpler past, the article tracks the growing popularity of shave ice even as it marks a sense of its disappearance: the small beach stands and mom-and-pop stores that had once served rural and peri-urban communities had grown into or been replaced by lucrative corporate franchises. The changing geography of local refreshment was illustrated by companies like Island Snow, a youthful upstart established in 1979, which attracted tourist dollars with branded merchandise and outlets in places like Waikīkī's International Marketplace and Las Vegas, Nevada.

Shared nostalgia for childhood experiences of shave ice becomes, in turn, a way to consolidate "local" claims to Hawai'i through anxieties about displacement in the present. Conceptualized in 1979 by the sociologist Fred Davis as a "painful yearning to return home," nostalgia—at least the American variety exploited by the twentieth-century advertising industry—emerged as a collective affect in the postwar era. His theorization, broken down into a few key characteristics, is useful here for parsing out what initially appears to be benign laments for yesteryear but ends up cogently articulating how locals' own histories of racialized oppression and exclusion from the United States get rewritten as a "simpler" time. Davis defines nostalgia as a social emotion anchored in a first-person experience; as such, it has the capacity to define a sense of community belonging through shared affect. In doing so, nostalgia is always produced through the present, with longings for the past compelled by the political and social context from which those feelings emerge.[68] It is, as Elspeth Probyn describes, both "a structure of feeling" and "an event" constituted by origins.[69] Often, those feelings come to be expressed through food because it is both sensory (i.e., experienced individually) and shared (i.e., experienced communally).[70]

Animated by anxieties around social and economic change in Hawai'i, including worry over impending losses of local culture and expressions of aloha as social norms, childhood memories of shave ice emblematized poststatehood nostalgia—what locals sometimes refer to as "small-kid time"—to index halcyon days of prestatehood rural life. For example, a July 30, 1974, feature article entitled "The Shave Ice Is the Same but the Price Has Changed" leveraged images of ambiguously racialized children enjoying their favorite flavors, while the story itself quotes senior citizens who long for the cheap and simply flavored shave ice of their childhoods, creating discursive and visual connections between an uncomplicated past and an innocent, if indeterminate, present.[71] Likewise, Keiko Ohnuma argues that "rather than political identity, aloha as pronounced by Asian Locals carries a tone of wishful nostalgia for the culture-wide 'small-kid time' before Asian immigrants were coerced into renouncing their homelands . . . or modeling the dominant capitalist paradigm as evidence of their rehabilitation." For Ohnuma, this yearning for childhood innocence becomes a "fetishization of the wound" that disavows Asian complicity in the settler colonial project, even as the temporal location of "small-kid time" coincides with Native Hawaiian colonization.[72] Dovetailing with a phenomenon that Adria Imada refers to as "settler-colonial nostalgia," in which the appropriation of Indigenous cultural forms shores up dispossessive logics, "small-kid time" envisions an ahistorical and uncomplicated past.

These references to childhood belonging, as an extension of aloha state ideologies, proliferated in popular media outlets of the 1970s and 1980s; they continue to frame narratives of shave ice businesses that, in the present day, have expanded from mom-and-pop stores to national franchises. The "about" section of Island Snow's website, for example, narrates that the company's owner grew up in Kailua, O'ahu, the location of its flagship store, with a "dream to own a business one day that would be a fun gathering place for friends and ohana [sic] (family). A business that would spread the 'Aloha spirit,' a feeling that is so unique to Hawai'i."[73] In this way, temporal locations of childhood anchor sentimental expressions of colonial politics so as to render them innocent and benign.

PLAYING WITH SHAVE ICE'S RACIAL IMAGINARIES

Shave ice's alignment with childhood makes possible an easy segue to forms of merchandising and marketing that allow consumers to engage with the racial and national narratives of Hawai'i in the present day. In 2011 and 2017, the American Girl doll company introduced two mixed-race Hawaiian dolls, Kanani Akina and Nanea Mitchell, whose characters, story lines, and accessories are prominently embellished with shave ice, offering consumers ways to play with "Hawaiian" culture through proscribed narratives centered around childhood, leisure, and American nationalism. Kanani, introduced in 2011 as part of the limited-release "Girl of the Year" series, is a contemporary Hawaiian-Japanese-Haole girl from the island of Kaua'i. Nanea, created in 2017, is one of the company's historical characters from the BeForever collection. Significantly, American Girl does not offer a doll of solely Hawaiian descent, even though the company has produced many other dolls that are not of mixed race.[74] Each doll comes with multivolume chapter books that are linked to extensive accessory collections, which can be purchased in addition to the base dolls. As with all American Girl characters, the dolls serve as centerpieces of complex story lines that often trade "upon nostalgic nationalist ideals" to promote values aligned with young female empowerment.[75]

While Kanani's and Nanea's stories reflect different time periods and problematics, there are key consistencies that suggest how mixed-race Hawaiian identities are domesticated and made consumable for broad audiences that may or may not have a personal connection to Hawai'i (though American Girl develops product lines in accordance with consumer demand for multiethnic representation). In particular, Kanani's and Nanea's stories thread nationalist sentiment into themes of friendship, family, and community service to produce coherent American identities for the dolls despite racial and geographic liminality. These themes remain consistent across the different time frames for their story lines, drawing parallels between a protostatehood past set during World War II and a poststatehood present located in rural Kaua'i.[76] In this sense, characters like Kanani and Nanea are teaching tools as much as they are playthings.

Shave ice figures prominently in both of Kanani's books, which are set in her family's store, Akina's Shave Ice and Sweet Treats, a space that serves as a marker of both indigeneity and ethnic multiculturalism: the store, her book says, was built by her great-grandfather in a rural Kaua'i sugar plantation town established in the nineteenth century. Described as a kind of cabinet of curiosity, its interior draws from the ethnic makeup of the plantation community that once patronized it. An illustration shows Japanese sticky rice balls in the display counter, a red Chinese dragon and Hawaiian quilt patterns adorning the back wall, and, in the foreground, a pair of dazzled white tourists who have come for shave ice, which Kanani's father expertly produces from the shop's machine. In time, Kanani takes over the family's shave ice stand—a mobile extension of the store—which she uses to generate funds to support the protection of the endangered Hawaiian monk seal, thus facilitating moral pedagogies about environmental protection through entrepreneurship. Significantly, Kanani's activism serves touristic experiences of Hawai'i by enhancing refreshment and leisure practices while simultaneously enlisting the patronage of visitors in the preservation of Hawai'i's endemic wildlife.

For Nanea, shave ice operates as a narrative device for resolving the racial tensions at the heart of her story, which is set in the aftermath of the Japanese bombing of Pearl Harbor (Pu'uloa). Chapter 4 of her introductory book, *Nanea: Growing Up with Aloha* (2017), begins with Nanea and her two friends—one white American, one Japanese American—indulging in their favorite shave ice flavors at the beach. By the end of that chapter, kamikaze planes and bombs drop from the sky. The intervening story grapples with Japanese internment, gendered wartime labor, and resource scarcity as Hawai'i is drawn squarely into the World War II Pacific theater of operations. As the story lines resolve near the end of the book, Nanea and her friends return to that same beach, sneaking through barbed wire barricades that now scar the waterline. This time, when they buy shave ice, they order three of the same: their favorite lemon, orange, and strawberry flavors layered to create "a rainbow." Bookended by sweetness and violence, this chapter operates as a pivotal moment in a story line that ultimately galvanizes shared American belonging across diverse racial identities.

In addition to reading the narratives crafted around each doll, American Girl consumers are encouraged to play out scenarios inspired by the books through the purchase of extensive accessory collections that reference the dolls' story lines and shape the possibilities of imaginative play. For Kanani and Nanea, these collections include wardrobes for the beach, "luau," and hula performances; pets (both dogs); and—most important—expensive built environments in which the dolls can be immersed. For these, doll-sized shave ice stands anchor the accessory lines in reference to the stories, though with outsize prominence in their accessory collections. Here, the importance of shave ice stands (as well as expressions of aloha as the key principle that guides the girls' behavior), despite the seventy-year gap between the temporal locations of the dolls, anchors their identities across time—nothing really changes about the roles they play or the material trappings of their imagined worlds—and thereby suggests indelible elements of Hawaiian personhood that fix them into feminized, infantilized, and working-class roles, thereby marking them as static even as they are normalized as American subjects.

Namely, the Hawaiian American Girl dolls do things that Natives and "locals" are expected to do, such as play at the beach, entertain with dance, share the spirit of aloha, and serve iced refreshments along with that spirit. They do these things within broader narratives that welcome the presence of settlers, both temporary and permanent, who assist the girls in resolving the conflicts in their stories in ways that locate their lives comfortably and unthreateningly within proscribed accounts of Hawai'i as a welcoming space for all Americans, and Hawaiians without indigeneity or political sovereignty. In doing so, the dolls symbolize the full appropriation of local identity by American nationalist multiculturalism, such that once-aberrant Kanaka Maoli and Asian identities become transformed into innocent, docile, and pleasant figures within accessible fictions of American assimilation and tolerance that anchor the overall mission of the American Girl dolls.

REINFORCING LOCAL TASTES IN THE POSTRACIAL STATE

Photographs taken of former US president Barack Obama during his annual Christmas vacations to the island of O'ahu often depict him holding a shave ice purchased from Kailua's Island Snow. Obama's love of shave ice is, in fact, the subject of hundreds of press photos taken across the eight years of his presidential holidays in my hometown, a once-sleepy beach community located about thirty minutes outside of Honolulu. This is Obama's favorite shave ice spot, a small surf apparel store and shave ice vendor located near one of the entrances to Kailua Beach Park, and a couple of miles down the road from the house he would rent.[77] When he visited while president, the media dutifully covered his appearances, including the syrup flavors he prefers (the store, which has doubled in size since the former president began his well-publicized visits, now offers a "Snowbama" flavor combination).[78] In the many photos of Obama and his family standing with their colorful cones in hand, he appears as the archetypal "local boy," casually waving a shaka to the crowd that gathers around him.[79] For many residents, Obama's Secret Service detail and motorcade were an exciting inconvenience. A joke circulates among Kailua residents: "What do you call it when Obama goes to get a shave ice? A road Barack."[80]

In this final example, I examine articulations of the American postra-

Figure 5.1. Barack Obama outside of Island Snow, Kailua, Hawaiʻi, December 31, 2013. Getty Images.

cial state as imagined through Barack Obama's relationship with Hawaiʻi, and as *imaged* through highly publicized shave ice consumption. Expanding outward from discourses around shave ice in particular, here I look beyond the cone to consider the political structures of colonialism that it becomes used to accessorize in the contemporary moment. In doing so, I want to interrogate not only how US imperialism has succeeded in appropriating the image of the multicultural Hawaiian local across media and consumer goods but, furthermore, how Obama, as an "archetypal 'local'" himself, embodies this new subjectivity in order to solidify and normalize the military occupation of Hawaiʻi.

Barack Obama's relationship to Hawaiʻi figures significantly into the making and unmaking of race and indigeneity within the settler state, particularly since, as Nitasha Tamar Sharma writes, he is "often read nationally as Black, and locally as multiracial."[81] Obama's positionality uniquely bridges racial politics across Hawaiʻi and the United States, revealing the ways in which racialization in the islands diverges from Black/white binaries overdetermined by continental histories of enslavement (even as the long shadow of the plantation economy stretches across the Pacific/Caribbean divide).[82] Erin Suzuki furthermore argues that the multiple ways that Obama has been read into narratives about race-making in Hawaiʻi—as a Black man, as a "Hawaiian native" (as the media would errantly label him), and as a mixed-race product of a multicultural upbringing—reflect the complexity with which local identity "unites, as well as divides Native and non-Native communities in Hawaiʻi."[83]

Although Obama was described by the media as America's "post-racial candidate" of the 2008 presidential election, his childhood in Hawaiʻi provoked public sentiments that at once denied and celebrated race.[84] Jonathan Okamura, for example, reveals the centrality of cultural performance in articulating Obama's ability to transcend and traverse multiple racial ethnic positions. On the continent, Asian American political organizations claimed Obama as their own—the first "Asian American president." In Hawaiʻi, folks recognized him as a "local boy." Without either Asian heritage or the multigenerational presence in the islands by which local identity is often indexed, that he is claimed by these overlapping groups speaks to the mutability of such categories in the service of political power.

While Okamura makes efforts to separate Obama's Asian Americanness from his localness, it is also useful to understand how these designations overlap: in the post–World War II era, Asian Americans emerged as "model minorities," and Hawaiʻi emerged as a "model multiethnic society" in which Asian Americans were the population majority. Okamura writes, "As is the case with multiculturalism in general, Hawaii's version flattens power and status differences among ethnic groups and obscures the persisting inequality among them, much to the disadvantage of the subordinate groups, including Native Hawaiians, Filipino Americans, and Samoans. Comparable to how colour-blind post-racialism serves to maintain white dominance in the continental United States, multicultural post-racialism perpetuates White, Chinese American and Japanese American power and privilege in the United States."[85] Within this complex racial landscape, Obama as a political figure converges with his personal genealogy as a mixed-race (former) resident of Hawaiʻi. In images in which he coolly bodysurfs Hawaiʻi's shorebreaks or delights in some Island Snow with his daughters, Obama's celebratory performance of Hawaiʻi localism expresses embodied investments in American power and privilege, rather than affinity with Hawaiʻi on its own terms as an Indigenous nation under military occupation.

Behind public rhetoric and media narrations of Obama's local tastes, Hawaiʻi's militarization was quietly reinforced. Island Snow—and even the town of Kailua—was strategically chosen for presidential leisure. Kailua Bay is flanked by the US Kaneohe Marine Corps Base Hawaii in Kāneʻohe, one of the largest military installations on the island, but certainly not the only one: 22.4 percent of Oʻahu is controlled by the military, and overall Hawaiʻi is the most militarized state in the nation.[86] The primary bases of the island are connected by an interstate highway system, the most recent installment being the H-3, completed in 1997, which connects the Kāneʻohe base with Hickam Air Force Base near Honolulu Harbor. The former president's vacation home, which he rented every year, notably sits in a location that allowed his regular security team to receive additional support from the US Coast Guard and Marines: one side of the property is beachfront, another is lined by a canal. According to one reporter, Obama's stay in Kailua required that the "U.S. Coast Guard man two 30-foot speedboats mounted with high-powered firearms. Four men are stationed in each boat in the canal that leads into the ocean, which is lined with homes. Two smaller boats continuously patrol the waters fronting the presidential rentals. The U.S. Coast Guard Cutter is stationed off the tip of Kailua Bay and the Kaneohe Marine Corp Air Station."[87] Similar to Nanea's story line in the American Girl book series, military power provides a central and underlying foundation on which refreshment functions as multiculturalist statecraft. While not as overt as barbed wire barriers on the beach or gunboats in a canal, shave ice nevertheless appears complementary to, rather than in contrast to, broader nationalistic agendas that seek to affirm Hawaiʻi's place in the United States through multiracial or even postracial logics.

AESTHETICIZING INCLUSION IN THE RAINBOW STATE

In the decades following statehood, shave ice took on fresh significance for residents in Hawaiʻi who fortified their local identity against an influx of wealth and "mainland" newcomers. In part, celebrations of shave ice relied on a claim to earlier times—"small-kid time"—characterized by community resilience, simplicity, and low economic wealth. Much as Hawaiʻi's "melting pot" became an aspiration—albeit a complicated one—for the future of American society, shave ice coheres nationalist renditions of US "Hawaiian" subjectivity through food: for all of its specificity to Hawaiʻi's prestatehood past, it has been deployed to produce unexpectedly American narratives. Evoked throughout popular press editorial features that emerged in the 1970s and 1980s, such remembrances point to a degree of cultural production that at once reifies local identity for longtime Hawai'i residents and aligns with American nationalism.

Through the examples of the American Girl dolls and Barack Obama, shave ice is used to produce "Hawaiians" as an always already multiethnic category evacuated of indigeneity or Kanaka Maoli claims to place. As indigeneity is visually and ideologically subsumed within the broader categories of ethnicity through the image of the shave ice cone, Hawaiianness becomes obliquely depoliticized in the service of neutralizing Kanaka Maoli indigeneity and, in turn, implicitly turns on settler logics of possession. This is aestheticized through the ever-present marketability of rainbow imagery that can be seen not only through representations of shave ice but across Hawai'i's broader cultural landscape.[88]

It's Sunday at Puʻuhonua o Puʻuhuluhulu. The late-July sun is bright and warm, and the crowd is the biggest that it has been since the camp's establishment about a week prior. In some respects, it feels celebratory, with abundant food, joyful greetings between old friends, and musicians playing. But our jubilance is tempered by the seriousness of our collective purpose for gathering at the base of the Mauna Kea Access Road. This is sovereignty work.

Only a handful of days have gone by since eight kiaʻi, or protectors, chained themselves to a cattle grate that straddles the road leading up to the summit. Even fewer days have passed since thirty-eight kūpuna (elders) were arrested for obstructing the path along which heavy equipment must travel to begin construction of the Thirty Meter Telescope. Some at the camp bore markings from those days, with cheeks ruddied and lips cracked from intense sun exposure. Like many who arrived at the mauna after the Royal Order of Kamehameha designated Puʻuhuluhulu as a site of refuge, I had been watching the events unfold from afar. For days I watched livestreams on Instagram and Facebook in my sweltering New York City apartment, hoping that I might quell the tug on my naʻau (gut) that told me I had to be there. When I could no longer bear the force of it, I got on a plane to Hilo.

My childhood friend Amanda meets me during my layover at Honolulu International Airport and travels with me the rest of the way to the camp. When we arrive, we head straight back to check in with Aunty Uʻi, who has taken on the kuleana (responsibility) of managing the camp kitchen. There are about thirty to thirty-five people working there at any given time, and that morning it is pumping. Uʻi wears a light-blue baseball cap, which makes her easy to pick out in the crowd. Even though her eyes are bleary, they shine the color of gold. She never sits. Waves of food donations arrive, and we struggle to find space for everything.

Figure C.1. The refrigeration section at Puʻuhonua o Puʻuhuluhulu, July 29, 2019. Photograph by the author.

Canned goods pile up under folding tables. Trays of cooked rice form a mountain that we worry will either be crushed or turn before they can be eaten. Some of that rice goes straight to the cook who works all day in a tent set back from the rest of the main area. He's young and has the energy of someone who is used to long hours in a commercial kitchen. He makes vats of fried rice in an enormous wok that balances over a propane burner.

I soon join Amanda, who has taken on responsibility for the coolers that hold perishable donations. Because of everyone's generosity, we are short on coolers, and there aren't enough places to put all the food, let alone the enormous bags of ice that have also been donated. We work against time and perishability, worried about keeping meat and dairy cold enough in the highly variable weather at the camp's elevation.[1] Without running water or electricity, this becomes a manual task. We play an elaborate game of Tetris: gallon-sized resealable bags of shredded meat—much of it coming off rotisserie chickens that folks bring in from Costco or KTA—are packed into several coolers; about half of the thirty-odd others are filled with cold cuts for making sandwiches;

cooked Hawaiian food occupies a few more; some just hold the ice we are desperately trying to keep frozen.

Our bodies become exhausted by the physicality of this work. The ice chests must be constantly drained of melt and repacked. We carry this gray water by bucket to the dish-washing station, where it gets heated and reused for scrubbing. A woman and her preteen son volunteer with us for a few hours, and together we arrange the coolers into some kind of logical order, writing out labels and attaching them with duct tape, then rewriting and retaping them when the mist soaks them through. Amanda is already thinking about how to hand her kuleana over to whoever will appear and take up her role when she must return to Oʻahu in a couple of days.

In the early weeks of Puʻuhuluhulu, these coolers, brought up from people's homes for indefinite use on the mauna, provide critical infrastructure. A stroke of good fortune brings Dernie to camp, a Kanaka originally from Maui Island, who quickly takes over Amanda's position and her careful inventory system. She stays until January.

While the coolers remain important features of the kitchen throughout the length of the encampment, under Dernie's watch the cooling systems grow in capacity and elaboration: first a funnel and drain system to decant ice melt into 5-gallon buckets from the coolers to, eventually, an insulated trailer with a generator-powered air conditioner and a 250-gallon water tank for gray water disposal.

As the refrigeration system becomes more sophisticated, the work of thermal management intensifies. Dernie later explained to me that as her time at Puʻuhuluhulu went on, "making sure everything stays cold became almost like an obsession for me." She described how, before heading home every weekend to shower and do laundry, she would ensure that the coolers were packed to the top with ice and the generator had enough gas to keep running over the weekend; then, upon her return, she would immediately tend to the melt that had accumulated over those two days. Dernie remarked on how the rhythms and the acoustics of the camp found their way into her subconscious as she became ever attuned to her daily labor. Like others who spent the majority of their days in the kitchen, from sunrise to sundown, she came to internalize the sound of the generator that powered the walk-in's air-conditioning unit. "Most of us in the kitchen," she said, "were kind of in tune to hearing the generator running in the back of our head that when it would stop it's like 'Ah! Go out there, the generator's out of gas!'"[2]

Attending to the rhythm of the generator, or the ongoing labor required to inventory food and its expiration dates, also reflects the hidden organizational labor of food work—what Marjorie Devault calls the work of "keeping things in mind"—that makes the kuleana of an alaka'i difficult to share, even if discrete tasks can occasionally be delegated.[3] Dynamics like these produced intense emotional experiences of responsibility, obligation, and care that hinged on managing thermal infrastrucutres. These struggles to keep food cold enough to safely feed a movement, to attend with devotion to perishability and spoilage, unfolded, significantly, in the shadow of Hawai'i's tallest mountain, the realm where our akua of ice and snow have ruled since time immemorial.

Since those few days at Pu'uhuluhulu, I have sat with the weight of these ice-filled coolers as one end point of the global cold chain in Hawai'i and wondered what the promises and limits of thermal management might offer for decolonial struggles over land and sovereignty. In what ways, I wonder, do "artificial" ice and refrigeration constrain the conditions of possibility within movements that call for deoccupation, demilitarization, and the dismantling of the settler state?[4] In what ways do they support activist and movement spaces? What place does refrigeration have within Indigenous futures that move beyond settler capitalism, when coldness has played such an intimate role in these systems of oppression?

BEYOND REFRIGERATION

Less than a year after Pu'uhuluhulu was established, the encampment's footprint winnowed down to a few tents. In March 2020, the COVID-19 epidemic sent much of the world—at least those privileged enough to do so—indoors, physically and socially distanced from each other. In the interest of public safety and with no immediate construction slated, the pu'uhonua requested that visitors "refrain from visiting the camp until the crisis has passed this critical stage."[5] Much of the camp, including the kitchen area, which had grown substantially since my days there, was dismantled.

In the months that followed, the coolers that had seemed like such a minor detail in the movement to halt the ongoing development of Maunakea became an outsize symbol of the modern food system's precarity in which overreliance on imported foods has constrained the resilience of local communities against large system failures. In many ways, the virus brought these layers of perishability and perishing into full view, revealing, as many pointed out, the everyday dependencies on inequitable and racialized labor systems required to keep American households provisioned.

Following national trends, Hawai'i residents began stocking up on shelf-stable foods, including rice and Spam, which experienced a record-setting uptick in sales.[6] Faltering confidence in cold infrastructures caused many to lean on international supply chains instead of Hawai'i farms: perishability represented but one more uncertainty in uncertain times. Local producers of goods, like fruits, vegetables, and livestock, struggled to sell products before spoilage, having lost much of their sales when hotels shut down and tourists stopped coming; the Hawai'i Emergency Management Agency began scouring the islands for available cold storage in emptied schools and at private catering companies.[7]

This phenomenon is not unique to Hawai'i, and so it's perhaps worth elaborating for a moment on how Hawai'i shares particularly thermal forms of food insecurity with other places enmeshed in US imperialism. Hawai'i's story looks a lot like ones that might also be told about Samoa, the Federated States of Micronesia, the Republic of the Marshall Islands, Cuba, the Philippines, and Puerto Rico. Conditions of dependency and debt, writes José I. Fusté, are hallmarks of places imprinted by US expansionism from 1898 onward: precarious economies beholden to US jurisdiction. The "moving parts" of American colonial formations, Fusté writes, are akin to "tectonic-like encounters between colonized sites and the subaltern populations in them that have been overdetermined by the dominant discourses and social forces of US empire."[8] Indebtedness manifests in myriad stressors on the food system, setting into motion food laborer migrations, turns toward industrial diets, collapsing local ecosystems, and many other choices that communities must make in order to ensure short-term survival over long-term abundance. And so, even if specific histories cannot be collapsed into one another, considering Hawai'i's food system as part of a broader imperial project brings these intersecting transcolonial formations into focus: these dynamics are at once structural and infrastructural, systemic and material.

After Hurricanes Maria in 2016 and Irma in 2017, people in Puerto Rico survived without access to electricity (and thus refrigeration) for months, dependent on shelf-stable food aid shipped from the United States (and the United States only, per trade restrictions under the Jones Act).[9] In Cuba, unstable infrastructures foster not only feelings of anxiety around food safety but also a kind of tolerance for rancid perishables. Cubans, Hanna Garth writes, "often wonder: would food that was brought into the city on a refrigerated truck be guaranteed to have been kept at the right temperature when so often those trucks broke down or their systems failed?"[10] Examples go on and on: in the Far North and the Deep South, in inner cities and rural townships, the availability of affordable and fresh foods marks an apartheid system.[11] This is a colonial condition of life within the settler state, and in Hawai'i it is profoundly felt every time the islands brace for an emergency. The fragility of the cold chain reveals itself everywhere: in the smarting wakes of natural disasters and epidemics, and through the dull pain of ongoing colonialism and racial capitalism. Who receives access to fresh foods (and under what conditions) brings structures of power to bear on the body's daily hungers.

As the virus raged on, supply chain pressure points ached. By September 2020, local news outlets in Hawai'i reported that refrigerators and freezers were back-ordered. New appliances, when they did arrive in the archipelago, had already been presold to those with their names on long wait lists.[12] Other US cities experienced the same shortages, with production slowing as factories implemented social distancing protocols.[13] In addition, demands on the domestic kitchen increased and appliances broke down, and anxieties over food shortages fixated on the freezer as an insurance policy against end times.[14] Beholden to these domestic appliances, the care work of feeding is hobbled by these vast and precarious global networks. As the terminal link in a "cold chain" that has played a crucial and overdetermined role in the way people eat, the freezers and refrigerators normatively essential to modern survival emerged out of the background noise of daily life.[15] Beyond the home, refrigeration would soon become the fulcrum on which emergence from the global pandemic turned.

By December 2020, the first distributions of highly perishable vaccines for the novel coronavirus fanned out across the United States, entirely reliant on cold, requiring storage at −70°C: a neat convergence of technological advancements born of the twentieth-century food system. Joanna Radin notes that key technologies for cold chain transport, originally created by cattle breeders for artificial insemination, now underpins biomedical supply chains (the word *vaccination* comes from the Latin for cow).[16] Expensive "ultracold" storage units, corralled into "freezer farms," served as distribution points for vaccines packed into specialized thermoses destined for places lacking the resources to have their own "ultracold" freezers.[17] The thermal environments of the cold chain—computerized reefers for bananas or beef or milk or lifesaving vaccines—provide illusions of abundance that fall apart in times of ecological rupture (like hurricanes or pandemics).

And still, Hawai'i remains relatively privileged in relation to other sites under US colonial rule.

The pu'uhonua on Maunakea illustrates how, and when, refrigerators and infrastructures of the cold converge with, and sit in tension with, struggles for territorial sovereignty and Indigenous self-determination. I am interested in how this can help us to understand concepts like food sovereignty, which aim to speak back to these systems of overdependence that this book describes. In the years since I experienced the kitchen space of this encampment, I have come back—again and again—to thinking about how thermal dependence, while a reality in the present day, does not necessarily impede the care, collaboration, and nourishment required to realize sovereign futures, even if those forms of care work and food work might not, on the surface, look like food sovereignty as most envision it.

Donated food flowing into the camp represented a diversity of community resources: huge buckets of fried chicken and chili from fast-casual restaurants, cardboard boxes of fruits picked from backyard trees, pallets of shelf-stable snack foods, and canned goods grabbed from home pantries. And so the collaborative forms of sustenance that converged in the mauna's kitchen were produced through financially constrained realities for many Kānaka Maoli and other residents, who struggle mightily against the increasingly high cost of living in Hawai'i. In local parlance, these constraints often translate into the philosophy to "cook what get," by using what's on hand and available, whether it's produce from a farmers market, canned goods, fish from the ocean, or other food foraged from the land.[18] While this range of foods may not conform to what is sometimes idealized as a decolonized or decolonial diet, such an approach to community food resource pooling reflects important networks of care and resilience that profoundly support decolonial futures.[19]

Settler foodscapes and the cold chains that help to maintain them thereby also help in the political refusal of land theft and capitalist development, and this tension sits at the heart of what Winona LaDuke and Deborah Cowen theorize as Wiindigo infrastructures. Calling forward Ruth Wilson Gilmore's assertion that white supremacy operates as a structure of feeling as well as a material infrastructure of being, LaDuke and Cowen propose that "Indigenous social infrastructures offer ways of thinking beyond capitalist accumulation."[20] Because resources at the camp explicitly do not serve a capitalist function, resource management takes on particular significance as a tool of anticolonial critique and resistance. In places like the kitchens at Puʻuhuluhulu, food is a central anchor for decolonizing praxis; feeding people makes strategic occupation possible on a daily level.[21] Given that mobilizations of protectorship safeguard Indigenous territories from development projects that build what we might think of as "critical infrastructures" for settler futurity, and, also, that contemporary food systems are heavily infrastructural themselves, movement kitchens have the power to exceed the dictates of settler food systems, even if and when they are also beholden to them.[22]

Today the protection of Maunakea requires nothing less than the constant vigilance of kiaʻi who have committed to standing in the way of further desecration and capitalist development. But, as many have pointed out, Puʻuhonua o Puʻuhuluhulu is about much more than a telescope. Thinking alongside the labor and community care within the spaces of the encampment also offers important insights for the affective dimensions of Indigenous resource management within movement spaces. Kitchen labor is one important but underexamined facet of this work because of the ways that it responds to, engages with, and pushes at settler infrastructures and normative relationships with sustenance, commensality, and abundance. The kitchen that grew at the base of the Mauna Kea Access Road made visible how particular infrastructures can support Indigenous world-making, despite their complicated colonial legacies. Each cooler bearing a family's name written with black permanent marker, each melting bag of ice, and each plastic bag of cold cuts exists as proof of the deep love that Kanaka have for their Hawaiʻi and for each other. Even when it doesn't look like food sovereignty in the textbook sense of the word, it is sovereignty at its most potent: a refusal of the state, of capitalist development, and a deep engagement with what it means to practice decolonization using "what get."

MANAGING MELT

Taking this into account, I wonder, what can our attention to thermal infrastructures tell us about the food systems on which many of our daily lives rely, and to which nothing less than disaster reminds us? Most scholarship on infrastructure provides frameworks for parsing their complexity as material, affective, technological, multiscalar, and promissory objects of analysis, but it does not tell us what to do with them, about where infrastructures fit in a future that refuses the legacies of their making.[23] Infrastructures, we know, are always in the process of falling apart. Often, when they falter, people describe them as "crumbling" in order to evoke a sense of brittleness and breakage, of substrates less firm than imagined that cause the structure to shift and eventually crack.[24] In Shannon Mattern's meditation on infrastructural care, for example, she writes that "infrastructures fail everywhere, all the time. Some people will even tell you that it's okay if [they] crumble."[25] Keeping infrastructures intact requires maintenance. The work of tending is necessary but undervalued: there are no great breakthroughs or rewards, other than the very fact that such labors keep things going for just a little while longer, forestalling the unforgiving effects of time. Breakage, however, may not be the inevitable end to an infrastructural world. As Ruth Wilson Gilmore so powerfully advises, "Any kind of infrastructure, whatever it is . . . means that it underlies what we can produce. . . . I don't mean productivity in the capitalist sense. I mean productivity, what we can do."[26] What Gilmore is saying here, I believe, is that infrastructures need not overdetermine the limits of our world-making.

In keeping with Gilmore's assessment, I wonder about letting our focus on breakage and repair stray for a moment, and instead training our attention on melt as a condition of our current times that might hold some utility in thinking about Indigenous futures beyond the *longue durée* of thermal colonialism. I say this carefully, and in recognition that we are, after all, currently living in a time of melt despite—or, more accurately, precisely because of—global commitments to thermal regulation. The energy infrastructures that produce cold in some places (from kitchens and business offices to refrigerated shipping containers) exemplify our efforts to control environments despite, and often in ignorance of, increasingly untenable human geographies at large.[27]

As climate crisis emerges as a singular concern for human futures, the rapid disappearance of ice is often used to visualize that urgency, with time-lapse photography projects speeding up the otherwise imperceptible process of glacial melt in places like Antarctica, Greenland, Alaska, and Australia and photo essays showing Pacific Island nations with low-lying atolls building seawalls to stave off the inevitable rise in ocean levels. Even so, as others have pointed out, such narratives about glacial melt tend to warn of a possible future for the global North rather than a critical present for Indigenous peoples, from the Marshall Islands to Yupik territory in western Alaska.[28]

And yet, melt's refusal to remain fixed, the way that it insists on our tending and attention, simultaneously gestures toward a future beyond refrigeration. I wish to speculatively venture that melt, like the melting ice in the coolers at Puʻuhonua o Puʻuhuluhulu, offers a way to think not only about anticolonial struggle but also about interdependence and calibration: a phase state change that does not shatter but re-forms bonds at a molecular level. For Indigenous archipelagic peoples, melt can remind us of shared struggles across vast geographies. For others, it might serve as a reminder that temperature will always resist stasis. On Maunakea, melt offers a way for us to think about ambience and animacy, and the profound enormousness of kuleana to protect delicate and life-sustaining environments against overdevelopment. Instead of desperately holding together the pieces of a crumbling infrastructure that was never designed to serve us, the environmental intimacies of melt might guide us toward worlds persistently calling for our return, ones predicated on change and growth—worlds that also require our maintenance and care.

NOTE ON ʻŌLELO HAWAIʻI USAGE

1. Mary Kawena Pukui and Samuel H. Elbert, *Hawaiian Dictionary*, rev. and enl. ed. (Honolulu: University of Hawaiʻi Press, 1986). For an extended discussion of the politics of translation within Hawaiian historiography, see Noenoe K. Silva, *Aloha Betrayed: Hawaiian Resistance to American Colonialism* (Durham, NC: Duke University Press, 2004).

2. I am paraphrasing Marie Alohalani Brown here. For an excellent discussion of the genealogy of these terms, their common usage, and the politics of distinct terms, see Marie Alohalani Brown, "He ʻŌlelo Wehehe: An Explanation for Readers," in *Facing the Spears of Change: The Life and Legacy of John Papa ʻĪʻī* (Honolulu: University of Hawaiʻi Press, 2016), ix–xiii.

INTRODUCTION

1. Bonanza Saloon, advertisement, *Ka Lahui Hawaii*, May 4, 1876, 2.

2. In referring to "the cold," I aim to distinguish it from temperature as a generalized thing. Instead, I see cold as a specific material articulation of temperature in relation to settler colonization.

3. According to Pukui and Elbert, the kind of numbness indicated by *māʻeʻele* could describe a number of feelings, including being deeply moved by love, being grief-stricken, and numbness during pregnancy. Pukui and Elbert, *Hawaiian Dictionary*, 218.

4. This point about how certain objects and cultural practices are invisibilized as they are assimilated into daily life is inspired by Geoffrey C. Bowker and Susan Leigh Star, *Sorting Things Out: Classification and Its Consequences* (Cambridge, MA: MIT Press, 2000); and Michel Foucault, *The Order of Things: An Archaeology of the Human Sciences* (New York: Vintage Books, 1994).

5. Browse books on Hawaiʻi and you will find a staggering number of titles that include the word *paradise* both sincerely and ironically.

6. The main islands of Hawaiʻi are located about twenty-five hundred miles from Japan and thirty-two hundred miles from the California coast.

7. At the same time, because of the archipelago's mountainous volcanic topography, it features ten of the earth's fourteen climatic zones (including a periglacial climate at the summit of Maunakea, Hawaiʻi's highest peak at 13,803 feet).

Derek Paiva, "Hawaii Has 10 of the World's 14 Climate Zones: An Explorer's Guide to Each of Them," *Hawai'i Magazine*, November 10, 2015.

8. Marie Sanderson, ed., *Prevailing Trade Winds: Climate and Weather in Hawai'i* (Honolulu: University of Hawai'i Press, 1993), 1.

9. As William Cronon writes in his essay on the cultural production of "wilderness": "As we gaze into the mirror it holds up for us, we too easily imagine that what we behold is Nature when in fact we see the reflection of our own unexamined longings and desires." William Cronon, "The Trouble with Wilderness; or, Getting Back to the Wrong Nature," in *Uncommon Ground: Toward Reinventing Nature*, ed. William Cronon (New York: Norton, 1995), 7. Also see Dipesh Chakrabarty, "The Climate of History: Four Theses," *Critical Inquiry* 35, no. 2 (2009): 197–222; Eric T. Jennings, *Curing the Colonizers: Hydrotherapy, Climatology, and French Colonial Spas* (Durham, NC: Duke University Press, 2006); Marsha E. Ackermann, *Cool Comfort: America's Romance with Air-Conditioning* (Washington, DC: Smithsonian Books, 2010).

10. For more on Edenic ideas about the tropics and colonialism, see Richard H. Grove, *Green Imperialism: Colonial Expansion, Tropical Island Edens and the Origins of Environmentalism, 1600–1860* (Cambridge: Cambridge University Press, 2003).

11. George Gilbert, *The Death of Captain James Cook* (Honolulu: Paradise of the Pacific Press, 1926), 5.

12. James Jackson Jarves, *History of the Hawaiian or Sandwich Islands: Embracing Their Antiquities, Mythology, Legends, Discovery by Europeans in the Sixteenth Century, Re-discovery by Cook, with Their Civil, Religious, and Political History* (Boston: Tappan and Dennet, 1843), 17.

13. Manley Hopkins, *Hawaii: The Past, Present, and Future of Its Island-Kingdom* (London: Longman, 1862), 351.

14. Warwick Anderson, "Climates of Opinion: Acclimatization in Nineteenth-Century France and England," *Victorian Studies* 35, no. 2 (1992): 135–57; Richard Eves, "Going Troppo: Images of White Savagery, Degeneration, and Race in Turn-of-the-Century Colonial Fictions of the Pacific," *History and Anthropology* 11, nos. 2–3 (1999): 351–85.

15. Karen Ordahl Kupperman, "Fear of Hot Climates in the Anglo-American Colonial Experience," *William and Mary Quarterly* 41, no. 2 (1984): 213–40.

16. Ikuko Asaka, *Tropical Freedom: Climate, Settler Colonialism, and Black Exclusion in the Age of Emancipation* (Durham, NC: Duke University Press, 2017).

17. David N. Livingstone, "Tropical Climate and Moral Hygiene: The Anatomy of a Victorian Debate," *British Journal for the History of Science* 32, no. 1 (1999): 109. Also see Warwick Anderson, *Colonial Pathologies: American Tropical Medicine, Race, and Hygiene in the Philippines* (Durham, NC: Duke University Press, 2006).

18. Jessica Wang, "Agricultural Expertise, Race, and Economic Development: Small Producer Ideology and Settler Colonialism in the Territory of Hawai'i, 1900–1917," *History and Technology* 36, nos. 3–4 (2020): 316–17.

19. Patrick Wolfe, "Settler Colonialism and the Elimination of the Native," *Journal of Genocide Research* 8, no. 4 (2006): 387–409; Lorenzo Veracini, *Settler*

Colonialism: A Theoretical Overview (New York: Palgrave Macmillan, 2010). There are too many to list here, but some other texts I rely on to understand the relationship between land and settler colonialism include Mishuana R. Goeman, "Land as Life: Unsettling the Logics of Containment," in *Native Studies Keywords*, ed. Stephanie Nohelani Teves, Andrea Smith, and Michelle H. Raheja (Tucson: University of Arizona Press, 2015), 71–89; Aileen Moreton-Robinson, *The White Possessive: Property, Power, and Indigenous Sovereignty* (Minneapolis: University of Minnesota Press, 2015); and Robert Nichols, "Theft Is Property! The Recursive Logic of Dispossession," *Political Theory* 46, no. 1 (2017): 3–28. My point about aesthetics refers to literatures produced about Hawai'i for the tourism industry, which retain images of Native Hawaiian peoples as a backdrop or scaffold for white pleasure. Take, for example, how a Hawai'i Tourism Bureau advertising campaign from 1972 describes the island of Kaua'i as "a garden of Eden [that] fed, clothed, and sheltered the children of Hawai'i." Accompanied by a photograph of a lush, unpopulated forest, narratives of Hawaiian primitivism and anachronism complement visions of an unspoiled nature awaiting discovery by the Western tourist. J. D. Goss, "Placing the Market and Marketing Place: Tourist Advertising of the Hawaiian Islands, 1972–92," *Environment and Planning D: Society and Space* 11, no. 6 (1993): 674.

20. Teresia Teaiwa, "Reading Paul Gauguin's *Noa Noa* with Epeli Hau'ofa's *Kisses in the Nederends*: Militourism, Feminism, and the 'Polynesian' Body," in *Inside Out: Literature, Cultural Politics, and Identity in the New Pacific*, ed. Vilsoni Hereniko and Rob Wilson (Lanham, MD: Rowman and Littlefield, 1999), 249–63.

21. Ty P. Kāwika Tengan, "Re-membering Panalā'au: Masculinities, Nation, and Empire in Hawai'i and the Pacific," *Contemporary Pacific* 20, no. 1 (2008): 27–53; Margaret Jolly, "Contested Paradise: Dispossession and Repossession in Hawai'i," *Contemporary Pacific* 30, no. 2 (2018): 355–77.

22. Maile Renee Arvin, *Possessing Polynesians: The Science of Settler Colonial Whiteness in Hawai'i and Oceania* (Durham, NC: Duke University Press, 2019).

23. Maile Renee Arvin, "Pacifically Possessed: Scientific Production and Native Hawaiian Critique of the 'Almost White' Polynesian Race" (PhD diss., UC San Diego, 2013); Graham E. L. Holton, "Heyerdahl's Kon Tiki Theory and the Denial of the Indigenous Past," *Anthropological Forum* 14, no. 2 (2004): 163–81; Arvin, *Possessing Polynesians*, 56.

24. Jen Rose Smith develops the term *temperate normativity* in "'Exceeding Beringia': Upending Universal Human Events and Wayward Transits in Arctic Spaces," *Environment and Planning D: Society and Space* 39, no. 1 (2021): 158–75. Also see Rafico Ruiz, *Slow Disturbance: Infrastructural Mediation on the Settler Colonial Resource Frontier* (Durham, NC: Duke University Press, 2021).

25. Crosby specifically makes this statement to explain how early colonialists brought many crops with them in order to grow food in the Americas, believing that eating Indigenous foods might affect their "civility." Alfred Crosby, *The Columbian Exchange: Biological and Cultural Consequences of 1492* (Westport, CT: Greenwood, 1972), 70.

26. Asaka, *Tropical Freedom*.

27. The first shipment of ice by "Ice King" Frederic Tudor left Charleston to St. Pierre in French Martinique in 1805. Marc Herold, "Ice in the Tropics: The Export of 'Crystal Blocks of Yankee Coldness' to India and Brazil," *Revista Espaco Academico*, March 1, 2012.

28. Herold, "Ice in the Tropics."

29. See David G. Dickason, "The Nineteenth-Century Indo-American Ice Trade: An Hyperborean Epic," *Modern Asian Studies* 25, no. 1 (1991): 53–89.

30. Ackermann, *Cool Comfort*; William Cronon, *Nature's Metropolis: Chicago and the Great West* (New York: Norton, 1991); Susanne Freidberg, *Fresh: A Perishable History* (Cambridge, MA: Belknap Press, 2009); Amy Bentley, "Islands of Serenity: Gender, Race, and Ordered Meals during World War II," *Food and Foodways* 6, no. 2 (1996): 131–56.

31. Jonathan Rees, *Refrigeration Nation: A History of Ice, Appliances, and Enterprise in America* (Baltimore, MD: Johns Hopkins University Press, 2013), 186–87.

32. Ackermann, *Cool Comfort*. Scott Lauria Morgensen argues that biopolitics, in fact, constitutes a feature of settler colonialism, writing that "Western law incorporates Indigenous peoples while simultaneously pursuing their elimination. . . . These historical processes ultimately enact biopower as a persistent activity of settler states that were never decolonised and of the global regimes that extend and naturalise their power." Scott Lauria Morgensen, "The Biopolitics of Settler Colonialism: Right Here, Right Now," *Settler Colonial Studies* 1, no. 1 (2011): 53–54.

33. Mark Rifkin, "Settler Common Sense," *Settler Colonial Studies* 3, nos. 3–4 (2013): 322–40.

34. Henry David Thoreau, *Walden; or, Life in the Woods* (Boston, MA: Ticknor and Fields, 1854), 223.

35. Manu Vimalassery [Karuka], Juliana Hu Pegues, and Alyosha Goldstein, "Introduction: On Colonial Unknowing," *Theory and Event* 19, no. 4 (2016): n.p.

36. Dean Itsuji Saranillio, *Unsustainable Empire: Alternative Histories of Hawai'i Statehood* (Durham, NC: Duke University Press, 2018), 74.

37. While settler colonialism is one of the primary theoretical frameworks used in this book, I see it as one that overlaps with racial capitalism and empire, as Karuka, Hu Pegues, and Goldstein describe in "Introduction: On Colonial Unknowing."

38. Nicole Starosielski, *Media Hot and Cold* (Durham, NC: Duke University Press, 2021); Catherine Fennell, *Last Project Standing: Civics and Sympathy in Post-welfare Chicago* (Minneapolis: University of Minnesota Press, 2015); Michelle Murphy, *Sick Building Syndrome: Environmental Politics, Technoscience, and Women Workers* (Durham, NC: Duke University Press, 2006).

39. Rifkin, "Settler Common Sense."

40. Nicole Starosielski calls these forms of settler colonial embodiments "thermocultures," or "the modes by which temperature is managed and organized in embodied and culturally specific ways." Nicole Starosielski, "Thermocultures of

Geological Media," *Cultural Politics* 12, no. 3 (2016): 306; also see Starosielski, *Media Hot and Cold*, 1–2.

41. Peter Atkins, "Temperature," in *Chemistry: Foundations and Applications*, ed. J. J. Lagowski (New York: Macmillan Reference USA, 2004), 4:206–9.

42. This range was established around 1742. "Celsius Temperature Scale," *Encyclopædia Britannica Online*, accessed July 23, 2015, http://www.britannica.com/technology/Celsius-temperature-scale. For a longer discussion of the history of temperature measurement, see Gino Segre, *A Matter of Degrees: What Temperature Reveals about the Past and Future of Our Species* (New York: Penguin Books, 2003).

43. "Cold, n.," OED Online, June 2015, Oxford University Press, http://www.oed.com/view/Entry/36100.

44. The first definition under "cold, adj." in the *Oxford English Dictionary* is "The proper adjective expressing a well-known quality of the air or of other substances exciting one of the primary physical sensations, due to the abstraction of heat from the surface of the body: of a temperature sensibly lower than that of the living human body." "Cold, adj.," OED Online, September 2015, Oxford University Press, http://www.oed.com/view/Entry/36101.

45. Catherine Fennell, "'Project Heat' and Sensory Politics in Redeveloping Chicago Public Housing," *Ethnography* 12, no. 1 (2011): 40–64.

46. *Anu* and *'āmu'emu'e* in Pukui and Elbert, *Hawaiian Dictionary*, 26, 23.

47. The first definition of "cool" in the *Oxford English Dictionary* is "of or at a relatively low temperature; moderately cold, esp. agreeable or refreshingly so (in contrast with heat and cold)." "Cool, adj., adv., and int.," OED Online, June 2015, Oxford University Press, http://www.oed.com/view/Entry/40978.

48. "Cool," in Pukui and Elbert, *Hawaiian Dictionary*, 420. This connection between coolness and sexual passion is reflected in an analysis that Kimo Alama Keaulana and Scott Whitney give of the 1930s song "Niu Haohao" ("Young Coconut") about a cold alcoholic drink that, translated, goes: "The young coconut spoonmeat, / So cool, so cool, / Cool for the throat to savor, / Gently restraining the voicebox, / Sliding, slipping, sliding / Is the water from the continent." As they remind readers, "One should remember that Hawaiians, living in the tropics, always pictured hospitality and pleasure as cool, whereas persons from temperate zone cultures tend to describe the same experiences as warm." There are many similarities that can be drawn here between this song and the advertisement for Bonanza Saloon with which this section opens. Kimo Alama Keaulana and Scott Whitney, "Ka wai kau mai o Maleka 'Water from America': The Intoxication of the Hawaiian People," *Contemporary Drug Problems* 17 (1990): 183.

49. This is a complex point that could take up a book-length discussion on its own, though it is beyond the focus of this project. A recent debate over the colonial expectations of the performance of aloha stemmed from an online video that went viral in 2014 and can be accessed on YouTube at https://youtu.be/zGoYEI8aIm8. The video, which shows an altercation between a Native Hawaiian man and a group of white settlers at Kalama Beach, Maui Island, provoked heated discussion about Hawaiian identity, expressions of aloha, and histories

of displacement. For an illuminating analysis, refer to Noelani Arista and Judy Kertész, "Aloha Denied," *Hawai'i Independent*, February 25, 2014, http://hawaii independent.net/story/aloha-denied. See also Adria L. Imada, *Aloha America: Hula Circuits through the U.S. Empire* (Durham, NC: Duke University Press, 2012); Keiko Ohnuma, "'Aloha Spirit' and the Cultural Politics of Sentiment as National Belonging," *Contemporary Pacific* 20, no. 2 (2008): 365–94; and Stephanie Nohelani Teves, "We're All Hawaiians Now: Kanaka Maoli Performance and the Politics of Aloha" (PhD diss., University of Michigan, 2012).

50. An examination of taste as a form of cultural distinction is useful here as an aside. To think about the politics of taste, I implicitly draw on works by Pierre Bourdieu, Claude Lévi-Strauss, and Mary Douglas—foundational theoreticians for the field of food studies—which establish taste as a socially conditioned and aesthetic practice used to articulate difference. Cuisines, they argue, operate as classificatory schemas that sort the moral from the immoral, the high class from the low, and the civilized from the savage. Such theories, however, treat flavor as a relatively neutral category separate from the more complex elaborations of taste. See Pierre Bourdieu, *Distinction: A Social Critique of the Judgement of Taste* (Cambridge, MA: Harvard University Press, 1984); Claude Lévi-Strauss, "The Culinary Triangle," *Parisian Review* 33, no. 4 (1966): 586–95; Mary Douglas, *Food in the Social Order: Studies of Food and Festivities in Three American Communities* (London: Routledge, 2003). For an in-depth discussion of works that engage the sensory dimensions of food culture, see David E. Sutton, "Food and the Senses," *Annual Review of Anthropology* 39 (2010): 209–33.

51. The colonial forms of refreshment I identify here are distinct from environmentally ready modes of refreshment that have long been part of traditional Hawaiian life, such as swimming or surfing in the ocean, or bathing in valley streams. These continue to be part of Hawai'i's pleasures for Kānaka, other locals, and tourists alike; they certainly exist alongside cocktails, ice creams, and shave ice as part of a broad field of thermal engagements with the islands specifically, and the tropics more generally. What distinguish them are the spatial relationships they articulate, such as immersion versus consumption. Distinct from ecological relationships grounded in Hawaiian concepts of aloha 'āina—akin to a love of land—freezing and refrigeration technologies (and the pleasures they offer) are premised on ideas of regulation and control. This point about aloha 'āina as both a relational and spatial practice comes from Candace Fujikane, *Mapping Abundance for a Planetary Future: Kanaka Maoli and Critical Settler Cartographies in Hawai'i* (Durham, NC: Duke University Press, 2021), 18.

52. R. Eccles, L. Du-Plessis, Y. Dommels, and J. E. Wilkinson, "Cold Pleasure: Why We Like Ice Drinks, Ice-Lollies, and Ice Creams," *Appetite* 71 (2013): 358.

53. Conducted in order to support increased US military presence in the Middle East, these tests sought to understand why soldiers stationed in the desert tended to dehydrate, failing to drink enough water if it was not served cold. D. Engell and E. Hirsch, "Environmental and Sensory Modulation of Fluid Intake on Humans," in *Thirst*, ed. D. J. Ramsay and D. Booth (London: Springer-Verlag, 1991), 383.

54. B. L. Sandick, D. B. Engell, and O. Maller, "Perception of Drinking Water Temperature and Effects for Humans after Exercise," *Physiology and Behavior* 32, no. 5 (1984): 851–55.

55. D. Boulze, P. Montastruc, and M. Cabanac, "Water Intake, Pleasure, and Water Temperature in Humans," *Physiology and Behavior* 30, no. 1 (1983): 97–102.

56. D. A. Zellner, W. F. Stewart, P. Rozin, and J. M. Brown, "Effect of Temperature and Expectations on Liking for Beverages," *Physiology and Behavior* 44, no. 1 (1988): 61–68. The neuroscientist Gordon Shepherd describes how brains can become conditioned to manifest cravings—essentially food desires that transcend hunger and "pleasant" taste. Gordon M. Shepherd, *Neurogastronomy: How the Brain Creates Flavor and Why It Matters* (New York: Columbia University Press, 2012), 165.

57. It's also worth noting that some cultures, particularly in Asia, will advise against the consumption of cold food and drink in order to manage individual health. See Linda C. Koo, "The Use of Food to Treat and Prevent Disease in Chinese Culture," *Social Science and Medicine* 18, no. 9 (1984): 757–66.

58. Alison K. Ventura and Julie A. Mennella, "Innate and Learned Preferences for Sweet Taste during Childhood," *Clinical Nutrition and Metabolic Care* 14, no. 4 (2011): 379–84.

59. These communities continue to be systemically racialized through biomedical and genomic research. For more, see Anthony Ryan Hatch, *Blood Sugar: Racial Pharmacology and Food Justice in Black America* (Minneapolis: University of Minnesota Press, 2016).

60. Sidney W. Mintz, *Sweetness and Power* (New York: Viking, 1985).

61. Ashanté M. Reese, "Tarry with Me: Reclaiming Sweetness in an Anti-Black World," *Oxford American*, no. 112 (Spring 2021), https://www.oxfordamerican.org/magazine/issue-112-spring-2021/tarry-with-me.

62. At the end of this book I expand my scope to Hawaiʻi's urbanizing rural spaces (many of which, into the twentieth century, have become increasingly urbanized themselves). There are, however, important exceptions to this trend. See Davianna Pōmaikaʻi McGregor, *Nā Kuaʻāina: Living Hawaiian Culture* (Honolulu: University of Hawaiʻi Press, 2007); Mehana Blaich Vaughan, *Kaiāulu: Gathering Tides* (Eugene: University of Oregon Press, 2018).

63. Gavan Daws, "Honolulu in the 19th Century: Notes on the Emergence of Urban Society in Hawaiʻi," *Journal of Pacific History* 2 (1967): 77.

64. This point is inspired by Ann Laura Stoler, *Carnal Knowledge and Imperial Power: Race and the Intimate in Colonial Rule* (Berkeley: University of California Press, 2002).

65. To echo Penelope Edmonds, *Urbanizing Frontiers: Indigenous Peoples and Settlers in 19th-Century Pacific Rim Cities* (Vancouver: University of British Columbia Press, 2010), 239.

66. Ray Jerome Baker, *Honolulu Then and Now: A Photographic Record of Progress in the City of Honolulu. Illustrated with 172 Original Photographic Prints* (Honolulu: R. J. Baker, 1941), plate 64.

67. The body of literature I refer to here excludes the dynamic debates over race, sovereignty, and politics occurring within Hawaiian print culture, which were prolific across the nineteenth century. See David A. Chang, *The World and All the Things upon It: Native Hawaiian Geographies of Exploration* (Minneapolis: University of Minnesota Press, 2016). For more on the politics of identity and "Hawaiianness," see J. Kēhaulani Kauanui, *Hawaiian Blood: Colonialism and the Politics of Sovereignty and Indigeneity* (Durham, NC: Duke University Press, 2008).

68. *Appleton's Illustrated Hand-Book of American Winter Resorts* (New York: D. Appleton and Company, 1895), 120.

69. Kyla Schuller argues in *The Biopolitics of Feeling* that "sentimentalism [as an aesthetic mode, epistemology, and ontology] served to explain how an originally separate individual could be affectively and politically reconciled to its material coexistence with the external environment it depended on for self-constitution." Kyla Schuller, *The Biopolitics of Feeling: Race, Sex, and Science in the Nineteenth Century* (Durham, NC: Duke University Press, 2018), 4.

70. Schuller, *Biopolitics of Feeling*, 15.

71. A concise overview of Hawai'i's colonization appears in Walter H. Hixson's "'Spaces of Denial': American Settler Colonialism in Hawai'i and Alaska," in his *American Settler Colonialism: A History* (New York: Palgrave Macmillan, 2013), 145–66.

72. Asserted in the foundational work of Haunani-Kay Trask, the self-indigenization of "locals" presents yet another wave of foreign claims over Native Hawaiian lands. "They claim Hawai'i as their own," she writes, "denying indigenous history, their long collaboration in our continued dispossession, and the benefits therefrom." Trask suggests, in turn, that substituting "local" for "immigrant" (as a gloss for "settler") produces an effect in which immigrant claims to belonging are normalized through the frameworks of American nationalism. "Simply said," she writes, "'locals' want to be 'Americans.'" Haunani-Kay Trask, "Settlers of Color and 'Immigrant' Hegemony: 'Locals' in Hawai'i," *Amerasia Journal* 26, no. 2 (2000): 2, 20.

73. See Nitasha Tamar Sharma, *Hawai'i Is My Haven: Race and Indigeneity in the Black Pacific* (Durham, NC: Duke University Press, 2021); Seri Kau'ikealaula Luangphinith, "Homeward Bound: Settler Aesthetics in Hawai'i's Literature," *Texas Studies in Literature and Language* 48, no. 1 (2006): 54–78; Candace Fujikane and Jonathan Y. Okamura, *Asian Settler Colonialism: From Local Governance to the Habits of Everyday Life in Hawai'i* (Honolulu: University of Hawai'i Press, 2008).

74. Glen Grant and Dennis M. Ogawa, "Living Proof: Is Hawai'i the Answer?," *Annals of the American Academy of Political and Social Science* 530, no. 1 (1993): 147.

75. The tensions at play between the commodification of aloha and Hawaiian cultural forms are powerfully unpacked in Stephanie Nohelani Teves, *Defiant Indigeneity: The Politics of Hawaiian Performance* (Chapel Hill: University of North Carolina Press, 2018).

76. Important to the landscapes of race and power that I'm describing here are

the theorizations of Asian settler colonialism produced by Hawaiʻi-based schol-ars. See Fujikane and Okamura, *Asian Settler Colonialism*.

77. US Census Bureau, "Hawaii: 2000," DP-1. *Profiles of General Demographic Characteristics*, May 2001, https://www.census.gov/library/publications/2001/dec/2kh.html.

78. "Oʻahu Land Divisions," in Kamehameha Schools, *Hawaiian Place Names: The Significance of Hawaiian Sites, Their Locations, and Interpretation of Their Names* 2, no. 1 (1987), http://manoa.hawaii.edu/coe/kulia/resources/ahupuaa_maps/OahuAhupuaa.pdf.

79. Though Honolulu continues to serve as Hawaiʻi's central urban hub, the is-lands are becoming increasingly urbanized overall, with Hawaiʻi's *Civil Beat* re-porting that 92 percent of residents now live in an urban area known to be one of the most expensive in the United States. HNN Staff, "No Surprises Here: Ha-waii Named Priciest State in the Nation," *Hawaii News Now*, July 12, 2018; Sean Connelly, "Urbanism as Island Living in Honolulu," *Civil Beat*, August 21, 2014, https://www.civilbeat.org/2014/08/urbanism-as-island-living-in-honolulu/.

80. Shawn Malia Kanaʻiaupuni, Wendy M. Kekahio, Kāʻeo Duarte, and Bran-don C. Ledward, "Material and Economic Well-Being," in *Ka Huakaʻi: 2014 Native Hawaiian Educational Assessment* (Honolulu: Kamehameha Publishing, 2014), 88–134. Also see Williamson Chang and Abbey Seitz, "It's Time to Acknowledge Native Hawaiians' Special Right to Housing," *Civil Beat*, January 8, 2021, https://www.civilbeat.org/2021/01/its-time-to-acknowledge-native-hawaiians-special-right-to-housing/. Studies of urban indigeneity, like those by Penelope Ed-monds, Ann Laura Stoler, and Maria John, reveal the ways that the city operates as a complex site of Indigenous world-making, in which expressions of self-determination respond to, navigate, and often exceed the demands of settler so-ciety. Edmonds, *Urbanizing Frontiers*; Stoler, *Carnal Knowledge and Imperial Power*; Maria John, "Sovereign Bodies: Urban Indigenous Health and the Politics of Self-Determination in Seattle and Sydney, 1950–1980" (PhD diss., Columbia Uni-versity, 2016).

81. Elizabeth Povinelli, *The Cunning of Recognition: Indigenous Alterities and the Making of Australian Multiculturalism* (Durham, NC: Duke University Press, 2002); Audra Simpson, "Whither Settler Colonialism?," *Settler Colonial Studies* 6, no. 4 (2016): 438–45. Also see Glen Coulthard, *Red Skin, White Masks: Rejecting the Colo-nial Politics of Recognition* (Minneapolis: University of Minnesota Press, 2014).

82. Silva, *Aloha Betrayed*; Saranillio, *Unsustainable Empire*.

83. Here Wolfe borrows from Deborah Bird Rose, *Hidden Histories: Black Stories from Victoria River Downs, Humbert River, and Wave Hill Stations* (Canberra: Ab-original Studies Press, 1991), 46. Wolfe, "Settler Colonialism," 388. Scott Lauria Morgensen argues that biopolitics, in fact, constitutes a feature of settler colo-nialism, writing that "Western law incorporates Indigenous peoples while simul-taneously pursuing their elimination. . . . These historical processes ultimately enact biopower as a persistent activity of settler states that were never decol-onised and of the global regimes that extend and naturalise their power." Scott

Lauria Morgensen, "The Biopolitics of Settler Colonialism: Right Here, Right Now," *Settler Colonial Studies* 1, no. 1 (January 2011): 53–54.

84. Freidberg, *Fresh*.

85. Rees, *Refrigeration Nation*, 7.

86. Susanne Freidberg, "Moral Economies and the Cold Chain," *Historical Research* 88, no. 239 (February 2015): 126.

87. Shane Hamilton, *Trucking Country: The Road to America's Wal-Mart Economy* (Princeton, NJ: Princeton University Press, 2008); Rees, *Refrigeration Nation*.

88. Scholars of infrastructure, as anthropologist Brian Larkin points out, often erroneously preface their studies by echoing Susan Leigh Star's assertion that infrastructures are, by nature, invisible until they break down. Larkin argues that this notion is "fundamentally inaccurate" for several reasons, including the fact that lived reality is shaped by "an embodied experience governed by the ways infrastructures produce the ambient conditions of everyday life: our sense of temperature, speed, florescence, and the ideas we have associated with these conditions." Brian Larkin, "The Politics and Poetics of Infrastructure," *Annual Review of Anthropology* 42 (2013): 336.

89. The rest of Hawai'i's food—around 88.4 percent—is imported, primarily from continental US distribution hubs located more than 2,300 miles away in California. Of the imported foods to Hawai'i, approximately 81 percent comes from the continental United States and the rest from other foreign markets. Matthew K. Loke and PingSun Leung, "Hawai'i's Food Consumption and Supply Sources: Benchmark Estimates and Measurement Issues," *Agricultural and Food Economics* 1, no. 10 (2013): n.p.

90. The Hawai'i State House self-sufficiency bill HB2703 HD2 as quoted in George Kent, "Food Security in Hawai'i," in *Food and Power in Hawai'i: Visions on Food Democracy*, ed. Aya Hirata Kimura and Krisnawati Suryanata (Honolulu: University of Hawai'i Press, 2016), 39.

91. "Hawaii May Be the Happiest State, but It Also Has the Highest Food Prices," *USA Today*, March 21, 2019.

92. Thomas C. Frohlich, "Where You'll Pay the Most in Electric Bills," *24/7 Wall St.* (blog), accessed July 11, 2019, https://247wallst.com/special-report/2019/01/24/where-youll-pay-the-most-in-electric-bills-3/.

93. This is not unique to Hawai'i: nearly all of the island "possessions" of the United States are beholden to American cold chains. I address this more fully in the conclusion.

94. This thermal system links "households to global networks of frozen food provisioning and to discourses and ideologies of care, convenience, health, well-being and family life." Jenny Rinkinen, Elizabeth Shove, and Mattijs Smits, "Cold Chains in Hanoi and Bangkok: Changing Systems of Provision and Practice," *Journal of Consumer Culture* 19, no. 3 (2019): 379–97.

95. Jayna Omaye, "O'ahu in 1978: Housing Prices on the Rise in Hawai'i," *Honolulu Magazine*, June 6, 2019, https://www.honolulumagazine.com/oahu-in-1978-housing-prices-on-the-rise-in-hawaii/.

96. The ʻohana unit must also be attached by roof to the existing house, containing only a "wet bar" in lieu of a kitchen. Ryan Shidaki, "Multigenerational Living in the Urban High-Rise: Designing for Hawaiʻi's Extended Family" (PhD diss., University of Hawaiʻi, 2009).

97. "The Cost of Living in Hawaiʻi 2020: The Ultimate Guide to the Price of Paradise," *Dwell Hawaiʻi* (blog), May 23, 2020, https://www.dwellhawaii.com /blog/what-cost-living-hawaii-2020/.

98. Cathy Possedi, "Accessory Dwelling Units Become Legal in Honolulu County," *Hawaiʻi Life Real Estate Brokers* (blog), September 22, 2015, https: //www.hawaiilife.com/blog/accessory-dwelling-units-legal-in-honolulu/.

99. Nicole E. Johns, "The Wealth (and Health) of Nations: Estimating Inequality to Better Estimate Health" (paper presented at the annual conference of Global Health Metrics and Evaluation: Data, Debates, Directions, Seattle, WA, June 18, 2013).

100. Emily Yates-Doerr, "Refrigerator Units, Normal Goods," *Limn* 4 (2014), https://limn.it/articles/refrigerator-units-normal-goods/.

101. Christina Jedra, "Hawaiʻi Is No Longer No. 1 for Homelessness. New York Is Worse," *Civil Beat*, January 7, 2020, https://www.civilbeat.org/2020/01/hawaii -is-no-longer-no-1-for-homelessness-new-york-is-worse/. Police regularly sweep the encampments that line city sidewalks and beaches in an effort to diminish the visibility of systemic impoverishment. Christina Jedra, "Hawaiʻi Increases Funding for Homeless Sweeps," *Civil Beat*, June 26, 2020, https://www.civilbeat .org/2020/06/hawaii-increases-funding-for-homeless-sweeps/.

102. In sharp contrast to the bureaucratically defined single-family home, Tatiana Kalaniopua Young writes movingly that for houseless community members living in Puʻuhonua o Waiʻanae, an encampment on the west shore of Oʻahu, "'home' was defined as 'places where you feel like returning to' and 'places of safety.'" "Home Is What We Make It," in *The Value of Hawaiʻi 3: Hulihia, the Turning*, ed. Noelani Goodyear-Kaʻōpua, Craig Howes, Jonathan Kay Kamakawiwoʻole Osorio, and Aikko Yamashiro (Honolulu: University of Hawaiʻi Press, 2020), 176. See also Kalaniopua Young, "Constellations of Rebellion: Home, Makeshift Economies and Queer Indigeneity" (PhD diss., University of Washington, 2019). For more on the intimate regulation of public life in Hawaiʻi, see Gaye Chan and Nandita Sharma, "Eating in Public" (lecture, Department of Social and Cultural Analysis, New York University, New York, October 27, 2015).

103. Bianca Isaki, "HB 645, Settler Sexuality, and the Politics of Local Asian Domesticity in Hawaiʻi," *Settler Colonial Studies* 1, no. 2 (2011): 82–102.

1. A PREHISTORY OF THE ARTIFICIAL COLD

1. I choose to primarily spell the name Maunakea as a single word that denotes the mountain as a proper noun, since in the Hawaiian language, Mauna Kea could refer to any "white mountain." However, Hawaiians also commonly refer to the mountain as Mauna a Wākea, or the Mountain of Wākea, the primordial father of earthy life. In testimony submitted in opposition to the TMT during the 2016

contested case hearings, Dr. Kū Kahakalau explained, "Based on a mele hānau, or birth chant for Kauikeaouli, Mauna Kea, Mauna a Kea, or Mauna a Wakea—all of these names can be used interchangeably—is such an entity, a sacred child of the highest birth. The chant states, "O hānau ka mauna a Kea, ʻōpuʻu aʻe ka mauna a Kea ʻO Wakea ke kāne, ʻo Papa, ʻo Walinuʻu ka wahine. Hānau Hoʻohōkū he wahine. Hānau Hāloa, he aliʻi. Hānau ka mauna. He keiki mauna na Kea.ʻ This primary source substantiates that Mauna Kea is a child of the gods, it's not just a mauna, or mountain, it is an aliʻi, a chief, it is an akua, a god, it is sacred." Kū Kahakalau, written direct testimony, Contested Case Hearing 2, October 26, 2016, https://dlnr.hawaii.gov/mk/files/2016/10/B.06a-wdt-Kahakalau.pdf.

2. Image from the UKIRT webcam, owned by the University of Arizona, published in Colin M. Stewart, "Rare July Snowfall Blankets Mauna Kea; Protesters Say It's a Sign," *Hawaii Tribune-Herald*, July 18, 2015, http://hawaiitribune-herald.com/news/local-news/rare-july-snowfall-blankets-mauna-kea-protesters-say-it-s-sign.

3. Protectmaunakea, Instagram photo, July 17, 2015, https://Instagram.com/p/5PyWQIPwJB/.

4. Stewart, "Rare July Snowfall."

5. "Timeline," TMT International Observatory, accessed April 20, 2021, https://www.tmt.org/page/timeline.

6. Iokepa Casumbal-Salazar, *First Light: Kanaka ʻŌiwi Resistance to Telescopes on Mauna a Wākea* (Minneapolis: University of Minnesota Press, forthcoming); David Uahikeaikaleiʻohu Maile, "On Being Late: Cruising Mauna Kea and Unsettling Technoscientific Conquest in Hawaiʻi," *American Indian Culture and Research Journal* 45, no. 1 (2021): 95–122; Noelani Goodyear-Kaʻōpua, "Protectors of the Future, Not Protestors of the Past: Indigenous Pacific Activism and Mauna a Wākea," *South Atlantic Quarterly* 116, no. 1 (2017): 184–94; Emalani Case, *Everything Ancient Was Once New: Indigenous Persistence from Hawaiʻi to Kahiki* (Honolulu: University of Hawaiʻi Press, 2021).

7. Uahikea Maile, "Ka Lei o ka Lanakila: Grasping Victory at Maunakea," *Abolition Journal*, July 17, 2020, https://abolitionjournal.org/ka-lei-o-ka-lanakila/.

8. Leanne Betasamosake Simpson, *As We Have Always Done: Indigenous Freedom through Radical Resistance* (Minneapolis: University of Minnesota Press, 2017). Also see Kim TallBear, "Why Interspecies Thinking Needs Indigenous Standpoints," *Fieldsights*, November 18, 2011, https://culanth.org/fieldsights/why-interspecies-thinking-needs-indigenous-standpoints; Robin Wall Kimmerer, *Braiding Sweetgrass: Indigenous Wisdom, Scientific Knowledge, and the Teachings of Plants* (Minneapolis: Milkweed Editions, 2015); Vanessa Watts, "Indigenous Place-Thought and Agency amongst Humans and Non Humans (First Woman and Sky Woman Go on a European Tour!)," *Decolonization* 2, no. 1 (2003): 20–34; Julie Cruikshank, *Do Glaciers Listen? Local Knowledge, Colonial Encounters, and Social Imagination* (Vancouver: University of British Columbia Press, 2005).

9. Eva Illouz, *Cold Intimacies: The Making of Emotional Capitalism* (Cambridge: Polity, 2007). What I am identifying here about settler capitalism and affect is

part of the premise of Illouz's work, though the core argument that she is making here is about the twentieth-century infusion of emotional investment by workers in corporate America. Lauren Berlant offers a smart discussion of this in *Cruel Optimism* (Durham, NC: Duke University Press, 2011), 217–18.

10. See Andrew Curley's argument about how various interlocking infrastructures operate as a "colonial beachhead" in the Navajo nation, "Infrastructures as Colonial Beachheads: The Central Arizona Project and the Taking of Navajo Resources," *Environment and Planning D: Society and Space* 39, no. 3 (2021): 387–404; Traci Brynne Voyles, *Wastelanding: Legacies of Uranium Mining in Navajo Country* (Minneapolis: University of Minnesota Press, 2015); Rafico Ruiz, *Slow Disturbance: Infrastructural Mediation on the Settler Colonial Resource Frontier* (Durham, NC: Duke University Press, 2021); Nick Estes and Jaskiran Dhillon, *Standing with Standing Rock: Voices from the #NoDAPL Movement* (Minneapolis: University of Minnesota Press, 2019); Anne Spice, "Fighting Invasive Infrastructures: Indigenous Relations against Pipelines," *Environment and Society* 9, no. 1 (2018): 40–56.

11. Nick Estes, *Our History Is the Future: Standing Rock versus the Dakota Access Pipeline, and the Long Tradition of Indigenous Resistance* (New York: Verso, 2019), 75. For more on how ideas of manifest destiny are brought to bear specifically on Indigenous water resources, see Melanie K. Yazzie and Cutcha Risling Baldy, "Introduction: Indigenous Peoples and the Politics of Water," *Decolonization* 7, no. 1 (2018): 1–18.

12. For more on masculinist aesthetics of imperial landscapes across the Pacific, including Hawai'i, see Vernadette Vicuña Gonzalez, *Securing Paradise: Tourism and Militarism in Hawai'i and the Philippines* (Durham, NC: Duke University Press, 2013).

13. Alison Kelly, "The Construction of Masculine Science," *British Journal of Sociology of Education* 6, no. 2 (1985): 133–54. In her expansive and moving discussion of the cleaving of emotional attachment and scholarly discourse about Maunakea, Emalani Case writes about revising her stance on describing Maunakea's sacredness, after previously thinking that doing so would diminish her scholarly credibility. She states, "To talk about Mauna Kea, therefore, is to talk about spirit. It is to use words like 'sacred' and to draw on emotions born of connection and relationship that are too often disregarded in academic discourse. Further, it is to use stories that are frequently categorized as 'myth,' a category that has not served Indigenous peoples well as myths tend to be read as fantastical or make-believe." Emalani Case, "I ka Piko, To the Summit: Resistance from the Mountain to the Sea," *Journal of Pacific History* 54, no. 2 (2019): 172.

14. See Noenoe K. Silva, *The Power of the Steel-Tipped Pen: Reconstructing Native Hawaiian Intellectual History* (Durham, NC: Duke University Press, 2017); Brandy Nālani McDougall, *Finding Meaning: Kaona and Contemporary Hawaiian Literature* (Tucson: University of Arizona Press, 2016).

15. Fujikane, *Mapping Abundance for a Planetary Future*, 87–89.

16. Among a large body of literature on Kanaka epistemologies about kalo and its relationship to Hawai'i's food system, some excellent pieces include Walter

Ritte Jr. and Leʻa Malia Kanehe, "Kuleana No Haloa (Responsibility for Taro): Protecting the Sacred Ancestor from Ownership and Genetic Modification," in *Pacific Genes and Life Patents*, ed. Aroha Te Pareake Mead and Steven Ratuva (Wellington, New Zealand: Call of the Earth Llamado de la Tierra, 2007), 130–37; Brandy Nālani McDougall, "Kaona, Connectivity to Papa, Wākea, and Hāloa Naka," in *Finding Meaning*, 86–120; Hōkūlani K. Aikau and Donna Ann Kameha'ikū Camvel, "Cultural Traditions and Food: Kānaka Maoli and the Production of Poi in the Heʻeʻia Wetland," *Food, Culture, and Society* 19, no. 3 (2016): 539–61.

17. Fujikane, *Mapping Abundance for a Planetary Future*, 87–89.

18. University of Hawaiʻi at Hilo, "Final Environmental Impact Statement, Vol. 1: Thirty Meter Telescope Project," May 8, 2010, http://www.malamamaunakea .org/uploads/management/plans/TMT_FEIS_vol1.pdf.

19. University of Hawaiʻi at Hilo, "Final Environmental Impact Statement," 1.

20. This definition is extrapolated from Pukui and Elbert, *Hawaiian Dictionary*; and Kepa Maly and Onaona Maly, *"Mauna Kea—Ka Piko Kaulana O Ka ʻĀina": A Collection of Native Traditions, Historical Accounts, and Oral History Interviews for: Mauna Kea, the Lands of Kaʻohe, Humuʻula, and the ʻĀina Mauna on the Island of Hawaiʻi* (Hilo: Office of Mauna Kea Management, 2005), 18.

21. This according to S. N. Haleole's first installment of "Ka Moolelo O Laieikawai," in *Kuokoa*, in which he writes, "He umikumamawalu makahiki me ekolu malama ka malamaiaʻna o keia Moolelo Kaao, e ka mea nana e hoopuka nei keia moolelo maloko o kana Buke Moolelo, e hoomaka ana ma ka malama o Augate, M. H. 1844." His transcription is the earliest known written record of this moʻolelo taken from its oral form, which had been passed down from person to person. According to Maly and Maly, the story circulated as a serial for the newspaper *Kuokoa* from November 29, 1862, to April 11, 1863; Martha Beckwith translated the pieces first as a PhD dissertation at Columbia University (1918) and published it thereafter. S. N. Haleole, *The Hawaiian Romance of Laieikawai*, trans. Martha Warren Beckwith (Washington, DC: Government Printing Office, 1918). Also see note in entry 2537 in David W. Forbes, comp., *Hawaiian National Bibliography, 1780–1900*, vol. 3, *1851–1880* (Honolulu: University of Hawaiʻi Press, 2001), 348.

22. It is important to note here that Beckwith's translation, offered in her book side by side with the *Kuokoa* text, makes choices that privilege certain interpretations that flatten or abridge the original meaning (for example, in this line the Hawaiian word *hewa* is translated as "sin," rather than a less doctrinal rendering of the word as "wrongdoing" or "error"). Summarized here from Martha Beckwith's translation, *Hawaiian Romance of Laieikawai*, 200. In *Finding Meaning*, Brandy Nālani McDougall uses Beckwith as an example of how translations are shaped by colonial politics; here I try to use Beckwith carefully by checking translations against other publications of *Ka Moolelo o Laieikawai*, though I recognize the limitations of my fluency in ʻōlelo Hawaiʻi may, in turn, limit my interpretations.

23. Hinaikamalama chants about the heat as well, saying, "The heat, ah! The heat / The heat of my love stifles me. / Its quivering touch scorches my heart, /

the sick old heat of the winter, / the fiery heat of the summer, / the dripping heat of the summer season, / the heat compels me to go. / I must go." Beckwith, *Hawaiian Romance of Laieikawai*, 202.

24. There are multiple versions of this moʻolelo with different elaborations. Here I use Maly and Maly's translation of Haleole's text from *Kuokoa*, chap. 18 (January 17, 1863). Maly and Maly, *Mauna Kea*, 23.

25. For more on the politics of interpretation, the multivalence of ʻōlelo Hawaiʻi, and the circulation of cultural knowledge through Hawaiian-language newspapers, see Silva, *Power of the Steel-Tipped Pen*.

26. Leon Noʻeau Peralto, "Portrait. Mauna a Wākea: Hānau ka Mauna, the Piko of Our Ea," in *A Nation Rising: Hawaiian Movements for Life, Land, and Sovereignty*, ed. Noelani Goodyear-Kaʻōpua, Ikaika Hussey, and Erin Kahunawaikaʻala Wright (Durham, NC: Duke University Press, 2014), 233.

27. Jonathan Goldberg-Hiller and Noenoe K. Silva, "Sharks and Pigs: Animating Hawaiian Sovereignty against the Anthropological Machine," *South Atlantic Quarterly* 110, no. 2 (2011): 435.

28. Fujikane, *Mapping Abundance for a Planetary Future*, 91.

29. E. Kalani Flores, quoted in Fujikane, *Mapping Abundance for a Planetary Future*, 102.

30. "About Mauna Kea Observatories," University of Hawaiʻi Institute for Astronomy, accessed March 13, 2017, https://www.ifa.hawaii.edu/mko/about_maunakea.shtml.

31. John Stickler, "Thirty Meter Telescope Could Boost Hawaii Island's Economy," *Hawaii Business Magazine*, September 2013, http://www.hawaiibusiness.com/thirty-meter-telescope-could-boost-hawaii-islands-economy/.

32. University of Hawaiʻi Institute for Astronomy website, accessed March 16, 2017, https://www.ifa.hawaii.edu/mko/telescope_table.shtml.

33. Dennis Overbye, "Under Hawaiʻi's Starriest Skies, a Fight over Sacred Ground," *New York Times*, October 3, 2016, https://www.nytimes.com/2016/10/04/science/hawaii-thirty-meter-telescope-mauna-kea.html?_r=0.

34. David Millward, "Protesters Halt Groundbreaking Ceremony for Mammoth Hawaiian Telescope," *Telegraph*, October 9, 2014, http://www.telegraph.co.uk/news/worldnews/northamerica/usa/11152624/Protests-halt-groundbreaking-ceremony-for-mammoth-Hawaiian-telescope.html.

35. For a comprehensive timeline, see "Timeline of Mauna Kea Legal Actions since 2011," Kahea: The Hawaiian-Environmental Alliance, accessed March 16, 2017, http://kahea.org/issues/sacred-summits/timeline-of-events.

36. Marie Alohalani Brown, "Mauna Kea: Hoʻomana Hawaiʻi and Protecting the Sacred," *Journal for the Study of Religion, Nature, and Culture* 10, no. 2 (2016): 150–70; Goodyear-Kaʻōpua, "Protectors of the Future."

37. In addition to Brown and Goodyear-Kaʻōpua, see Iokepa Casumbal-Salazar, "Multicultural Settler Colonialism and Indigenous Struggle in Hawaiʻi: The Politics of Astronomy on Mauna a Wākea" (PhD diss., University of Hawaiʻi, 2014); Peralto, "Mauna a Wākea"; and David Uahikeaikaleiʻohu Maile, "Science, Time,

and Mauna a Wākea: The Thirty-Meter Telescope's Capitalist-Colonialist Violence," *Red Nation*, May 13, 2015, https://therednation.org.

38. Coulthard, *Red Skin, White Masks*.

39. Krisnawati Suryanata, "Products from Paradise: The Social Construction of Hawai'i Crops," *Agriculture and Human Values* 17 (2000): 181–89; Gary Y. Okihiro, *Pineapple Culture: A History of the Tropical and Temperate Zones* (Berkeley: University of California Press, 2009).

40. For an excellent analysis of how those tropes were operationalized through the promotion of Hawaiian culture, see Imada, *Aloha America*.

41. Janeen Arnold Costa, "Paradisical Discourse: A Critical Analysis of Marketing and Consuming in Hawai'i," *Consumption Markets and Culture* 1, no. 4 (1998): 303–46.

42. Sun Kwok, *Stardust: The Cosmic Seeds of Life* (London: Springer, 2013), 65.

43. D. Morrison, R. E. Murphy, D. P. Cruikshank, W. M. Sinton, and T. Z. Martin, "Evaluation of Mauna Kea, Hawaii, as an Observatory Site," *Publications of the Astronomical Society of the Pacific* 85, no. 505 (1973): 255–57.

44. Quoted in Casumbal-Salazar, "Multicultural Settler Colonialism," 173.

45. Quoted in Stickler, "Thirty Meter Telescope Could Boost Hawaii Island's Economy."

46. There is a strong distinction that should be emphasized between Hawaiian understandings of natural elements and Western commoditization. If one takes an Indigenous approach to thinking about snow, it becomes clear that landscape and natural elements have active dialectical relationships with Kānaka Maoli; elements like snow and lava are commanded by akua. To further strengthen this point, it's important to mention that akua are known to mate with humans and produce human offspring of the highest chiefly rank. Pukui and Elbert, *Hawaiian Dictionary*, 15; Group 70 International, *Mauna Kea Science Reserve Master Plan* (Honolulu: [Group 70 International], 2000).

47. Charles Wilkes, *Voyage round the World* (Philadelphia: Geo. W. Gorton, 1849), 500.

48. Reprinted in William Ellis, *The Journal of William Ellis: Narrative of a Tour of Hawaii, or Owhyhee; with Remarks on the History, Traditions, Manners, Customs, and Language of the Inhabitants of the Sandwich Islands*, Honolulu Advertiser Reprint Edition (Honolulu: Honolulu Advertiser, 1963), 292.

49. Wolfe, "Settler Colonialism"; Ned Blackhawk, *Violence over the Land: Indians and Empires in the Early American West* (Cambridge, MA: Harvard University Press, 2006).

50. James Macrae, *With Lord Byron at the Sandwich Islands in 1825: Being Extracts from the MS Diary of James Macrae* (Honolulu: W. F. Wilson, 1922), 55.

51. Macrae, *With Lord Byron at the Sandwich Islands*, 55.

52. "Notes of the Week," *Pacific Commercial Advertiser*, October 23, 1862.

53. "Notes of the Week."

54. Audra Simpson, "On Ethnographic Refusal: Indigeneity, Voice, and Colonial Citizenship," *Junctures*, December 9, 2007, 69.

55. Sustainable Resources Group, Int'l., *Public Access Plan for the UH Management Areas on Mauna Kea* (Hilo: Office of Mauna Kea Management, 2010), 3-2.

56. These logics continue to this day through the operation of the Hawaiʻi Space Exploration Analog and Simulation (HI-SEAS) experimental station on Maunaloa, which since 2013 has been used to document the effects of space habitation. Sara Jensen Carr, "Alien Landscapes: NASA, Hawaiʻi, and Interplanetary Occupation," *Avery Review* 50 (2021), http://www.averyreview.com/issues/50/alien-landscapes.

57. Teaiwa, "Reading Paul Gauguin's *Noa Noa*." For more on this, see discussion of militourism in Hawaiʻi in the introduction.

58. Gonzalez, "The Machine in the Garden," in *Securing Paradise*, especially 170.

59. For more on the relationship between the Hawaiian shirt and American empire, see Christen Tsuyuko Sasaki, "Threads of Empire: Militourism and the Aloha Wear Industry in Hawaiʻi," *American Quarterly* 68, no. 3 (2016): 643–67; Amanda Kooser, "Space Station Crew Dons Matching Hawaiian Shirts to Greet New Astronauts," *CNET*, June 8, 2018, https://www.cnet.com/news/space-station-iss-crew-dons-matching-hawaiian-shirts-to-greet-new-astronauts/. Some additional examples, of which there are plenty, include the Hawaiian shirt patterned with pinup girls worn by scientist Matt Taylor to a press conference announcing the successful landing of a Rosetta module on a comet, reported in Rich Lowry, "We Landed on a Comet, and Feminists Are Angry about a Shirt," *New York Post*, November 17, 2014, https://nypost.com/2014/11/17/the-outrage-machine-insande-ado-about-sexist-shirt/.

60. Musk retweeted a journalist's photo of the Brownsville SpaceX campus, showing two of its Starships next to an A-frame structure, writing, "Real pic of 2 ships next to Starbase Tiki Bar on right." Elon Musk, Twitter post, June 17, 2021, 2:47 p.m., https://twitter.com/elonmusk/status/1405597886826512386.

61. The conceptual overlap between Hawaiʻi, outer space, and midcentury kitsch comes together wildly in Elvis Presley's televised concert "Aloha from Hawaii via Satellite" (1973), which used lunar imagery in some of its promotional material. Thank you to Kiri Salaita for bringing this to my attention.

62. Dave Smith, "Big Island's Role in Apollo Missions Remembered," *Big Island Now*, May 9, 2014, http://bigislandnow.com/2014/05/29/big-islands-role-in-apollo-missions-commemorated/.

63. Donald A. Beattie, *Taking Science to the Moon: Lunar Experiments and the Apollo Program* (Baltimore, MD: Johns Hopkins University Press, 2001), 187.

64. Luanne Pfeifer, "The Admirable Snowman of Mauna Kea," *Ski*, November 1971, 68.

65. Moreton-Robinson, "Bodies That Matter on the Beach," in *White Possessive*, 33–46.

66. Josh Lerman, "Hawaii Not?," *Skiing*, February 1992, 30. I do not read this quote as referring directly to Native Hawaiians but instead as erasing the distinction between Kanaka Maoli and residents of Hawaiʻi who replace "original Hawaiians."

67. Lerman, "Hawaii Not?," 30.

68. This point comes from Mischa Rahder, who beautifully observes, "Simulation 'fills the raw space' in a way that reimagines it as a different kind of raw space that is already elsewhere, a kind of fractal frontier in which each site of expansion contains all of its future/infinite unfoldings." Personal communication, April 10, 2021.

69. It is important to note here that the lands on which the Mauna Kea Science Reserve sits are part of the Hawaiian Kingdom's Crown and Government Lands, seized in a government coup in 1893 and renamed as public lands after US annexation in 1898. The notion of public land, then, is predicated on the "perception of [US] legitimacy." Iokepa Casumbal-Salazar, "A Fictive Kinship: Making 'Modernity,' 'Ancient Hawaiians,' and the Telescopes on Mauna Kea," *Native American and Indigenous Studies* 4, no. 2 (2017): 8–9. Thank you to J. Kēhaulani Kauanui for clarifying this point for me.

70. Martin Elvis, "After Apollo: The American West in Devising a New Space Policy," *Harvard International Review* 33, no. 4 (Spring 2012): 39.

71. Elvis, "After Apollo," 41.

72. Klaus Dodds and Christy Collis, "Post-colonial Antarctica," in *Handbook on the Politics of Antarctica*, ed. K. Dodds, A. D. Hemmings, and P. Roberts (Cheltenham: Edward Elgar, 2017), 50.

73. Dodds and Collis, "Post-colonial Antarctica," 50.

74. Dodds and Collis, "Post-colonial Antarctica," 56.

75. Ellis, *Journal of William Ellis*, 292.

76. Stickler, "Thirty Meter Telescope."

77. For a complete list of telescopes, including mirror size and national and institutional affiliation, see "Mauna Kea Telescopes," University of Hawai'i Institute for Astronomy website, accessed March 21, 2017, https://www.ifa.hawaii .edu/mko/telescope_table.shtml.

78. Gary H. Sanders, "The Thirty Meter Telescope (TMT): An International Observatory," *Journal of Astrophysics and Astronomy* 34 (2013): 81.

79. Ikaika Ramones, "OHA Backs Down from Contesting the TMT Sublease," *Hawai'i Independent*, July 17, 2014, http://hawaiiindependent.net/story/oha-backs -down-from-contesting-the-tmt-sublease.

80. Will Caron, "Mauna Kea and the Awakening of the Lāhui," *Hawai'i Independent*, April 26, 2015, http://hawaiiindependent.net/story/mauna-kea-and-the -awakening-of-the-lahui; quoted by Stickler, "Thirty Meter Telescope."

81. Stephanie Nohelani Teves, "Aloha State Apparatuses," *American Quarterly* 67, no. 3 (2015): 705–26; Lisa Kahaleole Hall, "Hawaiian at Heart and Other Fictions," *Contemporary Pacific* 17, no. 2 (2005): 404–13. Also see No'u Revilla and Jamaica Heolimeleikalani Osorio, "Aloha Is Deoccupied Love," in *Detours: A Decolonial Guide to Hawai'i*, ed. Hōkūlani K. Aikau and Vernadette Vicuña Gonzalez (Durham, NC: Duke University Press, 2019): 125–31.

82. *The Heart of Aloha: A Way Forward Maunakea*, pamphlet, September 2019,

https://casca.ca/wp-content/uploads/2019/10/Maunakea-The-Heart-of
-Aloha.pdf (emphasis added).

83. See Revilla and Osorio, "Aloha Is Deoccupied Love." In it, they write, "Deoc-cupied love believes in decolonization and does not surrender sovereignty. Deoc-cupied love is ea, beginning in our manawa and always, always rising" (126).

84. Adam Fish, "Native American Sacred Spaces and the Language of Capital-ism," *Future Anterior* 2, no. 1 (2005): 42.

85. Fish, "Native American Sacred Spaces," 42.

86. Robert Nichols, *Theft Is Property! Dispossession and Critical Theory* (Durham, NC: Duke University Press, 2020); Fish, "Native American Sacred Spaces," 42; David Treuer, "Return the National Parks to the Tribes," *Atlantic*, April 12, 2021, https://www.theatlantic.com/magazine/archive/2021/05/return-the-national -parks-to-the-tribes/618395/.

87. Cover image for special issue, Michelle Erai and Scott Lauria Morgensen, eds., "Karangatia: Calling Out Gender and Sexuality in Settler Societies," *Settler Colonial Studies* 2, no. 2 (2012).

88. Scott Lauria Morgensen, "Theorizing Gender, Sexuality, and Settler Colo-nialism: An Introduction," *Settler Colonial Studies* 2, no. 2 (2012): 2.

89. Morgensen, "Theorizing Gender," 2.

90. As a further example of American preoccupations with Native peoples and outer space, an academic article from 1987 mused that "because Native Ameri-cans have a different perspective of the world, they can offer us alternative ways of seeing ourselves in relationship to the natural world and help us answer the question of what constitutes appropriate behavior—in outer space, as well as on earth." M. Jane Young, "'Pity the Indians of Outer Space': Native American Views of the Space Program," *Western Folklore* 46, no. 4 (1987): 270.

91. The English-language version is the one that most people refer to, though the original text in Spanish reads: "Muchos años después, frente al pelotón de fu-silamiento, el coronel Aureliano Buendía había de recordar aquella tarde remota en que su padre lo llevó a conocer el hielo." Gabriel García Márquez, *One Hundred Years of Solitude* (New York: Avon, 1970), 1. It's also worth noting here that the Spanish *conocer* also means "to meet" or "to become acquainted with," suggesting a more lateral form of encounter, though those who have connected this text to my work here have certainly been drawing on the book's English translation.

2. VICE, VIRTUE, AND FROZEN NECESSITIES

1. As discussed in the introduction. Philip Chadwick Foster Smith, *Crystal Blocks of Yankee Coldness: The Development of the Massachusetts Ice Trade from Fred-erick Tudor to Wenham Lake, 1806–1880* (Wenham, MA: Wenham Historical Asso-ciation and Museum, 1962).

2. Here I am echoing Jodi Byrd's theorization of transit as a mode of empire that divorces Indigenous peoples from territories and then, in turn, racializes "Indianness" in such a way that ice could not be seen as inherently indigenous by

the middle of the nineteenth century. Jodi A. Byrd, *The Transit of Empire: Indigenous Critiques of Colonialism* (Minneapolis: University of Minnesota Press, 2011).

3. For an excellent history of early kingdom politics, see Noelani Arista, *The Kingdom and the Republic: Sovereign Hawaiʻi and the Early United States* (Philadelphia: University of Pennsylvania Press, 2019).

4. Silva, *Aloha Betrayed*; J. Kēhaulani Kauanui, *Paradoxes of Hawaiian Sovereignty: Land, Sex, and the Colonial Politics of State Nationalism* (Durham, NC: Duke University Press, 2018).

5. Rees reports that Tudor's largest foreign market, India, peaked in 1856 with 146,000 tons shipped that year, though the ice trade continued to grow domestically in American markets until the end of the nineteenth century. Rees, *Refrigeration Nation*, 23–24. Although Tudor struggled to profit directly from exports in the international market, he eventually succeeded in making a small fortune off of lakeside real estate that he purchased for ice harvesting. Gavin Weightman, *The Frozen Water Trade: A True Story* (New York: Hyperion, 2003), 173.

6. In addition to C. H. Lewers's successful application for a business license in 1858, there were at least four other license applications that were not granted, including applications from N. S. Bailey, D. D. Miller, and Thomas K. Park of New York in 1852; Cyrus W. Jones and Charles G. Davis in 1856; Captain John Paty in 1858; and Henry Hackfeld and J. C. Pfluger in 1861.

7. Thomas G. Thrum, "Honolulu Yesterdays," in *Hawaiian Almanac and Annual for 1931* (Honolulu: Thos. G. Thrum, 1930), 33–34.

8. At this time, the term *hotel* referred to a place for socialization and entertainment more than sleeping accommodations. Laws put into effect in the years 1845–46 determined that places "for the ordinary entertainment of sailors" would be called inns or victualing houses, and that a hotel would be "a house of public entertainment for the higher classes of society." In 1856 "respectable" retailers, including Cutrell, Bartlett, and Macfarlane, complained that the inadequate enforcement of harsh liquor license laws fostered illegal competition with "numerous illicit vendors diffused among all the classes of society." Richard A. Greer, "Grog Shops and Hotels: Bending the Elbow in Old Honolulu," *Hawaiian Journal of History* 28 (1994): 46–48.

9. A Florida physician, John Gorrie, filed the earliest ice machine patents in the United States and England in 1851, but the machines did not go into production. George D. Howe, "The Father of Modern Refrigeration," *Publications of the Florida Historical Society* 1, no. 4 (1909): 19–23.

10. The notice is specifically directed toward "the gentlemen of Honolulu, Captains of vessels, and strangers visiting Oahu." "Notice," *Polynesian*, August 24, 1850, 59.

11. "Notice," 59; advertisement, *Polynesian*, November 16, 1850, 108. The cargo, perplexingly, does not appear in any other records in contemporary publications. This may be simply due to a lack of reporting, or perhaps the cargo didn't last long enough for it to make significant news. *Polynesian*, September 21, 1850, 74; *Polynesian*, December 14, 1850, 123.

12. "Ice," *Polynesian*, June 26, 1852. The notice furthermore reports, "A few tons of ice were brought to this port from San Francisco by the bark Harriet T. Bartlet [*sic*], Capt. Hereen, and a part sold by our friend Thompson, at his auction, on Tuesday. This is the first importation of the kind, in any quantity, to this market." "Ice," 26. Only the mail, and not the ice, cargo of the *Harriet T. Bartlett* gets mention in the announcement of its arrival in the *Polynesian*, June 19, 1852, indicating general sentiments around the relative importance of ice to news from abroad. It's unclear whether the speedy Boston-based ship transported the small cargo on speculation or at the behest of a prospecting businessman. *New-York Daily Tribune*, March 30, 1846. It seems that subsequent shipments aboard the *Harriet T. Bartlett* never materialized, or at least the newspapers failed to report it.

13. Samuel Greene Wheeler Benjamin, *The Life and Adventures of a Free Lance* (Burlington, VT: Free Press, 1914), 64. The *Polynesian* notes that the bark was captained by "Edward Hereen" (also spelled Heeren in *The Friend*'s "Marine Journal," July 2, 1852).

14. Hereen probably bought a small quantity on speculation, hoping for a quick sale while taking on fresh supplies. "Seaborne Commerce of Pacific Coast of North America in Pioneer Days," *Monthly Review Mercantile Trust Company of California*, October 15, 1923, 218. During these years, the company shipped an estimated fifty thousand tons of natural ice to California, and particularly to the trade hub of San Francisco. The Russian American Commercial Ice Company reportedly sold the ice for $25 to $35 per ton (a good deal cheaper than the $75 per ton that could be bought from Boston by way of Cape Horn) and sold to consumers for five cents per pound. Sven D. Haakanson and Amy F. Steffian, *Giinaquq Like a Face: Suqpiaq Masks of the Kodiak Archipelago* (Fairbanks: University of Alaska Press, 2009), 45. One publication reports that San Francisco's first ice shipment arrived via the *Backus* on April 11, 1852, along with eight hundred pounds of halibut at the consignment of the newly formed Pacific Ice Company. Louis J. Rasmussen, *San Francisco Ship Passenger Lists: November 7, 1851–June 17, 1852* (Baltimore, MD: Genealogical Publishing, 2003), 244.

15. *Polynesian*, October 14, 1854; Thomas G. Thrum, *Hawaiian Almanac and Annual for 1914* (Honolulu: Thos. G. Thrum, 1913), 52. Additional details of the icehouse's structure cannot be found in the popular press, government documents, or city maps, though it continued to change hands for some time afterward and was eventually occupied as a shipwright's shop run by George Emmes. Thomas G. Thrum, *Hawaiian Almanac and Annual for 1882* (Honolulu: Thos. G. Thrum, 1882), 9.

16. One of the company's notices claimed that "the Agents will be prepared to furnish Ice at the Houses of all who may desire this indispensable luxury." Shipments advertised via the American brigs *Mallory* and *Noble*. *Polynesian*, October 28, 1854; November 4, 1854; and February 3, 1855. News of the icehouse built in anticipation of its arrival reached as far as California in "Further from the Sandwich Islands," *Sacramento Daily Union*, November 9, 1854, 3.

17. Circular, "Swan & Clifford . . ." [Honolulu 1855], Hawai'i State Archives, Honolulu, Hawai'i (hereafter HSA). Also see Forbes, *Hawaiian National Bibliography*, 3:156.

18. "How Ice Was Had Here in Old Pioneer Days," *Advertiser*, April 19, 1903.

19. Ralph Kuykendall calls the second volume of his *Hawaiian Kingdom* trilogy *Twenty Critical Years*. Ralph S. Kuykendall, *The Hawaiian Kingdom*, vol. 2, *Twenty Critical Years, 1854–1874* (Honolulu: University of Hawai'i Press, 1953). Sally Engle Merry also makes this reference in *Colonizing Hawai'i: The Cultural Power of Law* (Princeton, NJ: Princeton University Press, 2000), 4.

20. Daws, "Honolulu in the 19th Century," 83; also see Sumner J. LaCroix and James Roumasset, "The Evolution of Private Property in Nineteenth-Century Hawai'i," *Journal of Economic History* 50, no. 4 (1990): 829–52.

21. Kauanui, *Paradoxes of Hawaiian Sovereignty*, 18.

22. The historical literature on the Māhele is extensive; here I use Stuart Banner, "Preparing to Be Colonized: Land Tenure and Legal Strategy in Nineteenth-Century Hawai'i," *Law and Society Review* 39, no. 2 (2005): 281.

23. Kuykendall, *Hawaiian Kingdom*, 2:19–20.

24. Ray Jerome Baker, *Honolulu in 1853* (Honolulu: Ray Jerome Baker, 1950), 6.

25. Daws explains that during the period of the Māhele, "the outlines of a town committed to western property practices became visible." Daws, "Honolulu in the 19th Century," 80n11.

26. Banner, "Preparing to Be Colonized," 284.

27. Peter Corney, *Voyages in the Northern Pacific* (Honolulu: Thos. G. Thrum, 1896), 99.

28. Baker reports that in the year 1853, 110 vessels entered the harbor and Honolulu's custom receipts numbered over $100,000, with total kingdom revenue of $234,169. Baker, *Honolulu in 1853*, 5.

29. Samuel S. Hill, *Travels in the Sandwich and Society Islands* (London: Chapman and Hall, 1856), 96.

30. "Improvements and Changes in and about Honolulu," *Polynesian*, October 17, 1840, 74–75.

31. Don Hibbard, *Designing Paradise: The Allure of the Hawaiian Resort* (New York: Princeton Architectural Press, 2006), 8. For more on the sex trade in early nineteenth-century Honolulu, see Catherine 'Īmaikalani Ulep, "Women's Exchanges: The Sex Trade and Cloth in Early Nineteenth-Century Hawai'i" (master's thesis, University of Hawai'i, 2017). For more on the concomitant feminization of Hawai'i and its people in relation to tourism, see Imada, *Aloha America*.

32. The cargo arrived on the American clipper *Yankee*, along with letters and dry goods. *Polynesian*, October 25, 1856, 98–99. Cutrell owned both a liquor retail business and a boardinghouse called the Union Hotel. The Merchant's Exchange appears to have operated as a tavern only, although the Union Hotel and the Merchant's Exchange may have operated under the same roof. Richard A. Greer, "Cunha's Alley—the Anatomy of a Landmark," *Hawaiian Journal of History* 2 (1968): 144, 149–50. The concoctions would have been familiar to many hollow-

legged colonialists; contemporary reports from Australia list beverages of the same name. For example, a "stone fence" contained ginger beer and brandy, and a "smash" was composed of ice, brandy, and water. "The Literature of the Bottle," *Titan*, January–June 1859, 506.

33. An 1856 petition signed by a dozen or so liquor license holders, including Cutrell, complained about the "numerous illicit vendors diffused among all the classes of society" that they believed were negatively affecting the profitability of their business. Greer, "Grog Shops and Hotels," 47. Even though a limited number of liquor licenses were available, options for cheap brandies abounded, dispensed liberally by back-alley grog shops to those with less capital. The American sea captain E. E. Adams wrote in 1850, "Wherever I go [in Honolulu], I meet men lying on the floors, in the streets, in the forecastles, perfectly helpless and senseless; but brandy is so CHEAP." "Honolulu—Cheap versus Dear Spirits," quoted from the *Honolulu Friend* in *Bristol Temperance Herald*, January 1851, 91.

34. *Polynesian*, October 25, 1856, 98.

35. *Pacific Commercial Advertiser*, February 26, 1857; October 30, 1856.

36. While advertisements like Cutrell's for the Merchant's Exchange seem to speak to a general audience, the implicit omission of Kānaka from imaginaries of tropical leisure would have been obvious at the time. Native Hawaiians experienced exclusion from spaces like the Merchant's Exchange on ideological, legal, and economic levels, which prevented most Kānaka from purchasing alcoholic drinks, even if they had sufficient money to do so.

37. "View of Honolulu from the Harbor, No. 1," Hawaiian Historical Society Historical Photograph Collection, http://www.huapala.net/items/show/4711; reprinted in Baker, *Honolulu in 1853*.

38. It's difficult to pinpoint the exact location of the Merchant's Exchange since coordinates do not appear in newspaper advertisements and buildings of this time tended to change hands rather rapidly. In Richard Greer's detailed history of Cunha's Alley, located between Merchant and King Streets, he traces Cutrell's ownership of a building that is either the Merchant's Exchange or the Union Hotel (or both). Greer, "Cunha's Alley," 144.

39. The complex relationship between Native American peoples and alcohol has been well documented. On alcohol as a tool of Indigenous oppression, see Peter C. Mancall, *Deadly Medicine: Indians and Alcohol in Native America* (Ithaca, NY: Cornell University Press, 1995); William E. Unrau, *White Man's Wicked Water: The Alcohol Trade and Prohibition in Indian Country* (Lawrence: University Press of Kansas, 1996). On Native-led temperance movements and mutual support structures for alcoholism recovery, see William W. White, "The History of Recovered People as Wounded Healers: I. From Native American to the Rise of the Modern Alcoholism Movement," *Alcoholism Treatment Quarterly* 18, no. 1 (2000): 1–23.

40. Kuykendall refers to this as an 1837 law "rejecting the Catholic religion." Ralph S. Kuykendall, *The Hawaiian Kingdom*, vol. 1, *Foundation and Transformation, 1874–1893* (Honolulu: University of Hawai'i Press, 1938), 163–64. Also see Kealani

Cook, *Return to Kahiki: Native Hawaiians in Oceania* (Cambridge: Cambridge University Press, 2018), 53.

41. Rufus Anderson, *A Heathen Nation Evangelized: History of the Sandwich Islands Mission* (Cambridge, MA: H. O. Houghton, 1870), 177–78.

42. Merry, *Colonizing Hawai'i*; Marilyn Brown, "'Āina under the Influence: The Criminalization of Alcohol in 19th-Century Hawai'i," *Theoretical Criminology* 7, no. 1 (2003): 89–110.

43. Jennifer Fish Kashay, "'We Will Banish the Polluted Thing from Our Houses': Missionaries, Drinking, and Temperance in the Sandwich Islands," in *The Role of the American Board in the World: Bicentennial Reflections on the Organization's Missionary Work, 1810–2010*, ed. Clifford Putney and Paul T. Burlin (Eugene, OR: Wipf and Stock, 2012), 308.

44. Lorrin A. Thurston, *The Liquor Question in Hawaii—What Should Be Done about It?* (Honolulu: Social Science Association, 1909), 2–3. Also discussed in Kuykendall, *Hawaiian Kingdom*, 1:161.

45. Kuykendall, *Hawaiian Kingdom*, 1:162.

46. This perspective is illustrated well in the writings of the missionary Hiram Bingham, who stated, "The demon of intemperance, so terrible in heathen nations, still held a cruel sway, and threatened ruin to many, but to none, perhaps, more than the monarch of the isles. So disgusting and abominable the doings of the destroyer, even in the family of the king, and so determined were a class of human agents (who knew better) to encourage and confirm the king in his drinking habits, that the missionaries, anxious for him and those who hasted [*sic*] with him in this way to ruin, could have taken their lives in their hands to lay siege to this stronghold of Satan." Hiram Bingham, *A Residence in Twenty-One Years in the Sandwich Islands* (1847; New York: Praeger, 1969). Also see Thurston, *Liquor Question in Hawaii*, 3; Brown, "'Āina under the Influence," 97–99; Kuykendall, *Hawaiian Kingdom*, 1:161–63; Greer, "Grog Shops."

47. For more on the "Laplace Affair," see Mary Ellen Birkett, "Forging French Policy in the Pacific," *French Colonial History* 8 (2007): 155–69.

48. Kuykendall, *Hawaiian Kingdom*, 1:166.

49. Encouraged by temperance reformers in 1846, the Hawaiian Kingdom proposed amendments to treaty agreements made with France and England in 1839 and 1844, respectively, that included the prohibition of liquor importation. After a wholly unsatisfactory debate with representatives of the two powers, including complaints of favoritism, the kingdom not only allowed alcohol importation but eventually lowered the tariffs outlined in their first concession. Ralph S. Kuykendall, *The Hawaiian Kingdom*, vol. 3, *The Kalakaua Dynasty, 1874–1893* (Honolulu: University of Hawai'i Press, 1967), 372–73. Also see "The Struggle for Equitable Treaties," in Kuykendall, *Hawaiian Kingdom*, 1:368–82.

50. *Laws of His Majesty Kamehameha IV, King of the Hawaiian Islands, Passed by the Nobles and Representatives, at Their Session* (Honolulu: Hawaiian Government, 1855), 15. A good analysis of what trade agreements did to the Hawaiian economy, and ultimately its political independence, can be found in Sumner J. LaCroix and

Christopher Grandy, "The Political Instability of Reciprocal Trade and the Overthrow of the Hawaiian Kingdom," *Journal of Economic History* 57, no. 1 (1997): 161–89.

51. Brown, "'Āina under the Influence," 92; Greer, "Grog Shops and Hotels," 46; Hawaiian Government, *Penal Code of the Hawaiian Islands* (Honolulu: Government Press, 1850), 101.

52. Hawaii Supreme Court, *Annual Report of the Chief Justice* (Honolulu: Hawaii Administration of Justice, 1854), 3.

53. Gavan Daws, "Decline of Puritanism at Honolulu in the Nineteenth Century," *Hawaiian Journal of History* 1 (1967): 37.

54. Brown, "'Āina under the Influence," 95.

55. William H. Mulligan Jr., "Cold Water Army," in *The SAGE Encyclopedia of Alcohol: Social, Cultural, and Historical Perspectives*, ed. Scott C. Martin and William White (Thousand Oaks, CA: Sage, 2015), 415–16; William P. White, "A Historic Nineteenth Century Character," *Journal of the Presbyterian Historical Society (1901–1903)* 10, no. 5 (1920): 161–74.

56. Laura Fish Judd, *Honolulu: Sketches of Life: Sketches of the Social, Political, and Religious in the Hawaiian Islands from 1828–1861* (New York: Anson D. F. Randolph and Company, 1880), 78.

57. Rufus Anderson, *History of the Sandwich Islands Mission* (Boston: Congregational Publishing Society, 1870), 174.

58. "Letter from Mr. Armstrong, November 7, 1843," *Missionary Herald* 40 (1844): 192.

59. The militarism embedded in American Indian educational institutions has been well documented. For primary source material on philosophical approaches in their time, see Richard Henry Pratt, *Battlefield and Classroom: Four Decades with the American Indian, 1867–1904*, ed. Robert M. Utley (Norman: University of Oklahoma Press, 1964). For Indigenous critical analyses, see K. Tsianina Lomawaima, *They Called It Prairie Light: The Story of Chilocco Indian School* (Lincoln: University of Nebraska Press, 1994); and Jon Reyhner and Jeanne Eder, *American Indian Education: A History* (Norman: University of Oklahoma Press, 2004).

60. Tengan, "Re-membering Panalā'au," 27–53. Also see Lee D. Baker, "Missionary Positions," in *Globalization and Race: Transformations in the Cultural Production of Blackness*, ed. Kamari Maxine Clarke and Deborah A. Thomas (Durham, NC: Duke University Press, 2006), 37–54; Keith Camacho and Laurel A. Monnig, "Uncomfortable Fatigues," in *Militarized Currents: Toward a Decolonized Future in Asia and the Pacific*, ed. Setsu Shigematsu and Keith L. Camacho (Minneapolis: University of Minnesota Press, 2010), 147–80; and Brendan Hokowhitu, "Tackling Māori Masculinity: A Colonial Genealogy of Savagery and Sport," *Contemporary Pacific* 16 (2004): 259–84.

61. Tengan, "Re-membering Panalā'au," 29.

62. Joy Schulz, "Empire of the Young: Missionary Children in Hawai'i and the Birth of U.S. Colonialism in the Pacific" (PhD diss., University of Nebraska, 2011), 130–31.

63. See Kupperman, "Fear of Hot Climates"; Livingstone, "Tropical Climate and Moral Hygiene."

64. For the relationship between alcohol and climate, see Michael R. Hill, "Temperateness, Temperance, and the Tropics: Climate and Morality in the English Atlantic World, 1555–1705" (PhD diss., Georgetown University, 2013). For more on the tandem production of sugar and rum, see David Eltis, "New Estimates of Exports from Barbados and Jamaica, 1665–1701," *William and Mary Quarterly* 52, no. 4 (1995): 631–48.

65. Entry 1368 "[Temperance Badge]," in David W. Forbes, comp., *Hawaiian National Bibliography, 1780–1900*, vol. 2, *1831–1850* (Honolulu: University of Hawai'i Press, 2000), 334.

66. "A Cold Water Army," *Youth's Dayspring* 4, no. 11 (November 1853): 164.

67. This was one of many "temperance houses" erected in Honolulu across the 1830s, 1840s, and 1850s that offered room and board for sailors on leave who might otherwise abuse substances. Greer, "Grog Shops and Hotels," 40. For more see Gerrit P. Judd IV, *Dr. Judd: Hawaii's Friend. A Biography of Gerrit Parmele Judd, 1803–1873* (Honolulu: University of Hawai'i Press, 1960).

68. *Polynesian*, September 15, 1855.

69. S. A. Judd to L. Fish, [October 1855], Bishop Museum Archives, Honolulu, Hawai'i.

70. As Osorio notes, the racial politics of alcohol consumption became central to political struggles around the Bayonet Constitution of 1887, under the reign of Kalākaua. He writes, "Although there was no suggestion that alcohol consumption by haole in any way affected their ability to govern or vote, the ascribing of widespread alcoholism to the kānaka also came with its own 'proof.'" Jonathan Kamakawiwo'ole Osorio, *Dismembering Lāhui: A History of the Hawaiian Nation to 1887* (Honolulu: University of Hawai'i Press, 2002), 229.

71. James O'Meara, "Schemes to Annex the Sandwich Islands," *Californian* 4 (1881): 257–58.

72. For an extended discussion of the drinking behaviors of Kamehameha III, see Kashay, "We Will Banish."

73. Honolulu newspapers corroborate an arrival of the *Sea Bird* as a vessel intended for use as an interisland steamer on October 16 (not October 14). *Polynesian*, November 1, 1856, 102.

74. Records show that Cutrell advertised as the proprietor of the Merchant's Exchange as early as February 1856. Greer, "Cunha's Alley," 143.

75. O'Meara, "Schemes to Annex the Sandwich Islands," 264.

76. See Chauncey C. Bennett, "Death of King Kamehameha III," in *Sketches of Hawaiian History and Honolulu Directory* (Honolulu: C. C. Bennett, 1871), 38; *Polynesian*, December 30, 1854, 134. If one reads contemporary accounts that circulated through the popular press at the time of the mō'ī's (monarch's) death—around mid-December 1854—it is difficult to ascertain exactly what happened. Newspaper articles generally focus on reactions: the grief of his nation,

funeral details, and the business of appointing his successor, but they actually say very little about the king's extended illness or his swift decline. Private correspondence from the time connects the king's death to alcoholism. For example, the missionary John S. Emerson wrote in a letter to his son Samuel, "The King Kamehameha III died a bout [*sic*] one month since, disease *mania potu*"—a nineteenth-century term to describe alcoholism. John S. Emerson to Samuel Emerson, letter, January 23, 1855, Bishop Museum Archives.

77. This was illustrated most obviously by Kamehameha III's proclamation published December 8 of that year in the *Polynesian*, which affirmed his commitment to the kingdom's sovereignty. See Kuykendall, *Hawaiian Kingdom*, 1:426. Kamehameha III's ultimate decision on whether to cease annexation negotiations before his death remains unclear. According to archival evidence referenced by Kuykendall, cabinet members were under the impression that all negotiations had been terminated. Meeting minutes, however, show that the discussion had simply been tabled for further consideration. Certainly, no prepared annexation document had been waiting for signature.

78. News coverage about Kamehameha III's death and funerary rites reflects these broader discourses about civility in ways that are, even today, anguishing. Haole newspapers wrote approvingly about restrained public conduct during the funeral, in which traditional expressions of mourning (such as knocking out one's front teeth) were relatively absent. Even so, the *Polynesian* reported that at the corner of Nuʻuanu and Beretania Streets in Honolulu, "a long low wail arose from the thousands congregated there." Quoted in Ralph Thomas Kam, *Death Rites and Hawaiian Royalty: Funerary Practices in the Kamehameha and Kalākaua Dynasties, 1819–1953* (Jefferson, NC: McFarland, 2017), 59.

79. Merze Tate's book provides an overview of the debates around Hawaiian annexation throughout the second half of the nineteenth century. See Merze Tate, *Hawaii: Reciprocity or Annexation* (East Lansing: Michigan State University Press, 1968).

80. On nineteenth-century Hawaiian history, see Silva, *Aloha Betrayed*; Osorio, *Dismembering Lāhui*.

81. "A Few Words about Ice," *Pacific Commercial Advertiser*, October 21, 1858 (emphasis added).

82. The year this was published also saw the opening of an ice cream parlor on the corner of Nuʻuanu and Chaplain Streets by Mr. William Huddy, "where pleasant rooms and gentlemanly attendance greet the lady and gentleman visitors." *Pacific Commercial Advertiser*, November 11, 1858.

83. Wendy A. Woloson, *Refined Tastes: Sugar, Confectionery, and Consumers in Nineteenth-Century America* (Baltimore, MD: Johns Hopkins University Press, 2002), 84.

84. Woloson, *Refined Tastes*, 85.

85. On cookbooks, see Megan J. Elias, *Food on the Page: Cookbooks and American Culture* (Philadelphia: University of Pennsylvania Press, 2017), 14–16. On the ide-

alization of womanhood, shaped around the values of piety, purity, domesticity, and submissiveness, see Barbara Welter, "The Cult of True Womanhood: 1820–1860," *American Quarterly* 18, no. 2 (1966): 151–74.

86. *Polynesian*, November 4, 1854. Horace Crabb advertised "Ice Cream!" to be served at 7:30 p.m. on the same date.

87. Woloson, *Refined Tastes*, 78.

88. Jonathan Stainback Wilson, "Health Department," *Godey's Lady's Book* 57 (1858): 560.

89. Isabella Mary Beeton, *The Book of Household Management* (London: S. O. Beeton, 1861), 761.

90. Mary Tylor Mann, *Christianity in the Kitchen* (Boston: Ticknor and Fields, 1857), 26–27.

91. "Danger of Ice Cream," *Polynesian*, November 18, 1854.

92. John Paty to Hawaiian Minister of the Interior, December 25, 1858, HSA.

93. Cyrus W. Jones and Charles G. Davis, Draft Agreement, 1856, HSA; C. W. Jones and C. G. Davis to the Privy Council of His Hawaiian Majesty, Privy Council Petitions, April 17, 1856, HSA.

94. "Cool," *Polynesian*, March 20, 1858.

95. Charles E. Peterson, "Pioneer Architects and Builders of Honolulu," *Annual Report of the Hawaiian Historical Society* 72 (1964): 12; "A Honolulu Hardware Store," *Hardware Dealer's Magazine* 40 (1913): 1237.

96. Per details indexed in the Hawai'i State Archives card catalog under the heading "Ice," with incomplete reference to article in *Honolulu Advertiser*, February 1931.

97. *Polynesian*, October 16, 1858.

98. "Cool."

99. "ICE! ICE!," *Ka Hae Hawai'i*, November 3, 1858, 122.

100. "ICE! ICE!," 122.

101. "The Ice, and What Came of It," *Polynesian*, May 26, 1860.

102. C. H. Lewers to Hawaiian Minister of the Interior, March 18, 1861, HSA.

103. Hackfeld intended to export items like sugar, coffee, beef, and salt in return. H. Hackfeld and J. C. Pfluger to Hawaiian Minister of the Interior, March 25, 1861, HSA. For more on Hackfeld's business in Hawai'i, see "History of the House of H. Hackfeld & Co.," in *All about Hawaii: Thrum's Hawaiian Almanac and Annual for 1900* (Honolulu: Thos. G. Thrum, 1900), 43. In contrast, a note in *Paradise of the Pacific* regarding the death of Lewers's widow in Kansas City, Missouri, mentions that Lewers recalled that his ice cost him ten cents per pound. "The First Ice Importer," *Paradise of the Pacific*, November 1909, 23.

104. Cabinet Council Records, vol. 5, April 15, 1861, 217, HSA.

105. "Ice," *Saturday Press*, April 22, 1882.

3. MAKING ICE LOCAL

1. The mele "He Inoa No Kalani Ka Lakaua" was published twice in Hawaiian newspapers. The first publication, entitled "No Kaulilua," appeared in *Na Pupepa*

Kuokoa, March 20, 1875. The second, which I reproduce here, appeared in *Ka Leo o ka Lahui*, February 4, 1896; it varies slightly from the earlier publication but can be read more clearly. Here I use Tiffany Lani Ing's translation of the 1875 version because it gives a good dynamic translation and captures the broader contextual meaning of the mele. Tiffany Lani Ing, *Reclaiming Kalākaua: Nineteenth-Century Perspectives on a Hawaiian Sovereign* (Honolulu: University of Hawaiʻi Press, 2019), 130.

2. Ing, *Reclaiming Kalākaua*, 126–27.

3. In contrast to the chilliness of Kalākaua's journey to the United States in the winter of 1874–75, his welcome home blazed joyously warm: torches lined the street that ran between ʻĀinahou and the palace; the tower of Kawaihaʻo Church had been outfitted to look like a lighthouse; a bonfire raged at Pūowaina overlooking the city; and the phrase "Kalakaua-Imi-Pomaikai-Lahui" (Kalākaua searching for the good of the nation) topped ʻIolani in "fiery letters." A couple of days later, the mōʻī would give a public address reporting on successful negotiations for a treaty of reciprocity with the United States, which he believed would increase Hawaiʻi's economic prosperity and, perhaps, stay American plans for annexation. Ing, *Reclaiming Kalākaua*, 125–29.

4. See the chapter "Satisfied with Stones: Native Hawaiian Government Reorganization and the Discourses of Resistance," in Byrd, *Transit of Empire*, 147–84.

5. For more on the dynamics of this election, see chapter 1, "Kalākaua Becomes King," in Kuykendall, *Hawaiian Kingdom*, 3:3–16.

6. A useful discussion of the economic and political dynamics of US-Hawaiʻi reciprocity leading up to the treaty ratification in 1875 is found in LaCroix and Grandy, "Political Instability of Reciprocal Trade."

7. The 1875–76 treaty was ratified by the Hawaiian Kingdom on April 17, 1875, and by the United States on May 31. Treaties of reciprocity between Hawaiʻi and the United States were drafted in 1855, 1867, and 1875. In each draft, the American schedule lengthened without omitting any goods that may no longer have seemed relevant (which is probably why ice ended up on the 1875 draft). A major point of contention in negotiations was the proposed cession of "Pearl River Lagoon," later known as Pearl Harbor, which Kalākaua rejected as part of the 1875 draft but eventually conceded to in the treaty's 1887 renegotiation. As discussed in W. L. Green to Elisha Allen, October 14, 1874, Foreign Office and Executive Collection, HSA. Also see Kuykendall, *Hawaiian Kingdom*, 3:38–41; Osborne E. Hooley, "Hawaiian Negotiation for Reciprocity, 1855–1857," *Pacific Historical Review* 7, no. 2 (1938): 128–46; Donald Marquand Dozer, "The Opposition to Hawaiian Reciprocity, 1876–1888," *Pacific Historical Review* 14, no. 2 (1945): 157–83; John Patterson, "The United States and Hawaiian Reciprocity, 1867–1870," *Pacific Historical Review* 7, no. 2 (1938): 14–26.

8. Although the Hawaiian sugar industry prospered during the Civil War, when trade from the American South was interrupted, profits dipped again by the late 1860s because of high trade tariffs and increased sugar refinery competition on the California coast. Kuykendall, *Hawaiian Kingdom*, 3:18. The Reciprocity Treaty

restored prosperity in the Hawaiian sugar market, with Hawaiian sugar production doubling between 1870 and 1880 and almost tripling to 224.5 million pounds
annually between 1880 and 1890. LaCroix and Grandy, "Political Instability of Reciprocal Trade," 172. Also see John M. Liu, "Race, Ethnicity, and the Sugar Plantation System: Asian Labor in Hawai'i, 1850–1900," in *Labor Immigration under
Capitalism: Asian Workers in the United States before World War II*, ed. Lucie Cheng
and Edna Bonacich (Berkeley: University of California Press, 1984), 186–210;
J. A. Mollett, "Capital in Hawaiian Sugar: Its Formation and Relation to Labor
and Output, 1870–1957," *Agricultural Economics Bulletin* 21 (Honolulu: Hawai'i Agricultural Experiment Station, University of Hawai'i Mānoa, 1961); Edward D.
Beechert, *Working in Hawai'i: A Labor History* (Honolulu: University of Hawai'i
Press, 1985).

9. On the American side, opponents of reciprocity argued that treating with
Hawai'i would result in "unconstitutionality, [conflict with] most-favored-nation
treaties with other nations, and uncompensated loss of revenue to the Treasury."
David M. Pletcher, *Diplomacy of Involvement: American Economic Expansion across
the Pacific, 1784–1900* (Columbia: University of Missouri Press, 2001), 53. At the
time of enactment, kingdom supporters also viewed the agreement as insurance
against future American annexation, including Hawai'i's minister of foreign affairs William Lowthian Green, who exclaimed that "so long as this treaty with
the United States exists, the independence of this Kingdom is secured." Quoted
in Kuykendall, *Hawaiian Kingdom*, 3:29. Also see Pletcher, *Diplomacy of Involvement*, 56–57.

10. On American sugar interests and the Reciprocity Treaty, see, in addition to
Kuykendall, Tate, *Hawai'i*; Helen Geracimos Chapin's chapter on sugar and reciprocity, "'A New Era Has Dawned': Sugar Is King," in her *Shaping History: The Role
of Newspapers in Hawai'i* (Honolulu: Hawaiian Historical Society, 1996), 63–67;
and April Merleaux, *Sugar and Civilization: American Empire and the Cultural Politics of Sweetness* (Chapel Hill: University of North Carolina Press, 2015).

11. Noelani Goodyear-Ka'ōpua and Bryan Kamaoli Kuwada translate Nāwahī's
original statement, "ke 'ōlelo nei au he ku'ikahi kā'ili aupuni a kā'ili pono lāhui
kēia e ho'onele 'ia ai ka noho ali'i i kona mana kumu mai ka pō mai," as "I say
to you that this is a nation-snatching treaty, one that will steal from us our national rights and leave our throne bereft of its foundational mana, granted to it
from the depths of Pō, the darkness." For an extended discussion, see Noelani
Goodyear-Ka'ōpua and Bryan Kamaoli Kuwada, "Making 'Aha: Independent Hawaiian Pasts, Presents, and Futures," *Dædalus* 147, no. 2 (2018): 54. Sugar also mo-
tivated US treaties with the Philippines and Puerto Rico, which would become
territories or possessions, too. Merleaux, *Sugar and Civilization*.

12. Article IV of the Reciprocity Treaty. For more on Kanaka Maoli perspectives
on reciprocity and a detailed unpacking of Kalākaua's relationship to sugar planters, see Osorio, *Dismembering Lāhui*, 167–69.

13. In their words specifically, "the presence of a settler population intent on
making a territory their permanent home while continuing to enjoy metropoli-

tan living standards." Caroline Elkins and Susan Pederson, "Settler Colonialism: A Concept and Its Uses," in their *Settler Colonialism in the Twentieth Century* (New York: Routledge, 2005), 2.

14. There are no known records of ice shipments to Hawai'i during the 1870s or 1880s. While the 1855 version of the treaty does not list ice in its schedules, the 1867 draft negotiations include ice, along with an expanded schedule of commodity goods. Manuscript description of 1867 Reciprocity Treaty negotiations, unsigned, n.d., Foreign Office and Executive Collection, HSA. LaCroix and Grandy explain that the profits to American manufacturers would be negligible: "The tariff revenues on manufactured goods lost by Hawai'i's government would be transferred to Hawai'i consumers and sugar plantations purchasing machines and parts." Instead, the benefit to America rested in both the exclusion of other countries from Hawai'i trade and the potential to leverage treaty renegotiations for control of Pearl Harbor. LaCroix and Grandy, "Political Instability of Reciprocal Trade," 171.

15. This statistic is available only up to 1890 because trade that year was interrupted by the McKinley Tariff. Richard D. Weigle, "Sugar and the Hawaiian Revolution," *Pacific Historical Review* 16, no. 1 (1947): 41–58.

16. Anne McClintock, *Imperial Leather: Race, Gender, and Sexuality in the Colonial Contest* (New York: Routledge: 1995), 31–34.

17. Kuykendall, *Hawaiian Kingdom*, 2:94.

18. Kuykendall, *Hawaiian Kingdom*, 2:95–97.

19. Maturin Murray Ballou, *Travels under the Southern Cross: Travels in Australia, Tasmania, New Zealand, Samoa, and Other Pacific Islands*, 2nd ed. (Boston: Houghton Mifflin, 1887), 19.

20. For more on how ideas of American progress were yoked to civility, see Michael Adas, *Dominance by Design: Technological Imperatives and America's Civilizing Mission* (Cambridge, MA: Harvard University Press, 2006).

21. Rev. George L. Cheney, "Hawaii," *Unitarian Register*, January 6, 1898, 8–9.

22. Osorio, *Dismembering Lāhui*, 146.

23. I borrow this point from Philip J. Deloria's *Indians in Unexpected Places* (Lawrence: University Press of Kansas, 2004). See especially his conclusion, "The Secret History of Indian Modernity," 224–40.

24. Kamanamaikalani Beamer, *No Mākou Ka Mana: Liberating the Nation* (Honolulu: Kamehameha Publishing, 2014), 181, citing Silva, *Aloha Betrayed*, 90; also see Kealani R. Cook, "Kahiki: Native Hawaiian Relationships with Other Pacific Islanders, 1850–1915" (PhD diss., University of Michigan, 2001).

25. Kuykendall, *Hawaiian Kingdom*, 3:67; Carol Wilcox, *Sugar Water: Hawai'i's Plantation Ditches* (Honolulu: University of Hawai'i Press, 1998), 63.

26. George F. Nellist, *The Discovery and Development of Artesian Water* (Honolulu: Board of Water Supply, City and County of Honolulu, 1953), [2–3].

27. William Adams Simons, *The Hawaiian Telephone Story* (Honolulu: Hawaiian Telephone Company, [1958]).

28. See Silva, *Power of the Steel-Tipped Pen*. Honolulu's piped water system be-

gan in the 1840s to support the whaling industry; significant improvements were made in 1860–61 and 1879. Its functionality remained limited until the 1920s. Robert C. Schmitt, "Pipes, Pools, and Privies: Some Notes on Early Island Plumbing," *Hawaiian Journal of History* 16 (1982): 150–51.

29. For more on the history of the development of refrigeration technology in the United States, see Oscar Edward Anderson, *Refrigeration in America: A History of a New Technology and Its Impact* (Princeton, NJ: Princeton University Press, 1953).

30. In chapter 2, I mentioned an alleged ice machine that was advertised briefly. I have not been able to locate further information about that machine, however, so I choose this as the most likely "first."

31. "Ice," *Hawaiian Gazette*, October 11, 1871. Smith's announcement that the machine had been "altered to suit the temperature of the water in this climate . . . at great expense" indicates that he had been prototyping in California. "Manufactured Ice," *Hawaiian Gazette*, August 16, 1871; "Manufactured Ice," *Hawaiian Gazette*, October 4, 1871. The *A.S.R.E. Journal* credits Smith with inventing "the plate system of ice-making." "Review: Experiments on Cold Storage Insulation," *A.S.R.E. Journal* 2, no. 3 (November 1915): 70–71.

32. Joseph A. Nickerson Jr. and Geraldine D. Nickerson, *Chatham Sea Captains in the Age of Sail* (Charleston, SC: History Press, 2008), 86; "Review: Experiments on Cold Storage Insulation," 71.

33. At the time, this was a government-owned tract of land that would undergo significant dredging and expansion to take advantage of the ever-growing maritime commerce feeding into the downtown area. For an overview of the changes to the Honolulu waterfront that year, see *Pacific Commercial Advertiser*, December 16, 1871.

34. Honolulu's Judge Albert Francis Judd began receiving regular five-pound deliveries of ice to his home three days per week, according to receipts issued to A. F. Judd from the Honolulu Ice Manufactory dated July 14 and September 8, 1872, Bishop Museum Archives. Additionally, customers on neighboring islands could request shipments "at same rate" packed in boxes insulated with sawdust (with the cost of the box refunded if the box was returned to the factory). *Hawaiian Gazette*, April 3, 1872. Also see "Ice Manufacture," *Pacific Commercial Advertiser*, September 30, 1871; and "Manufactured Ice," *Hawaiian Gazette*, October 4, 1871.

35. Rees reports that in the final decades of the nineteenth century, "few other countries had anywhere near as many of the giant mechanical ice machines as the United States did because most countries did not have consumer ice industries. Rees, *Refrigeration Nation*, 47. Likewise, Roger Thévenot explains that until 1900, instances of artificial ice usage outside of brewing and the meat trade were generally very minor. Roger Thévenot, *History of Refrigeration throughout the World* (Paris: International Institute of Refrigeration, 1979), 53.

36. Woolrich reports this number as five, and Rees reports eight. Willis Raymond Woolrich, *The Men Who Created Cold: A History of Refrigeration* (New York:

Exposition Press, 1967), 45; Rees, *Refrigeration Nation*, 44. Woolrich furthermore writes that ice machines would remain relatively few into the 1890s, even after they came into regular manufacture, with only 189 in operation across the United States in 1889.

37. Thévenot argues that in the third quarter of the nineteenth century, the field of refrigeration belonged to the British, American, and French (and one Scotsman named James Harrison, who lived in Australia). Thévenot, *History of Refrigeration*, 130–31. Ice machines, however, emerged much earlier than this as prototypes. A notable example is Thomas Masters's successful display of an ice-making machine at the 1851 Great Exhibition in London. An illustration of Masters's machine can be found in the "General Hardware" section of the *Official Descriptive and Illustrated Catalog: Great Exhibition of the Works of Industry of All Nations*, vol. 2 (London: Spicer Brothers, 1851), 658. For more on the history of refrigeration, see Thévenot, *History of Refrigeration*; Rees, *Refrigeration Nation*; Mikael Hård, *Machines Are Frozen Spirit: The Scientification of Refrigeration and Brewing in the 19th Century—a Weberian Interpretation* (Frankfurt am Main: Campus Verlag, 1994); Anderson, *Refrigeration in America*; Woolrich, *Men Who Created Cold*.

38. Experiments in refrigerated meat transportation began as early as 1876, spurring on the establishment of cold chain "links" both in the United States and abroad. Places like Texas, Australia, New Zealand, and Argentina, with their large cattle industries, required substantial quantities of ice for packing and shipping meat to the American Northeast and Great Britain. Thévenot, *History of Refrigeration*, 79.

39. Woolrich writes: "The most inviting sources [of meat] were the hot-climate producing nations, and these could only be reached by water" (*Men Who Created Cold*, 39). Not only did refrigeration extend the food chain, but food systems adapted to the cold chain. Rebecca J. H. Woods, *The Herds Shot round the World: Native Breeds and the British Empire, 1800–1900* (Chapel Hill: University of North Carolina Press, 2017). Also see Roger Horowitz, *Putting Meat on the American Table: Taste, Technology, Transformation* (Baltimore, MD: Johns Hopkins University Press, 2006); Hård, *Machines Are Frozen Spirit*, 57.

40. Cronon, *Nature's Metropolis*; Keith Farrar, *To Feed a Nation: A History of Australian Food Science and Technology* (Collingwood, Victoria: CISRO, 2005), 52.

41. Rycroft arrived in Hawai'i in 1864, taking a job at Honolulu Iron Works, which manufactured custom agricultural machinery (he later enlisted the company's help in constructing his ice factory). Okihiro, *Pineapple Culture*, 108; Honolulu Iron Works Company, *Some Sugar Factories Built and Equipped by the Honolulu Iron Works Company* ([Honolulu]: Honolulu Iron Works Company, 1924). In 1866, Rycroft began a plumbing and retail business out of a storefront on King Street, according to an advertisement in *Pacific Commercial Advertiser*, February 17, 1866. For more on Rycroft, see "An Old Timer: Robert Rycroft Comes to Honolulu," *Hawaiian Gazette*, March 9, 1900, 5; and Peter Kaeo, *News from Moloka'i: Letters between Peter Kaeo and Queen Emma, 1873–1876* (Honolulu: University of Hawai'i

Press, 1976), 219. An 1873 advertisement for the Fountain Saloon describes it as an "Ice Cream and Lunch Room," having "Iced Soda and Ginger Pop always on hand." *Pacific Commercial Advertiser*, July 26, 1873.

42. Rycroft established Honolulu's Fountain Saloon in 1873 and sold it to J. W. Crowell after taking over the ice business. "Notice," *Pacific Commercial Advertiser*, February 6, 1875. Honolulu Ice Works was located along Nuʻuanu Valley stream, which runs toward Honolulu Harbor down the Koʻolau mountain range. The lot formerly belonged to Captain Thomas Cummins, a British ship captain who came to Hawaiʻi in 1828. Riánna Williams, "John Adams Cummins: Prince of Entertainers," *Hawaiian Journal of History* 30 (1996): 153–68. Government documents show that the minister of the interior granted use of the location on the condition that "there should be no waste of water," because the stream also functioned as a major fresh water source for the downtown area. Charles T. Gulick to Robert Rycroft, October 14, 1874, HSA. Shipping records show that by the end of the same November of Smith's departure, Rycroft received a cargo of machine parts and refrigerant containing "1 case fittings, 14 bundles iron pipes, 1 package castings, and 10 cs. Amonia [sic]" from San Francisco. "Imports," *Pacific Commercial Advertiser*, November 28, 1874. No other specifics about Rycroft's machine could be found.

43. "Ice, Once More," *Pacific Commercial Advertiser*, March 27, 1875.

44. Rycroft's cash-and-carry was initially located at the Fountain Saloon and later at the Family Market on King Street. Advertisements, *Pacific Commercial Advertiser*, August 7 and May 1, 1875. His ice factory promised an output of two tons per day, producing solid blocks of "excellent quality" ice between ten and four hundred pounds in size. "Ice," *Hawaiian Gazette*, March 31, 1873. Smith's machine may have been dismantled and repurposed: newspapers published a note reporting that the engine "formerly used at the Ice factory at the esplanade" was being transported for use at the Hāmākua Sugar Mill. "Ice, Ice," *Friend*, June 1, 1875, 41.

45. After selling his ice business, Rycroft left for Brisbane, Australia, where he established its first ammonia ice machine. "An Old Timer: Robert Rycroft Comes to Honolulu," 5. Biographical details are a bit sketchy, but it appears that Rycroft didn't leave for long, returning to Hawaiʻi in 1877 and settling in the Puna district of Hawaiʻi Island. David Sox, "Rycroft's Pohoiki: A 19th Century Boat Landing," *Historic Hawaiʻi News*, September 1981, 4. In 1901, Rycroft started a mineral and soda water plant on Sheridan Street, Honolulu. "New Plants and Improvements," *Ice and Refrigeration*, August 1901, 82. Wilder was a well-known figure in Honolulu, through various business and political relationships. Wilder partnered with C. H. Lewers (a former ice importer) in April 1872 to buy the lumber business of the late James I. Dowsett, naming it Wilder & Co. It was under this business name that Wilder managed interisland shipping for the kingdom before purchasing the government-owned boats *Likelike* and *Kilauea* in 1877 at auction. Ray Jerome Baker, *Honolulu in 1870: A Series of Ten Rare and Hitherto Unpublished Photographs* ([Honolulu]: [R. J. Baker], [1951]), 14–15; George F. Nellist, *The Story of Hawaiʻi and Its Builders* (Honolulu: Honolulu Star Bulletin, 1925), 871–72.

46. Honolulu residents seemed hopeful that Wilder & Co.'s updates to the machinery would help ice supply reliability, with newspapers writing that "the arrangements for manufacture have been so perfected that there is now hardly any possibility of interruption in the supply." *Hawaiian Gazette*, July 25, 1877. The Hawaiian-language newspaper *Ka Nupepa Kuokoa* likewise reported in August 1876 that repairs made under Wilder's ownership assured a resumed and reliable supply, writing, "Me he mea la ma keia hope aku, e holopono mau ana ka halihali ana, aole hoi ke kamukumuku." (It seems from this point on, the delivery of ice should return to normal, [and] there won't be any decrease in supply.) *Ka Nupepa Kuokoa*, August 12, 1876. Business seemingly proceeded without incident for several years, with the press reporting little about Wilder's Honolulu Ice Works, aside from advertisements and ice cream parlor notices.

47. See *Ka Nupepa Kuokoa*, July 29, 1876; *Ka Lahui Hawai'i*, May 4, 1876; *Ka Lahui Hawai'i,* August 16, 1877; "Wai Hui o Ka Hau!," *Ka Lahui Hawai'i*, March 1, 1877.

48. The large complex included an engine, two gas pumps, a boiler, and a freezing room. "A Visit to the Ice Works," *Daily Bulletin*, August 16, 1884. This article also contains extensive information on the freezing process using ammonia and iron pipe coils.

49. *Daily Bulletin*, July 11, 1882. J. W. Robertson's was located at 19 and 21 Merchant Street and was used as a print shop for the company's small broadside, which later expanded to become the *Daily Evening Bulletin* newspaper, a precursor to the *Honolulu-Star Bulletin* (today the *Star Advertiser*). David W. Forbes, comp., *Hawaiian National Bibliography, 1780–1900*, vol. 4, *1881–1900* (Honolulu: University of Hawai'i Press, 2003), 27; Bill Bryson, *At Home: A Short History of Private Life* (London: Doubleday, 2010), 71–73.

50. "Ice," *Friend*, December 5, 1881, 105.

51. *Daily Bulletin*, July 11, 1882.

52. "A Visit to the Ice Works," *Daily Bulletin*, August 16, 1884. Despite early unspecified "delays and difficulties," Foster began selling "Pure Artesian Ice" from his own shop located at 81 Fort Street in downtown Honolulu, which offered ice delivery at the beginning of March 1882. Advertisement in David Kalākaua, *King Kalakaua's Tour round the World: A Sketch of Incidents of Travel* (Honolulu: Pacific Commercial Advertiser, 1881), 28. Also see *Daily Bulletin*, February 28, 1882. Although production faltered for the first few months, their horse-drawn carriages soon delivered ice "to all parts of the city and suburbs at all hours of the day," including interisland deliveries. *Daily Bulletin*, June 30, 1882. The companies struggled both internally and against each other for a stable market share for several years before eventually merging. Reports of "ice famines" in Honolulu were often countered with assurances of functioning factories or announcements of repair. See "Ice! Ice!," *Daily Bulletin*, August 26, 1882; *Saturday Press* [supplement], September 23, 1882; *Daily Bulletin*, September 19, 1884. For more information on the merger, see *Daily Bulletin*, February 20, 1884. After the merger, Wilder shuttered the Mānoa factory and made major updates to his Nu'uanu facility. For public announcements about customer accounts, see *Daily Bulletin*, November 6, 1883. Up-

dates to the Nuʻuanu factory included a new engine and ammonia cooler designed by E. W. Tucker, the chief engineer of the Wilder Steamship Company. "A New Invention," *Pacific Commercial Advertiser*, July 20, 1886; *Hawaiian Gazette*, October 4, 1883; "The Honolulu Ice Works," *Saturday Press*, July 5, 1884. Rees explains that, even into the 1890s, many refrigeration companies lacked knowledgeable engineers who could effectively repair and update equipment, but Tucker's improvements to the Nuʻuanu ice factory appear to have come independently and without foreign instruction. Rees, *Refrigeration Nation*, 46. The new factory was massive, composed of several buildings that held a condenser measuring 100 feet around and 30 feet high; six water tanks 10 feet long, 4 feet wide, and 22 inches deep; a boiler 6 feet long and 16 feet high; and two storerooms, one 18 feet square and 9 feet deep, and the other 9 feet long and 18 feet high with the same depth, with a total capacity for 100 tons of ice. "Wilder's Ice Works," *Daily Bulletin*, October 17, 1884.

53. *Pacific Commercial Advertiser*, May 1, 1875; *Pacific Commercial Advertiser*, April 10, 1875.

54. I interpret na mea akamai, or "smart things," to mean "technology." "Eia Ka Hau Paa," *Ka Nupepa Kuokoa*, March 27, 1875.

55. Arthur Johnstone writes, "Nay, I have a dim recollection of having seen two decades gone Wilder's black, iron-bound chests on the local steamers between islands, which will account for the cooling cups not infrequently enjoyed in plantation porch and wayside hostel throughout the group." Arthur Johnstone, "Storied Nuuanu," in *Hawaiian Almanac and Annual for 1906*, ed. Thomas G. Thrum (Honolulu: Thos. G. Thrum, 1905), 162.

56. "Our Hilo Letter," *Pacific Commercial Advertiser*, July 13, 1872.

57. Parama Roy, *Alimentary Tracts: Appetites, Aversions, and the Postcolonial* (Durham, NC: Duke University Press, 2010), 7.

58. "The Day of Jubilee—Wednesday," *Friend [Jubilee Supplement to the Friend]* 20 (June 18, 1870): 56.

59. *Pacific Commercial Advertiser*, March 17, 1886.

60. This can be dated to probably sometime in the mid-1870s, as determined by the narrative that follows in the book. Malcolm Brown, *Reminiscences of a Pioneer Kauai Family, with References and Anecdotes of Early Honolulu* (Honolulu: Thos. McVeagh, 1918), 14.

61. This was the age of arctic exploration, which was chronicled extensively in newspapers around the globe. On arctic exploration and the world news, see Hampton Sides, *In the Kingdom of Ice: The Grand and Terrible Polar Voyage of the uss Jeanette* (New York: Anchor Books, 2014). For the role of Hawaiian men in the whaling industry and their labor in the Arctic, see chapter 3, "Kealoha in the Arctic," in Gregory Rosenthal, *Beyond Hawaiʻi: Native Labor in the Pacific World* (Berkeley: University of California Press, 2018), 82–104.

62. "Ka Hau," *Ka Lahui Hawaii*, August 9, 1877.

63. Translated from the sentence "Ma ke kau wela ma Amerika, o kau hau kekahi mea e pono ai ka noho ana o kanaka." Later in the article the author refers to "Honolulu nei," using the locational to indicate that they are placing them-

selves in the islands (roughly meaning, "here in Honolulu"). "Ka Hau," *Ka Lahui Hawaii*, August 9, 1877.

64. *Ka Lahui Hawaiʻi*, August 16, 1877. It's not clear whether the illustration used for this story was repurposed from somewhere else or was produced specifically for this story; this is perhaps one reason why the author's description does not seem to always align with the image.

65. "ICE!," *Sam Sly's African Journal: A Register of Facts, Fiction, News, Literature, Commerce, and Amusement*, January 11, 1849, n.p.; "Effects of Cold in Arctic Regions," *The Country Gentleman*, May 28, 1863, 360.

66. Kaori O'Connor, "The Hawaiian Luau," *Food, Culture, and Society* 11, no. 2 (2008): 161.

67. William R. Bliss, *Paradise in the Pacific* (New York: Sheldon and Company, 1873), 40. Archival photographs from the Kalākaua era show Western and Hawaiian styles blended together during royal entertainments. See, in particular, a lūʻau at the Mōʻī's Boathouse ca. 1883, photograph call no. PPWD-15-5-008, HSA.

68. Christine Skwiot, *The Purposes of Paradise: U.S. Tourism and Empire in Cuba and Hawaiʻi* (Philadelphia: University of Pennsylvania Press, 2010).

69. For good descriptions of soda fountain and ice cream parlor environments in the 1870s and 1880s in the United States, see Anne Cooper Funderberg, *Chocolate, Strawberry, and Vanilla: A History of American Ice Cream* (Bowling Green, OH: Bowling Green State University Popular Press, 1995). While generally accepted as a space for "polite" female society, its rise in gendered public culture meant that it was also understood, and policed, as, a potential space of transgression. For an extended discussion of this aspect of ice cream parlors and racial discourse at the turn of the century, see Bill Ellis, "Whispers in an Ice Cream Parlor: Culinary Tourism, Contemporary Legends, and the Urban Interzone," *Journal of American Folklore* 122, no. 483 (2009): 53–74. As a corollary to these discussions of temperature, gender, and public space, also note the early use of air-conditioning in American department stores, as discussed in Ackerman, *Cool Comfort*.

70. Hibbard, *Designing Paradise*, 29.

71. *Hawaiian Gazette*, November 20, 1878.

72. Arvin, *Possessing Polynesians*, 64.

73. Kristin M. McAndrews refers to this phenomenon as "gastrodiplomacy." For more on how this operated within the Hawaiian Kingdom, see Kristin M. McAndrews, "King David Kalakaua's Last Diplomatic Dinner: A Discussion of the Rhetoric of the Menu" (presentation at the Dublin Gastronomy Symposium, Dublin Institute of Technology, Dublin, May 31–June 1, 2016).

74. A survey of the collection of menus at the Hawaiʻi State Archives suggests that prior to the 1870s ice cream was not featured regularly, or at all, at fancy events; after 1875, ice cream appears on nearly all the menus.

75. "Dinner at U.S. Legation," menu, August 25, 1875, HSA.

76. "Menu de Diner a l'Hotel Hawaiʻi," menu, September 17, 1875, HSA.

77. "Day Book, July 1, 1884–August 31, 1886," 429, vol. 34, Correspondence and Record Books of the Chamberlain, HSA.

78. McAndrews, "King David Kalakaua's Last Diplomatic Dinner."

79. Isabella Lucy Bird, *The Hawaiian Archipelago: Six Months among the Palm Groves, Coral Reefs, and Volcanoes of the Sandwich Islands* (New York: J. Putnam's Sons, 1881), 2.

80. Bird, *Hawaiian Archipelago*, 174–78.

81. Bird, *Hawaiian Archipelago*, 180.

82. See Beamer's overview of the Kalākaua reign in *No Mākou Ka Mana*, 176–90, and in Silva, *Aloha Betrayed*, 90–91. In discussing the sumptuous caliber of palace festivities during this time, Ralph Kuykendall has also suggested that the Hawaiian monarchy adopted high pageantry in the same tradition as the British in order to consecrate power in the eyes of both Hawaiians and the American-born who had become so heavily involved in Hawai'i politics. Kuykendall, *Hawaiian Kingdom*, 3:261.

83. One arc lamp was installed at 'Iolani, one at the government building, another at the palace gate, and two on the perimeter bordering King Street. A local insurance executive named Charles Otto Berger had tested the "apparatus and wires" the day before, in anticipation of the public exhibition. "Electric Light," *Pacific Commercial Advertiser*, July 22, 1886.

84. "Electric Light," *Daily Bulletin*, July 22, 1886, 3.

85. "Archives Scrap-book #1," David Forbes, Inventories, pt. II, M-486, HSA.

86. Liza Keānuenueokalani Williams and Vernadette Vicuña Gonzalez, "Indigeneity, Sovereignty, Sustainability, and Cultural Tourism: Hosts and Hostages at 'Iolani Palace, Hawai'i," *Journal of Sustainable Tourism* 25, no. 5 (2017): 668–83.

87. Kalākaua signed the Bayonet Constitution only a few months after his jubilee. An effort led by the Hawai'i Reform Party's Sanford B. Dole and Lorrin A. Thurston, both American sugar planters, the document instituted a revised constitutional monarchy that significantly constrained monarchial power. The constitution is named after the weapons that Hawai'i's Reform Party used to force the agreement. Forbes explains, "The new constitution provided for a continuance of the monarchy, but it effectively stripped the monarch of much of his power. While the king was still able to appoint his cabinet, the cabinet members were by this document now responsible to the legislature. The king's veto could be overruled by a two-thirds vote, and the higher house of the legislature, the Nobles, were henceforth to be elected, not appointed by the monarch." Forbes, *Hawaiian National Bibliography*, 4:232–33.

88. For a brilliant analysis of the rhetorical power of this speech, see Brandy Nālani McDougall, "'We Are Not American': Competing Rhetorical Archipelagos in Hawai'i," in *Archipelagic American Studies*, ed. Brian Russell Roberts and Michelle Ann Stevens (Durham, NC: Duke University Press, 2017), 259–78.

89. This song, first titled "Hymn of Kamehameha I," is now considered the Hawaiian national anthem. Composed in 1875 by the German bandmaster Henry Berger, with lyrics set by Kalākaua, the song honors the leadership of Kamehameha I. For more on the Royal Hawaiian Band and Henry Berger, see David W. Bandy, "Bandmaster Henry Berger and the Royal Hawaiian Band," *Hawaiian Journal of History* 24 (1990): 69–90.

90. Stacy L. Kamehiro, "'Iolani Palace: Spaces of Kingship in Late Nineteenth-Century Hawai'i," *Pacific Studies* 29, nos. 3–4 (2006): 1–3; Stacy L. Kamehiro, *The Arts of Kingship: Hawaiian Art and National Culture of the Kalākaua Era* (Honolulu: University of Hawai'i Press, 2009); Beamer, *No Mākou Ka Mana*. For an outline of the critiques of Kalākaua, see Kristin Zambucka's short biography, *Kalakaua: Hawaii's Last King* (Honolulu: Mana Publishing, 2002), and Helena G. Allen's *Kalakaua: Renaissance King* (Honolulu: Mutual Publishing, 1995). A critique of the king contemporary to his time is also instructive, written the year after the kingdom overthrow. For more, see William de Witt Alexander, *Kalakaua's Reign: A Sketch of Hawaiian History* (Honolulu: Hawaiian Gazette Company, 1894).

91. Michel Foucault, *Security, Territory, Population: Lectures at the Collège de France, 1977–1978*, ed. Michel Senellart, trans. Graham Burchell (New York: Picador, 2007), 315.

4. COLD AND SWEET

1. Daryl Huff, "State Legalizes Hand-Pounded Poi: Governor Signs Bill to Allow Sales of Poi Made Traditional Way," KITV Honolulu, November 23, 2010, http://www.kitv.com/r/28275745/detail.html; Martha Cheng, "Got Pa'i 'ai? Hand-Pounded Pa'i 'ai Now Legal," *Honolulu Magazine*, November 29, 2011, http://www.honolulumagazine.com/Honolulu-Magazine/Biting-Commentary/November-2011/Got-pa'i'ai-Hand-pounded-pa'i'ai-now-legal/.

2. Hawaii Senate Bill 101, "Hand-pounded Poi; Exemption," June 16, 2011, https://legiscan.com/HI/text/SB101/2011.

3. Daryl Huff, "Health Officials Restrict Poi Pioneer: Supporters of Traditional Poi Challenge Health Department," KITV Honolulu, November 23, 2010, http://www.kitv.com/r/25903451/detail.html.

4. Heather Paxson, "Post-Pasteurian Cultures: The Microbiopolitics of Raw-Milk Cheese in the United States," *Cultural Anthropology* 23, no. 1 (2008): 15–47.

5. Following the true name of the Republic and Territory of Hawaii, I write it here with the 'okina omitted. For more on Native Hawaiian resistance to annexation, see Silva, *Aloha Betrayed*. Also see Noelani Goodyear-Ka'ōpua, "Hawai'i: An Occupied Country," *Harvard International Review* 35, no. 3 (2014): 58–62.

6. Tom Coffman, *The Island Edge of America: A Political History of America* (Honolulu: University of Hawai'i Press, 2003), 7–8.

7. Frank Fox, *Problems of the Pacific* (London: Williams and Norgate, 1912), 145.

8. Kauanui, *Hawaiian Blood*; Merry, *Colonizing Hawai'i*; David Keanu Sai, *Ua Mau Ke Ea—Sovereignty Endures: An Overview of the Political and Legal History of the Hawaiian Islands* (Honolulu: Pū'ā Foundation, 2011).

9. Arvin, *Possessing Polynesians*, 68.

10. For more on how settler colonialism manifests as white possession, see Moreton-Robinson, *White Possessive*.

11. *Laws of the Republic of Hawaii Passed by the Legislature at Its Session, 1898* (Honolulu: Republic of Hawaii, 1898), 47–51. This first application of a pure food law in Hawai'i technically came under the laws of the Republic of Hawaii, the provi-

sional government set up after the kingdom's overthrow, but its implementation was nearly simultaneous with the founding of the territorial government. The legislature approved the law on May 16, 1898, and the Newlands Resolution to annex Hawai'i was approved July 7, 1898. For more on the Newlands Resolution, see Alfred S. Hartwell, "The Organization of a Territorial Government for Hawaii," *Yale Law Review* 9, no. 3 (1899): 107–13 (in which he makes a fascinating and deeply racialized argument about the difference in governmental needs between Hawai'i and other US possessions—that because of the American citizens living in Hawai'i, it should be treated more like "Arizona, New Mexico, Oklahoma, and Alaska" rather than like "Puerto Rico, Cuba, the Philippines, and Guam" [107]). The questionable legality of the Newlands Resolution has been the subject of important literature on Hawai'i's history. See J. Kēhaulani Kauanui, "'A Blood Mixture Which Experience Has Shown Furnishes the Very Highest Grade of Citizen Material': Selective Assimilation in a Polynesian Case of Naturalization to U.S. Citizenship," *American Studies* 45, no. 3 (2004): 33–48; Noenoe K. Silva, "I Kū Mau Mau: How Kānaka Maoli Tried to Sustain National Identity within the United States Political System," *American Studies* 45, no. 3 (2004): 9–31; and Ramon Lopez-Reyes, "Hawaiian Sovereignty," *Peace Review* 12, no. 2 (2000): 311–18.

12. Many parallels can be made here between ice cream as a "pure food" in Hawai'i and milk in the American Northeast, if one is to look at concerns over race, cleanliness, modernity, and immigration. See E. Melanie DuPuis, *Nature's Perfect Food: How Milk Became America's Drink* (New York: New York University Press, 2002), 68. For the text of the Wiley Act, see "Federal Food and Drugs Act of 1906," US Food and Drug Administration website, accessed October 3, 2014, http://www.fda.gov/regulatoryinformation/legislation/ucm148690.htm. On Wiley and the making of the act itself, see Oscar E. Anderson, *Health of a Nation: Harvey W. Wiley and the Fight for Pure Food* (Chicago: University of Chicago Press, 1958).

13. Many works on the pure food and drug laws of 1906 establish a connection with the "not entirely coincidental" enactment of the Meat Inspection Act passed through Congress on the same day. See Lorine Swainston Goodwin, *The Pure Food, Drink, and Drug Crusaders, 1879–1914* (Jefferson, NC: McFarland, 2006); Ruth C. Engs, ed., *The Progressive Era's Health Reform Movement: A Historical Dictionary* (Westport, CT: Praeger).

14. For a fascinating overview of the social and economic factors behind the formation of the pure food and drug policies, see Marc T. Law and Gary D. Libecap, "The Determinants of Progressive Era Reform: The Pure Food and Drugs Act of 1906," in *Corruption and Reform: Lessons from America's Economic History*, ed. Edward L. Glaeser and Claudia Goldin (Chicago: University of Chicago Press, 2006), 319–42. As the American food chain grew longer and more complex, the unspoken social contracts between producers and consumers of more insular communities deteriorated. These attitudes are once again popular within American culture, as illustrated, for example, by Michael Pollan's widely read *The Omnivore's Dilemma: A Natural History of Four Meals* (New York: Penguin Books, 2006). Scholars use the term *food chain* to describe the complex movement of food from

farm (or manufacturer) to table. See especially Warren Belasco and Roger Horowitz, eds., *Food Chains: From Farmyard to Shopping Cart* (Philadelphia: University of Pennsylvania Press, 2009), based on a conference held at the Hagley Museum and Library in 2006.

15. Law and Libecap, "Determinants of Progressive Era Reform."

16. KC Councilor, "Feeding the Body Politic: Metaphors of Digestion in Progressive Era US Immigration Discourse," *Communication and Critical/Cultural Studies* 14, no. 2 (2017): 139–59. Also see Kyla Wazana Tompkins, *Racial Indigestion: Eating Bodies in the 19th Century* (New York: New York University Press, 2012); David Cisneros, "Contaminated Communities: The Metaphor of 'Immigrant as Pollutant' in Media Representations of Immigration," *Rhetoric and Public Affairs* 11, no. 4 (2008): 569–601.

17. Michael McGerr, *A Fierce Discontent: The Rise and Fall of the Progressive Movement in America, 1870–1920* (New York: Simon and Schuster, 2003), 163. The battle for pure food and drugs was in large part waged in the popular press, and particularly in women's publications, thus reflecting Benedict Anderson's thesis on media's role in modern nation making in *Imagined Communities: Reflections on the Origin and Spread of Nationalism* (London: Verso, 1983). Also see Benjamin R. Cohen, *Pure Adulteration: Cheating on Nature in the Age of Manufactured Food* (Chicago: University of Chicago Press, 2021), 203. Sylvia Lovegren explains, "The Pure Food and Drug Act of 1906 marked the beginning of effective U.S. federal regulation of food and drug labeling and assurance of a safe food supply. It prohibited the false labeling or adulteration of foods and drugs transported interstate; as such, it was limited in scope. Items produced and sold within a state or territory came under only local laws." Sylvia Lovegren, "Pure Food and Drug Act," in *The Oxford Encyclopedia of Food and Drink in America,* ed. Andrew F. Smith (New York: Oxford University Press, 2004), 484–85. Also see Ilyse D. Barkan, "Industry Invites Regulation: The Passage of the Pure Food and Drug Act of 1906," *American Journal of Public Health* 75 (1985): 18–26.

18. Anderson, *Imagined Communities.*

19. "Honolulu Delicacies," *American Kitchen Magazine* 9, no. 1 (April 1898): xvi.

20. Notably, the Newlands Resolution used to annex Hawai'i to the United States is a resolution and not a treaty, thereby delegitimating US occupation of Hawai'i. Jennifer M. L. Chock, "One Hundred Years of Illegitimacy: International Legal Analysis of the Illegal Overthrow of the Hawaiian Monarchy, Hawai'i's Annexation, and Possible Reparations," *University of Hawaii Law Review* 17 (1995): 463.

21. "Honolulu Delicacies."

22. John R. Musick, *Hawai'i: Our New Possessions* (New York: Funk and Wagnalls Company, 1898), 67.

23. "The Poi Eater's Progress," *Latter-day Saints Millennial Star* 55 (June 5, 1893): 376–77.

24. Delight Sweetser, *One Way around the World* (Indianapolis: Bowen-Merrill Company, 1898), 22.

25. Mark Twain, *Roughing It* (New York: Harper and Brothers, 1899), 230–31.

26. On some of those early ideas about Hawaiian bodies and their foods, see Jennifer Fish Kashay, "Missionaries and Foodways in Early 19th-Century Hawai'i," *Food and Foodways: Explorations in the History and Culture of Human Nourishment* 17, no. 3 (2009): 159–80.

27. Thomas C. Leonard, *Illiberal Reformers: Race, Eugenics, and American Economics in the Progressive Era* (Princeton, NJ: Princeton University Press, 2017); Paul Boyer, *Urban Masses and Moral Order in America, 1820–1920* (Cambridge, MA: Harvard University Press, 1978).

28. DuPuis, *Nature's Perfect Food.*

29. Jeri Quinzio, *Of Sugar and Snow: A History of Ice Cream Making* (Berkeley: University of California Press, 2009), 101.

30. The *Ice Cream Trade Journal* described ice cream's centrality to Fourth of July celebrations, suggesting connections between the food and displays of American nationalism, writing, "Like the artificial making of ice, which can be made in times of no unusual rush and stored for use when a city demands ice at once, ice cream can now be made at leisure and stored for the demands of a Fourth of July crowd." "Value and Importance of the Ice Cream Industry," *Ice Cream Trade Journal* 6 (1910): 17. While Anglo-European cuisine had long been available in Honolulu, food as a form of cultural assimilation flourished in the territory. For example, European-style meals existed nearly as long as haole began missing their foodways after settling in the islands. Christian missionaries set out to teach New England baking and cooking as readily as religion to Hawaiians in the early 1800s, and as boardinghouses sprang up for whalers and business prospectors by the midcentury, fare catered to their stomachs. In one well-known mission's 1837 account of setting up a church in Hilo, the author writes that as the church was being built, "the women and children were cared for by Mrs. Coan and Mrs. Lyman, who taught them habits of neatness and cleanliness, and instructed them in such useful domestic arts as sewing and cooking, making dresses and braiding neat little straw hats." Belle M. Brain, *The Transformation of Hawaii: How American Missionaries Gave a Christian Nation to the World* (New York: Fleming H. Revell Co., 1898), 128–29. Edibles from places like Boston and San Francisco flooded into the port of Honolulu as regular shipping routes were established in the third quarter of the nineteenth century, and grocers regularly advertised newly arrived American and European provisions: fruit pies, teas, curried oysters, plum pudding, tinned codfish, macaroni, cheese, tapioca, ginger snaps, and boxes of raisins. Advertisement for Bolles & Co., *Daily Bulletin*, October 17, 1882.

31. Burton Holmes, *Burton Holmes Travelogue*, vol. 11 (Chicago: Travelogue Bureau, 1919), 29.

32. A piece entitled "In and about Honolulu," published in the *Overland Monthly*, maintained that "nothing about your surroundings [suggests] that you are in the Hawaiian Islands, rather than in New York or San Francisco," and that (in describing an ice cream shop) "judging from the number of feminine patrons congregating in and about the place you might think that a matinee had been let out

somewhere." Milo K. Temple, "In and about Honolulu," *Overland Monthly* (July–December 1908): 223. Also see "New Palm Café Opens Today," *Honolulu Star-Bulletin*, September 21, 1912.

33. In some cases, ice cream existed as the common food denominator in events where Hawaiian fare and haole fare were divided, with a table for each cuisine and with a single dessert table of ice creams. "Society," *Pacific Commercial Advertiser*, September 27, 1903, 6. It should be noted that lūʻau is not a traditional Hawaiian term for feast but goes back only to 1856, with its first usage found in the *Pacific Commercial Advertiser*. Pukui and Elbert, *Hawaiian Dictionary*, 214.

34. Also recommended was a first course of lomi lomi salmon served "in a large glass dish with [a] lump of ice." Jessie C. Turner and Agnes B. Alexander, *How to Use Hawaiian Fruit and Food Products*, 2nd ed. (Honolulu: Paradise-Pacific, 1912), 73. The volume, organized by ingredient, provides directions on how to prepare ice creams and sorbets from most of the fruits listed, such as pineapple, papaya, ʻōhiʻa ʻai (mountain apple), guava, and mango.

35. Charmian London, *Our Hawaii* (New York: Macmillan, 1917), 92.

36. Cuisine wasn't the only thing that distinguished the haole guests from their hosts: London and his wife sat at a table with chairs while the rest of the party ate while sitting on mats on the ground. London, *Our Hawaii*, 97.

37. Florence Margaret Lee, "Domestic Science in the Normal School of Hawaii," *Journal of Home Economics* 2, no. 6 (1910): 647.

38. This according to the recollections of Julia Bryant, who noted that butter remained rare even as ice cream became more popular. June Gutmanis and Julia Bryant, *Oral History Interview with Julia Bryant* (Honolulu: Center for Oral History, 1978), 104–5.

39. "A Kamehameha Native Luau," *Pacific Commercial Advertiser*, December 22, 1907. Examples like this are numerous. Letters written home to America from Carrie Prudence Winter, a young schoolteacher at the Kawaihaʻo Seminary, describe how Hawaiian and haole cuisines mixed particularly well for celebratory meals. The school's Christmas dinner on December 25, 1892, offered separate menus for adults and children, with the children's meal including decidedly more Hawaiian fare to suit the tastes of the Kānaka Maoli students. Winter writes, "The boys and girls had luaued fish and pig, pork, poi, oranges, cake, ice-cream and candy. . . . For the adults at the dinner, many of them Americans, their courses were as follows: "1st—soup. 2nd—fish, limes, potato. 3rd—Turkey and all that goes with it. 4th—chicken pie. 5th—salad. 6th—pie and cake. 7th—plum pudding. 8th—coffee. 9th—nuts, raisins. 10th—fruit. 11th—ice cream and cake." Sandra Bonura and Deborah Day, eds., *An American Girl in the Hawaiian Islands: Letters of Carrie Prudence Winter, 1890–1893* (Honolulu: University of Hawaiʻi Press, 2012), 250.

40. The long-running monthly *Paradise of the Pacific* (later retitled *Honolulu Magazine*) showcased Hawaiʻi to the world. Its first issue ran in 1888 under David Kalākaua's sponsorship and then continued its coverage of the business and social lives of the islands into the territorial period. At the height of its circu-

lation, its advertisements and articles painted a picture of a land with modern businesses, staggering beauty, and a Native culture at the pleasure and service of those who would either visit or invest. The monthly periodical's specially designed cover always reflected the lavishness inside: glossy photographs of elegant hotels; advertisements for modern Honolulu industries; and cheeky talk of Santa Claus, snow, and Christmas traditions as if those things might reflect the experiences of the majority of Hawai'i's residents rather than of the readers who flipped through the pages as if reading a catalog of tropical resources. The 1921 Christmas edition is decorated with red and white plumeria flowers on its cover and full-color reproductions of scenic paintings within.

41. Rawley's Ice Cream advertisement, *Paradise of the Pacific*, December 1921, 132.

42. The Hawai'i Board of Health was established under the reign of Kamehameha III through an 1851 ordinance that carried over into the territorial period. For a fascinating look at the intersection of epidemiology and tourism in Hawai'i, see Public Health Committee, *The Health Story in Hawaii* (Honolulu: Chamber of Commerce of Honolulu, 1947).

43. *Laws of the Territory of Hawaii* (Honolulu: Territory of Hawaii, 1903), 272.

44. An editorial published in the *Pacific Commercial Advertiser*, for example, stated that "the people of these Islands every year are becoming more dependent on imported foods . . . in fact, we are now entirely dependent." "Food and the Price of Wages," *Pacific Commercial Advertiser*, November 11, 1899, 4. The president for the Board of Health for the Hawaiian Kingdom began reporting on unsanitary poi factories and dairies as early as 1892. The legislature hired its first food commissioner, Dr. Edmund C. Shorey, "on or about" May 1, 1899. Robert A. Duncan took over the office between October 1, 1903, and 1910, making Blanchard, who served between July 20, 1910, and June 12, 1913, Hawai'i's third food commissioner. George H. Akau, "Hawaii's Food and Drug Laws," *Food, Drug, and Cosmetic Law Journal* 13, no. 9 (1958): 553–54, 556.

45. "The Pure Food Bill," *Pacific Commercial Advertiser*, February 26, 1906.

46. *Hawaiian Star*, February 28, 1911.

47. Much of this interest in food regulation came from emergent ideas of germ theory, which provided a scientifically "objective" standard by which to measure good food against bad food. Joel Mokyr and Rebecca Stein, "Science, Health, and Household Technology: The Effect of the Pasteur Revolution on Consumer Demand," in *The Economics of New Goods*, ed. Timothy F. Bresnahan and Robert J. Gordon (Chicago: University of Chicago Press, 1997), 161. Hawai'i also regulated milk under its "pure food" act and can easily be read as one example of a much larger US national movement to regulate food associated with particularly vulnerable groups, such as infants and young children. See especially DuPuis, *Nature's Perfect Food*; Kendra Smith Howard, *Pure and Modern Milk: An Environmental History since 1900* (Oxford: Oxford University Press, 2014).

48. "Inspection of Ice Cream to Be Rigid," *Hawaiian Star*, May 15, 1912.

49. Charles Wesley Dunn, ed., *Dunn's Pure Food and Drug Legal Manual* (New

York: Dunn's Pure Food and Drug Legal Manual Corporation, 1912–13), 1953; *Laws of the Territory of Hawaii Passed by the Legislature at Its Regular Session* (Honolulu: Bulletin Publishing Co., 1911), 103. The law is listed as Act 77 and shows two amendments and the addition of a new section that amended section 1043 to include the food standards.

50. These standards, in fact, allowed many poi samples to test consistently to satisfaction while ice cream lagged far behind. E. B. Blanchard to President and Members of the Board of Health, letter, October 27, 1911, Board of Health Records, HSA; *Hawaiian Gazette*, March 14, 1911.

51. In 1909, the American boxer Al Fellows speculated that Kānaka in Honolulu "are pretty fair but would hardly class with [American] boys. Maybe it's because they all eat 'poi,' a native concoction that tastes like billboard paste." "A Day of Excitement in the House of Representatives," *Pacific Commercial Advertiser*, June 8, 1901. Also see Hiʻilei Julia Hobart, "A 'Queer-Looking Compound': Race, Abjection, and the Politics of Hawaiian Poi," *Global Food History* 3, no. 2 (2017): 133–49.

52. "Report of the Food Commissioner and Analyst," *Report of the Board of Health of the Territory of Hawaii* (Honolulu: Bulletin Publishing Company, 1907), 159.

53. "Frozen Problem Fronts Duncan," *Pacific Commercial Advertiser*, October 21, 1909.

54. "Poi as Medium for Cholera Infection," *Hawaiian Gazette*, March 17, 1911; "Poi Proven to Be Source of Cholera," *Hawaiian Gazette*, April 18, 1911.

55. E. A. Mott-Smith to Hon. J. H. Coney, letter, March 7, 1911, Board of Health Records, HSA.

56. E. B. Blanchard to E. A. Mott-Smith, letter, April 18, 1911, Board of Health Records, HSA.

57. The Kailihi poi factory supplied poi rations to three distribution points within the city, at Pālama, "Kawaihau" (this may have been Kawaiahaʻo), and Mōʻiliʻili. E. B. Blanchard to E. A. Mott-Smith, letter, April 18, 1911, Board of Health Records, HSA. The territorial government made a number of provisions to make poi available to the public despite the shutdown. According to Board of Health records, "The Legislature . . . appropriated $2,000.00 for the purpose of making poi available at cost to those who could afford to pay, and free to those who could not pay. The same resolution also provided for the establishment of depots for the distribution of poi under these conditions. Poi is now being purchased and supplied and three depots . . . have been established in accordance with the concurrent resolution." E. A. Mott-Smith to Hon. J. H. Coney, letter, March 7, 1911, Board of Health Records, HSA. This was the case, at least, until the following month, when a controversial county ordinance transferred responsibility from the territorial officer over to a county health office. E. A. Mott-Smith to Hon. J. H. Coney, letter, March 7, 1911, Board of Health Records, HSA; "Health Situation Is Thrown into Confusion by Events of One Day," *Hawaiian Gazette*, April 14, 1911.

58. This was not the first time that city officials had cracked down on poi shops

across the city in the name of sanitation and public health, but it was certainly the largest and most controversial effort because of the widespread closures. See "May Close Poi Shops," *Pacific Commercial Advertiser*, December 31, 1902; and announcements in 1895 of poi shop closures after a cholera outbreak in Honolulu, *Evening Bulletin*, August 30, 1895.

59. "For Regulation of All Chinese Shops Here," *Hawaiian Gazette*, March 17, 1911 (emphasis added).

60. Julia Katz, "Ahuna and the Moʻo: Rethinking Chinese Success in Hawaiian Commercial Food Production," *Pacific Historical Review* 86, no. 4 (2017): 599–631.

61. Many Americans worried that Hawaiʻi would serve as a "stepping-stone" for Chinese to enter the county. There's a large body of literature on American xenophobia and Chinese exclusion. See especially Iris Chang, *The Chinese in America: A Narrative History* (New York: Viking, 2003); Andrew Gyroy, *Closing the Gate: Race, Politics, and the Chinese Exclusion Act* (Chapel Hill: University of North Carolina Press, 1998); and Matthew Frye Jacobson's excellent *Barbarian Virtues: The United States Encounters Foreign Peoples at Home and Abroad, 1876–1917* (New York: Hill and Wang, 2001). For how Chinese exclusion affected Hawaiʻi's population after annexation, see Donald Rowland, "The United Stated and the Contract Labor Question in Hawaii, 1862–1900," *Pacific Historical Review* 2, no. 3 (1933): 249–69; and Adam D. Burns, "A New Pacific Border: William H. Taft, the Philippines, and Chinese Immigration, 1898–1903," *Comparative American Studies* 9, no. 4 (2011): 309–24.

62. "Minutes of a Special Meeting of the Board of Health," April 10, 1911, Board of Health Records, HSA.

63. "Poi Keeps Up Quarantine," *Hawaiian Star*, March 29, 1911, 10.

64. E. B. Blanchard to E. A. Mott-Smith, letter, March 28, 1911, Board of Health Records, HSA. Blanchard also notes that he was unable to communicate sanitary regulations to the poi makers without the help of an interpreter.

65. *Hawaiian Gazette*, February 10, 1911.

66. Blanchard, tasked with overseeing the operation, tested the government-sanctioned poi against his newly devised standards: "First sample, sixty-five and a half per cent of water and thirty-four and a half per cent of solids; second sample, the same; third sample, sixty-one and seven-tenths per cent of water, and thirty-eight and three-tenths per cent of solids." "Analyses of Poi Show, as Rule, Very Poor Quality," *Hawaiian Gazette*, March 14, 1911. Although Mott-Smith asked Blanchard—at least unofficially—to provide accounts of any operational poi shops in order to assess public health risks, regardless of whether the territorial Board of Health had direct jurisdiction over fines and closures, much of the controversy focused on who would be tasked with the new poi inspector position. Mott-Smith felt that any county official tasked with the job would be prone to corruption, protesting the power transfer by insisting "there was an absolute necessity to have health matters in the hand of people who can and who will enforce the regulations fearlessly and without a display of cowardice which comes often to those who depend on their political positions from the electorate." E. A. Mott-

Smith to E. B. Blanchard, letter, April 4, 1911, Board of Health Records, HSA; "Health Situation Is Thrown into Confusion by Events of One Day," *Hawaiian Gazette*, April 14, 1911.

67. "Analyses of Poi Show, as Rule, Very Poor Quality."

68. "Ice Cream Tests," *Hawaiian Gazette*, February 10, 1911.

69. The percentage dropped to 12 percent for fruit or nut ice creams. E. B. Blanchard to [Attorney General of the Territory of Hawaii], letter, September 29, 1910, Board of Health Records, HSA.

70. Outgoing Letters, Food Commissioner, Board of Health Records, HSA.

71. At least seventy-seven of ninety-two vendors had recognizably Japanese or Chinese names as opposed to Caucasian names or simply establishment names (such as Hollister Drug Store or the Palm Café). This number doesn't take into account five missing letters, which may or may not have been Asian dealers (the letters are numbered in the upper-left corner, and the numbers indicate missing letters). Outgoing letters, Food Commissioner, Board of Health Records, HSA.

72. "Rapid Fire Work with Icecream [sic]," *Hawaiian Star*, May 17, 1912.

73. Although local newspapers reported on ice cream regulation generally, court cases specifically followed Japanese ice cream dealers. The dealers identified in the *Evening Bulletin* were H. Ono, S. Deai, Y. Kato, H. Inukai, and M. Maida. "Ice Cream Cases Are Postponed," *Evening Bulletin*, May 29, 1912.

74. "Of forty-seven tests made by Food Chemist A. W. Hansen in August, five or six were found below the required standard, but only one was declared dangerous to health." *Honolulu Star-Bulletin*, September 19, 1913.

75. Edward Blanchard, "Food Commissioner and Analyst Report," letter, June 19, 1913, Board of Health Records, HSA.

76. "Ice Cream Is Now What It Is Called," *Hawaiian Gazette*, May 2, 1911.

77. See Mrs. Hascall's recipe for "Ice Cream." On the same page, a recipe for "Philadelphia Ice Cream," submitted by Mrs. Chas. Grey, includes a quart of cream—perhaps indicating that this is what would make it Philadelphian. *The Hawaiian Cook Book* (Honolulu: Ladies of Fort Street Church, 1882), 55. Even in the book's fourth edition, published in 1896, the inclusion of gelatin in the basic ice cream recipe remains.

78. "Ice Cream Fat Controversy in Police Court," *Hawaiian Star*, August 9, 1911.

79. "Blanchard Will Hold Exhibit in Pure Ice Cream Campaign," *Hawaiian Star*, May 17, 1912.

80. The archives don't indicate what happened with this proposal.

81. "Not Conspiracy, Just a Contract," *Hawaiian Gazette*, March 21, 1911.

82. "Little Interviews," *Hawaiian Star*, May 8, 1911.

83. This quote is attributed to "Dickey," who is probably the prominent Hawai'i architect William Charles Dickey. "A Day of Excitement," *Pacific Commercial Advertiser*, June 8, 1901.

84. "A Day of Excitement."

85. Some in the senate meetings, including "Attorney Achi," believed that the crackdown on poi shops served purely financial purposes—appropriations

that funded poi inspectors in the past had dried up, and the closing of poi shops merely saved funds. *Hawaiian Gazette*, March 31, 1911.

86. Currie had assigned patient numbers to each case and reported his findings with a chart that traced the outbreak to the Mānoa stream as the common denominator. "Minutes of a Special Meeting of the Board of Health," April 15, 1911, Board of Health Records, HSA.

87. "Poi Proven to Be Source of Cholera," *Hawaiian Gazette*, April 18, 1911.

88. "New Regulation Now in Effect," *Hawaiian Gazette*, April 18, 1911.

89. "Pauoa and the Growth of the Taro: Food Supply of the City in Grave Danger," *Pacific Commercial Advertiser*, April 21, 1903.

90. I am building here on Mishuana R. Goeman, "Disrupting a Settler-Colonial Grammar of Place: The Visual Memoir of Hulleah Tsinhnahjinnie," in *Theorizing Native Studies*, ed. Audra Simpson and Andrea Smith (Durham, NC: Duke University Press, 2014), 235–65, and on Henri LeFebvre's theory of the cultural construction of space in *The Production of Space*, trans. Donald Nicholson-Smith (Oxford: Blackwell, 1991).

91. Jocelyn Linnekin, "The *Hui* Lands of Keanae: Hawaiian Land Tenure and the Great Mahele," *Journal of the Polynesian Society* 92, no. 2 (1983): 169–88; Krisnawati Suryanata, "Diversified Agriculture, Land Use, and Agrofood Networks in Hawaii," *Economic Geography* 78, no. 1 (2002): 71–86; Jonathan Goldberg-Hiller and Noenoe K. Silva, "The Botany of Emergence: Kanaka Ontology and Biocolonialism in Hawai'i," *Native American and Indigenous Studies* 2, no. 2 (2015): 1–26.

92. Huff, "Health Officials Restrict Poi Pioneer."

93. See Geoffrey M. White and Ty Kāwika Tengan, "Disappearing Worlds: Anthropology and Cultural Studies in Hawai'i and the Pacific," *Contemporary Pacific* 13, no. 2 (2001): 381–416.

94. Amy Brinker, "Passage of Poi Bill a Major Milestone for Hawai'i," *Civil Beat*, May 5, 2011, http://www.civilbeat.com/2011/05/10763-passage-of-poi-bill-a-major-milestone-for-hawaii/.

5. LOCAL COLOR, RAINBOW AESTHETICS

1. There are no substantial published histories of shave ice, but an overview and conjectures about its origins in Hawai'i are sketched out in Arnold Hiura, *Kau Kau: Cuisine and Culture in the Hawaiian Islands* (Honolulu: Watermark, 2009), 91–92.

2. Jens Manuel Krogstad, "Hawaii Is Home to the Nation's Largest Share of Multicultural Americans," Pew Research Center, June 17, 2015, https://www.pewresearch.org/fact-tank/2015/06/17/hawaii-is-home-to-the-nations-largest-share-of-multiracial-americans/.

3. Advertisement, Pacific Resources, Inc., *Star-Bulletin*, April 29, 1984, 24.

4. For a thorough exploration of pejorative food metaphors, see Irene López-Rodríguez, "Are We What We Eat? Food Metaphors in the Conceptualization of Ethnic Groups," *Linguistik* 69 (2014): 3–36.

5. Arvin, *Possessing Polynesians*, 96–97.

6. Arvin, *Possessing Polynesians*, 99.

7. Haunani-Kay Trask, "Settlers of Color and 'Immigrant' Hegemony: 'Locals' in Hawai'i," *Amerasia Journal* 26, no. 2 (2000): 1–24; Lisa Kahaleole Hall, "Which of These Things Is Not Like the Other: Hawaiians and Other Pacific Islanders Are Not Asian Americans, and All Pacific Islanders Are Not Hawaiian," *American Quarterly* 67, no. 3 (2015): 727–47. Also see Fujikane and Okamura, *Asian Settler Colonialism*; and Teves, "Aloha State Apparatuses." In the past few years there have been increasing critiques of anti-Micronesian racism as a facet of antiblackness within Hawai'i alongside calls for solidarity. See, for example, Craig Santos Perez, "Black Lives Matter in the Pacific," *Ethnic Studies Review* 43, no. 3 (2020): 34–38.

8. Rachel Laudan, *The Food of Paradise: Exploring Hawaii's Culinary Heritage* (Honolulu: University of Hawai'i Press, 1996), 77.

9. Jenn Rice, "Farm-to-Ice: Inside Hawaii's Artisanal Shave Ice Craze," *Vogue*, January 2, 2017, https://www.vogue.com/article/artisanal-shave-ice-hawaii -guide.

10. Dean Itsuji Saranillio, "Colliding Histories: Hawai'i Statehood at the Intersection of Asians 'Ineligible to Citizenship' and Hawaiians 'Unfit for Self-Government,'" *Journal of Asian American Studies* 13, no. 3 (2010): 291.

11. Richard L. Bowen, Linda J. Cox, and Morton Fox, "The Interface between Tourism and Agriculture," *Journal of Tourism Studies* 2, no. 2 (1991): 43–54.

12. Mallory Huard's examination of Dole pineapple's role in twentieth-century American imperialism underscores the plantation's lasting impact on Hawaiian tourism by noting the Dole cannery's continued function as a tourist destination despite the closure of its last factory in the early 1990s. Today, tourists can enjoy field tours and a "pineapple maze" on O'ahu's North Shore, even though the pineapple industry has long been offshore. Mallory Huard, "In Hawai'i, Plantation Tourism Tastes Like Pineapple," *EdgeEffects* (blog), November 12, 2019, https:// edgeeffects.net/dole-pineapple-plantation/.

13. Shana Klein, "'The Perfect Servant': Race, Hygiene, and Canning Machinery at the Dole Hawaiian Pineapple Company," *Food, Fatness, and Fitness: Critical Perspectives* (blog), August 1, 2019, http://foodfatnessfitness.com/2019/08/01/race -hygiene-and-pineapple-cannery/.

14. Costa, "Paradisical Discourse." For more on gender, colonialism, and Hawai'i's tourism industry, see Haunani-Kay Trask, "Lovely Hula Hands: Corporate Tourism and the Prostitution of Hawaiian Culture," *Border/Lines* 23 (1991), 22–34.

15. Glenn R. Carroll and Dennis Ray Wheaton, "Donn, Vic, and Tiki Bar Authenticity," *Consumption Markets and Culture* 22, no. 2 (2019): 157–82.

16. Pardilla, "You Deserve a Mai Tai"; Alicia Kennedy, "One Mai Tai, Hold the Colonialism, Please," *Eater*, October 7, 2019, https://www.eater.com/2019/10/7 /20895319/tiki-tropical-drinks-colonialism-appropriation-lost-lake-pina-colada.

17. Denis Dutton, "Kitsch," *Grove Art Online*, accessed July 31, 2020, https:// www.oxfordartonline.com.

18. Daniel Taulapapa McMullin, "Tiki Kitsch, American Appropriation, and the Disappearance of the Pacific Islander Body," *LUX* 2, no. 1 (2013): 1–6.

19. Trask, "Settlers of Color." Also see Fujikane and Okamura, *Asian Settler Colonialism*; and Dean Itsuji Saranillio, "Why Asian Settler Colonialism Matters: A Thought Piece on Critiques, Debates, and Indigenous Difference," *Settler Colonial Studies* 3 (2013): 280–94. The well-known Massie Case of 1931–32, which resulted in the false accusation of five men (and the murder of Joseph Kahahawai, one of those men) for the alleged rape of a white military wife, Thalia Massie, galvanized local identity against haole newcomers to the islands. As Jonathan Rosa and David Stannard have detailed, the Massie Case powerfully illustrated the racial and class consciousness that emerged at this time for Hawai'i's working-class communities of color, particularly those who lived in neighborhoods in and around Honolulu. Widely reported on during its time, and later commonly included in school curriculum as a case study for Hawai'i's race relations, the Massie Case has been used to understand the tensions between shared histories of racial and class oppression. John P. Rosa, "Local Story: The Massie Case Narrative and the Cultural Production of Local Identity in Hawai'i," *Amerasia Journal* 26, no. 2 (2000): 94. Also see David Stannard, *Honor Killing: Race, Rape, and Clarence Darrow's Spectacular Last Case* (New York: Penguin Books, 2006).

20. Trask, "Settlers of Color," 20. In this way, the study of Asian "local" identity is wedded to the endurance of American settler colonialism, even as it attempts to articulate something other than "Asian American," identity which is grounded in "mainland" contexts. Jonathan Okamura, "Why There Are No Asian Americans in Hawai'i: The Continuing Significance of Local Identity," in *Asian American Family Life and Community*, ed. Franklin Ng (New York: Routledge, 2014), 161–78.

21. Trask, "Settlers of Color." Also see Judy Rohrer, *Staking Claim: Settler Colonialism and Racialization in Hawai'i* (Tucson: University of Arizona Press, 2016).

22. Philip Gleason, "The Melting Pot: Symbol of Fusion or Confusion?," *American Quarterly* 16, no. 1 (1964): 22.

23. Arvin, *Possessing Polynesians*, 100. Also see Romanzo Colfax Adams, *Interracial Marriage in Hawaii: A Study of the Mutually Conditioned Processes of Acculturation and Amalgamation* (New York: Macmillan, 1937).

24. Sidney Lewis Gulick, *Mixing the Races in Hawaii: A Study of the Coming Neo-Hawaiian American Race* (Honolulu: Hawaiian Board Book Rooms, 1937), quoted in John Chock Rosa, "'The Coming of the Neo-Hawaiian American Race': Nationalism and Metaphors of the Melting Pot in Popular Accounts of Mixed-Race Individuals," in *The Sum of Our Parts: Mixed-Heritage Asian Americans*, ed. Teresa Williams-León and Cynthia L. Nakashima (Philadelphia: Temple University Press, 2001), 52.

25. Rosa, "'The Coming of the Neo-Hawaiian American Race,'" 52.

26. Arvin, *Possessing Polynesians*, 122–23.

27. See Rosa, "Local Story."

28. Arvin, *Possessing Polynesians*, 98.

29. For more on the Big Five and Hawai'i's sugar oligopolies, see Carol A. Mac-

Lennan, *Sovereign Sugar: Industry and Environment in Hawai'i* (Honolulu: University of Hawai'i Press, 2014). On union movements, see Moon-Kie Jung, *Reworking Race: The Making of Hawaii's Interracial Labor Movement* (New York: Columbia University Press, 2006).

30. Forced on Kalākaua by a group of haole, this constitution reduced monarchial power while empowering the Hawaiian legislature, which would become filled with wealthy, landed haole. Gregory Rosenthal, "Bayonet Constitution (1887)," in *Imperialism and Expansionism in American History: A Social, Political, and Cultural Encyclopedia and Document Collection*, vol. 1, ed. Chris J. Magoc and David Bernstein (Santa Barbara: ABC-CLIO, 2016), 255–56.

31. Saranillio, "Colliding Histories," 295.

32. Saranillio, "Colliding Histories," 287.

33. Saranillio, "Colliding Histories," 300–301.

34. Trask, "Settlers of Color," 2.

35. Okamura writes that Hawai'i locals believe that "the overall quality of life in Hawaii measured in terms of human relationships cannot be found anywhere else in the world." Jonathan Y. Okamura, "Aloha Kanaka Me Ke Aloha 'Aina: Local Culture and Society in Hawai'i," *Amerasia Journal* 7 (1980): 131.

36. Okamura, "Aloha Kanaka."

37. Davianna Pōmaika'i McGregor, "Statehood: Catalyst of the Twentieth-Century Kanaka 'Ōiwi Cultural Renaissance and Sovereignty Movement," *Journal of Asian American Studies* 13, no. 3 (2010): 313–14.

38. Haunani-Kay Trask, "Birth of the Modern Hawaiian Movement: Kalama Valley, O'ahu," *Hawaiian Journal of History* 21 (1987): 126–53.

39. For an excellent overview of twentieth-century Hawaiian movements and class struggles in Hawai'i, see Noelani Goodyear-Ka'ōpua, "Introduction," in *A Nation Rising: Hawaiian Movements for Life, Land, and Sovereignty*, ed. Noelani Goodyear-Ka'ōpua, Ikaika Hussey, and Erin Kahunawaika'ala (Durham, NC: Duke University Press, 2014), 1–34.

40. As Stephanie Nohelani Teves argues, the appropriation of the Native Hawaiian concept of aloha likewise found its place in American statecraft as a performance of Foucauldian self-discipline through the popular designation of Hawai'i as the "Aloha State," through which Hawai'i's culturally diverse people are compelled to produce an always welcoming, always embracing space despite underlying racial tensions. Teves, "Aloha State Apparatuses," 711–15.

41. One fascinating example pertinent to Hawai'i is the emergence of Hawai'i regional cuisine, which I don't have the space to adequately treat here. See LeeRay Costa and Kathryn Besio, "Eating Hawai'i: Local Foods and Placemaking in Hawai'i Regional Cuisine," *Social and Cultural Geography* 12, no. 8 (2011): 839–54. Also see Kristin M. McAndrews, "Incorporating the Local Tourist at the Big Island Poke Festival," in *Culinary Tourism*, ed. Lucy Long (Lexington: University Press of Kentucky, 2004), 114–27. For scholarship on the intimate links between food and identity across racial, ethnic, cultural, and national categories, see Sidney W. Mintz and Christine M. Du Bois, "The Anthropology of Food and

Eating," *Annual Review of Anthropology* 31 (2002): 99–199; Amy B. Trubek, *Haute Cuisine: How the French Invented the Culinary Profession* (Philadelphia: University of Pennsylvania Press, 2000); Richard R. Wilke, "'Real Belizean Food': Building Local Identity in the Transnational Caribbean," *American Anthropologist* 101, no. 2 (1999): 244–55; Arjun Appadurai, "How to Make a National Cuisine: Cookbooks in Contemporary India," *Comparative Studies in Society and History* 30, no. 1 (1988): 3–24; and Jeffrey M. Pilcher, *¡Que Vivan los Tamales! Food and the Making of Mexican Identity* (Albuquerque: University of New Mexico Press, 1998).

42. Rachel Laudan, "Homegrown Cuisines or Naturalized Cuisines? The History of Food in Hawaii and Hawaii's Place in Food History," *Food, Culture, and Society* 19, no. 3 (2016): 437–59.

43. Laudan, *Food of Paradise*, 23.

44. See Claude Lévi-Strauss's classic and confounding essay "The Culinary Triangle," *Parisian Review* 33, no. 4 (1966): 586–95.

45. Laudan, *Food of Paradise*, 5.

46. Hiura notes, particularly, the ice deliveries that kept Hawai'i refrigerators cold before home electrification and the arrival of ice planers used to make that characteristic shave. Hiura, *Kau Kau*, 91–92.

47. While many communities around the world eat some form of iced dessert, Hawaiian shave ice is understood to descend from Japanese kakigōri, which refreshed elite classes from about the tenth or eleventh century. Whitney Filoon, "Shave Ice, Explained," *Eater* (blog), May 24, 2018, https://www.eater.com/2018/5/24/17376180/shave-ice-shaved-ice-kakigori-dessert-bao-bing-halo-halo.

48. Hiura, *Kau Kau*, 91–92.

49. Filoon, "Shave Ice, Explained."

50. Pioneer Mill Company, "Lahaina Ice Company Financial Reports, 1902–1942," Hawai'i Sugar Planter's Association, Hamilton Library, University of Hawai'i.

51. Pioneer Mill Company, "Lahaina Ice Company Financial Reports."

52. *Statutes of the United States of America, Passed at the Second Session of the Sixtieth Congress, 1908–1909*, pt. 1 (Washington, DC: Government Printing Office, 1909) 609.

53. F. P. McIntyre to the Manager, Honokaa Sugar Company and Pacific Sugar Mill, May 12, 1923, HSC & PSM Stores, C., F. A. Schaefer & Co., 1923, Hamilton Library.

54. "Store Business," May 21, 1923, HSC & PSM Stores, C., F. A. Schaefer & Co., 1923, Hamilton Library; "Store Business," May 9, 1923, HSC & PSM Stores, C., F. A. Schaefer & Co., 1923, Hamilton Library.

55. Violet Hew Zane, "Oral History Interview with Violet Hew Zane," interview by Warren Nishimoto on March 1, 1980, in Lower Pā'ia, Maui (Honolulu: University of Hawai'i at Mānoa Center for Oral History, 1980), 244. Zane's father owned Hew Fat Kee, a long-running store and restaurant in Lower Pā'ia, Maui.

56. I have not been able to find out about price differences between the two.

57. Coffman, *Island Edge of America*.

58. Coffman, *Island Edge of America*, 207.

59. Okamura, "Aloha Kanaka," 132. Locals distinguished themselves from "tourists, mainland Haoles, immigrants, land developers, or big business in general," as those who did not share the same appreciation of Hawai'i's uniqueness.

60. Coffman, *Island Edge of America*, 208.

61. The nickname first appeared in 1923, when the appearance of a rainbow over the football field coincided with an unexpected victory against Oregon State. "Hawaii to Keep 'Rainbow' in Name," *Associated Press*, May 14, 2013; Heather Diamond, *American Aloha: Cultural Tourism and the Negotiation of Tradition* (Honolulu: University of Hawai'i Press, 2008), 59.

62. Susan Yim, "Hawaii's Ethnic Rainbow: Shining Colors, Side by Side," *Honolulu Advertiser*, January 5, 1992, 31–34; and Susan Yim, "Growing Up 'Hapa': Interracial Marriage, Chop Suey Society," *Honolulu Advertiser*, January 5, 1992, 31–34.

63. Yim, "Hawaii's Ethnic Rainbow," 34.

64. Teves, "Aloha State Apparatuses," 715.

65. Strategic sampling of keywords in these newspapers across the twentieth century shows that most instances where "shave ice" is mentioned—at least until the early 1970s—come from advertisements or buy-and-sells for shave ice machines and equipment. Such instances reflect common consumption but do not elaborate cultural meaning. Ice cream also had a discourse increase during this period, but less dramatically so, although with the more voluminous general discourse on ice cream, one or two editorial features would not impact the graph so much.

66. This sample excludes Japanese-, Chinese-, or Hawaiian-language papers, which also circulated and would certainly have communicated specific tastes, ideas, and preferences.

67. Phil Mayer, "The Island's Shave Ice Business Is Not Cooling," *Star-Bulletin*, May 19, 1988, 3.

68. Fred Davis, *Yearning for Yesterday: A Sociology of Nostalgia* (New York: Free Press, 1979).

69. Elspeth Probyn, "Suspended Beginnings: Of Childhood and Nostalgia," GLQ 2 (1995): 439–65.

70. Susan L. Holak and William J. Havlena, "Feelings, Fantasies, and Memories: An Examination of the Emotional Components of Nostalgia," *Journal of Business Research* 42 (1998): 217–26.

71. Patsy Matsuura, "The Shave Ice Is the Same but the Price Has Changed," *Advertiser*, July 30, 1974, 13.

72. Ohnuma, "Aloha Spirit," 377.

73. "About," Island Snow, https://islandsnow.com/pages/copy-of-about-us.

74. The American Girl Doll Company does have a Nez Perce doll, Kaya'aton'my, or "Kaya," who was introduced in 2002. Kaya's story line is set in 1764.

75. Stefania Borghini et al., "Why Are Themed Brand Stores So Powerful? Retail Brand Ideology at *American Girl Place*," *Journal of Retailing* 85, no. 3 (2009): 3.

76. Kirby Larson, *Nanea: Growing Up with Aloha* (Middletown, WI: American

Girl, 2017); Lisa Yee, *Aloha, Kanani* (Middletown, WI: American Girl, 2011); Lisa Yee, *Good Job, Kanani* (Middletown, WI: American Girl, 2017).

77. Obama's vacation house is located within a beachfront estate on Kailuana Place named Paradise Point Estates, off of the main thoroughfare of Kalaheo Avenue, which terminates at the intersection where Island Snow is located. It is coincidental, but perhaps significant, that the property used to be owned by the family of Harold K. L. Castle, which eventually became the powerful real estate development firm and Big Five sugar company Castle & Cooke.

See Candy Evans, "Exclusive Pics: Inside Obama's Hawaiian Hideaway," AOL *Real Estate* (blog), December 31, 2009, http://realestate.aol.com/blog/2009/12/31 /exclusive-pics-inside-obamas-hawaiian-hideaway/; Lawrence Downs, "My Kailua," *New York Times*, September 2, 2011, http://nyti.ms/1DkEX1y.

78. Maeve Reston, "Obama Visits Favorite Shave Ice Shop before a Private New Year's Eve," *Los Angeles Times*, December 31, 2013.

79. The shaka sign, made by extending the little finger and the thumb from an otherwise closed fist is the universal symbol for "hang loose," akin to "take it easy." For more, read June Watanabe, "Wherever It Came From, Shaka Sign Part of Hawai'i," *Star-Bulletin*, March 31, 2002, http://archives.starbulletin.com/2002 /03/31/news/kokualine.html.

80. Credit for this joke goes to a lifetime Kailua resident, Steven Parker. I can attest to the truth in this humor—I grew up in one of Kailua's small neighborhoods that can only be accessed by the two-lane road that meets Island Snow from the opposite direction. During Obama's visits as US president, it was near impossible to pass the intersection to get into town.

81. Nitasha Tamar Sharma, *Hawai'i Is My Haven: Race and Indigeneity in the Black Pacific* (Durham, NC: Duke University Press, 2021), 11.

82. To counteract widespread associations in Hawai'i between blackness and military employment, for example, Black locals like Obama tend to "emphasize their localness," writes Sharma, in order to perform belonging to Hawai'i. Sharma, *Hawai'i Is My Haven*, 75.

83. Erin Suzuki, *Ocean Passages: Navigating Pacific Islander and Asian American Literatures* (Philadelphia: Temple University Press, 2021), 128.

84. Jonathan Y. Okamura, "Barack Obama as the Post-racial Candidate for a Post-racial America: Perspectives from Asian America and Hawai'i," *Patterns of Prejudice* 45, nos. 1–2 (2011): 133–53.

85. Okamura, "Barack Obama," 149–50.

86. In or around 2009 the name of the base was officially changed to Marine Corps Base Hawaii. In 2004, the US Department of Defense reported that the military controls 236,303 acres of land in the State of Hawai'i, with 161 total military installations. On the island of O'ahu, the acreage constitutes 22.4 percent of land area, making it one of the most militarized places in the nation. US Department of Defense, Office of the Deputy Under Secretary of Defense (Installations & Environment), Base Structure Report, Fiscal Year 2004 Baseline, accessed February 12, 2006, http://www.acq.osd.mil/ie/ irm/index.html. On the

consequences of this militarization on Kanaka Maoli self-determination, see Haunani-Kay Trask, "Politics in the Pacific Islands: Imperialism and Native Self-Determination," *Amerasia* 16, no. 1 (1990): 1–19.

87. Malia Zimmerman, "Obama's Million Dollar Hawaiian Vacation: Costs to Taxpayers Detailed," *Hawai'i Reporter*, December 28, 2010, http://www.hawaii reporter.com/president-obamas-million-dollar-plus-trip-to-hawaii-costs-to -taxpayers-detailed.

88. Jonathan Y. Okamura, "The Illusion of Paradise: Privileging Multiculturalism in Hawai'i," in *Making Majorities: Constituting the Nation in Japan, Korea, China, Malaysia, Fiji, Turkey, and the United States* (Stanford, CA: Stanford University Press, 1998), 264–84.

CONCLUSION

1. Across the years that activists have been protecting Maunakea, social media posts have noted the presence of Poli'ahu, a deity who materializes as snow. For more on this, see Hi'ilei Julia Hobart, "At Home on the Mauna: Ecological Violence and Fantasies of Terra Nullius on Maunakea's Summit," *Native American and Indigenous Studies* 6, no. 2 (2019): 30.

2. Dernie Waikiki, Zoom interview by author, September 19, 2020.

3. Majorie Devault, "Conflict and Deference," in *Food and Culture: A Reader*, 2nd ed., ed. Carole Counihan and Penny Van Estrick (New York: Routledge, 1997), 180–99.

4. This question is informed, in part, by Hannah Landecker's observation that the freezer, once novel and now banal, shapes the conditions of possibility for cloned life. Hannah Landecker, "Living Differently in Time: Plasticity, Temporality, and Cellular Biotechnologies," in *Technologized Images, Technologized Bodies*, ed. Jeanette Edwards, Penelope Harvey, and Peter Wade (New York: Berghahn Books, 2010), 217.

5. Press release, the Pu'uhuluhulu 'Ohana, March 14, 2020, https://static1 .squarespace.com/static/5d34aee654c6af0001463826/t/5e6dcc8973af576a4f80f33d /1584254091540/COVID-19+Puuhuluhulu.pdf.

6. Jenny Powers, "Sales of the 'Everlasting,' Beloved Product Spam Have Skyrocketed during Coronavirus as Long-Time Fans Stock Up," *Business Insider*, May 21, 2020, https://www.businessinsider.com/hormel-foods-spam-sales -skyrocketed-pandemic-bloggers-fans-stock-up-2020-5.

7. Andrew Gomes, "COVID-19 Is New Pestilence for Hawaii Farmers," *Star Advertiser*, April 20, 2020, https://www.staradvertiser.com/2020/04/20/hawaii-news /covid-19-is-new-pestilence-for-hawaii-farmers/.

8. José I. Fusté, "Repeating Islands of Debt: Historicizing the Transcolonial Relationality of Puerto Rico's Economic Crisis," *Radical History Review* 128 (2017): 94.

9. Adriana Garriga-López, "Puerto Rico: The Future in Question," *Shima* 13, no. 2 (2019): 183.

10. Hanna Garth, *Food in Cuba: The Pursuit of a Decent Meal* (Palo Alto, CA: Stanford University Press, 2020), 77.

11. The term *food apartheid* comes from food activist Karen Washington. See Anna Brones, "Karen Washington: It's Not a Food Desert, It's Food Apartheid," *Guernica*, May 7, 2018.

12. Sara Mattison, "Refrigerator, Freezer Stock Impacted by COVID-19," KHON2, September 16, 2020, https://www.khon2.com/coronavirus/refrigerator -freezer-stock-impacted-by-covid-19/.

13. Or, as they shut down in the wake of outbreaks. See, as one example of many, Gosia Wozniacka, "Poor Conditions at Meatpacking Plants Have Long Put Workers at Risk. The Pandemic Makes It So Much Worse," *Civil Eats*, April 17, 2020.

14. Alina Selyukh, "Why It's So Hard to Buy a New Refrigerator These Days," Hawai'i Public Radio, September 22, 2020, https://www.hawaiipublicradio.org /post/shortage-new-refrigerators-leaves-appliance-shoppers-out-cold#stream/o.

15. *Normative* operates as a keyword here, with attention to who is not afforded the "necessity" of refrigeration, as well as the invisibilized conditions of peoples and homelands from which the raw materials of biotechnology are extracted. Macarena Gómez-Barris, *The Extractive Zone: Social Ecologies and Decolonial Perspectives* (Durham, NC: Duke University Press, 2017).

16. Joanna Radin, "The Secret Weapon for Distributing a Potential Covid-19 Vaccination," *Washington Post*, November 12, 2020, https://www.washington post.com/outlook/2020/11/12/secret-weapon-distributing-potential-covid-19 -vaccine/. For more on cryopolitics and the biomedical industry's relationship with Indigenous peoples, see Emma Kowal and Joanna Radin, "Indigenous Biospecimen Collections and the Cryopolitics of Frozen Life," *Journal of Sociology* 51, no. 1 (2015): 63–80.

17. Pranav Baskar, "What Is a Cold Chain? And Why Do So Many Vaccines Need It?," NPR, February 24, 2021, https://www.npr.org/sections/goatsandsoda/2021 /02/24/965835993/what-is-a-cold-chain-and-why-do-so-many-vaccines-need-it.

18. This is a favorite refrain of notable local chef Mark Noguchi. "The Great Equalizer: Chef Gooch on the Power of Good Food," *Olukai* (blog), October 31, 2019, https://olukai.com/blogs/news/the-greatequalizer-chef-gooch-on-the -power-of-good-food.

19. There is robust scholarship around the importance of centering Indigenous foods as pathways to health and even decolonization, which this chapter does not deny the validity of; there are also crucial connections to be made about the revitalization of Indigenous cuisine's connection to territorial sovereignty. Some recent and important examples related to Hawai'i include essays by Charlie Reppun, Noa Kekuewa Lincoln, and the staff at Kua'āina Ulu 'Auamo, published in Noelani Goodyear-Ka'ōpua, Craig Howes, Jonathan Kay Kamakawiwo'ole Osorio, and Aiko Yamashiro, eds. *The Value of Hawai'i 3: Hulihia, the Turning* (Honolulu: University of Hawai'i Press, 2020).

20. Winona LaDuke and Deborah Cowen, "Beyond Wiindigo Infrastructure," *South Atlantic Quarterly* 119, no. 2 (2020): 245. They powerfully state that "infra-

structure is the *how* of settler colonialism, and the settler colony is where the Wiindigo runs free."

21. Food sovereignty broadly speaks to concerns over community health, traditional knowledges, land rights, cultural resurgence, and environmental sustainability for Indigenous communities. Devon Mihesuah and Elizabeth M. Hoover, *Indigenous Food Sovereignty in the United States: Restoring Cultural Knowledge, Protecting Environments, and Regaining Health* (Norman: University of Oklahoma Press, 2019).

22. Spice, "Fighting Invasive Infrastructures," 48.

23. Vivian Choi gives an excellent overview of infrastructure studies and its many foci in "Infrastructures of Feeling: The Sense and Governance of Disasters in Sri Lanka," in *Disastrous Times: Beyond Environmental Crisis in Urbanizing Asia*, ed. Eli Elinoff and Tyson Vaughan (Philadelphia: University of Pennsylvania Press, 2020), 83–101. For more on infrastructures as a dispossessive force, see Dana E. Powell, *Landscapes of Power: Politics and Energy in the Navajo Nation* (Durham, NC: Duke University Press, 2018); Andrew Needham, *Power Lines: Phoenix and the Making of the American Southwest* (Princeton, NJ: Princeton University Press, 2014); Spice, "Fighting Invasive Infrastructures."

24. Others have theorized water infrastructures as "leaky" to describe the challenge of repair, indicating that these aging infrastructures fall apart like a sieve. Nikhil Anand, "Leaky States: Water Audits, Ignorance, and the Politics of Infrastructure," *Public Culture* 27, no. 2 (2015): 305–30.

25. Shannon Mattern, "Maintenance and Care," *Places Journal* (November 2018), https://doi.org/10.22269/181120.

26. Ruth Wilson Gilmore, "Beyond Pipeline and Prisons: Infrastructures of Abolition with Ruth Wilson Gilmore and Winona LaDuke," keynote conversation, Ryerson University Social Justice Week, October 26, 2020.

27. I am thinking specifically here about the work of James Balog and his documentary film *Chasing Ice* (2012). I write more about this phenomenon in detail in Hiʻilei Julia Hobart, "Atomic Histories and Elemental Futures across Indigenous Oceans," *Media+Environment* 3, no. 1 (2021): 1–19.

28. Smith, "'Exceeding Beringia'"; Carol Farbotko, "Wishful Sinking: Disappearing Islands, Climate Refugees, and Cosmopolitan Experimentation," *Asia Pacific Viewpoint* 51, no. 1 (2010): 47–60.

Ackermann, Marsha E. *Cool Comfort: America's Romance with Air-Conditioning.* Washington, DC: Smithsonian Books, 2002.

Adams, Romanzo Colfax. *Interracial Marriage in Hawaii: A Study of the Mutually Conditioned Processes of Acculturation and Amalgamation.* New York: Macmillan, 1937.

Adas, Michael. *Dominance by Design: Technological Imperatives and America's Civilizing Mission.* Cambridge, MA: Harvard University Press, 2006.

Aikau, Hōkūlani K., and Donna Ann Kamehaʻikū Camvel. "Cultural Traditions and Food: Kānaka Maoli and the Production of Poi in the Heʻeʻia Wetland." *Food, Culture, and Society* 19, no. 3 (2016): 539–61.

Akau, George H. "Hawaii's Food and Drug Laws." *Food, Drug, and Cosmetic Law Journal* 13, no. 9 (1958): 551–63.

Alexander, William de Witt. *Kalakaua's Reign: A Sketch of Hawaiian History.* Honolulu: Hawaiian Gazette Company, 1894.

Allen, Helena G. *Kalakaua: Renaissance King.* Honolulu: Mutual Publishing, 1995.

Anand, Nikhil. "Leaky States: Water Audits, Ignorance, and the Politics of Infrastructure." *Public Culture* 27, no. 2 (2015): 305–30.

Anderson, Benedict. *Imagined Communities: Reflections on the Origin and Spread of Nationalism.* London: Verso, 1983.

Anderson, Oscar Edward. *Health of a Nation: Harvey W. Wiley and the Fight for Pure Food.* Chicago: University of Chicago Press, 1958.

Anderson, Oscar Edward. *Refrigeration in America: A History of a New Technology and Its Impact.* Princeton, NJ: Princeton University Press, 1953.

Anderson, Rufus. *A Heathen Nation Evangelized: History of the Sandwich Islands Mission.* Cambridge, MA: H. O. Houghton, 1870.

Anderson, Rufus. *History of the Sandwich Islands Mission.* Boston: Congregational Publishing Society, 1870.

Anderson, Warwick. "Climates of Opinion: Acclimatization in Nineteenth-Century France and England." *Victorian Studies* 35, no. 2 (1992): 135–57.

Anderson, Warwick. *Colonial Pathologies: American Tropical Medicine, Race, and Hygiene in the Philippines.* Durham, NC: Duke University Press, 2006.

Appadurai, Arjun. "How to Make a National Cuisine: Cookbooks in Contemporary India." *Comparative Studies in Society and History* 30, no. 1 (1988): 3–24.

Appleton's Illustrated Hand-Book of American Winter Resorts. New York: D. Appleton and Company, 1895.

Arista, Noelani. *The Kingdom and the Republic: Sovereign Hawai'i and the Early United States*. Philadelphia: University of Pennsylvania Press, 2019.

Arista, Noelani, and Judy Kertész. "Aloha Denied." *Hawaii Independent*, February 25, 2014. https://thehawaiiindependent.com/story/aloha-denied.

Arnold, David. *The Tropics and the Traveling Gaze: India, Landscape, and Science, 1800–1856*. Seattle: University of Washington Press, 2006.

Arvin, Maile Renee. "Pacifically Possessed: Scientific Production and Native Hawaiian Critique of the 'Almost White' Polynesian Race." PhD diss., uc San Diego, 2013.

Arvin, Maile Renee. *Possessing Polynesians: The Science of Settler Colonial Whiteness in Hawai'i and Oceania*. Durham, NC: Duke University Press, 2019.

Asaka, Ikuko. *Tropical Freedom: Climate, Settler Colonialism, and Black Exclusion in the Age of Emancipation*. Durham, NC: Duke University Press, 2017.

Atkins, Peter. "Temperature." In *Chemistry: Foundations and Applications*, edited by J. J. Lagowski, vol. 4, 206–9. New York: Macmillan Reference USA, 2004.

Baker, Lee D. "Missionary Positions." In *Globalization and Race: Transformations in the Cultural Production of Blackness*, edited by Kamari Maxine Clarke and Deborah A. Thomas, 37–54. Durham, NC: Duke University Press, 2006.

Baker, Ray Jerome. *Honolulu in 1853*. Honolulu: Ray Jerome Baker, 1950.

Baker, Ray Jerome. *Honolulu in 1870: A Series of Ten Rare and Hitherto Unpublished Photographs*. [Honolulu]: [R. J. Baker], [1951].

Baker, Ray Jerome. *Honolulu Then and Now: A Photographic Record of Progress in the City of Honolulu. Illustrated with 172 Original Photographic Prints*. Honolulu: R. J. Baker, 1941.

Ballou, Maturin Murray. *Travels under the Southern Cross: Travels in Australia, Tasmania, New Zealand, Samoa, and Other Pacific Islands*. 2nd ed. Boston: Houghton Mifflin, 1887.

Bandy, David W. "Bandmaster Henry Berger and the Royal Hawaiian Band." *Hawaiian Journal of History* 24 (1990): 69–90.

Banner, Stuart. "Preparing to Be Colonized: Land Tenure and Legal Strategy in Nineteenth-Century Hawai'i." *Law and Society Review* 39, no. 2 (2005): 273–314.

Barkan, Ilyse D. "Industry Invites Regulation: The Passage of the Pure Food and Drug Act of 1906." *American Journal of Public Health* 75 (1985): 18–26.

Baskar, Pranav. "What Is a Cold Chain? And Why Do So Many Vaccines Need It?" NPR, February 24, 2021. https://www.npr.org/sections/goatsandsoda/2021/02/24/965835993/what-is-a-cold-chain-and-why-do-so-many-vaccines-need-it.

Beamer, Kamanamaikalani. *No Mākou Ka Mana: Liberating the Nation*. Honolulu: Kamehameha Publishing, 2014.

Beattie, Donald A. *Taking Science to the Moon: Lunar Experiments and the Apollo Program*. Baltimore, MD: Johns Hopkins University Press, 2001.

Beckwith, Martha. *Hawaiian Mythology*. Alexandria, VA: Library of Alexandria, 1970.

Beechert, Edward D. *Working in Hawai'i: A Labor History*. Honolulu: University of Hawai'i Press, 1985.

Beeton, Isabella Mary. *The Book of Household Management*. London: S. O. Beeton, 1861.

Belasco, Warren, and Roger Horowitz, eds. *Food Chains: From Farmyard to Shopping Cart*. Philadelphia: University of Pennsylvania Press, 2009.

Benjamin, Samuel Greene Wheeler. *The Life and Adventures of a Free Lance*. Burlington, VT: Free Press, 1914.

Bennett, Chauncey C. "Death of King Kamehameha III." In *Sketches of Hawaiian History and Honolulu Directory*, 38. Honolulu: C. C. Bennett, 1871.

Bentley, Amy. "Islands of Serenity: Gender, Race, and Ordered Meals during World War II." *Food and Foodways* 6, no. 2 (1996): 131–56.

Berlant, Lauren. *Cruel Optimism*. Durham, NC: Duke University Press, 2011.

Bingham, Hiram. *A Residence in Twenty-One Years in the Sandwich Islands*. 1847. New York: Praeger, 1969.

Bird, Isabella Lucy. *The Hawaiian Archipelago: Six Months among the Palm Groves, Coral Reefs, and Volcanoes of the Sandwich Islands*. New York: J. Putnam's Sons, 1881.

Birkett, Mary Ellen. "Forging French Policy in the Pacific." *French Colonial History* 8 (2007): 155–69.

Blackhawk, Ned. *Violence over the Land: Indians and Empires in the Early American West*. Cambridge, MA: Harvard University Press, 2009.

Bliss, William R. *Paradise in the Pacific*. New York: Sheldon and Company, 1873.

Bonura, Sandra, and Deborah Day, eds. *An American Girl in the Hawaiian Islands: Letters of Carrie Prudence Winter, 1890–1893*. Honolulu: University of Hawai'i Press, 2012.

Borghini, Stefania, Nina Diamond, Robert V. Kozinets, Mary Ann McGrath, Albert M. Muñiz Jr., and John F. Sherry Jr. "Why Are Themed Brand Stores So Powerful? Retail Brand Ideology at *American Girl Place*." *Journal of Retailing* 85, no. 3 (2009): 363–75.

Boulze, D., P. Montastruc, and M. Cabanac. "Water Intake, Pleasure, and Water Temperature in Humans." *Physiology and Behavior* 30, no. 1 (1983): 97–102.

Bourdieu, Pierre. *Distinction: A Social Critique on the Judgement of Taste*. Cambridge, MA: Harvard University Press, 1984.

Bowen, Richard L., Linda J. Cox, and Morton Fox. "The Interface between Tourism and Agriculture." *Journal of Tourism Studies* 2, no. 2 (1991): 43–54.

Bowker, Geoffrey C., and Susan Leigh Star. *Sorting Things Out: Classification and Its Consequences*. Cambridge, MA: MIT Press, 2000.

Boyer, Paul. *Urban Masses and Moral Order in America, 1820–1920*. Cambridge, MA: Harvard University Press, 1978.

Brain, Belle M. *The Transformation of Hawaii: How American Missionaries Gave a Christian Nation to the World*. New York: Fleming H. Revell Co., 1898.

Brinker, Amy. "Passage of Poi Bill a Major Milestone for Hawaii." *Honolulu Civil*

Beat, May 5, 2011. http://www.civilbeat.com/2011/05/10763-passage-of-poi-bill
-a-major-milestone-for-hawaii/.

Brones, Anna. "Karen Washington: It's Not a Food Desert, It's Food Apartheid."
Guernica, May 7, 2018.

Brower, Andrea. "Hawai'i: GMO Ground Zero." *Capitalism, Nature, Socialism* 26,
no. 1 (2016): 68–86.

Brown, Malcolm. *Reminiscences of a Pioneer Kauai Family, with References and Anecdotes of Early Honolulu*. Honolulu: Thos. McVeagh, 1918.

Brown, Marie Alohalani. "He 'Ōlelo Wehehe: An Explanation for Readers." In *Facing the Spears of Change: The Life and Legacy of John Papa 'Ī'i*, ix–xiii. Honolulu:
University of Hawai'i Press, 2016.

Brown, Marie Alohalani. "Mauna Kea: Ho'omana Hawai'i and Protecting the
Sacred." *Journal for the Study of Religion, Nature, and Culture* 10, no. 2 (2016):
150–70.

Brown, Marilyn. "'Āina under the Influence: The Criminalization of Alcohol in
19th-Century Hawai'i." *Theoretical Criminology* 7, no. 1 (2003): 89–110.

Bryson, Bill. *At Home: A Short History of Private Life*. London: Doubleday, 2010.

Burns, Adam D. "A New Pacific Border: William H. Taft, the Philippines, and Chinese Immigration, 1898–1903." *Comparative American Studies* 9, no. 4 (2011):
309–24.

Byrd, Jodi A. *The Transit of Empire: Indigenous Critiques of Colonialism*. Minneapolis: University of Minnesota Press, 2011.

Camacho, Keith, and Laurel A. Monnig. "Uncomfortable Fatigues." In *Militarized
Currents: Toward a Decolonized Future in Asia and the Pacific*, edited by Setsu Shi-
gematsu and Keith L. Camacho, 147–80. Minneapolis: University of Minnesota
Press, 2010.

Caron, Will. "Mauna Kea and the Awakening of the Lahui." *Hawai'i Independent*,
April 26, 2015. https://thehawaiiindependent.com/story/mauna-kea-and-the
-awakening-of-the-lahui.

Carr, Sara Jensen. "Alien Landscapes: NASA, Hawai'i, and Interplanetary Occupation." *Avery Review* 50 (2021). http://www.averyreview.com/issues/50/alien
-landscapes.

Carroll, Glenn R., and Dennis Ray Wheaton. "Donn, Vic, and Tiki Bar Authenticity." *Consumption Markets and Culture* 22, no. 2 (2019): 157–82.

Carroll, Rick. "Frozen Assets: The Shave Ice Syrup Tycoon of Hawaii." *Advertiser*,
August 8, 1985, 21.

Case, Emalani. *Everything Ancient Was Once New: Indigenous Persistence from Hawai'i to Kahiki*. Honolulu: University of Hawai'i Press, 2021.

Case, Emalani. "I ka Piko, To the Summit: Resistance from the Mountain to the
Sea." *Journal of Pacific History* 54, no. 2 (2019): 166–81.

Casumbal-Salazar, Iokepa. "A Fictive Kinship: Making 'Modernity,' 'Ancient Hawaiians,' and the Telescopes on Mauna Kea." *Native American and Indigenous
Studies* 4, no. 2 (2017): 1–30.

Casumbal-Salazar, Iokepa. *First Light: Kanaka ʻŌiwi Resistance to Telescopes on Mauna a Wākea*. Minneapolis: University of Minnesota Press, forthcoming.

Casumbal-Salazar, Iokepa. "Multicultural Settler Colonialism and Indigenous Struggle in Hawaiʻi: The Politics of Astronomy on Mauna a Wākea." PhD diss., University of Hawaiʻi, 2014.

"Celsius Temperature Scale." *Encyclopædia Britannica Online*. Accessed July 23, 2015. http://www.britannica.com/technology/Celsius-temperature-scale.

Chakrabarty, Dipesh. "The Climate of History: Four Theses." *Critical Inquiry* 35, no. 2 (2009): 197–222.

Chan, Gaye, and Nandita Sharma. "Eating in Public." Lecture, Department of Social and Cultural Analysis, New York University, New York, October 27, 2015.

Chang, David A. *The World and All the Things upon It: Native Hawaiian Geographies of Exploration*. Minneapolis: University of Minnesota Press, 2016.

Chang, Iris. *The Chinese in America: A Narrative History*. New York: Viking, 2003.

Chang, Williamson, and Abbey Seitz. "It's Time to Acknowledge Native Hawaiians' Special Right to Housing." *Civil Beat*, January 8, 2021. https://www.civilbeat.org/2021/01/its-time-to-acknowledge-native-hawaiians-special-right-to-housing/.

Chapin, Helen Geracimos. *Shaping History: The Role of Newspapers in Hawaiʻi*. Honolulu: University of Hawaiʻi Press, 1996.

Cheney, George L., Rev. "Hawaii." *Unitarian Register*, January 6, 1898, 8–9.

Cheng, Martha. "Got Paʻi ʻai? Hand-Pounded Paʻi ʻai Now Legal." *Honolulu Magazine*, November 29, 2011. http://www.honolulumagazine.com/Honolulu-Magazine/Biting-Commentary/November-2011/Got-paʻiʻai-Hand-pounded-paʻiʻai-now-legal/.

Chock, Jennifer M. L. "One Hundred Years of Illegitimacy: International Legal Analysis of the Illegal Overthrow of the Hawaiian Monarchy, Hawaiʻi's Annexation, and Possible Reparations." *University of Hawaii Law Review* 17 (1995): 463–512.

Choi, Vivian. "Infrastructures of Feeling: The Sense and Governance of Disasters in Sri Lanka." In *Disastrous Times: Beyond Environmental Crisis in Urbanizing Asia*, edited by Eli Elinoff and Tyson Vaughan, 83–101. Philadelphia: University of Pennsylvania Press, 2020.

Cisneros, David. "Contaminated Communities: The Metaphor of 'Immigrant as Pollutant' in Media Representations of Immigration." *Rhetoric and Public Affairs* 11, no. 4 (2008): 569–601.

Coffman, Tom. *The Island Edge of America: A Political History of America*. Honolulu: University of Hawaiʻi Press, 2003.

Cohen, Benjamin R. *Pure Adulteration: Cheating on Nature in the Age of Manufactured Food*. Chicago: University of Chicago Press, 2021.

Connelly, Sean. "Urbanism as Island Living in Honolulu." *Civil Beat*, August 21, 2014. https://www.civilbeat.org/2014/08/urbanism-as-island-living-in-honolulu/.

Cook, Kealani R. "Kahiki: Native Hawaiian Relationships with Other Pacific Islanders, 1850–1915." PhD diss., University of Michigan, 2001.

Cook, Kealani R. *Return to Kahiki: Native Hawaiians in Oceania*. Cambridge: Cambridge University Press, 2018.

Corney, Peter. *Voyages in the Northern Pacific*. Honolulu: Thos. G. Thrum, 1896.

Costa, Janeen Arnold. "Paradisical Discourse: A Critical Analysis of Marketing and Consuming in Hawai'i." *Consumption Markets and Culture* 1, no. 4 (1998): 303–46.

Costa, LeeRay, and Kathryn Besio. "Eating Hawai'i: Local Foods and Placemaking in Hawai'i Regional Cuisine." *Social and Cultural Geography* 12, no. 8 (2011): 839–54.

Coulthard, Glen. *Red Skin, White Masks: Rejecting the Colonial Politics of Recognition*. Minneapolis: University of Minnesota Press, 2014.

Councilor, KC. "Feeding the Body Politic: Metaphors of Digestion in Progressive Era US Immigration Discourse." *Communication and Critical/Cultural Studies* 14, no. 2 (2017): 139–59.

Cronon, William. *Nature's Metropolis: Chicago and the Great West*. New York: Norton, 1991.

Cronon, William. "The Trouble with Wilderness; or, Getting Back to the Wrong Nature." In *Uncommon Ground: Toward Reinventing Nature*, edited by William Cronon, 7–28. New York: Norton, 1995.

Crosby, Alfred. *The Columbian Exchange: Biological and Cultural Consequences of 1492*. Westport, CT: Greenwood, 1972.

Cruikshank, Julie. *Do Glaciers Listen? Local Knowledge, Colonial Encounters, and Social Imagination*. Vancouver: University of British Columbia Press, 2005.

Curley, Andrew. "Infrastructures as Colonial Beachheads: The Central Arizona Project and the Taking of Navajo Resources." *Environment and Planning D: Society and Space* 39, no. 3 (2021): 387–404.

Davis, Fred. *Yearning for Yesterday: A Sociology of Nostalgia*. New York: Free Press, 1979.

Daws, Gavan. "Decline of Puritanism at Honolulu in the Nineteenth Century." *Hawaiian Journal of History* 1 (1967): 31–42.

Daws, Gavan. "Honolulu in the 19th Century: Notes on the Emergence of Urban Society in Hawai'i." *Journal of Pacific History* 2 (1967): 77–96.

Deloria, Philip J. *Indians in Unexpected Places*. Lawrence: University Press of Kansas, 2004.

Devault, Majorie. "Conflict and Deference." In *Food and Culture: A Reader*, 2nd ed., edited by Carole Counihan and Penny Van Estrick, 180–99. New York: Routledge, 1997.

Diamond, Heather. *American Aloha: Cultural Tourism and the Negotiation of Tradition*. Honolulu: University of Hawai'i Press, 2008.

Dickason, David G. "The Nineteenth-Century Indo-American Ice Trade: A Hyperborean Epic." *Modern Asian Studies* 25, no. 1 (1991): 53–89.

Dodds, Klaus, and Christy Collis. "Post-colonial Antarctica." In *Handbook on the*

Politics of Antarctica, edited by K. Dodds, A. D. Hemmings, and P. Roberts, 50–68. Cheltenham: Edward Elgar, 2017.

Douglas, Mary. *Food in the Social Order: Studies of Food and Festivities in Three American Communities*. London: Routledge, 2003.

Downs, Lawrence. "My Kailua." *New York Times*, September 2, 2011. http://nyti.ms/1DkEX1y.

Dozer, Donald Marquand. "The Opposition to Hawaiian Reciprocity, 1876–1888." *Pacific Historical Review* 14, no. 2 (1945): 157–83.

Dunn, Charles Wesley, ed. *Dunn's Pure Food and Drug Legal Manual*. New York: Dunn's Pure Food and Drug Legal Manual Corporation, 1912–13.

DuPuis, E. Melanie. *Nature's Perfect Food: How Milk Became America's Drink*. New York: New York University Press, 2002.

Dutton, Denis. "Kitsch." *Grove Art Online*. Accessed July 31, 2020. https://www.oxfordartonline.com.

Eccles, R., L. Du-Plessis, Y. Dommels, and J. E. Wilkinson. "Cold Pleasure: Why We Like Ice Drinks, Ice-Lollies, and Ice Creams." *Appetite* 71 (2013): 357–60.

Edmonds, Penelope. *Urbanizing Frontiers: Indigenous Peoples and Settlers in 19th-Century Pacific Rim Cities*. Vancouver: University of British Columbia Press, 2010.

Elias, Megan J. *Food on the Page: Cookbooks and American Culture*. Philadelphia: University of Pennsylvania Press, 2017.

Elkins, Caroline, and Susan Pederson. *Settler Colonialism in the Twentieth Century*. New York: Routledge, 2005.

Ellis, Bill. "Whispers in an Ice Cream Parlor: Culinary Tourism, Contemporary Legends, and the Urban Interzone." *Journal of American Folklore* 122, no. 483 (2009): 53–74.

Ellis, William. *The Journal of William Ellis: Narrative of a Tour of Hawaii, or Owhyhee; with Remarks on the History, Traditions, Manners, Customs, and Language of the Inhabitants of the Sandwich Islands*. Honolulu Advertiser Reprint Edition. Honolulu: Honolulu Advertiser, 1963.

Eltis, David. "New Estimates of Exports from Barbados and Jamaica, 1665–1701." *William and Mary Quarterly* 52, no. 4 (1995): 631–48.

Elvis, Martin. "After Apollo: The American West in Devising a New Space Policy." *Harvard International Review* 33, no. 4 (Spring 2012): 38–43.

Engell, D., and E. Hirsch. "Environmental and Sensory Modulation of Fluid Intake on Humans." In *Thirst*, edited by D. J. Ramsay and D. Booth, 382–90. London: Springer-Verlag, 1991.

Engs, Ruth C., ed. *The Progressive Era's Health Reform Movement: A Historical Dictionary*. Westport, CT: Praeger.

Estes, Nick. *Our History Is the Future: Standing Rock versus the Dakota Access Pipeline, and the Long Tradition of Indigenous Resistance*. New York: Verso, 2019.

Estes, Nick, and Jaskiran Dhillon. *Standing with Standing Rock: Voices from the #NoDAPL Movement*. Minneapolis: University of Minnesota Press, 2019.

Evans, Candy. "Exclusive Pics: Inside Obama's Hawaiian Hideaway." *AOL Real Es-*

tate (blog), December 31, 2009. http://realestate.aol.com/blog/2009/12/31
/exclusive-pics-inside-obamas-hawaiian-hideaway/.

Eves, Richard. "Going Troppo: Images of White Savagery, Degeneration, and Race in Turn-of-the-Century Colonial Fictions of the Pacific." *History and Anthropology* 11, nos. 2–3 (1999): 351–85.

Farbotko, Carol. "Wishful Sinking: Disappearing Islands, Climate Refugees, and Cosmopolitan Experimentation." *Asia Pacific Viewpoint* 51, no. 1 (2010): 47–60.

Farrar, Keith. *To Feed a Nation: A History of Australian Food Science and Technology.* Collingwood, Victoria: CISRO, 2005.

Fennell, Catherine. *Last Project Standing: Civics and Sympathy in Post-welfare Chicago.* Minneapolis: University of Minnesota Press, 2015.

Fennell, Catherine. "'Project Heat' and Sensory Politics in Redeveloping Chicago Public Housing." *Ethnography* 12, no. 1 (2011): 40–64.

Filoon, Whitney. "Shave Ice, Explained." *Eater* (blog), May 24, 2018. https://www
.eater.com/2018/5/24/17376180/shave-ice-shaved-ice-kakigori-dessert-bao
-bing-halo-halo.

Fish, Adam. "Native American Sacred Spaces and the Language of Capitalism." *Future Anterior* 2, no. 1 (2005): 40–49.

Forbes, David W., comp. *Hawaiian National Bibliography, 1780–1900.* Vol. 2, *1831–1850.* Honolulu: University of Hawai'i Press, 2000.

Forbes, David W., comp. *Hawaiian National Bibliography, 1780–1900.* Vol. 3, *1851–1880.* Honolulu: University of Hawai'i Press, 2001.

Forbes, David W., comp. *Hawaiian National Bibliography, 1780–1900.* Vol. 4, *1881–1900.* Honolulu: University of Hawai'i Press, 2003.

Foucault, Michel. *The Order of Things: An Archaeology of the Human Sciences.* New York: Vintage Books, 1994.

Foucault, Michel. *Security, Territory, Population: Lectures at the Collège de France, 1977–1978.* Edited by Michel Senellart. Translated by Graham Burchell. New York: Picador, 2007.

Fox, Frank. *Problems of the Pacific.* London: Williams and Norgate, 1912.

Freidberg, Susanne. *Fresh: A Perishable History.* Cambridge, MA: Belknap Press, 2009.

Freidberg, Susanne. "Moral Economies and the Cold Chain." *Historical Research* 88, no. 239 (February 2015): 125–37.

Frohlich, Thomas C. "Where You'll Pay the Most in Electric Bills." *24/7 Wall St.* (blog). Accessed July 11, 2019. https://247wallst.com/special-report/2019/01
/24/where-youll-pay-the-most-in-electric-bills-3/.

Frost, Alan. "New South Wales as Terra Nullius: The British Denial of Aboriginal Land Rights." *Historical Studies* 19, no. 77 (1981): 513–23.

Fujikane, Candace. *Mapping Abundance for a Planetary Future: Kanaka Maoli and Critical Settler Cartographies in Hawai'i.* Durham, NC: Duke University Press, 2021.

Fujikane, Candace, and Jonathan Y. Okamura, eds. *Asian Settler Colonialism: From*

Local Governance to the Habits of Everyday Life in Hawai'i. Honolulu: University of Hawai'i Press, 2008.

Funderberg, Anne Cooper. *Chocolate, Strawberry, and Vanilla: A History of American Ice Cream*. Bowling Green, OH: Bowling Green State University Popular Press, 1995.

Fusté, José I. "Repeating Islands of Debt: Historicizing the Transcolonial Relationality of Puerto Rico's Economic Crisis." *Radical History Review* 128 (2017): 91–119.

García Márquez, Gabriel. *One Hundred Years of Solitude*. New York: Avon, 1970.

Garriga-López, Adriana. "Puerto Rico: The Future in Question." *Shima* 13, no. 2 (2019): 174–92.

Garth, Hanna. *Food in Cuba: The Pursuit of a Decent Meal*. Palo Alto, CA: Stanford University Press, 2020.

Gilbert, George. *The Death of Captain James Cook*. Honolulu: Paradise of the Pacific Press, 1926.

Gleason, Philip. "The Melting Pot: Symbol of Fusion or Confusion?" *American Quarterly* 16, no. 1 (1964): 20–46.

Goeman, Mishuana R. "Disrupting a Settler-Colonial Grammar of Place: The Visual Memoir of Hulleah Tsinhnahjinnie." In *Theorizing Native Studies*, edited by Audra Simpson and Andrea Smith, 71–89. Durham, NC: Duke University Press, 2014.

Goeman, Mishuana. "Land as Life: Unsettling the Logics of Containment." In *Native Studies Keywords*, edited by Stephanie Nohelani Teves, Andrea Smith, and Michelle H. Raheja, 71–89. Tucson: University of Arizona Press, 2015.

Goldberg-Hiller, Jonathan, and Noenoe K. Silva. "The Botany of Emergence: Kanaka Ontology and Biocolonialism in Hawai'i." *Native American and Indigenous Studies* 2, no. 2 (2015): 1–26.

Goldberg-Hiller, Jonathan, and Noenoe K. Silva. "Sharks and Pigs: Animating Hawaiian Sovereignty against the Anthropological Machine." *South Atlantic Quarterly* 110, no. 2 (2011): 429–46.

Gomes, Andrew. "COVID-19 Is New Pestilence for Hawaii Farmers." *Star Advertiser*, April 20, 2020. https://www.staradvertiser.com/2020/04/20/hawaii-news/covid-19-is-new-pestilence-for-hawaii-farmers/.

Gómez-Barris, Macarena. *The Extractive Zone: Social Ecologies and Decolonial Perspectives*. Durham, NC: Duke University Press, 2017.

Gonzalez, Vernadette Vicuña. *Securing Paradise: Tourism and Militarism in Hawai'i and the Philippines*. Durham, NC: Duke University Press, 2013.

Goodwin, Lorine Swainston. *The Pure Food, Drink, and Drug Crusaders, 1879–1914*. Jefferson, NC: McFarland, 2006.

Goodyear-Ka'ōpua, Noelani. "Hawai'i: An Occupied Country." *Harvard International Review* 35, no. 3 (2014): 58–62.

Goodyear-Ka'ōpua, Noelani. "Protectors of the Future, Not Protestors of the Past: Indigenous Pacific Activism and Mauna a Wākea." *South Atlantic Quarterly* 116, no. 1 (2017): 184–94.

Goodyear-Kaʻōpua, Noelani, Craig Howes, Jonathan Kay Kamakawiwoʻole Osorio, and Aiko Yamashiro, eds. *The Value of Hawaiʻi 3: Hulihia, the Turning*. Honolulu: University of Hawaiʻi Press, 2020.

Goodyear-Kaʻōpua, Noelani, Ikaika Hussey, and Erin Kahunawaikaʻala, eds. *A Nation Rising: Hawaiian Movements for Life, Land, and Sovereignty*. Durham, NC: Duke University Press, 2014.

Goodyear-Kaʻōpua, Noelani, and Bryan Kamaoli Kuwada. "Making ʻAha: Independent Hawaiian Pasts, Presents, and Futures." *Dædalus* 147, no. 2 (2018): 49–59.

Goss, J. D. "Placing the Market and Marketing Place: Tourist Advertising of the Hawaiian Islands, 1972–92." *Environment and Planning D: Society and Space* 11, no. 6 (1993): 663–88.

Grant, Glen, and Dennis M. Ogawa. "Living Proof: Is Hawaiʻi the Answer?" *Annals of the American Academy of Political and Social Science* 530, no. 1 (1993): 137–54.

Greer, Richard A. "Cunha's Alley—the Anatomy of a Landmark." *Hawaiian Journal of History* 2 (1968): 142–52.

Greer, Richard A. "Grog Shops and Hotels: Bending the Elbow in Old Honolulu." *Hawaiian Journal of History* 28 (1994): 35–68.

Group 70 International. *Mauna Kea Science Reserve Master Plan*. Honolulu: [Group 70 International], 2000.

Grove, Richard H. *Green Imperialism: Colonial Expansion, Tropical Island Edens and the Origins of Environmentalism, 1600–1860*. Cambridge: Cambridge University Press, 2003.

Gulick, Sidney Lewis. *Mixing the Races in Hawaii: A Study of the Coming Neo-Hawaiian American Race*. Honolulu: Hawaiian Board Book Rooms, 1937.

Gutmanis, June, and Julia Bryant. *Oral History Interview with Julia Bryant*. Honolulu: Center for Oral History, 1978.

Gyroy, Andrew. *Closing the Gate: Race, Politics, and the Chinese Exclusion Act*. Chapel Hill: University of North Carolina Press, 1998.

Haakanson, Sven D., and Amy F. Steffian. *Giinaquq Like a Face: Suqpiaq Masks of the Kodiak Archipelago*. Fairbanks: University of Alaska Press, 2009.

Haleole, S. N. *The Hawaiian Romance of Laieikawai*. Translated by Martha Warren Beckwith. Washington, DC: Government Printing Office, 1918.

Haleole, S. N. "Ka Moolelo O Laieikawai." *Kuokoa*, November 29, 1862.

Hall, Lisa Kahaleole. "Hawaiian at Heart and Other Fictions." *Contemporary Pacific* 17, no. 2 (2005): 404–13.

Hall, Lisa Kahaleole. "Which of These Things Is Not Like the Other: Hawaiians and Other Pacific Islanders Are Not Asian Americans, and All Pacific Islanders Are Not Hawaiian." *American Quarterly* 67, no. 3 (2015): 727–47.

Hamilton, Shane. *Trucking Country: The Road to America's Wal-Mart Economy*. Princeton, NJ: Princeton University Press, 2008.

Hård, Mikael. *Machines Are Frozen Spirit: The Scientification of Refrigeration and Brewing in the 19th Century—a Weberian Interpretation*. Frankfurt am Main: Campus Verlag, 1994.

Hartwell, Alfred S. "The Organization of a Territorial Government for Hawaii." *Yale Law Review* 9, no. 3 (1899): 107–13.

Hatch, Anthony Ryan. *Blood Sugar: Racial Pharmacology and Food Justice in Black America*. Minneapolis: University of Minnesota Press, 2016.

The Hawaiian Cook Book. Honolulu: Ladies of Fort Street Church, 1882.

Hawaiian Government. *Penal Code of the Hawaiian Islands*. Honolulu: Government Press, 1850.

Hawaii Supreme Court. *Annual Report of the Chief Justice*. Honolulu: Hawaii Administration of Justice, 1854.

Henrich, K. M., L. J. Y. Hsu, C. B. Johnson, Y. Jokura, M. Rider, and J. E. Maddock. "Food Security Issues for Low-Income Hawai'i Residents." *Asia Pacific Journal of Public Health* 20, suppl. (2008): 64–69.

Herold, Marc. "Ice in the Tropics: The Export of 'Crystal Blocks of Yankee Coldness' to India and Brazil." *Revista Espaco Academico*, March 1, 2012.

Hibbard, Don. *Designing Paradise: The Allure of the Hawaiian Resort*. New York: Princeton Architectural Press, 2006.

Hill, Michael R. "Temperateness, Temperance, and the Tropics: Climate and Morality in the English Atlantic World, 1555–1705." PhD diss., Georgetown University, 2013.

Hill, Samuel S. *Travels in the Sandwich and Society Islands*. London: Chapman and Hall, 1856.

Hiura, Arnold. *Kau Kau: Cuisine and Culture in the Hawaiian Islands*. Honolulu: Watermark, 2009.

Hixson, Walter H. *American Settler Colonialism: A History*. New York: Palgrave Macmillan, 2013.

HNN Staff. "No Surprises Here: Hawaii Named Priciest State in the Nation." *Hawaii News Now*, July 12, 2018.

Hobart, Hi'ilei Julia. "At Home on the Mauna: Ecological Violence and Fantasies of Terra Nullius on Maunakea's Summit." *Native American and Indigenous Studies* 6, no. 2 (2019): 30–50.

Hobart, Hi'ilei Julia. "Atomic Histories and Elemental Futures across Indigenous Oceans." *Media+Environment* 3, no. 1 (2021): 1–19.

Hobart, Hi'ilei Julia. "A 'Queer-Looking Compound': Race, Abjection, and the Politics of Hawaiian Poi." *Global Food History* 3, no. 2 (2017): 133–49.

Hokowhitu, Brendan. "Tackling Māori Masculinity: A Colonial Genealogy of Savagery and Sport." *Contemporary Pacific* 16 (2004): 259–84.

Holak, Susan L., and William J. Havlena. "Feelings, Fantasies, and Memories: An Examination of the Emotional Components of Nostalgia." *Journal of Business Research* 42 (1998): 217–26.

Holmes, Burton. *Burton Holmes Travelogue*. Vol. 11. Chicago: Travelogue Bureau, 1919.

Holton, Graham E. L. "Heyerdahl's Kon Tiki Theory and the Denial of the Indigenous Past." *Anthropological Forum* 14, no. 2 (2004): 163–81.

"A Honolulu Hardware Store." *Hardware Dealer's Magazine* 40 (1913): 1237.

Honolulu Iron Works Company. *Some Sugar Factories Built and Equipped by the Honolulu Iron Works Company.* [Honolulu]: Honolulu Iron Works Company, 1924.

Hooley, Osborne E. "Hawaiian Negotiation for Reciprocity, 1855–1857." *Pacific Historical Review* 7, no. 2 (1938): 128–46.

Hopkins, Manley. *Hawaii: The Past, Present, and Future of Its Island-Kingdom.* London: Longman, 1862.

Horowitz, Roger. *Putting Meat on the American Table: Taste, Technology, Transformation.* Baltimore, MD: Johns Hopkins University Press, 2006.

Howard, Kendra Smith. *Pure and Modern Milk: An Environmental History since 1900.* Oxford: Oxford University Press, 2014.

Howe, George D. "The Father of Modern Refrigeration." *Publications of the Florida Historical Society* 1, no. 4 (1909): 19–23.

Huard, Mallory. "In Hawai'i, Plantation Tourism Tastes Like Pineapple." *EdgeEffects* (blog), November 12, 2019. https://edgeeffects.net/dole-pineapple -plantation/.

Huff, Daryl. "Health Officials Restrict Poi Pioneer: Supporters of Traditional Poi Challenge Health Department." KITV Honolulu, November 23, 2010. http:// www.kitv.com/r/25903451/detail.html.

Huff, Daryl. "State Legalizes Hand-Pounded Poi: Governor Signs Bill to Allow Sales of Poi Made Traditional Way." KITV Honolulu, November 23, 2010. http:// www.kitv.com/r/28275745/detail.html.

Illouz, Eva. *Cold Intimacies: The Making of Emotional Capitalism.* Cambridge: Polity, 2007.

Imada, Adria L. *Aloha America: Hula Circuits through the U.S. Empire.* Durham, NC: Duke University Press, 2012.

Ing, Tiffany Lani. *Reclaiming Kalākaua: Nineteenth-Century Perspectives on a Hawaiian Sovereign.* Honolulu: University of Hawai'i Press, 2019.

Isaki, Bianca. "HB 645, Settler Sexuality, and the Politics of Local Asian Domesticity in Hawai'i." *Settler Colonial Studies* 1, no. 2 (2011): 82–102.

Jacobson, Matthew Frye. *Barbarian Virtues: The United States Encounters Foreign Peoples at Home and Abroad, 1876–1917.* New York: Hill and Wang, 2001.

Jarves, James Jackson. *History of the Hawaiian or Sandwich Islands: Embracing Their Antiquities, Mythology, Legends, Discovery by Europeans in the Sixteenth Century, Re-discovery by Cook, with Their Civil, Religious, and Political History.* Boston: Tappan and Dennet, 1843.

Jedra, Christina. "Hawai'i Increases Funding for Homeless Sweeps." *Civil Beat,* June 26, 2020. https://www.civilbeat.org/2020/06/hawaii-increases-funding -for-homeless-sweeps/.

Jedra, Christina. "Hawai'i Is No Longer No. 1 for Homelessness. New York Is Worse." *Civil Beat,* January 7, 2020. https://www.civilbeat.org/2020/01/hawaii -is-no-longer-no-1-for-homelessness-new-york-is-worse/.

Jennings, Eric T. *Curing the Colonizers: Hydrotherapy, Climatology, and French Colonial Spas.* Durham, NC: Duke University Press, 2006.

John, Maria. "Sovereign Bodies: Urban Indigenous Health and the Politics of Self-Determination in Seattle and Sydney, 1950–1980." PhD diss., Columbia University, 2016.

Johns, Nicole E. "The Wealth (and Health) of Nations: Estimating Inequality to Better Estimate Health." Paper presented at the annual conference of Global Health Metrics and Evaluation: Data, Debates, Directions, Seattle, WA, June 18, 2013.

Johnstone, Arthur. "Storied Nuuanu." In *Hawaiian Almanac and Annual for 1906*, edited by Thomas G. Thrum, 160–68. Honolulu: Thos. G. Thrum, 1905.

Jolly, Margaret. "Contested Paradise: Dispossession and Repossession in Hawai'i." *Contemporary Pacific* 30, no. 2 (2018): 355–77.

Judd, Gerrit P., IV. *Dr. Judd: Hawaii's Friend. A Biography of Gerrit Parmele Judd, 1803–1873*. Honolulu: University of Hawai'i Press, 1960.

Judd, Laura Fish. *Honolulu: Sketches of Life: Sketches of the Social, Political, and Religious in the Hawaiian Islands from 1828–1861*. New York: Anson D. F. Randolph and Company, 1880.

Jung, Moon-Kie. *Reworking Race: The Making of Hawaii's Interracial Labor Movement*. New York: Columbia University Press, 2006.

Kaeo, Peter. *News from Molokai: Letters between Peter Kaeo and Queen Emma, 1873–1876*. Honolulu: University of Hawai'i Press, 1976.

Kahakalau, Kū. Written direct testimony. Contested Case Hearing 2, October 26, 2016. https://dlnr.hawaii.gov/mk/files/2016/10/B.06a-wdt-Kahakalau.pdf.

Kalākaua, David. *King Kalakaua's Tour round the World: A Sketch of Incidents of Travel*. Honolulu: Pacific Commercial Advertiser, 1881.

Kam, Ralph Thomas. *Death Rites and Hawaiian Royalty: Funerary Practices in the Kamehameha and Kalākaua Dynasties, 1819–1953*. Jefferson, NC: McFarland, 2017.

Kamehameha Schools. *Hawaiian Place Names: The Significance of Hawaiian Sites, Their Locations, and Interpretation of Their Names* 2, no. 1 (1987). http://manoa.hawaii.edu/coe/kulia/resources/ahupuaa_maps/OahuAhupuaa.pdf.

Kamehiro, Stacy L. *The Arts of Kingship: Hawaiian Art and National Culture of the Kalākaua Era*. Honolulu: University of Hawai'i Press, 2009.

Kamehiro, Stacy L. "'Iolani Palace: Spaces of Kingship in Late Nineteenth-Century Hawai'i." *Pacific Studies* 29, nos. 3–4 (2006): 1–32.

Kana'iaupuni, Shawn Malia, Wendy M. Kekahio, Kā'eo Duarte, and Brandon C. Ledward. "Material and Economic Well-Being." In *Ka Huaka'i: 2014 Native Hawaiian Educational Assessment*, 88–134. Honolulu: Kamehameha Publishing, 2014.

Kashay, Jennifer Fish. "Missionaries and Foodways in Early 19th-Century Hawaii." *Food and Foodways: Explorations in the History and Culture of Human Nourishment* 17, no. 3 (2009): 159–80.

Kashay, Jennifer Fish. "'We Will Banish the Polluted Thing from Our Houses': Missionaries, Drinking, and Temperance in the Sandwich Islands." In *The Role of the American Board in the World: Bicentennial Reflections on the Organization's*

Missionary Work, 1810–2010, edited by Clifford Putney and Paul T. Burlin, 287–311. Eugene, OR: Wipf and Stock, 2012.

Katz, Julia. "Ahuna and the Moʻo: Rethinking Chinese Success in Hawaiian Commercial Food Production." *Pacific Historical Review* 86, no. 4 (2017): 599–631.

Kauanui, J. Kēhaulani. "'A Blood Mixture Which Experience Has Shown Furnishes the Very Highest Grade of Citizen Material': Selective Assimilation in a Polynesian Case of Naturalization to U.S. Citizenship." *American Studies* 45, no. 3 (2004): 33–48.

Kauanui, J. Kēhaulani. *Hawaiian Blood: Colonialism and the Politics of Sovereignty and Indigeneity*. Durham, NC: Duke University Press, 2008.

Kauanui, J. Kēhaulani. *Paradoxes of Hawaiian Sovereignty: Land, Sex, and the Colonial Politics of State Nationalism*. Durham, NC: Duke University Press, 2018.

Keaulana, Kimo Alama, and Scott Whitney. "Ka wai kau mai o Maleka 'Water from America': The Intoxication of the Hawaiian People." *Contemporary Drug Problems* 17 (1990): 161–94.

Kelly, Alison. "The Construction of Masculine Science." *British Journal of Sociology of Education* 6, no. 2 (1985): 133–54.

Kennedy, Alicia. "One Mai Tai, Hold the Colonialism, Please." *Eater*, October 7, 2019. https://www.eater.com/2019/10/7/20895319/tiki-tropical-drinks -colonialism-appropriation-lost-lake-pina-colada.

Kent, George. "Food Security in Hawaiʻi." In *Food and Power in Hawaiʻi: Visions on Food Democracy*, edited by Aya Hirata Kimura and Krisnawati Suryanata, 36–53. Honolulu: University of Hawaiʻi Press, 2016.

Kessler, Lawrence. "No 'Perfect Garden': American Constructions of Hawaiian Landscapes and the Making of a Climatic Borderland." *Southern California Quarterly* 94, no. 3 (2012): 277–303.

Kimmerer, Robin Wall. *Braiding Sweetgrass: Indigenous Wisdom, Scientific Knowledge, and the Teachings of Plants*. Minneapolis: Milkweed Editions, 2015.

Klein, Shana. "'The Perfect Servant': Race, Hygiene, and Canning Machinery at the Dole Hawaiian Pineapple Company." *Food, Fatness, and Fitness: Critical Perspectives* (blog), August 1, 2019. http://foodfatnessfitness.com/2019/08/01 /race-hygiene-and-pineapple-cannery/.

Koo, Linda C. "The Use of Food to Treat and Prevent Disease in Chinese Culture." *Social Science and Medicine* 18, no. 9 (1984): 757–66.

Kooser, Amanda. "Space Station Crew Dons Matching Hawaiian Shirts to Greet New Astronauts." *CNET*, June 8, 2018. https://www.cnet.com/news/space -station-iss-crew-dons-matching-hawaiian-shirts-to-greet-new-astronauts/.

Kowal, Emma, and Joanna Radin. "Indigenous Biospecimen Collections and the Cryopolitcs of Frozen Life." *Journal of Sociology* 51, no. 1 (2015): 63–80.

Krogstad, Jens Manuel. "Hawaii Is Home to the Nation's Largest Share of Multicultural Americans." Pew Research Center, June 17, 2015. https://www .pewresearch.org/fact-tank/2015/06/17/hawaii-is-home-to-the-nations -largest-share-of-multiracial-americans/.

Kupperman, Karen Ordahl. "Fear of Hot Climates in the Anglo-American Colonial Experience." *William and Mary Quarterly* 41, no. 2 (1984): 213–40.

Kuykendall, Ralph S. *The Hawaiian Kingdom.* Vol. 1, *Foundation and Transformation, 1778–1854.* Honolulu: University of Hawai'i Press, 1938.

Kuykendall, Ralph S. *The Hawaiian Kingdom.* Vol. 2, *Twenty Critical Years, 1854–1874.* Honolulu: University of Hawai'i Press, 1953.

Kuykendall, Ralph S. *The Hawaiian Kingdom.* Vol. 3, *The Kalakaua Dynasty, 1874–1893.* Honolulu: University of Hawai'i Press, 1967.

Kwok, Sun. *Stardust: The Cosmic Seeds of Life.* London: Springer, 2013.

LaCroix, Sumner J., and Christopher Grandy. "The Political Instability of Reciprocal Trade and the Overthrow of the Hawaiian Kingdom." *Journal of Economic History* 57, no. 1 (1997): 161–89.

LaCroix, Sumner J., and James Roumasset. "The Evolution of Private Property in Nineteenth-Century Hawaii." *Journal of Economic History* 50, no. 4 (1990): 829–52.

LaDuke, Winona, and Deborah Cowen. "Beyond Wiindigo Infrastructure." *South Atlantic Quarterly* 119, no. 2 (2020): 243–68.

Landecker, Hannah. "Living Differently in Time: Plasticity, Temporality, and Cellular Biotechnologies." In *Technologized Images, Technologized Bodies*, edited by Jeanette Edwards, Penelope Harvey, and Peter Wade, 211–36. New York: Berghahn Books, 2010.

Larkin, Brian. "The Politics and Poetics of Infrastructure." *Annual Review of Anthropology* 42 (2013): 327–43.

Larson, Kirby. *Nanea: Growing Up with Aloha.* Middletown, WI: American Girl, 2017.

Laudan, Rachel. *The Food of Paradise: Exploring Hawaii's Culinary Heritage.* Honolulu: University of Hawai'i Press, 1996.

Laudan, Rachel. "Homegrown Cuisines or Naturalized Cuisines? The History of Food in Hawaii and Hawaii's Place in Food History." *Food, Culture, and Society* 19, no. 3 (2016): 437–59.

Law, Marc T., and Gary D. Libecap. "The Determinants of Progressive Era Reform: The Pure Food and Drugs Act of 1906." In *Corruption and Reform: Lessons from America's Economic History*, edited by Edward L. Glaeser and Claudia Goldin, 319–42. Chicago: University of Chicago Press, 2006.

Laws of His Majesty Kamehameha IV, King of the Hawaiian Islands, Passed by the Nobles and Representatives, at Their Session. Honolulu: Hawaiian Government, 1855.

Laws of the Republic of Hawaii Passed by the Legislature at Its Session, 1898. Honolulu: Republic of Hawaii, 1898.

Laws of the Territory of Hawaii. Honolulu: Territory of Hawaii, 1903.

Laws of the Territory of Hawaii Passed by the Legislature at Its Regular Session. Honolulu: Bulletin Publishing Co., 1911.

Lee, Florence Margaret. "Domestic Science in the Normal School of Hawaii." *Journal of Home Economics* 2, no. 6 (1910): 646–47.

Lee, Stephanie, Melissa Oshiro, Laura Hsu, Opal Vanessa Buchthal, and Tetine Sentell. "Public Health Hotline: Neighborhoods and Health in Hawai'i: Considering Food Accessibility and Affordability." *Hawai'i Journal of Medicine and Public Health* 71, no. 8 (2012): 232–37.

LeFebvre, Henri. *The Production of Space.* Translated by Donald Nicholson-Smith. Oxford: Blackwell, 1991.

Leonard, Thomas C. *Illiberal Reformers: Race, Eugenics, and American Economics in the Progressive Era.* Princeton, NJ: Princeton University Press, 2017.

Lerman, Josh. "Hawaii Not?" *Skiing*, February 1992, 30.

Lévi-Strauss, Claude. "The Culinary Triangle." *Parisian Review* 33, no. 4 (1966): 586–95.

Linnekin, Jocelyn. "The *Hui* Lands of Keanae: Hawaiian Land Tenure and the Great Mahele." *Journal of the Polynesian Society* 92, no. 2 (1983): 169–88.

Linnekin, Jocelyn. *Sacred Queens and Women of Consequence: Rank, Gender, and Colonialism in the Hawaiian Islands.* Ann Arbor: University of Michigan Press, 1990.

Liu, John M. "Race, Ethnicity, and the Sugar Plantation System: Asian Labor in Hawaii, 1850–1900." In *Labor Immigration under Capitalism: Asian Workers in the United States before World War II,* edited by Lucie Cheng and Edna Bonacich, 186–210. Berkeley: University of California Press, 1984.

Livingstone, David N. "Tropical Climate and Moral Hygiene: The Anatomy of a Victorian Debate." *British Journal for the History of Science* 32, no. 1 (1999): 93–110.

Loke, Matthew K., and PingSung Leung. "Hawai'i's Food Consumption and Supply Sources: Benchmark Estimates and Measurement Issues." *Agricultural and Food Economics* 1, no. 10 (2013): n.p.

Lomawaima, K. Tsianina. *They Called It Prairie Light: The Story of Chilocco Indian School.* Lincoln: University of Nebraska Press, 1994.

London, Charmian. *Our Hawaii.* New York: Macmillan, 1917.

Long, Lucy, ed. *Culinary Tourism.* Lexington: University Press of Kentucky, 2004.

Lopez-Reyes, Ramon. "Hawaiian Sovereignty." *Peace Review* 12, no. 2 (2000): 311–18.

López-Rodríguez, Irene. "Are We What We Eat? Food Metaphors in the Conceptualization of Ethnic Groups." *Linguistik* 69 (2014): 3–36.

Lovegren, Sylvia. "Pure Food and Drug Act." In *The Oxford Encyclopedia of Food and Drink in America,* edited by Andrew F. Smith, 484–85. New York: Oxford University Press, 2004.

Lowry, Rich. "We Landed on a Comet, and Feminists Are Angry about a Shirt." *New York Post*, November 17, 2014. https://nypost.com/2014/11/17/the-outrage -machine-insande-ado-about-sexist-shirt/.

Luangphinith, Seri Kau'ikealaula. "Homeward Bound: Settler Aesthetics in Hawai'i's Literature." *Texas Studies in Literature and Language* 48, no. 1 (2006): 54–78.

MacLennan, Carol A. *Sovereign Sugar: Industry and Environment in Hawai'i*. Honolulu: University of Hawai'i Press, 2014.

Macrae, James. *With Lord Byron at the Sandwich Islands in 1825: Being Extracts from the MS Diary of James Macrae*. Honolulu: W. F. Wilson, 1922.

Maile, David Uahikeaikalei'ohu. "Ka Lei o ka Lanakila: Grasping Victory at Maunakea." *Abolition Journal*, July 17, 2020. https://abolitionjournal.org/ka-lei-o-ka-lanakila/.

Maile, David Uahikeaikalei'ohu. "On Being Late: Cruising Mauna Kea and Unsettling Technoscientific Conquest in Hawai'i." *American Indian Culture and Research Journal* 45, no. 1 (2021): 95–122.

Maile, David Uahikeaikalei'ohu. "Science, Time, and Mauna a Wākea: The Thirty-Meter Telescope's Capitalist-Colonialist Violence." *Red Nation*, May 13, 2015. https://therednation.org.

Maly, Kepa, and Onaona Maly. *"Mauna Kea—Ka Piko Kaulana O Ka 'Āina": A Collection of Native Traditions, Historical Accounts, and Oral History Interviews for: Mauna Kea, the Lands of Ka'ohe, Humu'ula, and the 'Āina Mauna on the Island of Hawai'i*. Hilo: Office of Mauna Kea Management, 2005.

Mancall, Peter C. *Deadly Medicine: Indians and Alcohol in Native America*. Ithaca, NY: Cornell University Press, 1995.

Mann, Mary Tylor. *Christianity in the Kitchen*. Boston: Ticknor and Fields, 1857.

Matsuura, Patsy. "The Shave Ice Is the Same but the Price Has Changed." *Advertiser*, July 30, 1974, 13.

Mattern, Shannon. "Maintenance and Care." *Places Journal*, November 2018. https://doi.org/10.22269/181120.

Mattison, Sara. "Refrigerator, Freezer Stock Impacted by COVID-19." KHON2, September 16, 2020. https://www.khon2.com/coronavirus/refrigerator-freezer-stock-impacted-by-covid-19/.

Mayer, Phil. "The Island's Shave Ice Business Is Not Cooling." *Star-Bulletin*, May 19, 1988, 3.

McAndrews, Kristin M. "Incorporating the Local Tourist at the Big Island Poke Festival." In *Culinary Tourism*, edited by Lucy Long, 114–27. Lexington: University Press of Kentucky, 2004.

McAndrews, Kristin M. "King David Kalakaua's Last Diplomatic Dinner: A Discussion of the Rhetoric of the Menu." Presentation at the Dublin Gastronomy Symposium, Dublin Institute of Technology, Dublin, May 31–June 1, 2016.

McClintock, Anne. *Imperial Leather: Race, Gender, and Sexuality in the Colonial Contest*. New York: Routledge, 1995.

McDougall, Brandy Nālani. *Finding Meaning: Kaona and Contemporary Hawaiian Literature*. Tucson: University of Arizona Press, 2016.

McDougall, Brandy Nālani. "'We Are Not American': Competing Rhetorical Archipelagos in Hawai'i." In *Archipelagic American Studies*, edited by Brian Russell Roberts and Michelle Ann Stevens, 259–78. Durham, NC: Duke University Press, 2017.

McGerr, Michael. *A Fierce Discontent: The Rise and Fall of the Progressive Movement in America, 1870–1920*. New York: Simon and Schuster, 2003.

McGregor, Davianna Pōmaikaʻi. *Nā Kuaʻāina: Living Hawaiian Culture*. Honolulu: University of Hawaiʻi Press, 2007.

McGregor, Davianna Pōmaikaʻi. "Statehood: Catalyst of the Twentieth-Century Kanaka ʻŌiwi Cultural Renaissance and Sovereignty Movement." *Journal of Asian American Studies* 13, no. 3 (2010): 311–26.

McMullin, Daniel Taulapapa. "Tiki Kitsch, American Appropriation, and the Disappearance of the Pacific Islander Body." *LUX* 2, no. 1 (2013): 1–6.

Merleaux, April. *Sugar and Civilization: American Empire and the Cultural Politics of Sweetness*. Chapel Hill, NC: University of North Carolina Press, 2015.

Merry, Sally Engle. *Colonizing Hawaiʻi: The Cultural Power of Law*. Princeton, NJ: Princeton University Press, 2000.

Mihesuah, Devon, and Elizabeth M. Hoover. *Indigenous Food Sovereignty in the United States: Restoring Cultural Knowledge, Protecting Environments, and Regaining Health*. Norman: University of Oklahoma Press, 2019.

Millward, David. "Protesters Halt Groundbreaking Ceremony for Mammoth Hawaiian Telescope." *Telegraph*, October 9, 2014. http://www.telegraph.co.uk/news/worldnews/northamerica/usa/11152624/Protests-halt-groundbreaking-ceremony-for-mammoth-Hawaiian-telescope.html.

Mintz, Sidney W. *Sweetness and Power*. New York: Viking, 1985.

Mintz, Sidney W., and Christine M. Du Bois. "The Anthropology of Food and Eating." *Annual Review of Anthropology* 31 (2002): 99–199.

Mokyr, Joel, and Rebecca Stein. "Science, Health, and Household Technology: The Effect of the Pasteur Revolution on Consumer Demand." In *The Economics of New Goods*, edited by Timothy F. Bresnahan and Robert J. Gordon, 143–206. Chicago: University of Chicago Press, 1997.

Mollett J. A. "Capital in Hawaiian Sugar: Its Formation and Relation to Labor and Output, 1870–1957." *Agricultural Economics Bulletin* 21. Honolulu: Hawaiʻi Agricultural Experiment Station, University of Hawaiʻi Mānoa, 1961.

Moreton-Robinson, Aileen. *The White Possessive: Property, Power, and Indigenous Sovereignty*. Minneapolis: University of Minnesota Press, 2015.

Morgensen, Scott Lauria. "The Biopolitics of Settler Colonialism: Right Here, Right Now." *Settler Colonial Studies* 1, no. 1 (2011): 52–76.

Morgensen, Scott Lauria. "Theorizing Gender, Sexuality, and Settler Colonialism: An Introduction." *Settler Colonial Studies* 2, no. 2 (2012): 2–22.

Morrison, D., R. E. Murphy, D. P. Cruikshank, W. M. Sinton, and T. Z. Martin. "Evaluation of Mauna Kea, Hawaii, as an Observatory Site." *Publications of the Astronomical Society of the Pacific* 85, no. 505 (1973): 255–57.

Mulligan, William H., Jr. "Cold Water Army." In *The SAGE Encyclopedia of Alcohol: Social, Cultural, and Historical Perspectives*, edited by Scott C. Martin and William White, 415–16. Thousand Oaks, CA: Sage, 2015.

Murphy, Michelle. *Sick Building Syndrome: Environmental Politics, Technoscience, and Women Workers*. Durham, NC: Duke University Press, 2006.

Musick, John R. *Hawai'i: Our New Possessions*. New York: Funk and Wagnalls Company, 1898.

Needham, Andrew. *Power Lines: Phoenix and the Making of the American Southwest*. Princeton, NJ: Princeton University Press, 2014.

Nellist, George F. *The Discovery and Development of Artesian Water*. Honolulu: Board of Water Supply, City and County of Honolulu, 1953.

Nellist, George F. *The Story of Hawaii and Its Builders*. Honolulu: Honolulu Star Bulletin, 1925.

Nichols, Robert. *Theft Is Property! Dispossession and Critical Theory*. Durham, NC: Duke University Press, 2020.

Nichols, Robert. "Theft Is Property! The Recursive Logic of Dispossession." *Political Theory* 46, no. 1 (2017): 3–28.

Nickerson, Joseph A., Jr., and Geraldine D. Nickerson. *Chatham Sea Captains in the Age of Sail*. Charleston, SC: History Press, 2008.

Nonaka, Howard, and Francis Miyake. *Oral History Interview with Francis Miyake*. Honolulu: Center for Oral History, 1977.

O'Connor, Kaori. "The Hawaiian Luau." *Food, Culture, and Society* 11, no. 2 (2008): 149–72.

Official Descriptive and Illustrated Catalog: Great Exhibition of the Works of Industry of All Nations, vol. 2. London: Spicer Brothers, 1851.

Ohnuma, Keiko. "'Aloha Spirit' and the Cultural Politics of Sentiment as National Belonging." *Contemporary Pacific* 20, no. 2 (2008): 365–94.

Okamura, Jonathan Y. "Aloha Kanaka Me Ke Aloha 'Aina: Local Culture and Society in Hawai'i." *Amerasia Journal* 7 (1980): 119–37.

Okamura, Jonathan Y. "Barack Obama as the Post-racial Candidate for a Post-racial America: Perspectives from Asian America and Hawai'i." *Patterns of Prejudice* 45, nos. 1–2 (2011): 133–53.

Okamura, Jonathan Y. "The Illusion of Paradise: Privileging Multiculturalism in Hawai'i." In *Making Majorities: Constituting the Nation in Japan, Korea, China, Malaysia, Fiji, Turkey, and the United States*, edited by Dru D. Gladney, 264–84. Stanford, CA: Stanford University Press, 1998.

Okamura, Jonathan Y. "Why There Are No Asian Americans in Hawai'i: The Continuing Significance of Local Identity." In *Asian American Family Life and Community*, edited by Franklin Ng, 161–78. New York: Routledge, 2014.

Okihiro, Gary Y. *Island World: A History of Hawai'i and the United States*. Berkeley: University of California Press, 2008.

Okihiro, Gary Y. *Pineapple Culture: A History of the Tropical and Temperate Zones*. Berkeley: University of California Press, 2009.

Omaye, Jayna. "O'ahu in 1978: Housing Prices on the Rise in Hawai'i." *Honolulu Magazine*, June 6, 2019.

O'Meara, James. "Schemes to Annex the Sandwich Islands." *Californian* 4 (1881): 257–65.

Osorio, Jonathan Kamakawiwo'ole. *Dismembering Lāhui: A History of the Hawaiian Nation to 1887*. Honolulu: University of Hawai'i Press, 2002.

Overbye, Dennis. "Under Hawai'i's Starriest Skies, a Fight over Sacred Ground." *New York Times*, October 3, 2016. https://www.nytimes.com/2016/10/04 /science/hawaii-thirty-meter-telescope-mauna-kea.html?_r=0.

Paiva, Derek. "Hawaii Has 10 of the World's 14 Climate Zones: An Explorer's Guide to Each of Them." *Hawaii Magazine*, November 10, 2015.

Pardilla, Caroline. "You Deserve a Mai Tai—a Real One, That Is." *Eater*, November 10, 2016. https://www.eater.com/21348867/best-mai-tai-recipe-history.

Patterson, John. "The United States and Hawaiian Reciprocity, 1867–1870." *Pacific Historical Review* 7, no. 2 (1938): 14–26.

Paxson, Heather. "Post-Pasteurian Cultures: The Microbiopolitics of Raw-Milk Cheese in the United States." *Cultural Anthropology* 23, no. 1 (2008): 15–47.

Peralto, Leon No'eau. "Portrait. Mauna a Wākea: Hānau ka Mauna, the Piko of Our Ea." In *A Nation Rising: Hawaiian Movements for Life, Land, and Sovereignty*, edited by Noelani Goodyear-Ka'ōpua, Ikaika Hussey, and Erin Kahunawaika'ala Wright, 233–44. Durham, NC: Duke University Press, 2014.

Perez, Craig Santos. "Black Lives Matter in the Pacific." *Ethnic Studies Review* 43, no. 3 (2020): 34–38.

Peterson, Charles E. "Pioneer Architects and Builders of Honolulu." *Annual Report of the Hawaiian Historical Society* 72 (1964): 7–28.

Pfeifer, Luanne. "The Admirable Snowman of Mauna Kea." *Ski*, November 1971, 68.

Pilcher, Jeffrey M. *¡Que Vivan Los Tamales! Food and the Making of Mexican Identity*. Albuquerque: University of New Mexico Press, 1998.

Pletcher, David M. *Diplomacy of Involvement: American Economic Expansion across the Pacific, 1784–1900*. Columbia: University of Missouri Press, 2001.

Pollan, Michael. *The Omnivore's Dilemma: A Natural History of Four Meals*. New York: Penguin Books, 2006.

Possedi, Cathy. "Accessory Dwelling Units Become Legal in Honolulu County." *Hawai'i Life Real Estate Brokers* (blog), September 22, 2015. https://www .hawaiilife.com/blog/accessory-dwelling-units-legal-in-honolulu/.

Povinelli, Elizabeth. *The Cunning of Recognition: Indigenous Alterities and the Making of Australian Multiculturalism*. Durham, NC: Duke University Press, 2002.

Powell, Dana E. *Landscapes of Power: Politics and Energy in the Navajo Nation*. Durham, NC: Duke University Press, 2018.

Powers, Jenny. "Sales of the 'Everlasting,' Beloved Product Spam Have Skyrocketed during Coronavirus as Long-Time Fans Stock Up." *Business Insider*, May 21, 2020. https://www.businessinsider.com/hormel-foods-spam-sales -skyrocketed-pandemic-bloggers-fans-stock-up-2020-5.

Pratt, Richard Henry. *Battlefield and Classroom: Four Decades with the American Indian, 1867–1904*. Edited by Robert M. Utley. Norman: University of Oklahoma Press, 1964.

Probyn, Elspeth. "Suspended Beginnings: Of Childhood and Nostalgia." GLQ 2 (1995): 439–65.

Public Health Committee. *The Health Story in Hawaii*. Honolulu: Chamber of Commerce of Honolulu, 1947.

Pukui, Mary Kawena, and Samuel H. Elbert. *Hawaiian Dictionary.* Rev. and enl. ed. Honolulu: University of Hawaiʻi Press, 1986.

Quinzio, Jeri. *Of Sugar and Snow: A History of Ice Cream Making.* Berkeley: University of California Press, 2009.

Radin, Joanna. "The Secret Weapon for Distributing a Potential Covid-19 Vaccination." *Washington Post*, November 12, 2020. https://www.washingtonpost .com/outlook/2020/11/12/secret-weapon-distributing-potential-covid-19 -vaccine/.

Ramones, Ikaika. "OHA Backs Down from Contesting the TMT Sublease." *Hawaii Independent*, July 17, 2014. https://www.thehawaiiindependent.com/story /oha-backs-down-from-contesting-the-tmt-sublease.

Rasmussen, Louis J. *San Francisco Ship Passenger Lists: November 7, 1851–June 17, 1852.* Baltimore, MD: Genealogical Publishing, 2003.

Rees, Jonathan. *Refrigeration Nation: A History of Ice, Appliances, and Enterprise in America.* Baltimore, MD: Johns Hopkins University Press, 2013.

Reese, Ashanté M. "Tarry with Me: Reclaiming Sweetness in an Anti-Black World." *Oxford American*, no. 112 (Spring 2021). https://www.oxfordamerican .org/magazine/issue-112-spring-2021/tarry-with-me.

Reinecke, John, and Stanley Tsuzaki, eds. *Language and Dialect in Hawaii: A Sociolinguistic History to 1935.* Honolulu: University of Hawaiʻi Press, 1969.

Report of the Board of Health of the Territory of Hawaii. Honolulu: Bulletin Publishing Company, 1907.

Reston, Maeve. "Obama Visits Favorite Shave Ice Shop before a Private New Year's Eve." *Los Angeles Times*, December 13, 2013.

Revilla, Noʻu, and Jamaica Heolimeleikalani Osorio. "Aloha Is Deoccupied Love." In *Detours: A Decolonial Guide to Hawaiʻi*, edited by Hōkūlani K. Aikau and Vernadette Vicuña Gonzalez, 125–31. Durham, NC: Duke University Press, 2019.

Reyhner, Jon, and Jeanne Eder. *American Indian Education: A History.* Norman: University of Oklahoma Press, 2004.

Rice, Jenn. "Farm-to-Ice: Inside Hawaii's Artisanal Shave Ice Craze." *Vogue*, January 2, 2017. https://www.vogue.com/article/artisanal-shave-ice-hawaii-guide.

Rifkin, Mark. "Settler Common Sense." *Settler Colonial Studies* 3, nos. 3–4 (2013): 322–40.

Rinkinen, Jenny, Elizabeth Shove, and Mattijs Smits. "Cold Chains in Hanoi and Bangkok: Changing Systems of Provision and Practice." *Journal of Consumer Culture* 19, no. 3 (2019): 379–97.

Ritte, Walter, Jr., and Leʻa Malia Kanehe. "Kuleana No Haloa (Responsibility for Taro): Protecting the Sacred Ancestor from Ownership and Genetic Modification." In *Pacific Genes and Life Patents*, edited by Aroha Te Pareake Mead and Steven Ratuva, 130–37. Wellington, New Zealand: Call of the Earth Llamado de la Tierra, 2007.

Rohrer, Judy. *Staking Claim: Settler Colonialism and Racialization in Hawaiʻi.* Tucson: University of Arizona Press, 2016.

Rosa, John Chock. "'The Coming of the Neo-Hawaiian American Race': National-ism and Metaphors of the Melting Pot in Popular Accounts of Mixed-Race In-dividuals." In *The Sum of Our Parts: Mixed-Heritage Asian Americans*, edited by Teresa Williams-León and Cynthia L. Nakashima, 49–60. Philadelphia: Temple University Press, 2001.

Rosa, John P. "Local Story: The Massie Case Narrative and the Cultural Produc-tion of Local Identity in Hawai'i." *Amerasia Journal* 26, no. 2 (2000): 93–115.

Rose, Deborah Bird. *Hidden Histories: Black Stories from Victoria River Downs, Hum-bert River, and Wave Hill Stations*. Canberra: Aboriginal Studies Press, 1991.

Rosenthal, Gregory. "Bayonet Constitution (1887)." In *Imperialism and Expansion-ism in American History: A Social, Political, and Cultural Encyclopedia and Docu-ment Collection*, vol. 1, edited by Chris J. Magoc and David Bernstein, 255–57. Santa Barbara: ABC-CLIO, 2016.

Rosenthal, Gregory. *Beyond Hawai'i: Native Labor in the Pacific World*. Berkeley: University of California Press, 2018.

Rowland, Donald. "The United Stated and the Contract Labor Question in Ha-wai'i, 1862–1900." *Pacific Historical Review* 2, no. 3 (1933): 249–69.

Roy, Parama. *Alimentary Tracts: Appetites, Aversions, and the Postcolonial*. Durham, NC: Duke University Press, 2010.

Ruiz, Rafico. *Slow Disturbance: Infrastructural Mediation on the Settler Colonial Re-source Frontier*. Durham, NC: Duke University Press, 2021.

Sai, David Keanu. *Ua Mau Ke Ea—Sovereignty Endures: An Overview of the Political and Legal History of the Hawaiian Islands*. Honolulu: Pu'a Foundation, 2011.

Sanders, Gary H. "The Thirty Meter Telescope (TMT): An International Observa-tory." *Journal of Astrophysics and Astronomy* 34 (2013): 81–86.

Sanderson, Marie, ed. *Prevailing Trade Winds: Climate and Weather in Hawai'i*. Ho-nolulu: University of Hawai'i Press, 1993.

Sandick, B. L., D. B. Engell, and O. Maller. "Perception of Drinking Water Tem-perature and Effects for Humans after Exercise." *Physiology and Behavior* 32, no. 5 (1984): 851–55.

Saranillio, Dean Itsuji. "Colliding Histories: Hawai'i Statehood at the Inter-section of Asians 'Ineligible to Citizenship' and Hawaiians 'Unfit for Self-Government.'" *Journal of Asian American Studies* 13, no. 3 (2010): 283–309.

Saranillio, Dean Itsuji. *Unsustainable Empire: Alternative Histories of Hawai'i State-hood*. Durham, NC: Duke University Press, 2018.

Saranillio, Dean Itsuji. "Why Asian Settler Colonialism Matters: A Thought Piece on Critiques, Debates, and Indigenous Difference." *Settler Colonial Studies* 3 (2013): 280–94.

Sasaki, Christen Tsuyuko. "Threads of Empire: Militourism and the Aloha Wear Industry in Hawai'i." *American Quarterly* 68, no. 3 (2016): 643–67.

Schmitt, Robert C. "Pipes, Pools, and Privies: Some Notes on Early Island Plumb-ing." *Hawaiian Journal of History* 16 (1982): 149–70.

Schuller, Kyla. *The Biopolitics of Feeling: Race, Sex, and Science in the Nineteenth Cen-tury*. Durham, NC: Duke University Press, 2018.

Schulz, Joy. "Empire of the Young: Missionary Children in Hawaiʻi and the Birth of U.S. Colonialism in the Pacific." PhD diss., University of Nebraska, 2011.

Segre, Gino. *A Matter of Degrees: What Temperature Reveals about the Past and Future of Our Species*. New York: Penguin Books, 2003.

Selyukh, Alina. "Why It's So Hard to Buy a New Refrigerator These Days." Hawaiʻi Public Radio, September 22, 2020. https://www.hawaiipublicradio.org/post/shortage-new-refrigerators-leaves-appliance-shoppers-out-cold#stream/0.

Severson, Kim. "Squash, Rice, and Roadkill: Feeding the Fighters at Standing Rock." *New York Times*, November 16, 2016.

Sharma, Nitasha Tamar. *Hawaiʻi Is My Haven: Race and Indigeneity in the Black Pacific*. Durham, NC: Duke University Press, 2021.

Shepherd, Gordon M. *Neurogastronomy: How the Brain Creates Flavor and Why It Matters*. New York: Columbia University Press, 2012.

Shidaki, Ryan. "Multigenerational Living in the Urban High-Rise: Designing for Hawaii's Extended Family." PhD diss., University of Hawaiʻi, 2009.

Sides, Hampton. *In the Kingdom of Ice: The Grand and Terrible Polar Voyage of the USS Jeanette*. New York: Anchor Books, 2014.

Silva, Noenoe K. *Aloha Betrayed: Hawaiian Resistance to American Colonialism*. Durham, NC: Duke University Press, 2004.

Silva, Noenoe K. "I Kū Mau Mau: How Kānaka Maoli Tried to Sustain National Identity within the United States Political System." *American Studies* 45, no. 3 (2004): 9–31.

Silva, Noenoe K. *The Power of the Steel-Tipped Pen: Reconstructing Native Hawaiian Intellectual History*. Durham, NC: Duke University Press, 2017.

Simons, William Adams. *The Hawaiian Telephone Story*. Honolulu: Hawaiian Telephone Company, [1958].

Simpson, Audra. "On Ethnographic Refusal: Indigeneity, Voice, and Colonial Citizenship." *Junctures*, December 9, 2007, 67–80.

Simpson, Audra. "Whither Settler Colonialism?" *Settler Colonial Studies* 6, no. 4 (2016): 438–45.

Simpson, Leanne Betasamosake. *As We Have Always Done: Indigenous Freedom through Radical Resistance*. Minneapolis: University of Minnesota Press, 2017.

Skwiot, Christine. *The Purposes of Paradise: U.S. Tourism and Empire in Cuba and Hawaiʻi*. Philadelphia: University of Pennsylvania Press, 2010.

Smith, Dave. "Big Island's Role in Apollo Missions Remembered." *Big Island Now*, May 9, 2014. http://bigislandnow.com/2014/05/29/big-islands-role-in-apollo-missions-commemorated/.

Smith, Jen Rose. "'Exceeding Beringia': Upending Universal Human Events and Wayward Transits in Arctic Spaces." *Environment and Planning D: Society and Space* 39, no. 1 (2021): 158–75.

Smith, Philip Chadwick Foster. *Crystal Blocks of Yankee Coldness: The Development of the Massachusetts Ice Trade from Frederick Tudor to Wenham Lake, 1806–1880*. Wenham, MA: Wenham Historical Association and Museum, 1962.

Sox, David. "Rycroft's Pohoiki: A 19th Century Boat Landing." *Historic Hawai'i News*, September 1981, 4.

Spice, Anne. "Fighting Invasive Infrastructures: Indigenous Relations against Pipelines." *Environment and Society* 9, no. 1 (2018): 40–56.

Stannard, David. *Honor Killing: Race, Rape, and Clarence Darrow's Spectacular Last Case*. New York: Penguin Books, 2006.

Starosielski, Nicole. *Media Hot and Cold*. Durham, NC: Duke University Press, 2021.

Starosielski, Nicole. "Thermocultures of Geologic Media." *Cultural Politics* 12, no. 3 (2016): 293–309.

Statutes of the United States of America, Passed at the Second Session of the Sixtieth Congress, 1908–1909. Pt. 1. Washington, DC: Government Printing Office, 1909.

Stepan, Nancy Leys. *Picturing Tropical Nature*. Ithaca, NY: Cornell University Press, 2001.

Stewart, Colin M. "Rare July Snowfall Blankets Mauna Kea; Protesters Say It's a Sign." *Hawaii Tribune-Herald*, July 18, 2015. http://hawaiitribune-herald .com/news/local-news/rare-july-snowfall-blankets-mauna-kea-protesters -say-it-s-sign.

Stickler, John. "Thirty Meter Telescope Could Boost Hawaii Island's Economy." *Hawaii Business Magazine*, September 2013. http://www.hawaiibusiness.com /thirty-meter-telescope-could-boost-hawaii-islands-economy/.

Stoler, Ann Laura. *Carnal Knowledge and Imperial Power: Race and the Intimate in Colonial Rule*. Berkeley: University of California Press, 2002.

Suryanata, Krisnawati. "Diversified Agriculture, Land Use, and Agrofood Networks in Hawaii." *Economic Geography* 78, no. 1 (2002): 71–86.

Suryanata, Krisnawati. "Products from Paradise: The Social Construction of Hawaii Crops." *Agriculture and Human Values* 17 (2000): 181–89.

Sustainable Resources Group, Int'l. *Public Access Plan for the UH Management Areas on Mauna Kea*. Hilo: Office of Mauna Kea Management, 2010.

Sutton, David E. "Food and the Senses." *Annual Review of Anthropology* 39 (2010): 209–33.

Suzuki, Erin. *Ocean Passages: Navigating Pacific Islander and Asian American Literatures*. Philadelphia: Temple University Press, 2021.

Sweetser, Delight. *One Way around the World*. Indianapolis: Bowen-Merrill Company, 1898.

TallBear, Kim. "Why Interspecies Thinking Needs Indigenous Standpoints." *Fieldsights*, November 18, 2011. https://culanth.org/fieldsights/why-interspecies -thinking-needs-indigenous-standpoints.

Tate, Merze. *Hawaii: Reciprocity or Annexation*. East Lansing: Michigan State University Press, 1968.

Teaiwa, Teresia. "Reading Paul Gauguin's *Noa Noa* with Hau'ofa's *Kisses in the Nederends*: Militourism, Feminism, and the 'Polynesian' Body." In *Inside Out: Literature, Cultural Politics, and Identity in the New Pacific*, edited by Vilsoni Hereniko and Rob Wilson, 249–63. Lanham, MD: Rowman and Littlefield, 1999.

Temple, Milo K. "In and about Honolulu." *Overland Monthly*, July–December 1908, 219–23.

Tengan, Ty P. Kāwika. "Re-membering Panalāʻau: Masculinities, Nation, and Empire in Hawaiʻi and the Pacific." *Contemporary Pacific* 20, no. 1 (2008): 27–53.

Teves, Stephanie Nohelani. "Aloha State Apparatuses." *American Quarterly* 67, no. 3 (2015): 705–26.

Teves, Stephanie Nohelani. *Defiant Indigeneity: The Politics of Hawaiian Performance*. Chapel Hill: University of North Carolina Press, 2018.

Teves, Stephanie Nohelani. "We're All Hawaiians Now: Kanaka Maoli Performance and the Politics of Aloha." PhD diss., University of Michigan, 2012.

Thévenot, Roger. *History of Refrigeration throughout the World*. Paris: International Institute of Refrigeration, 1979.

Thoreau, Henry David. *Walden; or, Life in the Woods*. Boston: Ticknor and Fields, 1854.

Thrum, Thomas G. *All about Hawaiʻi: Thrum's Hawaiian Almanac and Annual for 1900*. Honolulu: Black and Auld, Printers, 1900.

Thrum, Thomas G. *Hawaiian Almanac and Annual for 1882*. Honolulu: Thos. G. Thrum, 1882.

Thrum, Thomas G. *Hawaiian Almanac and Annual for 1914*. Honolulu: Thos. G. Thrum, 1913.

Thrum, Thomas G. *Hawaiian Almanac and Annual for 1931*. Honolulu: Thos. G. Thrum, 1930.

Thurston, Lorrin A. *The Liquor Question in Hawaii—What Should Be Done about It?* Honolulu: Social Science Association, 1909.

Tompkins, Kyla Wazana. *Racial Indigestion: Eating Bodies in the 19th Century*. New York: New York University Press, 2012.

Trask, Haunani-Kay. "Birth of the Modern Hawaiian Movement: Kalama Valley, Oʻahu." *Hawaiian Journal of History* 21 (1987): 126–53.

Trask, Haunani-Kay. "Lovely Hula Hands: Corporate Tourism and the Prostitution of Hawaiian Culture." *Border/Lines* 23 (1991): 22–34.

Trask, Haunani-Kay. "Politics in the Pacific Islands: Imperialism and Native Self-Determination." *Amerasia* 16, no. 1 (1990): 1–19.

Trask, Haunani-Kay. "Settlers of Color and 'Immigrant' Hegemony: 'Locals' in Hawaiʻi." *Amerasia Journal* 26, no. 2 (2000): 1–24.

Treuer, David. "Return the National Parks to the Tribes." *Atlantic*, April 12, 2021. https://www.theatlantic.com/magazine/archive/2021/05/return-the-national -parks-to-the-tribes/618395/.

Trubek, Amy B. *Haute Cuisine: How the French Invented the Culinary Profession*. Philadelphia: University of Pennsylvania Press, 2000.

Turner, Jessie C., and Agnes B. Alexander. *How to Use Hawaiian Fruit and Food Products*. 2nd ed. Honolulu: Paradise-Pacific, 1912.

Twain, Mark. *Roughing It*. New York: Harper and Brothers, 1899.

Ulep, Catherine ʻĪmaikalani. "Women's Exchanges: The Sex Trade and Cloth in

Early Nineteenth-Century Hawaiʻi." Master's thesis, University of Hawaiʻi, 2017.

University of Hawaiʻi at Hilo. "Final Environmental Impact Statement, Vol. 1: Thirty Meter Telescope Project." May 8, 2010. http://www.malamamaunakea .org/uploads/management/plans/TMT_FEIS_vol1.pdf.

Unrau, William E. *White Man's Wicked Water: The Alcohol Trade and Prohibition in Indian Country, 1802–1892.* Lawrence: University Press of Kansas, 1996.

U.S. Census Bureau. "Hawaii: 2000." *DP-1. Profiles of General Demographic Characteristics,* May 2001. https://www.census.gov/library/publications/2001/dec /2kh.html.

Vaughan, Mehana Blaich. *Kaiāulu: Gathering Tides.* Eugene: University of Oregon Press, 2018.

Ventura, Alison K., and Julie A. Mennella. "Innate and Learned Preferences for Sweet Taste during Childhood." *Clinical Nutrition and Metabolic Care* 14, no. 4 (2011): 379–84.

Verancini, Lorenzo. *Settler Colonialism: A Theoretical Overview.* New York: Palgrave Macmillan, 2010.

Vimalassery [Karuka], Manu, Juliana Hu Pegues, and Alyosha Goldstein. "Introduction: On Colonial Unknowing." *Theory and Event* 19, no. 4 (2016): n.p.

Voyles, Traci Brynne. *Wastelanding: Legacies of Uranium Mining in Navajo Country.* Minneapolis: University of Minnesota Press, 2015.

Wang, Jessica. "Agricultural Expertise, Race, and Economic Development: Small Producer Ideology and Settler Colonialism in the Territory of Hawaiʻi, 1900–1917." *History and Technology* 36, nos. 3–4 (2020): 310–36.

Watanabe, June. "Wherever It Came From, Shaka Sign Part of Hawaii." *Honolulu Star-Bulletin,* March 31, 2002. http://archives.starbulletin.com/2002/03/31 /news/kokualine.html.

Watts, Vanessa. "Indigenous Place-Thought and Agency amongst Humans and Non Humans (First Woman and Sky Woman Go on a European Tour!)." *Decolonization* 2, no. 1 (2003): 20–34.

Weightman, Gavin. *The Frozen Water Trade: A True Story.* New York: Hyperion, 2003.

Weigle, Richard D. "Sugar and the Hawaiian Revolution." *Pacific Historical Review* 16, no. 1 (1947): 41–58.

Welter, Barbara. "The Cult of True Womanhood: 1820–1860." *American Quarterly* 18, no. 2 (1966): 151–74.

White, Geoffrey M., and Ty Kāwika Tengan. "Disappearing Worlds: Anthropology and Cultural Studies in Hawaiʻi and the Pacific." *Contemporary Pacific* 13, no. 2 (2001): 381–416.

White, William P. "A Historic Nineteenth Century Character." *Journal of the Presbyterian Historical Society (1901–1903)* 10, no. 5 (1920): 161–74.

White, William W. "The History of Recovered People as Wounded Healers: I. From Native American to the Rise of the Modern Alcoholism Movement." *Alcoholism Treatment Quarterly* 18, no. 1 (2000): 1–23.

Wilcox, Carol. *Sugar Water: Hawaii's Plantation Ditches*. Honolulu: University of Hawai'i Press, 1998.

Wilke, Richard. "'Real Belizean Food': Building Local Identity in the Transnational Caribbean." *American Anthropologist* 101, no. 2 (1999): 244–55.

Wilkes, Charles. *Voyage round the World*. Philadelphia: Geo. W. Gorton, 1849.

Williams, Liza Keānuenueokalani, and Vernadette Vicuña Gonzalez. "Indigeneity, Sovereignty, Sustainability, and Cultural Tourism: Hosts and Hostages at 'Iolani Palace, Hawai'i." *Journal of Sustainable Tourism* 25, no. 5 (2017): 668–83.

Williams, Riánna. "John Adams Cummins: Prince of Entertainers." *Hawaiian Journal of History* 30 (1996): 153–68.

Wilson, Jonathan Stainback. "Health Department." *Godey's Lady's Book* 57 (1858): 560–61.

Wolfe, Patrick. "Settler Colonialism and the Elimination of the Native." *Journal of Genocide Research* 8, no. 4 (2006): 387–409.

Woloson, Wendy A. *Refined Tastes: Sugar, Confectionery, and Consumers in Nineteenth-Century America*. Baltimore, MD: Johns Hopkins University Press, 2002.

Woods, Rebecca J. H. *The Herds Shot round the World: Native Breeds and the British Empire, 1800–1900*. Chapel Hill: University of North Carolina Press, 2017.

Woolrich, Willis Raymond. *The Men Who Created Cold: A History of Refrigeration*. New York: Exposition Press, 1967.

Wozniacka, Gosia. "Poor Conditions at Meatpacking Plants Have Long Put Workers at Risk. The Pandemic Makes It So Much Worse." *Civil Eats*, April 17, 2020.

Yates-Doerr, Emily. "Refrigerator Units, Normal Goods." *Limn* 4 (2014). https://limn.it/articles/refrigerator-units-normal-goods/.

Yazzie, Melanie K., and Cutcha Risling Baldy. "Introduction: Indigenous Peoples and the Politics of Water." *Decolonization* 7, no. 1 (2018): 1–18.

Yee, Lisa. *Aloha, Kanani*. Middletown, WI: American Girl, 2011.

Yee, Lisa. *Good Job, Kanani*. Middletown, WI: American Girl, 2017.

Yim, Susan. "Growing Up 'Hapa': Interracial Marriage, Chop Suey Society." *Honolulu Advertiser*, January 5, 1992, 31–34.

Yim, Susan. "Hawaii's Ethnic Rainbow: Shining Colors, Side by Side." *Honolulu Advertiser*, January 5, 1992, 31–34.

Young, M. Jane. "'Pity the Indians of Outer Space': Native American Views of the Space Program." *Western Folklore* 46, no. 4 (1987): 269–79.

Young, Tatiana Kalaniopua. "Constellations of Rebellion: Home, Makeshift Economies and Queer Indigeneity." PhD diss., University of Washington, 2019.

Young, Tatiana Kalaniopua. "Home Is What We Make It." In *The Value of Hawai'i 3: Hulihia, the Turning*, edited by Noelani Goodyear-Ka'ōpua, Craig Howes, Jonathan Kay Kamakawiwo'ole Osorio, and Aikko Yamashiro, 174–77. Honolulu: University of Hawai'i Press, 2020.

Zambucka, Kristin. *Kalakaua: Hawaii's Last King*. Honolulu: Mana Publishing, 2002.

Zane, Violet Hew. "Oral History Interview with Violet Hew Zane." Interview by

Warren Nishimoto on March 1, 1980, in Lower Pāʻia, Maui. Honolulu: University of Hawaiʻi at Mānoa Center for Oral History, 1980.

Zellner, D. A., W. F. Stewart, P. Rozin, and J. M. Brown. "Effect of Temperature and Expectation on Liking for Beverages." *Physiology and Behavior* 44 (1988): 61–68.

Zimmerman, Malia. "Obama's Million Dollar Hawaiian Vacation: Costs to Taxpayers Detailed." *Hawaii Reporter*, December 28, 2010. http://www.hawaii reporter.com/president-obamas-million-dollar-plus-trip-to-hawaii-costs-to -taxpayers-detailed.

annexation, 62–64, 75, 89, 93–95, 173n77, 175n3; and Hawai'i's food system, 101; Newlands Resolution, 93, 185n11, 187n20; and "public land," 164n69; and reciprocity, 73–74, 175n3; resistance to, 14. *See also* sovereignty

Antarctica, supposed neutrality of, 40–41. *See also* neutrality, supposed

Anthony, Daniel: and the "legalize pa'i 'ai movement," 91–92, 111. *See also* pa'i 'ai

Apollo Valley, 37–40. *See also* Maunakea; space exploration

Armstrong, Richard: and the Cold Water Army, 59. *See also* temperance: Cold Water Army

artesian wells, 75–76, 78–79, 181n52. *See also* water

artificial ice. *See* ice machines

Arvin, Maile: on American claims to territory and shifting racialization of Polynesian people, 6; on assimilationist projections, 118; on Kanaka Maoli engagement with Western racial logics, 86; on rainbows/melting pots and colonialism, 114; on white progressivism and the governance of Hawai'i, 94

Asian settler colonialism, 117–18, 128, 154n76, 196n20

assimilation, 5, 92–95; and American Girl dolls, 131; impossibility of, 94; and statehood, 118–20; of taste, 94–101, 110, 188n30. *See also* civilization/civility; dispossession, Indigenous

astronomy, and Maunakea, 23, 28, 30, 35, 38–39, 42–43. *See also* kuleana (responsibility); Maunakea; space exploration; Thirty Meter Telescope (TMT)

Aweau, Don: on preservation of Maunakea's summit as public benefit, 42. *See also* Thirty Meter Telescope (TMT); University of Hawai'i

Ballou, Maturin Murray: on Honolulu's early modernity, 75. *See also* Honolulu

Bayonet Constitution, 88, 119, 172n70, 184n87, 197n30. *See also* Kalākaua; settler colonialism

Beamer, Kamanamaikalani: on Hawaiian modernity and Western hegemony, 76

Beattie, Donald: on Maunakea as moon substitute, 38. *See also* Maunakea; space exploration

Beckwith, Martha: and the translation of *Ka Moolelo o Laieikawai*, 25–26, 160nn21–22. *See also* mo'olelo (stories)

Beeton, Isabella Mary: on the consumption of iced drinks in moderation, 66

belonging, 13–14, 32–33; and kinolau, 27; "legal" forms of, 17; multiethnic, as a form of American nationalism, 14; and nostalgia, 127–28; in poststatehood Hawai'i, 124–25, 127. *See also* multiculturalism

Berger, Henry: and the Hawaiian national anthem, 89, 184n89

Bergeron, Victor "Trader Vic" J.: and the Mai Tai, 116. *See also* Mai Tai (cocktail); tiki bars

Bingham, Hiram: on intemperance, 170n46. *See also* alcohol; temperance

biopolitics, 92–94; microbiopolitics, 92–93; and settler colonialism, 8, 104, 155n83

Bird, Isabella Lucy: on nineteenth-century Hawaiian civility, 86–87. *See also* civilization/civility

bitterness: of cold and taste ('āmu'emu'e), 10. *See also* cold

Black Lives Matter, 14. *See also* race; resistance

Blanchard, Edward: language limitations of, 192n64; and pure food regulation/standards, 101–9, 111, 190n44, 192n66. *See also* ice cream; poi; pure food

Blatchley, Dr. Abraham: and Maunakea, 32. *See also* Maunakea

Bliss, William: on Honolulu's cosmopolitanism, 85. *See also* Honolulu: cosmopolitanism of

Bonanza Saloon, 1–2, 151n48. *See also* Crowell, J. W.

Bourdieu, Pierre: on taste as socially conditioned, 152n50. *See also* taste

Brinker, Amy: on Indigenous food advo-

erasure, Indigenous, 13, 120. *See also* as-similation; dispossession, Indigenous; indigeneity; settler colonialism

Estes, Nick: on extractive and infrastructural regimes, 23

eugenics, and Kamehameha Schools, 94

evolutionary theory, and the tropical imaginary, 4–5

expectation: and access to freezing/refrigeration, 123; and mixed-race Hawaiian American Girl dolls, 131; of the performance of aloha, 151; and temperature preference, 11. *See also* taste; temperature

family: expanded networks of, 13; legal definitions of, 16, 157n96

Faulkner, Walter: and the electrification of ʻIolani Palace, 88. *See also* electricity; ʻIolani Palace: electrification of

Fellows, Al: on the effects of eating poi on Kānaka Maoli, 191n50. *See also* poi

Fish, Adam: on tourism and the aesthetic qualities of sacred sites, 43–44. *See also* sacred, the; tourism

fishing: and ice, 17. *See also* ice

Flores, E. Kalani: on akua and environmental protection, 27. *See also* akua (deity)

food apartheid, 142, 202n11

food chain, 95, 122, 179n39, 186n14

food preservation, and ice, 7, 68, 79. *See also* freezing; refrigeration: and freshness

food safety, 19, 91–93, 95, 101–6, 108–11, 142. *See also* health

food security: and refrigeration, 15–16, 140–42; and settler colonialism, 141

forgetting, and the ice trade, 51. *See also* memory

Fornander, Abraham: settler colonial logics of, 6. *See also* settler colonialism

Foster, W. E.: and ice production/manufacturing in Hawaiʻi, 78–79. *See also* ice machines

Fox, Frank: on American imperial expansion in the Pacific, 93–94. *See also* settler colonialism

freezing, 73, 77–80, 123, 152n51, 181n52, 201n4; and biomedical supply chains, 142–43. *See also* ice; infrastructure; refrigeration

Freidberg, Susanne: on the effects of refrigeration, 15. *See also* infrastructure; refrigeration

Fujikane, Candace: on the origins/creation of Maunakea, 24, 27. *See also* Maunakea; moʻolelo (stories)

Fusté, José I.: on dependency and debt as hallmarks of US expansionism, 141

García Márquez, Gabriel: *One Hundred Years of Solitude*, 45, 165n91. *See also* ice

Garth, Hanna: on Cubans and food safety, 142. *See also* food security

gender: and ice cream parlors, 65, 85–86, 183n69, 188n32; and Maunakea's summit, 35–39; and the military, 35; and saloons, 86; and settler colonialism, 24; and suffrage, 97; and temperance, 59; and temperature, 9–10, 24, 61, 72–73, 79; and wartime labor, 130

Gilbert, George: on the "delightful" climate on Maui, 4. *See also* climate; paradise

Gilmore, Ruth Wilson: on infrastructure, 145; on white supremacy, 143

glacial ice, 2; melting of, 145. *See also* ice; melting

Gleason, Philip: on the term *melting pot*, 118. *See also* melting pot

Goeman, Mishuana: on "settler-colonial grammar of place," 110. *See also* settler colonialism

Goldberg-Hiller, Jonathan: on kino-lau, 27

Gonzalez, Vernadette Vicuña: on ʻIolani Palace, 88; on the masculinized mobilities of the military, 35. *See also* ʻIolani Palace; military

Goodrich, Rev. Joseph: and Maunakea, 32–33. *See also* Maunakea

Goodyear-Kaʻōpua, Noelani, 176n11; on

the protectorship of Maunakea, 22. *See also* Maunakea; resistance

Gorrie, John: and the ice machine, 166n9. *See also* ice machines

Grant, Ulysses S., 72. *See also* Kalākaua

Great Māhele, the, 52–53, 168n25. *See also* Kamehameha III; land

Greer, Richard: on Cunha's Alley, 169n38. *See also* Cutrell, Peck; Merchant's Exchange (saloon)

Gulick, Sidney Lewis: on Hawai'i's "melting pot," 118. *See also* melting pot

Hackfeld, Henry, 174n103; and ice accessibility, 68–69. *See also* access: to ice

Haleole, S. N.: *Ka Moolelo o Laieikawai*, 25–26, 160n21. *See also* mo'olelo (stories)

Hall, Lisa Kahaleole: on multiculturalism discourses and inequity, 114; on settler-state leveraging of "aloha," 43. *See also* aloha, spirit of; multiculturalism; settler colonialism

Hawai'i, 147nn6–7; and agriculture, 3, 15, 19, 29–30, 76, 124; as "Aloha State," 114, 128, 197n40; and blackness, 13–14, 195n7, 200n82; climate of, 3–6, 15, 77; cost of living, 14–16, 143, 155n79; coup d'état (1893), 64, 75, 93, 164n69; dependence on imported food, 15–16, 140, 156n89, 156n94, 190n44; as exotic, 5, 98, 116; food culture of, 84–85; and France, 56–57, 85, 170n46; and futurity, 137–46; and localness, 13, 20, 113, 115, 117–21, 128, 131–35, 154n72, 196n20, 197n35, 199n59; and the military, 5, 8, 13, 23–24, 35–36, 74, 89, 93, 114, 132–34, 200n82, 200n86; as "model multiethnic society," 133; and multiculturalism, 12–14, 20, 98–99, 113–35; national anthem of, 89, 184n89; as paradise, 2–6, 13, 29–30, 124, 147n5, 148n19, 189n40; Republic of, 93, 99; territorial occupation, 8–9, 19, 91–112, 116, 119, 122, 185n11, 189n40, 190n42, 191n57; and tourism, 5, 13, 23–24, 35, 29–30, 35, 38–40, 65, 73, 85, 115–17, 120, 124, 141, 148n19, 152n51; and the United States, 8–9, 19, 63–64, 71–74, 175n3, 175nn6–8, 176n9, 176n11, 177n14

Hawaiian shirts, 36, 163n59. *See also* kitsch, Polynesian

Hawaii Five-O, 124

"Hawai'i Pono'ī" (song), 89, 184n89. *See also* Hawai'i

health: Board of Health, 92, 101, 103–4, 107–9, 190n42, 190n44, 191n57, 192n66; and climate, 4; vs. cold food and drink, 153n57; and food safety, 19, 91–93, 95, 101–6, 108–11, 142; and iced refreshment, 65–66; and Indigenous foods, 202n19; and race, 103–4; and refrigeration, 17, 142–43; vs. taste, 19, 108–9. *See also* cholera; COVID-19

heat: anxieties about, 65; and claims of inferiority, 59–60; and cold, 10, 81, 83–84, 151n44; "hot foreign light" (Kukui Wela Haole), 88; and love, 160n23; and meat, 68; and Poli'ahu, 26. *See also* Poli'ahu (akua)

Hereen, Captain Edward: and the ice trade, 167nn12–14. *See also* ice trade

Herold, Marc W.: on ice as luxury product in the tropics, 7. *See also* ice: as luxury

Heyerdahl, Thor: settler colonial logics of, 6. *See also* settler colonialism

hierarchies: of power, 5–6; of race, 5, 90, 94, 118; in sacredness, 31; of taste, 19, 96, 110, 95–96. *See also* race; sacred, the; taste

Hillebrand, Dr. William: on Kanaka Maoli presence on Maunakea, 33–34. *See also* Maunakea

Hinaikamalama: in *Ka Moolelo o Laieikawai*, 25–26, 160n23. See also *Ka Moolelo o Laieikawai*; mo'olelo (stories); Poli'ahu (akua)

Hiura, Arnold: and shave ice scholarship, 121, 194n1. *See also* shave ice

Holmes, Burton: on Honolulu as an American-like city, 98. *See also* Honolulu: as "American-like"

home: and climate control, 2; definitions of, 157n102; feeling at, in Hawai'i, 12, 14–15, 176n13; and ice, 66–69, 72–73, 77, 90, 167n16; and kitchens, 15–16, 157n96; and poi making, 104; and refrigeration,

infrastructure, 19, 75–76, 85, 90, 140–46; of cold (refrigeration, freezing), 2–3, 7–8, 12, 17, 72–73, 122–24, 140–43; as "colonial beachhead," 159n10; and extraction, 23; and invisibility, 156n88; maintenance of, 145–46; military, 23, 134; and Puʻuhonua o Puʻuhuluhulu, 139, 143; technological, 75–77, 79, 87–90; water, as "leaky," 203n24; Wiindigo (LaDuke/Cowen), 143–44, 202n20. *See also* cold chain; electricity; freezing; refrigeration

Ing, Tiffany Lani: on Kalākaua, 72, 174n1. *See also* Kalākaua

intermarriage, 13

intimacy: of food networks and domestic life, 15; between Kānaka Maoli and new-comers producing contested spaces, 12; spatial, of Honolulu, 55–56

inversion: of hot and cold, 81, 83–84; of temperature/emotion relationships, 10, 151n47. *See also* cold; heat; ice cream

ʻIolani Palace, 86–89, 175n3; electrification of, 76, 87–89, 184n83; and Liliʻuokalani, 88, 93. *See also* Kalākaua; Liliʻuokalani, Queen

Isaki, Bianca: on settler colonial home-making and Indigenous dispossession, 17. *See also* dispossession, Indigenous; home; settler colonialism

Island Snow, 127–28, 131–34. *See also* shave ice

Jarves, James Jackson: on Hawaiʻi's "salu-brious" climate, 4. *See also* climate; para-dise, Hawaiʻi as

Jones, Cyrus W.: and the importation of ice into Hawaiʻi, 54–55, 67, 166n6. *See also* ice trade

Judd, Gerrit P., 59. *See also* missionaries

Judd, Laura Fish: and the Cold Water Army, 59, 61. *See also* temperance: Cold Water Army

Kahahawai, Joseph: and the Massie Case, 118, 196n19

Kahakalau, Dr. Kū: on the names of Maunakea, 157n1. *See also* Maunakea

Kahoupokāne (akua), and Maunakea, 24. *See also* akua (deity); Maunakea; moʻolelo (stories)

kakigōri, 114, 121, 198n47. *See also* shave ice

Kalākaua, 71–90, 172n70, 174n1, 184n87, 197n30; drinking habits of, 62; and the Hale Nauā, 76; and ice cream, 86, 88–89; as lyricist, 185n90; on the moderniza-tion of Honolulu, 75–77; and the Papa Kūʻauhau Aliʻi o Nā Aliʻi Hawaiʻi, 76; and the *Paradise of the Pacific*, 189n40; and reciprocity with the US, 73–74, 175n3; and technological modernity, 87–89. *See also* Bayonet Constitution; ice cream; ʻIolani Palace

Kalama Valley protests, 120. *See also* real-estate development; resistance

kalo (taro), 24, 60, 91, 96–97, 102–3, 108–12. *See also* paʻi ʻai; poi

Kamehameha I, 52; and regulation of al-cohol, 56. *See also* Royal Order of Kame-hameha I

Kamehameha II, drinking habits of, 62

Kamehameha III: and annexation, 173n77; death and alcoholism of, 58, 62–64, 172n76, 172n78; and the Great Māhele, 52–53; Hale Aliʻi (palace), 54; and the Hawaiʻi Board of Health, 190n42; and the importation of ice, 49; and the regulation of alcohol, 57–58. *See also* alcohol

Kamehameha IV, 87; on reciprocity with the US, 73. *See also* reciprocity treaties

Kamehameha V, on reciprocity with the US, 73. *See also* reciprocity treaties; Royal Order of Kamehameha I

Kamehameha Schools: and eugenics, 94; and ice cream, 99. *See also* ice cream

Ka Moolelo o Laieikawai, 25–26, 160nn21–22. *See also* moʻolelo (stories)

Kanahele, Pua Kanakaʻole: on the sa-credness of Maunakea, 31. *See also* Maunakea; sacred, the

Kānaka Maoli (Native Hawaiian), 14, 154n67; exclusion of, 169n36; and ice consumption, 80–84; and knowledge,

Schuller, Kyla: on "plasticity of feeling," 13; on sentimentalism, 154n69

self-control: and haole, 57; and stereotypes of Kānaka Maoli, 56, 64; and stereotypes of women, 65–66. *See also* temperance

self-determination, 20, 143, 155n82; and food, 109, 111; and Maunakea, 29. *See also* self-governance; sovereignty

self-governance: and stereotypes of Kānaka Maoli, 4, 6, 58, 61–62, 93–94. *See also* self-determination; sovereignty

self-indigenization, of "locals," 154n72. *See also* indigeneity; local identity, in Hawai'i

settler colonialism, 2–18, 176n13; Asian, 117–18, 124–25, 128, 154n76, 196n20; and biopolitics, 8, 104, 155n83; and civility discourse, 4, 6–7, 13, 19, 52–53, 55–56, 62–64, 67–70, 72, 77, 80, 85–87, 94–100, 149n25, 172n78; and comfort, 6–10, 58, 69; and debt, 141; and domesticity, 16; and gender, 59; and ice, 47–49, 51, 84–87; and infrastructure, 159n10; and the leveraging of aloha, 42–43, 197n40; and measurement, 41; and multiculturalism ("rainbows" and "melting pots"), 114, 118; and narratives of "absence," 18, 22–24, 27–45, 148n19; and nostalgia, 126–31, 134–35; and notions of "paradise," 30; and politics of recognition, 14, 29, 34, 43; and private property, 16–17, 43–44, 94; and refreshment, 6–10, 92–112, 114, 126–28; and resource extraction, 4, 6–8, 23, 40–42; and the sensorium, 80–90; and taste, 48, 80, 96–112; and Western desires for sweetness, 11; and white progressivism, 94. *See also* missionaries; temperance

shaka, 200n79; of Obama, 131–32. *See also* Obama, Barack

Sharma, Nitasha Tamar: on blackness and the military in Hawai'i, 200n82; on national vs. local readings of Barack Obama, 132. *See also* military; Obama, Barack

shave ice, 10, 113–35, 152n51, 198nn46–47, 199n65; and Hawaiian multiculturalism, 20, 113–35; "ice shave," 115; and Indigenous dispossession, 20; Island Snow, 127–28, 131–34, 200n77, 200n80; and localness, 115, 120–24, 126, 131–35; media representations of, 20; nostalgia for, 126–28. *See also* kakigōri; multiculturalism; rainbow

Shaw, Amanda, 137–39. *See also* Maunakea; Pu'uhonua o Pu'uhuluhulu (encampment); resistance

Shepherd, Gordon: on cravings, 153n56

shipments: affordability of, 15; and the Jones Act, 141; of meat, 77, 179nn38–39; of pond water ice, 2, 7–8, 24, 48–51, 78–79, 82–83, 166n11, 167nn12–16, 199n65. *See also* ice; ice trade; steamships

Silva, Noenoe: on Hawaiian modernity and Western hegemony, 76; on kinolau, 27

Simpson, Audra: on ethnographic refusal, 34; on the politics of recognition within settler domination, 14. *See also* recognition; refusal; settler colonialism

Simpson, Leanne Betasamosake: on diplomatic relationships with the nonhuman world, 22. *See also* animacies, of Maunakea

Sinclair, Upton: *The Jungle*, 95. *See also* pure food

skiing, 23–24, 35, 38–40, 163n66. *See also* Maunakea; snow, mountain

slavery, 4, 7–9, 132; and desires for sweetness, 11–12; and plantations, 8–9, 117

Smith, David: and the ice machine, 77–78, 87, 178n31. *See also* ice machines

Smith, Jen Rose: on thermal colonialism, 6. *See also* settler colonialism

snow, mountain, 2, 18, 21–24, 25–26, 28, 31, 35, 38–40, 140, 162n46, 201n1. *See also* Maunakea; skiing

sounds: of generators, 138–39; of kitchen refrigerators, 15

sovereignty: and electricity/technology, 88; food, 20, 91–92, 111, 143–44, 203n21; movements, in Hawai'i, 14, 29, 89, 115,